THE CHRISTIAN WRITERS
MARKET GUIDE

2021

THE CHRISTIAN WRITERS
MARKET GUIDE

2021

Your Comprehensive Resource for Getting Published

STEVE LAUBE

THE CHRISTIAN WRITERS MARKET GUIDE 2021

ISBN – 978-162-184-1302 (paperback)
ISBN – 978-162-184-1319 (ebook)

Cover design by Five J's Design (*fivejsdesign.com*)
Typesetting by Jamie Foley (*jamiefoley.com*)
Edited by Lin Johnson

Printed in the United States of America.

Visit The Christian Writers Institute at *www.ChristianWritersInstitute.com*.

E-mail: *admin@christianwritersmarketguide.com*

Disclaimer: The information in this guide is provided by the individuals or companies through online questionnaires and email inquiries, as well as their websites and writers guidelines. The individuals or companies do not pay to be listed in the *Guide*. The entries in the *Guide* are not necessarily endorsed by Steve Laube or The Christian Writers Institute. Steve Laube and The Christian Writers Institute make every attempt to verify the accuracy of the information provided. The entries in the *Guide* are for information only. Any transaction(s) between a user of the information and the individuals or companies listed is strictly between those parties.

TABLE OF CONTENTS

PART 5: SUPPORT FOR WRITERS 237

FOREWORD

I assume you've accessed this resource treasure because you're serious about writing. You have a dream, and dreams are essential to execution and production. But if you're only a dreamer, you'll find yourself only talking about writing.

Want to really become a writer?

Writers write.

That said, I'm hoping, praying, that the stay-at-home crisis of 2020 is far in our rearview mirror by the time you read this. I don't know about you, but I found that despite the fact that I have worked from home for nearly three decades, when I was forced to stay home, I developed a serious case of cabin fever and looked for reasons to venture out.

A friend said when it was garbage day and he had to roll the trash cans to the curb, he was giddy about just deciding what to wear!

I confess I was excited about what all this home time might do for book sales. With seemingly unlimited time to read, wouldn't the book market explode?

Well, yes and no. Research shows that people indeed read more; but book sales, like those of so many other products, declined. Fortunately, by midyear we saw only about a one-percent decline; but still it was surprising.

And what did the quarantine do to your motivation to write more? Strangely, I found that having seemingly unlimited time to write made me procrastinate more. It made no sense, but I also found I was not alone. Almost every colleague commiserated over the same malady. Angst and uncertainty about the future had to be a contributor.

Was that the reason many publishers delayed releases of new books, brick-and-mortar bookstores closed, and autograph tours became virtually nonexistent?

Well, be encouraged. Publishers who pumped the brakes for months suddenly hit the accelerator in fall. Deals that had been delayed are operative again, and this situation can only bode well for 2021. After years of wringing our hands over the constant upheaval in the publishing industry, it's as if the marketplace held its breath for the better part of a year and is beginning to breathe again.

So, what will publishing look like now? I wouldn't dare prophesy about it, but one thing I'm certain of is that good writing will be needed as never before. Regardless the medium or vehicle you choose to get your prose to the public, cream will rise, quality will out.

So as you're leafing through this guide and enjoying that singular aroma of a newly published book, let it motivate you. Open your eyes to all possibilities out there. Are you blogging? Writing articles? Short stories? Writing a memoir? A how-to book? A Bible study or a devotional? Taking a shot at your first novel?

Wherever you find yourself on the spectrum of writers, commit to producing manuscripts that aim at the heart and soul. Give yourself to the craft, so you can do your best writing every time.

Your message, your theme, deserves a hearing.

–Jerry B. Jenkins
www.JerryJenkins.com

INTRODUCTION

WRITING IS A SERIOUS BUSINESS. It is also a serious calling. The privilege of having your words influence other people's thinking or inspiring their spirit is a gift from God. A number of publication opportunities for great writing from great authors exist. Traditional methods for publication remain, but the diversity of online opportunities are seemingly endless. In addition, independent-publication options have made it easier to see your byline on a book, a blog post, or an online magazine.

Since many Christian bookstores have closed, it may seem like the Christian publishing industry is shrinking; but it is not. It is simply changing. Therefore, you must research more effectively to find the best place for your work. The problem with online search engines is the immense number of results you receive. Then the results depend on that site's search-engine optimization and those who have paid to have their site show at the top. *The Christian Writers Market Guide* has curated the information for you. Now you can find what is targeted specifically for the Christian market and your areas of interest.

One of the biggest mistakes a writer can make is to ignore the guidelines of an agent, an editor, or a publisher. In the past, some publications dropped their listings in this guide because writers failed to follow the instructions posted on websites or in this guide. Editors are looking for writers who understand their periodicals or publishing houses and their unique approaches to the marketplace. This book will help you be such a writer. With a little time and effort, you can meet an editor's expectations, distinguish yourself as a professional, and sell what you write.

If you can, I recommend you attend a writers conference, whether virtual or in person. (We have many listed inside.) It is good to meet new people and become familiar with the best teachers in the industry. If you cannot get to a conference, consider exploring the courses available online at *ChristianWritersInstitute.com*. There are more than 110 to choose from, and you can enjoy them at any time on any device.

If this is the first time you've used this guide, read the "How to Use This Book" section. If you run into an unfamiliar term, look it up in the "Publishing Lingo" section in back and learn the terminology.

Please be aware that the information in this guide is provided by the companies or individuals through online questionnaires and email inquiries, as well as their websites and writers guidelines. The companies or individuals do not pay to be listed in the *Guide*. The entries in the *Guide* are not endorsed by me or The Christian Writers Institute. We make every attempt to verify the accuracy of the information provided. The entries in the *Guide* are for information only. Any transaction(s) between a user of the information and the individuals or companies listed is strictly between those parties.

May God bless your writing journey. We are on a mission to change the world, word by word. To that end, strive for excellence and make your work compelling and insightful. Great writing is still in demand. But it must be targeted, crafted, edited, critiqued, polished, and proofread until it shines.

My thanks go to Lin Johnson whose invaluable work makes this all possible. She keeps tabs throughout the year on market changes, so every listing is accurate to the best of our information at the time of publication. (Our online version of this guide, *ChristianWritersMarketGuide.com*, is updated regularly during the year.) As the administrator of the online and print editions, she is the genius behind the details. In addition, I would also like to acknowledge my wife, Lisa. Her love, support, and encouragement have been incalculable. We make a great team!

Steve Laube
President
The Christian Writers Institute
and
The Steve Laube Agency
24 W. Camelback Rd. A-635
Phoenix, AZ 85013
www.christianwritersinstitute.com
www.stevelaube.com

To update a listing or to be added to the next edition or online, go to *www.christianwritersmarketguide.com*. Click on the Get Listed tab, and fill out the form.

For direct-sales questions, email the publisher: *admin@christianwritersinstitute.com*

For books and courses on the writing craft, visit The Christian Writers Institute: *www.christianwritersinstitute.com*.

HOW TO USE THIS BOOK

THE CHRISTIAN WRITERS MARKET GUIDE 2021 IS DESIGNED to make it easier for you to sell your writing. It will serve you well if you use it as a springboard to become thoroughly familiar with the markets best suited to your writing style and areas of interest and expertise.

Start by getting acquainted with the setup of this guide.

Part 1 lists Christian royalty book publishers with contact information and what they are looking for. Notice that many houses accept manuscripts only from agents or through meeting with their editors at a writers conference. If you need a literary agent, check the agent listings in Chapter 16.

Since independent book publishing is a viable option today, Part 2 provides resources to help you. Chapter 2 lists independent book publishers, many of which provide all the services you need as packages or à la carte services. If you decide to publish on your own, Chapters 3 and 4 list design, production, and distribution services. You'll also want to hire a professional editor, so see Chapter 19 for help in this area.

Part 3 lists periodical—magazine, newspaper, and newsletter—publishers. Chapter 5 will help you find markets by topics (e.g., marriage, evangelism) and types (e.g., how-to, poetry, personal experience). Although these lists are not comprehensive, they provide a shortcut for finding appropriate markets for your ideas.

Cross-referencing may be helpful. For example, if you have an idea for a how-to article on parenting, look at the lists in both the how-to and parenting categories. Also, don't overlook writing on the same topic for different periodicals, such as money management for a general adult magazine, a teen magazine, a women's newsletter, and a magazine for pastors. Each would require a different slant, but you would get more mileage from one idea.

If you run into words in the listings that you are not familiar with, check "Publishing Lingo" at the back of the book.

In Part 4, "Specialty Markets," you'll find nonbook, nonperiodical markets like daily devotionals and drama. Here you can explore types of writing you may not have thought about but can provide a steady writing income.

As a writer, you'll need support to keep going. Part 5 provides information for various kinds of support.

One of the best ways to get published today is to meet editors at writers conferences. Check out Chapter 17 for a conference or seminar near you or perhaps in a location you'd like to visit. Before deciding which conference to attend, check the websites for who is on faculty, what houses are represented, and what classes are offered that can help you grow your craft and writing business. You may also want to factor in the size of the conference. Don't be afraid to stretch outside your comfort zone.

For ongoing support and feedback on your manuscripts, join a writers group. Chapter 18 lists groups by state. If you can't find one near you, consider starting one or join an online group.

Since editors and literary agents are looking for polished manuscripts, you may want to hire a professional editor. See Chapter 19 for people who offer a variety of editorial services, including coaching.

Whether you publish your book with a royalty house or go the independent route, you'll need to do most, if not all, of the promotion. If you want to hire a specialist with contacts, check out Chapter 20, "Publicity and Marketing Services." And if you need accounting or legal help, check out Chapter 21.

One way to promote your message and your books is through speaking. If you need help in this area—and most writers do—see Chapter 22, "Speaking Services." There you will find organizations and conferences that train speakers and/or connect them with groups looking for speakers.

Since writers who stagnate don't get published, check out Chapter 23 for education resources to help you improve your writing style, write different types of manuscripts, and learn the business of writing and publishing. You'll find a variety of free and paid resources, including podcasts and classes.

Entering a writing contest can boost your sales, supplement your writing income, lead to publication, and sometimes give you valuable feedback on your writing. Check out Chapter 24 for a list of contests by genre. Many of them are not Christian oriented, but you can enter manuscripts with a Christian worldview.

Once you get acquainted with this guide, start using it. After you identify potential markets for your ideas and/or manuscripts, read their writers guidelines. If these are available on the website, the URL is included. Otherwise, email or send (with a SASE) for a copy. Also study at least one sample copy of a periodical (information to obtain one is given in most listings) or the book publisher's website to see if your idea truly fits there. Never send a manuscript without doing this market study.

Above all, keep in mind that this guide is only a starting point for your research and change is the one constant in the publishing industry. It is impossible for any market guide to be 100 percent accurate since editors move around, publications and publishing houses close, and new ones open. But this guide is an essential tool for getting published in the Christian market and making an impact on God's Kingdom with your words.

PART 1

BOOK PUBLISHERS

BOOK PUBLISHERS

Before submitting your query letter or book proposal, it's critical that you read and follow a publisher's guidelines exactly. In many cases the guidelines are available on the website and a direct link is given in the listing. If you do not have a literary agent—and even if you do—check out a publisher thoroughly before signing a contract.

1517 MEDIA
See listings for Fortress Press, Broadleaf Books, and Beaming Books.

AADEON PUBLISHING COMPANY
PO Box 223, Hartford, CT 06141
www.aadeonmedia.com
- **Submissions:** Mail only. Query first. Nonfiction 140-200,000 words. Responds in six weeks. Only considers manuscripts that have been edited by a professional book copy editor.
- **Types and topics:** cultural and moral makeup of society in the US and its impact on Christianity
- **Guidelines:** *www.aadeonmedia.com/submissions.html*

ABINGDON PRESS
2222 Rosa L. Parks Blvd., Nashville, TN 37228-1306 | 615-749-6000
www.abingdonpress.com
Constance Stella, Bible, leadership, and theology
Paul Franklyn, academic books
- **Parent company:** United Methodist Publishing House
- **Denomination:** United Methodist
- **Submissions:** Submit proposal with sample chapters through the website. Publishes 120 titles per year; receives 2,000 submissions annually. Fewer than 5% of books from first-time authors. Accepts manuscripts through agents only for Christian living. Bible: CEB.

Royalty: begins at 7.5% on net

Types and topics: seasonal for Advent, Christmas, Mother's Day, and Father's Day; spiritual and personal growth; devotional; gift books; group Bible studies

Guidelines: *www.abingdonpress.com/submissions*

Tip: Looking for "any young and new voices that have active speaking and conference engagements, as well as blog and social-media followers."

AMBASSADOR INTERNATIONAL

411 University Ridge, Ste. B14, Greenville, SC 29601 | 864-751-4844, 864-751-4847

publisher@emeraldhouse.com | *www.ambassador-international.com*

Katie Cruice Smith, senior editor

Mission statement: dedicated to spreading the gospel of Christ and empowering Christians through the written word

Submissions: Submit proposal with three chapters through the website. Publishes fifty titles per year; receives 750 submissions annually. First-time authors: 50%. Accepts manuscripts through agents or authors. Length: 144 pages minimum. Considers simultaneous submissions. Responds in one month. Bible: KJV, NIV, ESV, NKJV, NASB.

Royalty: 15-20% of net, 25% for ebooks, no advance

Types and topics: theology, devotionals, biography, inspirational, children's, business, finance, topical, Bible studies; fiction for teens, new adults, and adults

Guidelines: *ambassador-international.com/submission-guidelines*

Tip: "We're most open to a book that has a clearly defined market and the author's total commitment to the project. We do well with first-time authors. We have full international coverage. Many of our titles sell globally."

AMERICAN CATHOLIC PRESS

16565 State St., South Holland, IL 60473-2025 | 708-331-5485

acp@acpress.org | *www.acpress.org, www.leafletmissal.com*

Father Michael Gilligan, editorial director

Denomination: Catholic

Submissions: Publishes four titles per year; receives ten submissions annually. Query first via mail. Average first printing 3,000. Publication within one year. No simultaneous submissions. Responds in two months. Bible: NAS.

Royalty: pays $25-100 for outright purchases only

Types and topics: only publishes material on the liturgy

Guidelines: *www.americancatholicpress.org/faq.html#faq5*

AMG PUBLISHERS

6815 Shallowford Rd., Chattanooga, TN 37421 | 423-894-6060
amandaj@amgpublishers.com | *www.amgpublishers.com*
Amanda Jenkins, author liaison

> **Parent company:** AMG International
> **Mission statement:** In 1980, AMG Publishers, Inc. was launched
> by AMG International to minister to people through the written
> word. Since its inception, AMG Publishers has become a leader
> in Christian publishing with the *Hebrew-Greek Key Word Study
> Bible,* award-winning youth fiction, exhaustive reference materials,
> multiple Bible studies, and patriotic literature.
> **Submissions:** Publishes six to ten titles per year; receives 100
> submissions annually. Email or mail proposal with sample chapters.
> Accepts manuscripts through agents or authors. First-time authors:
> 70%. Responds in three to six months. Bible version: prefers
> NASB 95, NKJV, ESV, or NIV.
> **Royalty:** starts at 14%, advance sometimes
> **Types and topics:** Bible study, devotional, Bible reference, Christian
> living topics if in Bible study or devotional format
> **Types of books:** hardcover, offset and POD paperback, ebook
> **Imprints:** Living Ink Books (youth fiction), God and Country Press
> (patriotic)
> **Guidelines:** *www.amgpublishers.com/index.php/author-guidelines*
> **Tip:** "We look for work that is theologically sound without
> denominational bias."

ANCIENT FAITH PUBLISHING

PO Box 748, Chesterton, IN 46304
khyde@ancientfaith.com | *www.ancientfaith.com/publishing*
Katherine Hyde, senior director, adult
Jane Meyer, children's book editor, jmeyer@ancientfaith.com

> **Mission statement:** to embrace the fullness of the Orthodox
> Christian faith, encourage the discipleship of believers, equip the
> faithful for ministry, and evangelize the unchurched
> **Denomination:** Eastern Orthodox
> **Submissions:** Publishes twelve to sixteen adult titles per year; receives
> 100 submissions annually. First-time authors: 50%. Length: 40-
> 100,000 words. Email query letter only. Responds in three months.
> Bible: NKJV. Must be an Orthodox Christian.
> **Royalty:** 10-15%, no advance
> **Types and topics:** Orthodox life, marriage and family, theology,
> spirituality, church history, memoir, biography/hagiography, Bible
> commentary, worship and sacraments, patristics, contemporary

issues—all from Eastern Orthodox perspective; children's/YA fiction, nonfiction, picture books

Also does: small booklets

Guidelines: *www.ancientfaith.com/publishing#af-resources*

Tip: "Read and follow the guidelines. Look through our website to see the kinds of books we publish. Do not submit material that is not intended specifically for an Eastern Orthodox audience."

ANEKO PRESS

PO Box 652, Abbotsford, WI 54405 | 715-223-3013
jeremiah@lspbooks.com | *www.anekopress.com*
Jeremiah Zeiset, president

Parent company: Life Sentence Publishing, Inc.

Mission statement: to publish books for ministry

Submissions: Niche is publishing ministry-related books. Publishes twenty titles per year; receives fifty. First-time authors: 20%. Length: 30,000-100,000 words. Prefers agent submissions. Submit proposal with full manuscript through the website. Responds in two weeks. Bible: KJV, ESV, NKJV.

Types of books: offset paperback, hardcover, ebook, audiobook; print run 1,000-5,000

Royalty: 30% net, no advance

Types and topics: Christian living

Guidelines: *anekopress.com/faq*

Tip: "The majority of our authors are in ministry as missionaries or other similar ministries."

ARMOUR BOOKS

PO Box 492, Corinda, QLD 4075, Australia
message through Facebook | *www.facebook.com/armourbooks.au*
Anne Hamilton

Mission statement: to publish quality books with a "kiss from God" at their heart

Submissions: Publishes three to five books per year; receives 50-100 submissions. Responds in two to four weeks. First-time authors: 50%. Length: maximum of 50,000 words. Inquire via email messenger first. No simultaneous submissions.

Type of books: POD

Royalty: 9-10%, sometimes offers advance

Types and topics: fantasy, science fiction, spiritual blockages to calling and healing

Guidelines: by email

Tip: "The golden rule: Support other authors as you would like to be supported."

ASCENDER BOOKS

proposals@newhopepublishers.com | *www.ironstreammedia.com*

Parent company: Iron Stream Media

Submissions: Authors must come from the Spirit-led community. Only accepts proposals through agents, author referrals, and conference meetings.

Types and topics: focused for a grace-inspired audience, spiritual growth, spiritual warfare, in-depth studies of Scripture, also includes online studies for churches and small groups

Guidelines: *www.ironstreammedia.com/submission-process*

ASHBERRY LANE

13607 Bedford Rd. N.E., Cumberland, MD 21502 | 866-245-2211

r.white@whitefire-publishing.com | *AshberryLane.com*

Roseanna White, senior fiction editor

Parent company: WhiteFire Publishing

Mission statement: Ashberry Lane is a romance line that specializes in "heartfelt stories of faith."

Submissions: Publishes five to ten books a year; receives fifty proposals annually. Length: 70,000-100,000. Email query only. Responds in three months. First-time book authors: 10%.

Types and topics: Only romance: romantic suspense, contemporary romance, historical romance

Royalty: 50% for ebooks, 10% of retail for print, advance sometimes ($500-2,000)

Types of books: hardcover, POD, ebook, audiobook

Guidelines: *ashberrylane.com/submissions*

Tip: "Please be familiar with our titles and mission."

ASPIRE PRESS

PO Box 3473, Peabody, MA 01961-3473 | 800-358-3111

info@hendricksonrose.com | *www.hendrickson.com/content/aspire-press*

Lynette Pennings, managing editor

Parent company: Hendrickson Publishers

Submissions: Publishes books that are "compassionate in their approach and rich with Scripture," giving "godly insight and counsel for those personally struggling and for believers who have a heart to minister and encourage others." Need credentials in helping others. Takes submissions only through agents or

conferences.
Types and topics: Christian living, counseling

AVE MARIA PRESS

PO Box 428, Notre Dame, IN 46556
submissions@mail.avemariapress.com | www.avemariapress.com
Heidi Hess Saxton, senior acquisitions editor

Parent company: Congregation of Holy Cross
Denomination: Catholic
Mission statement: to help people know, love, and serve God and to spread the gospel of Jesus through books and other resources
Submissions: Publishes forty to fifty books per year; receives hundreds. Email proposal with first chapter. Responds in four to six weeks. Accepts both agented and unagented proposals.
Types and topics: Catholic prayer and spirituality, family life, history, parish ministry, theology, no fiction or children's books
Guidelines: *www.avemariapress.com/manuscript-submissions*

B&H PUBLISHING GROUP

1 Lifeway Plaza, MSN 188, Nashville, TN 37234
www.bhpublishinggroup.com
Devin Maddox, director of trade books
Taylor Combs, associate publisher of Christian living and leadership
Ashley Gorman, women's publisher
Michelle Freeman, B&H Kids publisher
Anna Sargeant , B&H Kids associate publisher
Madison Trammel, director of academic books

Denomination: Southern Baptist
Parent company: LifeWay Christian Resources
Submissions: "Because we believe Every Word Matters, we seek to provide innovative, intentional content that is grounded in biblical truth." Agents only. Publishes ninety titles per year; receives thousands of submissions annually. First-time authors: 10%. Responds in two to three months. Bible version: CSB.
Royalty: on net, advance
Types and topics: Christian living, leadership, reference, women, Bible-study helps, church growth, college textbooks, evangelism, theology, marriage, parenting, worship, children's
Imprints: B&H Books, B&H Kids, B&H Academic, Holman Bibles, Broadman Church Supplies, B&H Español
Guidelines: none

Tip: "Be informed that the market in general is very crowded with the book you might want to wrtie. Do the research before submitting."

BAKER ACADEMIC

6030 E. Fulton Rd., Ada, MI 49301 | 616-676-9185
submissions@bakeracademic.com | *bakerpublishinggroup.com/bakeracademic*
Robert Hosack, senior aquisitions editor

Parent company: Baker Publishing Group
Submissions: Publishes fifty titles per year. First-time authors: 10%. Accepts manuscripts through agents, submission services, or editor's personal contacts at writers conferences.
Royalty: standard, advance
Types and topics: religious academic books, professional books for students and church leaders
Guidelines: *bakerpublishinggroup.com/bakeracademic/contact/ submitting-a-proposal*

BAKER BOOKS

6030 E. Fulton Rd., Ada, MI 49301 | 616-676-9185
bakerpublishinggroup.com/bakerbooks
Rebekah Guzman, editorial director
Brian Thomasson, senior acquisitions editor
Rachel Jacobson, acquisitions editor

Parent company: Baker Publishing Group
Submissions: No unsolicited proposals. Agents only.
Types and topics: family, parenting, business, leadership, marriage, Christian living, spiritual growth, personal growth, self-help, memoir/personal narrative, biography, cultural engagement, theology, apologetics, church life, ministry resources

BARBOUR PUBLISHING, INC.

PO Box 719, Uhrichsville, OH 44683 | 740-922-6045
submissions@barbourbooks.com | *www.barbourbooks.com*
Annie Tipton, senior acquisitions editor

Submissions: Agents only.
Types and topics: fiction, popular Bible reference, gift books, Christian classics, children's, practical Christian living
Guidelines: *www.barbourbooks.com/frequently-asked-questions*

BEAMING BOOKS

510 Marquette Ave., Minneapolis, MN 55403
www.beamingbooks.com
Andrew DeYoung, director of product development
Naomi Kreuger, aquisitions editor

Parent company: 1517 Media
Denomination: Evangelical Lutheran Church in America
Submissions: Agents only. Publishes twenty-four books per year; receives 250. First-time authors: 50%. Length: 500 words for picture book. Responds in three months. Bible: NIV, CEB.
Royalty: varies, advance
Types and topics: board books for ages birth-3, picture books for ages 3-8, activity books for ages 3-8, early reader and first chapter books for ages 5-9, nonfiction books for ages 5-9 and 8-12, fiction for ages 8-12, activity books for families, devotionals for ages 0-12 and families
Tip: "Look at what we've published before. Read a few of our books before submitting."

BETHANY HOUSE PUBLISHERS

11400 Hampshire Ave. S., Bloomington, MN 55438 | 952-829-2500
bakerpublishinggroup.com/bethanyhouse
Andy McGuire, editorial director
Raela Schoenherr, senior aquisitions editor

Parent company: Baker Publishing Group
Mission statement: to publish high-quality writings that represent historical Christianity and serve the diverse interests and concerns of evangelical readers
Submissions: Publishes seventy-five to eighty-five titles per year. Accepts manuscripts through agents only or writers met at conferences. No unsolicited submissions. Bible: NIV.
Types of books: offset paperback, hardcover, ebook
Royalty: varies by type of book and author, advance
Types and topics: devotionals, Christian living, family resources, theology, prayer; fiction: Amish, biblical, contemporary, contemporary and historical romance, historical, romantic suspense, Regency
Tip: "The best opportunities for new authors come via literary agencies, conferences, writing communities, and author referrals. Get connected."

BLING! ROMANCE

100 Missionary Ridge, Birmingham, AL 35242 | 888-811-9934
editor@blingromance.com | *shoplpc.com/bling-romance*
Jessica Nelson, acquisitions and managing editor

Parent company: Lighthouse Publishing of the Carolinas/Iron Stream Media

Submissions: Publishes eight books per year; receives forty proposals. First-time authors: 50%. Length: 80,000 words. Only accepts proposals from agents, author referrals, and conference meetings. Responds in three months. Bible: NIV.

Types of books: POD, ebook

Royalty: 40% net, no advance

Types and topics: romance fiction

Guidelines: *shoplpc.com/bling*

Tip: "At Bling! the first thing readers will notice is a solid, entertaining story. Think parables. The primary objective is to entertain and engage the contemporary reader. The stories are simultaneously character- and plot-driven, written by seasoned and debut novelists with unique voices. We seek clean, wholesome stories with God's moral truths woven into the story. Please avoid sermons in stories. Bling! sells into the general market."

BMH BOOKS

PO Box 544, Winona Lake, IN 46590 | 800-348-2756, 574-372-3098
lcgates@bmhbooks.com | *www.BMHbooks.com*
Liz Cutler Gates, executive director

Denomination: Grace Brethren

Submissons: Shows preference to Grace Brethren authors who have important and worthwhile messages that need to be heard. Trinitarian theology, dispensational eschatology, emphasis on exegesis. No unsolicited proposals. Publishes three to five titles per year; receives thirty submissions annually. First-time authors: 50%. Query first; no unsolicited manuscripts. Requires accepted manuscripts by email. Length: 50-75,000 words or 128-256 pages. Prefers not to consider simultaneous submissions. Responds in three months. Bible version: prefers KJV, NIV.

Royalty: 8-10% on retail, rarely pays an advance

Types and topics: theology, the church, pastoral helps, Bible studies, Christian home, devotional studies, Christian living, deeper life

Guidelines: *bmhbooks.com/guidelines-submitting-manuscripts*

Tip: "Most open to a small-group study book or text for Bible college/Bible institute and biblically based, timeless discipleship material."

BOLD VISION BOOKS

PO Box 2011, Friendswood, TX 77549-2011 | 832-569-4282
boldvisionbooks@gmail.com | *www.boldvisionbooks.com*
Karen Porter, acquisitions
Rhonda Rhea, aquisitions

Mission statement: We are small, but innovative—and aspiring to be astute and progressive in this changing industry.

Submissions: Publishes twenty to thirty titles per year; receives 100. First-time authors: 40%. Length: 50-90,000 words. Email query or proposal. Prefers submissions from agents and writers met at conferences. Responds in three months. Bible: NIV, NLT, NKJV.

Types of books: offset paperback, hardcover, POD, ebook; first print run 5,000-8,000

Royalty: 25-50%; advance sometimes ($1,000-5,000)

Types and topics: Christian living, creative nonfiction, fiction (contemporary, historical, romance, mystery), YA fiction

Imprints: Nuts 'n Bolts (craft books), Optasia Books (books from beloved pastors)

Guidelines: *www.boldvisionbooks.com/new-page*

Tip: "We are looking for well-crafted nonfiction manuscripts with a timeless message told in a fresh new way, using story techniques and strong Scripture backing. We would love to see your novel if it has a great theme and strong story."

BRAZOS PRESS

6030 E. Fulton Rd., Ada, MI 49301 | 616-676-9185
submissions@brazospress.com | *bakerpublishinggroup.com/brazospress*
Katelyn Beaty, acquisitions editor

Parent company: Baker Publishing Group

Submissions: Publishes books that creatively draw on the riches of our catholic Christian heritage to deepen our understanding of God's creation and inspire faithful reflection and engagement. Authors typically hold advanced degrees and have established publishing platforms.

Guidelines: *bakerpublishinggroup.com/brazospress/contact/submitting-a-proposal*

BRIDGE LOGOS

17750 N.W. 115th Ave., Bldg. 200, Ste. 220, Alachua, FL 32615 | 386-462-2525
swooldridge@bridgelogos.com | *www.bridgelogos.com*
Peggy Hildebrand, acquisitions editor

Submissions: Publishes classics, books by Spirit-filled authors, and inspirational books that appeal to the general evangelical market. Publishes forty titles per year; receives 200 submissions annually. First-time authors: 30%. Accepts manuscripts through agents or authors. Email proposal with three to five chapters. Length: 250 pages. Responds in six weeks. Prefers accepted manuscripts by email.

Royalty: 10% on net, rarely pays advance

Types and topics: Bible study, biographies of notable Christians, business, finance, personal money management, Christian living, contemporary issues, devotionals/personal growth, encouragement, eschatology, evangelism, families and marriage, Messianic work, material on our nation's heritage (history and patriotism), men's issues, political issues, prayer, singles, social issues, Spirit-filled topics, timely topics, unusual outreach ministries, women's issues, youth, African-American, Hispanic

Imprint: Synergy

Guidelines: *www.bridgelogos.com/Manuscript_Submission.html*

Tip: "Looking for well-written, timely books that are aimed at the needs of people and that glorify God. Have a great message, a well-written manuscript, and a specific plan and willingness to market your book. Looking for previously published authors with an active ministry who are experts on their subjects."

BRIMSTONE FICTION

1440 W. Taylor St., Ste. 449, Chicago, IL 60607 | 224-339-4159
brimstonefiction@gmail.com | *www.brimstonefiction.com*
Rowena Kuo, CEO and executive editor

Submissions: Brimstone Fiction is geared for YA through adult readers who enjoy speculative fiction and chiller thrillers with supernatural or paranormal elements. Publishes eight to twelve books per year; receives sixty proposals. First-time authors: 60%. Length: 60-100,000 words. Submit proposal with sample chapters or full manuscript by email or through the website. Prefers submissions from agents. Responds in six to eight weeks. Bible: NIV.

Types of books: POD, ebook

Royalty: 30% of profits, no advance

Types and topics: science fiction, YA fantasy and science fiction, suspense, mystery, action and adventure, romance, supernatural, paranormal, paranormal romance, paranormal suspense, contemporary women's, historical/medieval fiction, time travel

Also does: short and full-length films

Guidelines: *brimstonefiction.com/submission-guidelines*

Tip: "We welcome new and multipublished authors and/or authors with or without agents. If you have a good story, come and meet us at writers conferences or through our website."

BROADLEAF BOOKS

PO Box 1209, Minneapolis, MN 55440-1209 | 800-328-4648
submissions@broadleafbooks.com | *broadleafbooks.com*
Lil Copan, senior acquisitions editor

Parent company: 1517 Media
Submissions: Works primarily with agents but open to unsolicited proposals. Responds only if interested.
Types and topics: nonfiction books in the areas of religion and spirituality, social justice, personal growth, Christian living, and the intersections of religion and culture; theologically and socially liberal
Guidelines: *www.broadleafbooks.com/info/submissions*

BROADSTREET PUBLISHING

8646 Eagle Creek Cir., Ste. 210, Savage, MN 55378 | 855-935-2000
proposals@broadstreetpublishing.com | *www.broadstreetpublishing.com*
Tim Payne, editorial director

Submissions: Prefers working with agents but will work directly with authors. Publishes more than 100 titles per year.
Types and topics: biographies, Majestic Expressions adult coloring books, Christian living, fiction, devotionals, and Bible promise books
Imprint: Belle City Gifts (women's journals, devotional journals, and planners)
Guidelines: *broadstreetpublishing.com/contact*

CANDLELIGHT ROMANCE

100 Missionary Ridge, Birmingham, AL 35242 | 888-811-9934
editor@candlelightfiction.com | *shoplpc.com/candlelight-romance*

Parent company: Lighthouse Publishing of the Carolinas/Iron Stream Media
Submissions: Publishes four books per year; receives twenty proposals. First-time authors: 50%. Length: 55-80,000 words. Only accepts proposals from agents, author referrals, and conference meetings. Responds in three months. Bible: NIV.
Types of books: POD, ebook
Royalty: 40% net, no advance
Types and topics: inspirational contemporary romance fiction
Guidelines: *shoplpc.com/candlelight*
Tip: "At Candlelight we agree that a romance novel should first entertain. In doing so, the story should have a strong action plot, emotional plot, and faith plot. Candlelight envisions romance as a novel incorporating depth of character as relationships develop.

Romance can be exhibited in the worst of trials and circumstances or encased in a lovely evening of moonlight and roses. Candlelight stories may focus on a soft glow, an illumination of heart and soul, a flame of emotion, and/or a light to one's spiritual journey. Our realistic love stories are designed to entertain, encourage, inspire, and enlighten. We seek clean, wholesome stories with God's moral truths woven into the story. Please avoid sermons in stories. Candlelight sells into the general market."

CASCADE BOOKS

199 W. 8th Ave., Ste. 3, Eugene, OR 97401 | 541-344-1528
www.wipfandstock.com/imprint/cascade-3

Parent company: Wipf and Stock
Types of books: POD, ebook
Types and topics: theology, religion
Guidelines: *wipfandstock.com/submitting-a-proposal*

CASCADIA PUBLISHING HOUSE

126 Klingerman Rd., Telford, PA 18969
editor@CascadiaPublishingHouse.com | *CascadiaPublishingHouse.com*
Michael A. King, publisher, editor

Submissions: Query only by mail or email.
Types and topics: creative, thought-provoking, Anabaptist-related material
Guidelines: *www.cascadiapublishinghouse.com/submit.htm*
Tip: "All Cascadia books receive rigorous evaluation and some form of peer or consultant review."

CATHOLIC BOOK PUBLISHING HOUSE

77 W. End Rd., Totowa, NJ 07572 | 973-890-2400
info@catholicbookpublishing.com | *www.catholicbookpublishing.com*
Anthony Buono, editor

Denomination: Catholic
Submissions: Primarily assigns books but will look at mailed queries. No simultaneous submissions or submissions from agents. Responds in two to three months. Publication in twelve to fifteen months.
Royalty: negotiable
Imprint: Resurrection Press (see separate entry)
Types and topics: liturgical books, Bibles, missals, prayer books
Guidelines: *www.catholicbookpublishing.com/page/faq#manuscript*

CHALICE PRESS

483 E. Lockwood Ave., Ste. 100, St. Louis, MO 63119 | 800-366-3383
submissions@chalicepress.com | *chalicepress.com*
Brad Lyons, publisher

Submissions: Open to receiving any publishing proposal that "aligns with our mission to publish resources inviting all people into deeper relationship with God, equipping them as disciples of Jesus Christ, and sending them into ministries as the Holy Spirit calls them. Particularly interested in publishing content by and for women, young adults (age 18 to 35), and racial/ethnic cultures for our academic, congregational leadership, and general audiences." Submit proposal through website.

Types and topics: academic (homiletics, biblical studies, theology, Christian education); congregational leadership (preaching, evangelism, hospitality, leadership development, discipleship/equipping ministries); general (faith and life, inspiration/devotion, Bible study/application, mission/evangelism)

Guidelines: *www.chalicepress.com/AuthorGuidelines.aspx*

Tip: "Our theological tradition is evangelistic (we share with others our experience of God), inclusive (we are guests at a table where everyone is welcome), and mission-oriented (our gratitude to God compels us to serve others)."

CHARISMA HOUSE

600 Rinehart Rd., Lake Mary, FL 32746 | 407-333-0600
charismahouse@charismamedia.com | *www.charismahouse.com*
Kyle Duncan, VP of aquisitions and content development

Mission statement: to inspire and equip people to live a Spirit-led life and walk in the divine purpose for which they were called

Submissions: Accepts proposals only through agents. Publishes 150 titles per year; receives 1,500 submissions annually. First-time authors: 65%. Reprints books. Length: 55,000 words. Responds in one to two months.

Royalty: on net or outright purchase, advance

Topics and types: Charisma House: Charismatic/Pentecostal perspective on Christian living, work of the Holy Spirit, prophecy, prayer, Scripture, adventures in evangelism and missions, popular theology. Siloam: living in good health—body, mind, and spirit, including alternative medicine; diet and nutrition; and physical, emotional, and psychological wellness; prefers manuscripts from certified doctors, nutritionists, trainers, and other medical professionals. Frontline: contemporary political and social issues from a Christian perspective. Realms: adult Christian fiction in the supernatural, speculative genre, 80-120,000 words; also considers historical or biblical fiction if supernatural element is substantial. Excel: targeted toward success in the workplace and businesses.

CHICKEN SOUP FOR THE SOUL BOOKS

See listing in the periodicals section, "**Adult Markets.**"

CHOSEN

6030 E. Fulton Rd., Ada, MI 49301 | 616-676-9185
bakerpublishinggroup.com/chosen
Jane Campbell, editorial director
Kim Bangs, senior acquisitions editor
David Sluka, senior acquisitions editor

> **Parent company:** Baker Publishing Group
> **Mission statement:** Chosen Books is dedicated to being the premier publishing partner serving the Spirit-empowered community with thoughtful, accessible books that recognize the gifts and ministry of the Holy Spirit and help readers live more empowered and effective lives for Jesus Christ
> **Submissions:** Publishes thirty-six books annually. First-time authors: 10%. Length: 40-50,000 words. Email query letter or proposal with sample chapters. Responds in one month.
> **Types of books:** offset paperback, hardcover, ebook; first print run, 7,500
> **Royalty:** based on previous sales, advance
> **Types and topics:** nonfiction expositional, Spirit-empowered devotionals, Spirit-empowered gift books, spiritual warfare, deliverance, prophecy/prophetic, prayer/intercession, Israel/Messianic, missions/evangelism, Spirit-filled living/charismatic, Holy Spirit, healing, revival/renewal, biblical studies
> **Guidelines:** *bakerpublishinggroup.com/chosen/contact/preparing-a-proposal-for-chosen-books*
> **Tip:** "Explain your book in one compelling sentence that states clearly the single idea you are addressing, and describe the size of your platform (e.g., 100,000 followers on Facebook or Instagram)."

CHRISM PRESS

13607 Bedford Rd., Cumberland, MD 21502 | 301-876-4876
submissions@chrismpress.com | *www.chrismpress.com*
Rhonda Ortiz, editor
Karen Ullo, editor
Marisa Deshaies, editor

Parent company: WhiteFire Publishing

Mission statement: Chrism Press is dedicated to stories informed by Catholic and Orthodox Christianity that may not be able to find a home in either mainstream secular or Christian (evangelical) presses.

Submissions: Publishes five to ten books a year; receives sixty proposals annually. First-time book authors: 25%. Length: 60,000-100,000 words. Prefers submissions from agents and writers met at conferences. Submit query letter only. Responds in three months.

Types and topics: all genres of adult and young-adult fiction

Types of books: POD, ebook, audiobook

Royalty: 50% for ebooks, 10% for print, advance sometimes

Guidelines: *www.chrismpress.com/submissions*

Tip: "Chrism Press serves the Catholic and Orthodox Christian markets. We are open to submissions from authors outside these faiths, but please read our mission statement and submissions FAQ carefully to see if your work would be a good fit for us."

CHRISTIAN FOCUS PUBLICATIONS

Geanies House, Fearn, Tain, Ross-shire IV20 1TW, Scotland, UK | 01862 871011
submissions@christianfocus.com | *www.christianfocus.com*
Willie MacKenzie, director
Catherine MacKenzie, children's editor, Catherine.Mackenzie@christianfocus.com

Submissions: Submit proposal with two chapters by email or mail.

Types and topics: Christian Focus: popular works, including biographies, commentaries, basic doctrine, and Christian living. Mentor: written at a level suitable for Bible college and seminary students, pastors, and other serious readers, including commentaries, doctrinal studies, examination of current issues, and church history. Christian Heritage: classic writings from the past. Children's: Bible story books, devotionals, craft books, puzzle books, activity books, game books, material for family devotions, biography series (Trailblazers for ages 9-14, retells the stories of well-known Christians past and present; Torchbearers for ages 8-11 about real martyrs), and several fiction series

Imprint: CF 4 Kids

Guidelines: adults: *www.christianfocus.com/about/adult-guidelines* | children: *www.christianfocus.com/about/childrens-guidelines*

Tip: "Read our website please. Don't send us stuff we don't publish."

CLADACH PUBLISHING

PO Box 336144, Greeley, CO 80633 | 970-371-9530
cathy@cladach.com | www.cladach.com
Catherine Lawton, publisher, editor

Submissions: Publishes four titles per year; receives fifty proposals. First-time authors: 50%. Considers book proposals from authors met at writers conferences. Email query letter only. Length: 120-300 pages. Responds in three months. Bible: NIV, NRSV.

Types of books: offest and POD paperback, ebook, audiobook

Royalty: 10-20%, $100 advance

Types and topics: creative nonfiction, memoir, poetry, fiction (frontier, literary), nature writings, devotional, inner healing/wholeness

Guidelines: *cladach.com/authors*

Tip: "We are accepting very few unsolicited manuscripts."

CLC PUBLICATIONS

PO Box 1449, Fort Washington, PA 19034 | 215-542-1242
submissions@clcpublications.com | www.clcpublications.com
Dave Fessenden, editorial coordinator

Parent company: CLC Ministries International

Mission statement: books for the deeper life

Submissions: Publishes twelve titles per year; receives 200 submissions. First-time authors: 30%. Length: 144-320 pages, 35,000-80,000 words. Submit proposal with sample chapters or full manuscript via email, mail, or website form. Prefers submissions from agents and writers met at conferences. Cold contacts from authors: Use the website form. Responds in one to two months. Bible: ESV.

Types of books: offset paperback, ebook, audiobook; first print run 2,000-3,500

Royalty: 12-14% net, advance sometimes

Types and topics: Christian living, Christian growth, deeper life

Guidelines: *www.clcpublications.com/about/prospective-authors-submissions*

Tip: "We prefer a book that speaks to an international audience, not only North America."

COLLEGE PRESS PUBLISHING

PO Box 1132, 2111 N. Main St., Ste. C, Joplin, MO 64801 | 800-289-3300
collpressjoplin@gmail.com | www.collegepress.com

Denomination: Christian Churches/Churches of Christ

Submissions: Requires a query or proposal first. Responds in two to three months.

Types and topics: Bible studies, topical studies (biblically based), apologetic studies, historical biographies of Christians

Guidelines: *www.collegepress.com/pages/for-authors*

CROSSLINK PUBLISHING

558 E. Castle Pines Pkwy., Ste. B4117, Castle Rock, CO 80108 | 888-697-4851

publisher@crosslink.org | *www.crosslinkpublishing.com*

Rick Bates, managing editor

Parent company: CrossLink Ministries

Submissions: As a small publisher, it is author focused, processes are nimble, and it prides itself on having the most transparent and participative publishing process in the industry. Publishes thirty-five titles per year. Receives 500 submissions annually. First-time authors: 85%. Requires manuscript submission on the website. Length: 12-60,000 words. Responds in a week.

Royalty: 10% of retail, 20% for ebooks, no advance

Types and topics: adult fiction, Bible studies, devotional, inspirational, meditations, spiritual-growth areas

Imprint: New Harbor Press

Guidelines: *www.crosslinkpublishing.com/submit-a-manuscript*

Tip: "We are particularly interested in providing books that help Christians succeed in their daily walk (inspirational, devotional, small groups, etc.)."

CROSSRIVER MEDIA GROUP

PO Box 187, Brewster, KS 67732 | 816-752-2171

submissions@crossrivermedia.com | *www.crossrivermedia.com*

Debra L. Butterfield, editorial director, deb@crossrivermedia.com

Mission statement: to glorify God by providing high-quality books and materials that ignite a woman's relationship with God and inspire her to lead a life that honors Him

Submissions: Publishes four to six titles per year; receives sixty submissions annually. First-time authors: 50%. Accepts but doesn't require submissions through agents. Length: 30,000-85,000 words. Email proposal with sample chapters. Responds in three to four months. Bible: any except NIV.

Types of books: POD, ebook

Royalty: 10-15%, no advance

Types and topics: inspirational fiction for adults (contemporary, historical, romance), Christian living, spiritual growth

Guidelines: *www.crossrivermedia.com/about/manuscript-submissions*

Tip: "Know how your book fits our mission statement and include that information in your proposal."

THE CROSSROAD PUBLISHING COMPANY

submissions@crossroadpublishing.com | www.crossroadpublishing.com

Submissions: Open to unsolicited proposals; email submissions only. Responds in six to eight weeks. Accepts submissions from agents or authors.

Royalty: yes, no advance

Types and topics: spirituality, Christian living, theology

Guidelines: *www.crossroadpublishing.com/crossroad/static/for-authors*

Tip: "Our experience is that many authors have powerful and potentially life-changing ideas emerging from their training, study, and experience, but they have not identified the best way to communicate their wisdom. Your ideas are not new to you, but they are new to the person who will be reading your work. So before you send a submission, the most important thing is to do your own research about publishing in general and about the potential audience for your specific proposal."

CROSSWAY

1300 Crescent St., Wheaton, IL 60187 | 630-682-4300

submissions@crossway.org | www.crossway.org

Parent company: Good News Publishers

Mission: Our purpose is to publish gospel-centered, Bible-centered content that will honor our Savior and serve his Church. We seek to help people understand the massive implications of the gospel and the truth of God's Word, for all of life, for all eternity, and for the glory of God.

Submissions: Publishes seventy-five titles per year; receives five hundred annually. First-time authors: 1%. Length: 35,000-75,000 words. Email a query first, or submit it through the website. Responds in six to eight weeks if interested. Bible: ESV.

Types of books: hardcover, offset and POD paperback, ebook, audiobook

Royalty: negotiable, advance

Types and topics: biblical studies, Christian living, current issues, academic, professional

Guidelines: *www.crossway.org/submissions*

Tip: "Look at submission guidelines to be sure it is a genre we publish. Also be prepared with a well-written proposal. No Spanish queries please."

CSS PUBLISHING GROUP, INC.

5450 N. Dixie Hwy., Lima, OH 45807-9559 | 419-227-1818
editor@csspub.com | *www.csspub.com*
Missy Cotrell, managing editor

> **Submissions:** Serves the needs of pastors, worship leaders, and parish program planners in the broad Christian mainline of the American church. Prefers query first but will also look at proposals with a sample chapter(s) by email or mail. Publishes fifteen titles per year; receives 500-1,000 submissions annually. First-time authors: 50%. Length: 100-125 pages. Responds in three weeks to six months. Bible version: NRSV.
>
> **Royalty:** none, no advance, outright purchase
>
> **Types and topics:** lectionary-based resources for worship, preaching, group study, drama, and use with children (but not children's books); sermons, preaching, and worship resources for special seasons and days of the church year and special themes or emphasis; children's object lessons and sermons; resources for working with youth; pastoral aids, such as materials to assist in counseling; easy-to-perform dramas and pageants for all age groups, primarily for Advent/Christmas/Epiphany and Lent/Easter (no full-length plays); parish-tested materials for use in education, youth ministry, stewardship, and church growth; a few general titles
>
> **Guidelines:** *store.csspub.com/page.php?Custom%20Pages=10*
>
> **Imprints:** Fairway Press (see separate listing in "Independent Book Publishers"), B.O.D. (Books On Demand)
>
> **Tip:** "We're looking for authors who will help with the marketing of their books."

DAVID C. COOK

4050 Lee Vance Dr., Colorado Springs, CO 80918 | 719-536-0100
www.davidccook.org
Michael Covington, senior acquisitions and development editor
Susan McPherson, acquisitions (women, family)
Stephanie Bennett, acquisitions (teens, youth leaders)

> **Mission statement:** to equip the Church with Christ-centered resources for making and teaching disciples
>
> **Submissions:** Only proposals from agents and writers met at conferences. Publishes forty books per year; receives 1,200 proposals. First-time authors: 10%. Responds in one month. Bible: any. Length: 45-50,000 words.
>
> **Types of books:** offset paperback, hardcover, POD, ebook
>
> **Also does:** Sunday school curriculum, Standard Lesson Commentary
>
> **Royalty:** 12-22%, advance varies

Types and topics: Christian living, spiritual growth, discipleship, leadership, marriage, parenting, women's, men's, church resources, some picture books

Guidelines: *shop.davidccook.org/pages/frequently-asked-questions*

Tip: "We look for significant platform, excellent writing, and relevant content."

DISCOVERY HOUSE PUBLISHERS
See Our Daily Bread Publishing.

DIVINE MOMENTS BOOKS
See listing in periodicals section, "**Adult Markets**."

DOVE CHRISTIAN PUBLISHERS
PO Box 611, Bladensburg, MD 20710-0611 | 240-342-3293
editorial@dovechristianpublishers.com | www.dovechristianpublishers.com
Raenita Wiggins, acquisitions editor

Parent company: Kingdom Christian Enterprises

Mission statement: "We entertain, edify, equip and encourage people through products that glorify and honor Jesus Christ and His kingdom. In addition, we provide new and emerging Christian authors with a forum for their creative and kingdom-building voices."

Submissions: Submit proposal with full manuscript through the website. Publishes ten books per year; receives 300 proposals. First-time authors: 95%. Responds in three to four weeks. Length: 100-220 pages. Bible: NIV.

Books: POD, ebooks, hardcover

Royalty: 10-25%, no advance

Types and topics: Christian living, self-help, devotionals, relationships, fiction (romance, fantasy, suspense, historical, thrillers, biblical, adventure), children's, African-American

Guidelines: *www.dovechristianpublishers.com/publish-with-us*

Tip: "Author should establish a platform and familiarize themselves with book marketing and promotion prior to submission."

EERDMANS BOOKS FOR YOUNG READERS
4035 Park East Ct. S.E., Grand Rapids, MI 49546 | 800-253-7521
kmerz@eerdmans.com | www.eerdmans.com/youngreaders
Kathleen Merz, acquisitions and managing editor

Parent company: Wm. B. Eerdmans Publishing Co.

Mission statement: to engage young minds with books—books that are honest, wise, and hopeful; books that delight us with their storyline, characters, or good humor; books that inform, inspire, and entertain

Submissions: Submit by mail; prefers from agents. Send a proposal with three chapters for book length or complete manuscript for picture books. Publishes sixteen to twenty titles per year; receives 1,500 submissions annually. First-time authors: 5-10%. Length: picture books, 1,000 words; middle-grade books, 15-30,000 words. Publication within one year for novels, two to three years for picture books. Responds in four months if interested. Ethnic books: African-American.

Types of books: hardcover, ebook, audiobook

Royalty: on net, advance varies

Types and topics: picture books: animal, contemporary, folktales, history, humor, multicultural, nature/environment, poetry, religion, special needs, social issues; middle grade: adventure, contemporary, history, humor, multicultural, nature/environment, religion, social issues

Guidelines: *www.eerdmans.com/Pages/YoungReaders/EBYR-Guidelines.aspx*

Tip: "We strongly encourage writers and illustrators to become familiar with our publications and the general trade children's book market before submitting any material. Please review our books in our catalog, on our website, or at your local library or bookstore to determine whether your manuscript is appropriate for us."

WM. B. EERDMANS PUBLISHING CO.

4035 Park East Ct. S.E., Grand Rapids, MI 49546 | 800-253-7521, 616-459-4591

info@eerdmans.com | *www.eerdmans.com*

Andrew Knapp, aquisitions editor

Submissions: Publishes about 100 titles per year. Accepts manuscripts through agents or authors. Email proposal only. Responds in six weeks.

Royalty: yes, some advances

Topics and types: adult nonfiction, textbooks, reference, biblical studies, theology, religious history and biography, ethics, spirituality, Christian living, ministry, social issues, contemporary cultural issues

Imprint: Eerdmans Books for Young Readers (see separate listing)

Tip: "Review submission guidelines carefully and check website for suitability. Target readerships range from academic to semipopular.

We are publishing a growing number of books in Christian life, spirituality, and ministry."

eLECTIO PUBLISHING

4206 S. Mentor Ave., Springfield, MO 65804 | 972-987-0015
submissions@electiopublishing.com | *www.electiopublishing.com*

Submissions: Publishes sixty to 100 titles per year; receives 1,000 annually. First-time authors: 70-80%. Length: 25-100,000 words. Email full manuscript. Responds in three months.

Royalty: 20%, no advance

Types and topics: Christian living, fiction (historical, romance, mystery), Bible studies, memoir, YA, African-American, Hispanic

Tip: "Please read carefully the submissions guidelines listed on website."

ELK LAKE PUBLISHING, INC.

35 Dogwood Dr., Plymouth, MA 02360-3166 | 508-746-1734
Deb@ElkLakePublishingInc.com | *ElkLakePublishingInc.com*
Deb Haggerty, publisher & editor-in-chief
Linda Rondeau, senior acquisitions editor—fiction,
  LindaRondeau@gmail.com
Susan K. Stewart, senior acquisitions editor—nonfiction,
  SKStewart@elklakepublishinginc.com

Mission statement: To captivate our readers and carry them to places of escape, encouragement, education, and entertainment—to broaden their horizons and urge them to new heights. More than anything else, we want to point people to Jesus Christ.

Submissions: Publishes fifty titles per year; receives 150 plus. First-time authors: 85%. Length: fiction, 80-100,000 words. Email proposal with sample chapters, or submit them through the website form. Prefers submissions from agents or writers met at conferences. Replies in one month. Bible: NLT, ESV.

Types of books: POD, ebook, hardcover, audiobook

Royalty: 40%, no advance

Types and topics: romance to speculative fiction, contemporary to historical, children's, middle-grade, young adult; nonfiction with a twist; no Amish fiction, westerns, Bible studies, devotionals, poetry

Guidelines: *www.elklakepublishinginc.com/choose-best-publisher*

Tip: "Ensure the style sheet is followed as well as the guidelines. Ensure the proposal is free of errors and follows the guidelines completely."

EMPOWERED PUBLICATIONS, INC.

529 County Road 31, Millry, AL 36558 | 251-754-9335
editor@empoweredpublicationsinc.com | *www.empoweredpublicationsinc.com*

Denomination: Conservative Pentecostal (Assemblies of God, Church of God, independent Pentecostals)

Submissions: Publishes thirty-six titles per year; receives 500 annually. First-time authors: 80%. Length: 35,000 for nonfiction, 65-80,000 for fiction. Email or mail proposal with full manuscript. Replies in two weeks. Bible version: KJV.

Royalty: 8-30%

Types and topics: Christian living; theology; biographies; pneumatology; historical, biblical, contemporary fiction for all ages

Guidelines: *www.empoweredpublicationsinc.com/about-us.html*

Tip: "We prefer submissions from those with an established ministry, but will consider works from a lay person recommended by a minister personally known to us. Potential authors must agree with our Statement of Faith. No prosperity preaching."

ENCLAVE PUBLISHING

24 W. Camelback Rd. A-635, Phoenix, AZ 85013
acquisitions@enclavepublishing.com | *www.enclavepublishing.com*
Steve Laube, publisher and acquisitions editor

Mission: We publish out-of-this-world stories that are informed by a coherent theology.

Submissions: Enclave is a focused publisher of Christian fantasy and science fiction. Publishes twelve titles per year; receives more than 200 submissions annually. Responds in two to three months; if no reply, assume it is "No thank you." First-time authors: 20-30%. Submit proposal through the website form. Length: 80,000-140,000 words.

Types: hardcover, offset paperback, ebooks, audiobooks licensed out

Royalty: varies, no advance

Types and topics: only speculative fiction (sci-fi, fantasy, supernatural) for adults and YA

Imprint: Enclave Escape (YA)

Guidelines: *www.enclavepublishing.com/guidelines*

Tip: "Keep word count above 80,000 words and below 140,000. Too often we are sent books that are either far too short or extremely long."

EXEGETICA PUBLISHING

312 Greenwich #112, Lee's Summit, MO 64082

editor@exegeticapublishing.com | exegeticapublishing.com

Mission statement: Exegetica Publishing publishes high-quality books designed to help learners grow to understand the Bible and the biblical worldview. Since 2005 Exegetica has produced resources that encourage Christians and non-Christians alike to engage with the Bible, to understand the world around them, and to "taste and see that the Lord is good," as Psalm 34:8 exhorts.

Submissions: Publishes ten books a year; receives thirty submissions annually. First-time book authors: 10%. Length: 200-300 pages. Email proposal with sample chapters and curriculum vitae. Responds in three to four weeks. Bible: NASB, NKJV, ESV.

Types and topics: Bible/theology, academic, Christian living

Royalty: 10%, no advance

Types of books: offset paperback, ebook

Imprint: Grace Acres Press (see separate listing)

Guidelines: *exegeticapublishing.com/submit-a-proposal*

Tip: "Follow submission guidelines with solid biblical resources."

FAITH ALIVE CHRISTIAN RESOURCES

1700 28th St. S.E., Grand Rapids, MI 49508-1407 | 800-333-8300, 616-224-0728

rvanderhart@crcna.org | www.faithaliveresources.org
Ruth Vanderhart, managing editor

Denomination: Christian Reformed

Submissions: Submit by mail or email. Responds in one month.

Types and topics: educational curricula for children, teens, and adults; Bible studies; church leadership and training materials

FAITHWORDS

1 Franklin Park, 6100 Tower Cir., Ste. 210, Franklin, TN 37067 | 615-221-0996

www.faithwords.com

Parent company: Hachette Book Group

Submissions: Through agents only. Publishes seventy-five books per year; receives 350 proposals. First-time authors: 50%. Length: 50,000 words. Responds in one month. Bible: ESV, NIV.

Types of books: offset paperback, hardcover, ebook

Royalty: 10% and up, advance

Types and topics: for Christian women ages 25-45: parenting, marriage, Christian living, social issues, spiritual issues, African-

American, Hispanic
Guidelines: *www.hachettebookgroup.com/about/faqs/#submissions*
Tip: "Have a clear, well-written proposal and a solid platform."

FATHER'S PRESS

590 N.W. 1921 St. Rd., Kingsville, MO 64061-9312 | 816-566-0654
mike@fatherspress.com | *www.fatherspress.com*
Mike Smitley, editor

> **Submissions:** Accepts manuscripts only through authors; no agents. Send proposal. Responds in four weeks. Bible versions: KJV, ESV.
>
> **Types and topics:** fiction (contemporary or historical), historical nonfiction, reference, children's books, biblical studies, theology, ethics, literature, religious history, regional history, cookbooks, self-help, Christian counseling
>
> **Guidelines:** *fatherspress.com/submission-guidelines*
>
> **Tip:** "Father's Press is a rapidly-growing, full-service publishing company dedicated to publishing well-written works by dynamic, energetic new authors who are frustrated with the endless barriers that have historically locked talented authors out of the writing profession."

FIREFLY SOUTHERN FICTION

100 Missionary Ridge, Birmingham, AL 35242 | 407-414-8188
fireflysouthernfiction@aol.com | *shoplpc.com/firefly*
Eva Marie Everson, managing editor

> **Parent company:** Lighthouse Publishing of the Carolinas/Iron Stream Media
>
> **Mission:** Firefly Southern Fiction is story-driven with distinctly Southern characters living within the realm of Southern tradition, both historical and contemporary.
>
> **Submissions:** Publishes four books per year; receives twenty proposals. First-time authors: 20%. Length: 75-95,000 words. Prefers proposals from agents, or email proposal with sample chapters. Responds in three months.
>
> **Types of books:** offset paperback, ebook, audiobook
>
> **Royalty:** 40% net, no advance
>
> **Types and topics:** Southern fiction
>
> **Guidelines:** *shoplpc.com/firefly*
>
> **Tip:** "Know your audience, Southern people, Southern lifestyle, Southern history."

FIRST STEPS PUBLISHING

PO Box 571, Gleneden Beach, OR 97388 | 541-961-7641
rj@FirstStepsPublishing.com | *www.FirstStepsPublishing.com*
RJ McRoberts, senior acquisitions editor

> **Submissions:** Publishes three to five titles per year; receives 400-500 submissions. First-time authors: 90%. Length: children's, 700 words minimum; fiction and nonfiction, 50-80,000 words. Agent submissions only. Responds in two to three months but only to writers who adhere to proper submission guidelines. Bible: NKJV, NIV.
>
> **Types:** offset paperback, POD, ebook, audiobook
>
> **Royalty:** 15-35%, higher for special cases, no advance
>
> **Types and topics:** fiction: action/adventure, mystery, thriller, historical; adventure; true stories; memoir; biography; creative nonfiction
>
> **Imprints:** White Parrot Press (children), West Wind Press (middle grade, young adult)
>
> **Guidelines:** *www.firststepspublishing.com/get-published*
>
> **Tip:** "Our acquisition editors are the first readers who decide whether a manuscript is worth pursuing. Put your best foot forward, and edit your manuscript until you are happy with every single word. This includes your query letter and proposal. If these concepts are foreign to you, learn them. If you just 'wing it,' we'll know; and your submission will be rejected. Do you know your target audience? Why would your book sell? Do you have a platform? Taking the time to learn what a publisher is looking for in an author will improve your chances of acquisition."

FOCUS ON THE FAMILY

8605 Explorer Dr., Colorado Springs, CO 80995 | 719-531-5181
www.focusonthefamily.com
Larry Weeden, acquisitions

> **Submissions:** Accepts manuscripts only via established literary agents or manuscript services.
>
> **Types and topics:** family advice topics, including resources about specific elements of marriage and parenting, encouragement for women, and topics for seniors

FORTRESS PRESS

PO Box 1209, Minneapolis, MN 55440-1209
www.fortresspress.com
Beth Gaede, senior aquisitions editor, ministry, leadership, pastoral care, parish life

Ryan Hemmer, aquisitions editor, theology, culture, biblical studies, ethics, philosophy

Denomination: Evangelical Lutheran Church in America
Parent company: 1517 Media
Submissions: Submit via the online form.
Types and topics: scholarly works in biblical studies, theology, Christian history, spirituality, social justice, wisdom traditions, spiritual practices, Christian living, creativity, culture
Guidelines: *ms.fortresspress.com/downloads/Fortress_Press_ submissions_guidelines_document.docx*
Tip: "People in all stages of life hunger for meaning, understanding, spiritual growth, and to make a difference in the world. Fortress Press seeks to be an informed, valuable, and delightful companion—a change maker in readers' spiritual and intellectual journeys and a leader in key conversations. With fresh perspectives, compelling stories, and fearless explorations, our books inspire readers to build a better world."

FORWARD MOVEMENT

412 Sycamore St., Cincinnati, OH 45202-4110 | 800-543-1813
editorial@forwardmovement.org | www.forwardmovement.org
Richelle Thompson, managing editor, rthompson@forwardmovement.org

Denomination: Episcopal
Submissions: Focuses on discipleship. Submit through email. Responds in four to six weeks.
Also does: PDF downloads, smartphone applications
Types and topics: prayer, spiritual practices, stewardship, church traditions, emerging trends, Bible study
Guidelines: *www.forwardmovement.org/Pages/About/Writers_ Guidelines.aspx*

THE FOUNDRY PUBLISHING

PO Box 419527, Kansas City, MO 64141
thefoundrypublishing.com
René McFarland, consumer product editor

Denomination: Nazarene
Submissions: Mail proposal to Attn: Product Development.
Types and topics: Christian living, spiritual growth, ministry resources

FOUR CRAFTSMEN PUBLISHING

PO Box U, Lakeside, AZ 85929-0585 | 928-367-2076
info@fourcraftsmen.com | www.fourcraftsmen.com
CeCelia Jackson, editor in chief
Martin Jackson, publisher

Mission statement: publishing truth that works for Christian readers
Submissions: Publishes four to six books per year; receives five proposals. First-time authors: 100%. Length: 40-80,000 words. Submit proposal with sample chapters or full manuscript by email or mail. Responds in two weeks. Bible: NASB, NKJV, TLB, TEV.
Types of books: POD, ebook, offset paperback, hardcover; print run 500
Royalty: 10% print, 50-60% ebook, no advance
Types and topics: testimony, Scripture studies, Christian living, finances, Bible analysis, spiritual warfare
Guidelines: *fourcraftsmen.com/additional-info*
Tip: "Original work, not compilation of source quotes. Necessary quotes correctly attributed and permissions provided."

FRANCISCAN MEDIA

28 W. Liberty St., Cincinnati, OH 45202 | 800-488-0488, 513-241-5615
info@franciscanmedia.org | www.FranciscanMedia.org
Mark Lombard, director, acquisitions, MLombard@FranciscanMedia.org

Denomination: Catholic
Submissions: Seeks manuscripts that inform and inspire adult Catholics, other Christians, and all who are seeking to better understand and live their faith. Goal is to help people "Live in love. Grow in faith." Not accepting unsolicited manuscripts. Publishes twenty to thirty books per year. Submit proposal by email or mail. Responds in one to three months. Length: 25,000-50,000 words or 100-250 pages. Bible: NRSV. No simultaneous submissions.
Royalty: 10-14% on net, advance $1,000-3,000
Topics and types: Christian living, spiritual growth, fiction
Guidelines: *franciscanmedia.org/writers-guides*

FRIENDS UNITED PRESS

101 Quaker Hill Dr., Richmond, IN 47374 | 765-962-7573
friendspress@fum.org | friendsunitedmeeting.org
Kristina Evans, managing editor

Denomination: Quaker

Mission statement: to energize and equip Friends through the power of the Holy Spirit to gather people into fellowships where Jesus Christ is known, loved, and obeyed as Teacher and Lord

Submissions: Email proposal with two or three chapters; responds in one to three months. Publishes two to five books per year; receives twenty-five proposals. First-time authors: 50%. Length: 120-350 pages.

Types of books: offset paperback, POD, hardcover, ebook

Royalty: 10-15%, no advance

Types and topics: nonfiction, fiction (historical, juvenile), children, juvenile, Quakerism, Quaker history, Quaker thought

Guidelines: by email

Tip: "Must relate to the Religious Society of Friends (Quakers), currently or in the past, or be strongly related to the work of Friends United Meeting."

GRACE ACRES PRESS

PO Box 22, Larkspur, CO 80118 | 303-681-9995
Anne@GraceAcresPress.com | www.GraceAcresPress.com
Anne R. Fenske, publisher

Parent company: Exegetica Publishing

Mission statement: Growing Your Faith One Page at a Time

Submissions: Publishes six books per year; receives twenty. First-time authors: 75%. Length: 100-300 pages. Email or mail query letter only; or submit through the website. No agents. Responds in one month. Bible: NKJV, NIV.

Types of books: offset and POD paperback, hardcover, ebook; print run 500-2,000

Royalty: 10-15%, no advance

Types and topics: Bible study, evangelism, discipleship, missions, biography/memoir

Guidelines: by email

Tip: "Explain your contribution as a copartner in marketing your book."

GRACE PUBLISHING

PO Box 1233, Broken Arrow, OK 74013-1233 | 918-346-7960
editorial@grace-publishing.com | www.grace-publishing.com
Terri Kalfas, publisher

Parent company: The Jomága Group, LLC

Mission statement: To develop and distribute—with integrity and excellence—biblically based resources that challenge, encourage, teach, equip, and entertain Christians in their personal journeys. We are committed to providing the most effective resources possible for evangelism, discipleship, and spiritual growth and renewal. By publishing materials that help and encourage Christians everywhere to deepen their relationship with our Lord Jesus Christ, we hope to change the lives of believers and the people their lives touch.

Submissions: Publishes six to eight titles per year; receives 250 submissions. First-time authors: 10%. Length: varies, fiction 40-80,000 words. Email proposal with sample chapters. Responds in six months. Bible: any. First-time authors: 10%.

Types of books: POD, ebook

Royalty: varies, advance sometimes

Types and topics: Christian living, Bible study, memoir, anthologies

Imprint: Jomága House (Christian worldview, nonfiction, memoir)

Guidelines: *grace-publishing.com/manuscript-submission*

Tip: "Meet with a representative at a writers conference; know your subject; present in a professional way."

GROUP PUBLISHING, INC.

1515 Cascade Ave., Loveland, CO 80538 | 970-669-3836
submissions@group.com | *www.group.com*

Mission statement: We create experiences that help people grow in relationship with Jesus and each other.

Submissions: Publishes thirty titles per year; receives 200 submissions annually. First-time authors: 10%. Length: 128-250 pages. Email or mail proposal with sample chapters. Responds in three months. Bible: NLT.

Types of books: offset paperback, hardcover, ebook; print run 3,000

Royalty: 8-10% net, $2,000 advance sometimes

Topics and types: church resources, Christian living, curriculum

Guidelines: *grouppublishingps.zendesk.com/hc/en-us/articles/211878258-Submissions*

Tip: "Most open to innovative and practical resources involving active/interactive learning that will help change lives. Tell our readers something they don't already know in a way that they've not seen before."

GUARDIAN ANGEL PUBLISHING, INC.

12430 Tesson Ferry Rd. #186, St. Louis, MO 63128 | 314-276-8482
editorial_staff@guardianangelpublishing.com |
www.guardianangelpublishing.com

Submissions: Publishes thirty-six to seventy titles per year; receives 100+ submissions annually. First-time authors: 5-10%. Length: picture book, 100 words; storybook, up to 5,000 words;

chapter book, up to 25,000 words. Email complete manuscript. Responds in one to three months. Bible: no preference. Submit only during August.

Types of books: POD, ebook, CD, hardcover

Royalty: 30%, advance sometimes

Types and topics: all kinds of books for kids ages 2-12, nonfiction and fiction, Spanish and bilingual, ethnic audiences

Imprints: Wings of Faith, Chapbooks for Tweens, Littlest Angels, Academic Wings, Health & Hygiene, Animals & Pets, Angelic Harmony, Angel to Angel

Guidelines: *www.guardianangelpublishing.com/submissions.htm*

Tip: "Send your best story. Follow the directions and suggestions."

GUIDEPOSTS BOOKS

110 William St., Ste. 901, New York, NY 10038 | 212-251-8100
bookeditors@guideposts.org | *www.guideposts.org*
Jon Woodhams, editor
Rebecca Maker, acquisitions for Daily Guideposts

Submissions: Extremely limited acquisitions. Accepts manuscripts through agents only. Publishes twenty to thirty titles per year.

Types and topics: inspirational memoir; Christian living; contemporary women's fiction focusing on faith, family, and friendships

GUIDING LIGHT WOMEN'S FICTION

100 Missionary Ridge, Birmingham, AL 35242 | 888-811-9934
submissions@guidinglightfiction.com | *shoplpc.com/guiding-light*
Karin Beery, acquisitions and managing editor

Parent company: Lighthouse Publishing of the Carolinas/Iron Stream Media

Mission statement: to publish compelling stories, beautifully written

Submissions: Publishes maximum of eight books per year; receives 100 proposals. First-time authors: 50%, enjoys working with them. Length: 80-90,000 words. Only accepts proposals from agents, author referrals, and conference meetings. Responds in one to three months. Bible: NIV.

Types of books: POD, ebook, audiobook

Royalty: 40% net, no advance

Types and topics: women's fiction

Guidelines: *shoplpc.com/guiding-light-1*

Tip: "Be teachable. A willingness to learn will get you far."

HARAMBEE PRESS

100 Missionary Ridge, Birmingham, AL 35242 | 888-811-9934
harambeepresslpcbooks@gmail.com | *shoplpc.com/harambee-press*
Edwina Perkins, managing editor

> **Parent company:** Lighthouse Publishing of the Carolinas/Iron Stream Media
> **Mission statement:** giving voice to ethnic writers
> **Submissions:** Publishes four to eight books per year; receives sixty proposals. First-time authors: 50%. Length: 40-90,000 words. Email proposal with sample chapters. Only accepts proposals from agents, author referrals, and conference meetings. Responds in three months. Bible: NIV.
> **Types of books:** POD, ebook, audiobook
> **Royalty:** 40% on net, no advance
> **Types and topics:** marriage, Christian living, devotionals, memoirs, parenting; fiction: women's, romance, suspense, mystery; books for African-American, Hispanic, and Asian audiences
> **Guidelines:** *shoplpc.com/harambee*
> **Tip:** "Follow any additional instructions when asked."

HARBOURLIGHT BOOKS

PO Box 1738, Aztec, NM 87410
customer@harbourlightbooks.com | *www.pelicanbookgroup.com*
Nicola Martinez, editor-in-chief

> **Parent company:** Pelican Book Group
> **Mission:** Our primary ministry is to publish quality books that reflect the salvation and love offered by Jesus Christ. Our titles adhere to mainline Christianity but are enjoyed by Christians and non-Christians alike.
> **Submissions:** Novels 25-80,000 words. Interested in series ideas. Accepts unagented submissions. Responds in three to four months. Submit through the website form. Bible: NIV, NAB. Considers books for all ethnicities.
> **Types of books:** offset and POD paperback, hardcover, ebook, audiobook
> **Royalty:** 40% on download, 7% on print, advance sometimes
> **Types and topics:** fiction: action-adventure, mystery (cozy or other), suspense, crime drama, police procedural, family saga, westerns, women's
> **Guidelines:** *pelicanbookgroup.com/ec/index.php?main_page=page&id=57*

HARPERCOLLINS CHRISTIAN PUBLISHING

See Thomas Nelson, Tommy Nelson, Zonderkidz, and Zondervan.

HARPERONE

353 Sacramento St. #500, San Francisco, CA 94111-3653 | 415-477-4400
harperone.com
Gideon Weil, editorial director
> **Parent company:** HarperCollins Publishing
> **Submissions:** Requires manuscripts through agents only. Publishes
> seventy-five titles per year; receives 10,000 submissions annually. First-
> time authors: 5%. Length: 160-256 pages. Responds in three months.
> **Royalty:** 7.5-15% on retail, advance $20-100,000
> **Types and topics:** religion, spirituality

HARVEST HOUSE PUBLISHERS

PO Box 41210, Eugene, OR 97404-0322 | 800-547-8979
harvesthousepublishers.com
Kathleen Kerr, acquisitions editor
Kyle Hatfield, acquisitions editor, children and family
> **Submissions:** Requires submissions through agents.
> **Types and topics:** self-help (relationships, family, Christian living),
> Bible resources (Bible studies, topical studies), and full-color gift
> and children's books
> **Imprint:** Harvest House Kids (children), Ink & Willow (gift books,
> journals, cards, nontraditional books)
> **Guidelines:** *www.harvesthousepublishers.com/about/manuscript-
> submissions*

HENDRICKSEN PUBLISHERS

137 Summit St., PO Box 3473, Peabody, MA 01961
rbrown@hendrickson.com | www.hendrickson.com
Rick Brown, publisher
> **Submissions:** Works only through agents or direct contact at various
> conferences editors attend throughout the year (most notably, the
> AAR/SBL annual meeting).
> **Types and topics:** academic, Bible studies, marriage and parenting
> resources, new media and the arts, biblical studies and reference
> works for both pastors and thoughtful laypersons, devotionals,
> classic fiction, Christian classics, and prolife resources
> **Imprints:** Aspire Books, Rose Publishing, RoseKidz (see separate listings)
> **Guidelines:** *www.hendrickson.com/content/getting-published*

HERITAGE BEACON FICTION

100 Missionary Ridge, Birmingham, AL 35242 | 888-811-9934
editor@smittenromance.com | *shoplpc.com/heritage-beacon-historical-fiction*
Denise Weimer, managing editor

Parent company: Lighthouse Publishing of the Carolinas/Iron Stream Media

Submissions: Publishes six books per year; receives twenty proposals. First-time authors: 75%. Length: 65-80,000 words. Only accepts proposals from agents, author referrals, and conference meetings. Responds in one to two months. Bible: NIV.

Types of books: POD, ebook, audiobook

Royalty: 40% net, no advance

Types and topics: historical fiction

Guidelines: *shoplpc.com/heritage-beacon*

Tip: "Romance should be a subplot, rather than the main plot."

HOWARD BOOKS

1230 Avenue of the Americas, New York, NY 10020 | 212-698-7329
simonandschusterpublishing.com/howard-books
Peter Borland, acquisitions editor

Parent company: Simon & Schuster, Atria Publishing Group

Submissions: Does not accept, review, or return unsolicited manuscripts, except through agents. Publishes twenty-five books per year; receives 400 submissions. First-time authors: 25%. Responds in two months.

Types of books: offset paperback, hardcover, ebook, audiobook

Royalty: standard, advance

Types and topics: fiction, memoir, Christian living, spiritual growth

Guidelines: none

Tip: "Have a great idea, a large platform, and strong writing."

ILLUMINATEYA

100 Missionary Ridge, Birmingham, AL 35242 | 888-811-9934
illuminateYAsubmission@gmail.com | *shoplpc.com/illuminateYA*
Tessa Emily Hall, acquisitions editor

Parent company: Lighthouse Publishing of the Carolinas/Iron Stream Media

Mission statement: Our goal is to shed light on positive and inspiring books that engross readers in an entertaining journey from beginning to end. We don't shy away from reflecting today's authentic youth culture, yet we do so in a way that promotes good morals and values. Our stories touch teens' deepest needs, answer their life questions, sweep them away in a can't-put-me-down adventure, and portray their world with a thread of hope.

Submissions: Publishes four books per year; receives twenty-five proposals. First-time authors: 50%. Length: 50-95,000 words. Email proposal with sample chapters. Only accepts submissions from agents, author referrals, and conference meetings. Responds in one to three months. Bible: NIV.

Types of books: POD, ebook, audiobook

Royalty: 40% net, no advance

Types and topics: YA contemporary, historical, romance, fantasy, speculative, sci-fi

Guidelines: *www.illuminateya.com/submissions*

Tip: "Our YA novels are clean reads; no vulgar language or sex scenes. IlluminateYA seeks to change our culture by publishing books with strong moral values. We will consider inspirational themes but prefer stories that can reach the young, general-market reader."

IMAGE BOOKS

1745 Broadway, New York, NY 10019 | 212-782-9000
imagebooks@randomhouse.com | *crownpublishing.com/archives/imprint/image-catholic-books*
Gary Jansen, director

Parent company: Crown Publishing Group, which is part of Penguin Random House

Denomination: Catholic

Submissions: Takes submissions only from agents.

IRON STREAM BOOKS

100 Missionary Ridge, Birmingham, AL 35242 | 888-811-9934
proposals@newhopepublishers.com | *www.ironstreammedia.com*

Parent company: Iron Stream Media

Submissions: Only accepts proposals through agents, author referrals, and conference meetings. Email proposal. Length: 50,000-90,000. Responds in four months. Bible: NASB.

Types and topics: leadership, spiritual growth, business as mission, millennials, and specialty markets

Royalty: no advance

Guidelines: *www.ironstreammedia.com/submission-process*

Tip: "All submissions must follow the guidelines. No query letters."

IRON STREAM MEDIA

See Iron Stream Books; New Hope Publishers; and the imprints of Lighthouse Publishing of the Carolinas: Bling!, Candlelight Romance, Firefly Southern Fiction, Guiding Light Women's Fiction, Harambee Press, Heritage Beacon Fiction, IlluminateYA, Lamplighter Mysteries & Suspense, Smitten Historical Romance, Sonrise Devotionals, Straight Street Books, Trailblazer Western Fiction.

IVP

PO Box 1400, Downers Grove, IL 60515-1426 | 630-734-4000
email@ivpress.com | www.ivpress.com
Al Hsu, senior editor and acquisitions, IVP Books
Jon Boyd, editorial director, academic

> **Parent company:** InterVarsity Christian Fellowship
> **Submissions:** Publishes 100 titles per year; receives more than 1,000 submissions annually. First-time authors: 15%. Accepts manuscripts through agents or if you have had direct contact with an editor. Length: 50,000 words or 200 pages. Bible: NIV, NRSV.
> **Royalty:** negotiable on retail or outright purchase, negotiable advance
> **Types and topics:** IVP books are characterized by a thoughtful, biblical approach to the Christian life that transforms the hearts, souls, and minds of readers in the university, church, and the world, on topics ranging from spiritual disciplines to apologetics to current issues, to theology. Especially looking for ethnic writers (African-American, Hispanic, Asian-American).
> **Imprints:** IVP Academic, IVP Books, IVP Connect (Bible studies and small-group resources), IVP Formatio (spiritual formation), IVP Cresendo (women's books), IVP Praxis (ministry)
> **Guidelines:** *www.ivpress.com/submissions*
> **Tip:** "Most open to books written by pastors (though not collections of sermons) or other church staff, by professors, by leaders in Christian organizations. Authors need to bring resources for publicizing and selling their own books, such as a website, an organization they are part of that will promote their books, speaking engagements, well-known people they know personally who will endorse and promote their book, writing articles for national publication, etc."

JOURNEY FICTION

2657 Rungsted St., Las Vegas, NV 89142 | 702-570-3433
contact@journeyfiction.com | www.journeyfiction.com
Jennifer L. Farey, publisher

> **Mission statement:** Specializes in series fiction. We encourage binge

reading.

Submissions: Publishes twelve books per year; receives forty. First-time authors: 90%. Length: 70-80,000 words. Email proposal with sample chapters. Prefers series. Responds in two weeks. Bible: NKJV.

Types of books: POD, ebook, audiobook

Royalty: 50% of net sales, no advance

Types and topics: fiction only: contemporary and historical, romance, suspense, mystery, speculative

Guidelines: *www.journeyfiction.com/for-authors*

Tip: "We're looking for great characters with compelling stories. Let us see characters live out their faith (or struggle with it), rather than break out into sermons."

JOURNEYFORTH BOOKS

1430 Wade Hampton Blvd., Greenville, SC 29609 | 864-546-4600
journeyforth@bjupress.com | *www.journeyforth.com*
Nancy Lohr, acquisitions editor

Parent company: BJU Press

Mission statement: We publish youth fiction and biographies as well as teen and adult nonfiction that reflect a solidly biblical worldview and encourage Christians to live out their faith.

Submissions: Publishes six to eight titles per year; receives 150-200 submissions. First-time authors: 45%. Length: varies, see guidelines. Email proposal with sample chapters. Agent not necessary. Responds in three months. Bible: KJV, NKJV, ESV, NASB. Open to books for ethnic audiences.

Types of books: offset paperback, ebook

Royalty: 10-15%, variable advance sometimes

Types and topics: youth fiction: adventure, contemporary stories, historical fiction, mystery, family stories, animal stories, school stories; youth biographies; teen and adult Bible study and Christian living; marriage and family

Guidelines: *www.bjupress.com/books/freelance.php*

Tip: "We are looking for writing that has a fresh and engaging voice, but text that is not filled with jargon or idioms that would date the content quickly."

JUDSON PRESS

1075 First Ave., King of Prussia, PA 19406
editor@judsonpress.com | *www.judsonpress.com*
Rebecca Irwin-Diehl, editor

Parent company: American Baptist Home Mission Societies

BOOK PUBLISHERS | *Book Publishers*

Denomination: Baptist

Mission statement: committed to producing Christ-centered leadership resources for the transformation of individuals, congregations, communities, and cultures

Submissions: Publishes twelve titles per year; receives 300 submissions. First-time authors: 25%. Email or mail proposal with sample chapters. Responds in three to six months. Length: 128-244 pages. Bible: NRSV.

Types of books: offset paperback, ebook, POD; print run 2,500

Royalty: 10-15% net, advance sometimes

Types and topics: church resources, pastoral resources, Christian living, devotional, Baptist identity and history, worship resources, African-American, Asian, Hispanic, multicultural

Guidelines: *www.judsonpress.com/Pages/Info/For-Authors.aspx*

Tip: "Be clear about your audience; be proactive as a promotional partner; be passionate about what makes your project unique and compelling."

KREGEL PUBLICATIONS

2450 Oak Industrial Dr. N.E., Grand Rapids, MI 49505 | 616-451-4775

KPacquisitions@kregel.com | *www.kregel.com*

Janyre Tromp, development and acquisitions editor (fiction, women)

Joel Armstrong, acquisitions (nonfiction)

Submissions: Does not accept unsolicited proposals or manuscripts for review. Submit only through agents or manuscript-review services.

Types and topics: biblical studies, biography, Bible reference, children's, Christian living, church/ministry, fiction (YA, historical, romance, romantic suspense), marriage and family, theology, women's issues, self-help, parenting, Bible studies (prefers topical), discipleship, devotionals

Guidelines: *www.kregel.com/contact-us/submissions-policy*

LAMPLIGHTER MYSTERIES & SUSPENSE

100 Missionary Ridge, Birmingham, AL 35242 | 888-811-9934

lamplighterlpc@gmail.com | *shoplpc.com/lamplighter-1*

Darla Crass, managing editor

Parent company: Lighthouse Publishing of the Carolinas/Iron Stream Media

Submissions: Publishes five books per year; receives twenty proposals. First-time authors: 80%. Length: 65-80,000 words. Only accepts manuscripts from agents and writers met at conferences. Responds in one month. Bible: NIV.

Types of books: POD, ebook, audiobook
Royalty: 40% net, no advance
Types and topics: mystery, suspense
Guidelines: *shoplpc.com/pages.php?pageid=22*
Tip: "A good handle on plot and structure will be a strong advantage."

LEAFWOOD PUBLISHERS

ACU, PO Box 29138, Abilene, TX 79699 | 325-674-2720
manuscriptsubmissions@groupmail.acu.edu | *www.leafwoodpublishers.com*
Dr. Jason Fikes, editor

Parent company: Abilene Christian University
Denomination: Churches of Christ
Mission statement: to publish deeper books that make faith practical
Submissions: Publishes fifteen to twenty books per year; receives 100 proposals. First-time authors: 35%. Length: 55,000 words. Prefers working with agents. Response time: three to six months. Bible: NIV, ESV.
Types of books: offset paperback, ebook
Royalty: 14-16%, advance
Types and topics: Christian living, spirituality, social issues, leadership, church history, theology
Guidelines: *tinyurl.com/ybgt6bew*
Tips: "Know your readers. Your book is not for everyone. Be practical. Don't be afraid to go deep."

LEXHAM PRESS

1313 Commercial St., Bellingham, WA 98225
editor@lexampress.com | *www.lexhampress.com*
Dr. Brannon Ellis, publisher

Parent company: FaithLife Corporation, makers of Logos Bible Software
Submissions: Publishes print, ebooks, and innovative resources for Logos Bible Software. Will work directly with authors. Submit proposal and sample chapters through the website.
Types and topics: evangelical scholarly and pastoral works in the areas of biblical studies, including Bible reference and original language resources; biblical, historical, and systematic theology; and ministry resources
Guidelines: *www.lexhampress.com/manuscript-submission*

LIGHTHOUSE PUBLISHING

754 Roxholly Walk, Buford, CA 30518 | 770-709-2268
info@lighthousechristianpublishing.com | *www.lighthousechristianpublishing.com*
Sylvia Charvet, acquisitions editor

Parent company: Lighthouse eMedia and Publishing

Submissions: Publishes thirty books annually; receives 200. First-time authors: 80%. Length: 300-320 pages for fiction. Email proposal with full manuscript. Responds in four to six weeks. Bible: NAS.

Types of books: POD, ebook, audiobook

Royalty: 50%, no advance

Types and topics: all fiction and nonfiction, also African-American and Hispanic audiences

Imprint: Lone Oak Publishing (general market)

Tip: Looking for unique stories.

LIGHTHOUSE TRAILS PUBLISHING, LLC

PO Box 908, Eureka, MT 59917 | 406-889-3610
david@lighthousetrails.com | www.lighthousetrails.com
David Dombrowski, acquisitions editor

Mission statement: publishes books that bring clarity and light to areas of spiritual darkness or deception

Submissions: Publishes two to four titles per year; receives fifty to seventy-five submissions annually. First-time authors: 30%. Accepts manuscripts directly from authors. Length: 160-300 pages. Email proposal with two sample chapters as attachment, or mail it. Responds in two months. Bible: KJV.

Royalty: 12-17% of net, 20% of retail

Types and topics: stories of Christians who have risen above incredible and unusual challenges and even their own failures to illustrate God's amazing grace and strength to overcome, books about or by missionaries, fiction for all ages

Guidelines: *www.lighthousetrails.com/content/11-submit-manuscript*

Tip: "Any book we consider will not only challenge the more scholarly reader, but also be able to reach those who may have less experience and comprehension. Our books will include human interest and personal experience scenarios as a means of getting the point across. Read a couple of our books to better understand the style of writing we are looking for. We also have a doctrinal statement on our website that helps to define us."

LION HUDSON

Wilkinson House, Jordan Hill Rd., Oxford OX2 8DR, UK
submissions-non-fiction@lionhudson.com, submissions-fiction@lionhudson.com,
submissions-children@lionhudson.com | www.lionhudson.com
Colin Forbes, senior editorial manager

Parent company: AFD Group

Submissions: Publishes internationally; distributed in the US by

Kregel Publications. Email or mail a proposal and sample chapters or manuscript; mail only for children's books. If no response in three months, consider it a rejection.

Types and topics: Lion Books, Lion Children's Books, Lion Fiction: accessible books that reflect a Christian worldview to a general audience. Candle Books, Monarch Books: support Christian families, individuals, and communities in their devotional and spiritual lives

Guidelines: *www.lionhudson.com/page/submissions*

LITTLE LAMB BOOKS

PO Box 211724, Bedford, TX 76095 | 817-505-8719
subs@littlelambbooks.com | *www.littlelambbooks.com*
Rachel Pellegrino, publisher
Lindsay Schlegel, editor-at-large

Parent company: Lamb Publishing, LLC

Mission statment: to shepherd the next generation of readers by encouraging their faith in God, inspiring their love of reading, and delighting their imaginations through colorful and creative literary works

Submissions: Publishes three to five books per year; receives 120-180 proposals. First-time authors: 80%. Length: picture books, 500 words; chapter books, 1,500-5,000 words; middle grade, 30-60,000 words; YA, 50-80,000 words. Email proposal with sample chapters. Submissions are accepted only during February, June, and November. Responds in three to four months. Bible: NIV.

Types of books: offset paperback, hardcover, ebook, POD

Royalty: varies, no advance

Types and topics: Picture books (ages 4-8): character and biblical values, animals/nature, fables, holiday/seasonal, multicultural, family-oriented. Chapter books (ages 6-10): adventure, mystery, humor/comedy, history, friendships, family values. Middle grade (ages 10-14): contemporary, multicultural, fables/fantasy, historical, action/adventure, sports, mystery/suspense. YA (age 12+): contemporary, sweet romance, fantasy/royalty, some speculative fiction, historical, action/adventure, sports, travel, mystery/suspense.

Guidelines: *littlelambbooks.com/subs*

Also does: digital printables, T-shirts, travel mugs, coloring books, stickers, totes, trading cards, etc.

Tip: "We're seeking diverse and original stories from a biblical worldview that entertain, inspire, and engage young readers. Strong characters and settings, curious plots, and evergreen pitches capture our attention. Authors should follow our guidelines, but also be sure that your query has your synopsis, comparative titles, platform notes, and a hook that leaves us wanting more from you."

LITURGICAL PRESS

2950 St. John's Rd., PO Box 7500, Collegeville, MN 56321-7500
submissions@litpress.org | www.litpress.org

Denomination: Catholic
Submissions: Submit a proposal through the website form.
Types and topics: biography, vocation, commentaries, chidren's, church, discipleship, liturgy, marriage and family, prayer, preaching, Bible reference books, theology, spirituality
Guidelines: *www.litpress.org/Authors/submit_manuscript*

LOVE INSPIRED

195 Broadway, 24th floor, New York, NY 10007 | 212-207-7000
harlequin.submittable.com/submit | www.loveinspired.com
Tina James, executive editor
Melissa Endlich, senior editor
Emily Rodmell, editor
Shana Asaro, editor
Dina Davis, associate editor

Parent company: Harlequin, a division of HarperCollins Publishers
Mission statement: From contemporary romance to heart-stopping romantic suspense, Love Inspired books celebrate wholesome, inspirational romances that enrich the lives of each reader.
Submissions: Publishes 144 titles per year; receives 500-1,000. First-time authors: 15%. Submit proposal with sample chapters or full manuscript through the website. Agent not required. Responds in three months. Length: 55,000 words. Bible: KJV.
Royalty: on retail, competitive advance
Type of books: mass-market paperback
Types and topics: Love Inspired: contemporary romance; Love Inspired Suspense: contemporary romantic suspense
Guidelines: *harlequin.submittable.com/submit*
Tip: "We're looking for compelling stories with engaging characters, a sustained conflict, and an emotionally satisfying romance. The focus must always be on the hero and heroine as they overcome the obstacles in their paths to find love together."

LOVE2READLOVE2WRITE PUBLISHING, LLC
(L2L2 PUBLISHING)

PO Box 103, Camby, IN 46113
editor@love2readlove2writepublishing.com |
www.love2readlove2writepublishing.com
Michele Israel Harper, acquisitions editor

Submissions: Publishes four to six titles per year; receives 150-200 proposals. 20% from first-time authors. Length: 60-90,000. Email proposal with full manuscript. Replies in two to three months. Bible: NKJV. Agent not required though welcome.

Type of book: POD

Royalty: 50% of net, $50 advance

Types and topics: Christian or clean speculative fiction only: YA, fantasy, paranormal, supernatural, dystopian, science fiction; unique writing guides

Guidelines: *www.love2readlove2writepublishing.com/submissions*

Tip: "Be professional, be succinct, and know your audience."

LOYOLA PRESS

3441 N. Ashland Ave., Chicago, IL 60657 | 773-281-1818, 800-621-1008
durepos@loyolapress.com | *www.loyolapress.com*
Joseph Durepos, acquisitions editor

Denomination: Catholic

Submissions: Publishes twenty titles per year; receives 500 submissions annually. Accepts manuscripts directly from authors. Email proposal with sample chapters. Length: 25-75,000 words or 150-300 pages. Considers first-time authors without agents. Responds in three months. Bible: NRSV (Catholic edition).

Royalty: standard, reasonable advance

Types and topics: books that help people experience God in their lives more directly, that introduce the dynamics of the Spiritual Exercises and the Ignatian process of discernment and decision-making, and that open up Scripture as a way of encountering Jesus; books that introduce and explain Catholic tradition and the richness of our faith

Guidelines: *www.loyolapress.com/general/submissions*

Tip: "Looking for books and authors that help make Catholic faith relevant and offer practical tools for the well-lived spiritual life."

MASTER BOOKS

PO Box 726, Green Forest, AR 72638 | 800-999-3777
submissions@nlpg.com | www.masterbooks.com
Craig Froman, acquisitions editor
> **Parent company:** New Leaf Publishing Group
> **Submissions:** Publishes thirty to thirty-five titles per year. First-time
> authors: 10%. Accepts manuscripts directly from authors. Requires
> email submission with "Author's Proposal Document" on the
> website. Responds within three months or isn't interested. No
> simultaneous submissions.
> **Royalty:** varies on net, no advance
> **Types and topics:** young-Earth creation material for all ages, including
> apologetics, homeschool resources, science and the Bible, reference
> titles, and children's literature
> **Guidelines:** *www.nlpg.com/submissions*

MAURICE WYLIE MEDIA

143 Northumberland St., Belfast, Ireland BT13 2JF | 08456439319
author@MauriceWylieMedia.com | www.MauriceWylieMedia.com
> **Mission statement:** to provide inspirational Christian books with one
> goal: to give the best
> **Submissions:** Email proposal with sample chapters. Responds in two
> weeks. Publishes ten books per year. Receives twenty-five proposals
> per year. First-time book authors: 80%. Length: 60,000 words.
> Bible: NKJV.
> **Royalty:** 30-50%, sometimes gives advance
> **Types of books:** hardcover, offset and POD paperback, ebook,
> audiobook; first print run, 5,000 books
> **Types and topics:** all Christian nonfiction and fiction books
> **Guidelines:** *mauricewyliemedia.com/publishing*
> **Tip:** "We have one goal: to give you the best!"

MOMENTS BOOKS

See listing in the periodicals section, "**Adult Markets.**"

MOODY PUBLISHERS

820 N. LaSalle Blvd., Chicago, IL 60610 | 800-678-8812
www.moodypublishers.com
Judy Dunagan, acquisitions editor, judy.dunagan@moody.edu
Drew Dyck, acquisitions editor, drew.dyck@moody.edu
John Hinkley, acquisitions editor, john.hinkley@moody.edu
Duane Sherman, acquisitions editor, duane.sherman@moody.edu

Amy Simpson, acquisitions editor, amy.simpson@moody.edu

Parent company: Moody Bible Institute

Mission statement: to resource the church's work of discipling all people

Submissions: Publishes fifty to sixty titles per year; receives thousands of submissions annually. First-time authors: 20%. Does not accept unsolicited manuscripts in any category; must be submitted by a literary agent, an author who has published with Moody, a Moody Bible Institute employee, or a contact at a writers conference. Responds in one to two months. Bible: NASB, ESV, NKJV.

Royalty: on net, advances begin at $500

Types and topics: books need to fit one of these categories: marriage and family resources—how to be a better mom, dad, grandparent, etc.; church leaders—pastors, community care, leading in a church context; Bible study materials—how to better study God's Word, primarily for women and young people; Christian living—how to help people take that next step in the Christian life; and ministry partners—those who work to make a better world in some way from orphan care to responsible finances

Guidelines: *www.moodypublishers.com/about/contact*

Tip: "Most open to books that (1) have a great idea at the core, (2) are executed well, and (3) can demonstrate an audience clamoring for the content."

MOUNTAIN BROOK INK

White Salmon, WA | 509-493-3953
mountainbrookink@gmail.com | www.mountainbrookink.com
Miralee Ferrell, lead acquisitions editor

Mission statement: fiction you can believe in that embodies restoration and/or renewal

Submissions: Publishes twelve titles per year; receives fifty-plus proposals. First-time authors: 75%. Length: minimum 75,000 words, 75,000-90,000 words for YA. Email query letter if not a traditionally published book author. If traditionally published, email proposal with sample chapters. No single titles; prefers sets or series. Accepts submissions from agents and directly from authors. Replies in two months. Bible: KJV, NKJV, NIV.

Types of books: POD, ebook, audiobook

Royalty: 30-40%, no advance

Types and topics: fiction only—women's, historical, historical romance, contemporary romance, YA, cozy mystery, suspense/thrillers (with or without romance), biblical, speculative for middle grade and YA

Imprint: Mountain Brook Fire (speculative fiction)

Guidelines: *mountainbrookink.com/submission-guidelines-for-inquiries, fire.mountainbrookink.com/submission-guidelines*

Tip: "Send the best work you've done, preferably that's been edited so it shines."

MY HEALTHY CHURCH

1445 N. Boonville Ave., Springfield, MO 65802 | 800-641-4310, 417-831-8000

newproducts@myhealthychurch.com | *www.myhealthychurch.com*

Denomination: Assemblies of God

Submissions: Does not accept unsolicited manuscripts unless represented by an agent. Responds in two to three months.

Types and topics: church resources for kids, youth, and adults; small group studies

Guidelines: *myhealthychurch.com/store/startcat.cfm?cat=tWRITGUID*

Tip: "The content of all our books and resources must be compatible with the beliefs and purposes of the Assemblies of God."

NAVPRESS

3820 N. 30th St., Colorado Springs, CO 80904 | 719-598-1212

inquiries@navpress.com | *www.navpress.com*

Caitlyn Carlson, acquisitions editor

David Zimmerman, acquisitions editor

Parent company: The Navigators

Submissions: Publishes twenty titles per year; receives 1,000 proposals annually. First-time authors: 40%. Length: 40,000 words. Submissions only from agents, current authors, or authors known to the editors. Responds in two months.

Royalty: 16-22%, advance

Types and topics: Christian living, spiritual growth, devotionals, marriage, prayer, discipleship, parenting/grandparenting, leadership, counseling/psychology, evangelism, missions, apologetics, theology, church/ministry, women, men, relationships, dating, home/family, Bible studies

Guidelines: *www.navpress.com/faq*

Tip: "Proposals with strong discipleship elements are preferred. Authors should have a ministry platform that supports their discipleship elements. NavPress does not accept unsolicited manuscripts."

NEW GROWTH PRESS

PO Box 4485, Greensboro, NC 27404 | 336-378-7775
submissions@newgrowthpress.com | *www.newgrowthpress.com*
Cheryl White, director of acquisitions
Rush Witt, acquisitions editor, biblical counseling resources

Mission statement: to empower individuals, families, and churches to grow in their love for God, their love for others, and their ability to bring healing and hope to the world

Submissions: Will work directly with authors and agents. Email proposal. Responds in three months if interested.

Types and topics: small-group resources, family, parenting, counseling issues, sexual-identity issues, missions, renewal, fiction, illustrated children's books

Also does: minibooks, short, 24-page booklets that address one specific felt need

NEW HOPE PUBLISHERS

100 Missionary Ridge, Birmingham, AL 35252 | 866-266-8399
proposals@newhopepublishers.com | *www.newhopepublishers.com*

Parent company: Iron Stream Media

Submissions: Publishes twenty to twenty-five nonfiction and ten to fifteen fiction titles per year; receives more than 100. First-time authors: 20%. Length 40-50,000 words. Only accepts proposals through agents, author referrals, and conference meetings. Responds in four months. Bible: any.

Royalty: 12-14%; sometimes variable advance, depending on publishing history

Types and topics: spiritual growth, personal growth, leadership, Bible studies, fiction (women's, suspense, romantic suspense, contemporary and historical romance, seasonal, speculative), parenting, family

Imprint: New Hope Kidz (picture and board books for preschool and early readers, storybooks and Bibles for boys and girls)

Guidelines: *www.newhopepublishers.com/proposals*

Tip: "Proposals must be polished and free of errors. Marketing plans in proposal must show author's knowledge of market, platform, and genre. Please include previous sales figures (if any) and author's biography as related to book topic."

NEW LEAF PRESS

PO Box 726, Green Forest, AR 72638-0726 | 870-438-5288
submissions@newleafpress.net | www.nlpg.com/imprint/new-leaf-press
Craig Froman, acquisitions editor

> **Parent company:** New Leaf Publishing Group
> **Submissions:** Publishes thirty to thirty-five titles per year; receives 1,000 submissions annually. First-time authors: 10%. Accepts manuscripts directly from authors. Requires email submission with "Author's Proposal Document" on the website. Responds within three months or isn't interested.
> **Royalty:** on net, no advance
> **Types and topics:** Christian living, stewardship, reference titles, church ministry, family issues, some materials in Spanish
> **Guidelines:** *www.nlpg.com/submissions*
> **Tip:** "Always follow our online guidelines before submitting."

NORTH WIND PUBLISHING

PO Box 3655, Brewer, ME 04412 | 207-922-8435
info@northwindpublishing.com | www.northwindpublishing.com
Janet Robbins, publisher

> **Submissions:** Email or mail proposal with sample chapters. No agents. Responds in three months. Publishes one or two titles per year; receives ten. First-time authors: 70%. Length: 150 pages. Bible: NIV.
> **Type of books:** POD
> **Royalty:** 10-20%, no advance
> **Types and topics:** devotionals, Christian living
> **Guidelines:** none
> **Tip:** "Manuscripts must have already been professionally edited."

NORTHWESTERN PUBLISHING HOUSE

1250 N. 113th St., Milwaukee, WI 53226 | 800-662-6022, 414-615-5710
braunj@nph.wels.net | www.nph.net
John Braun

> **Denomination:** Wisconsin Evangelical Lutheran Synod
> **Submissions:** Mail proposal and manuscript, Attn: Manuscript Submissions.
> **Types and topics:** devotions, family and personal guidance, church history, Scripture studies like the popular People's Bible commentary series and the People's Bible Teachings series on doctrine
> **Guidelines:** *online.nph.net/manuscript-submission*

OLIVIA KIMBRELL PRESS

PO Box 470, Fort Knox, KY 40121-0470 | 859-577-1071
admin@oliviakimbrellpress.com | www.oliviakimbrellpress.com
Heather McCurdy, editor
Gregg Bridgeman, editor-in-chief

Submissions: Specializes in true-to-life, meaningful Christian fiction and nonfiction titles intended to uplift the heart and engage the mind. Primary focus on "Roman Road" small-group guides or reader's guides to accompany nonfiction and fiction. Fiction: finished manuscript only. Nonfiction: primarily completed and an outline. Email submission.

Types and topics: adult devotionals, family, Christian living, healthy living, cookbooks, fasting/feasts; fiction: speculative/science fiction, fantasy

Imprints: CAVË (historical fiction from the periods immediately before, during, or after the time of Christ), Sign of the Whale (biblical and/or Christian fiction primarily with speculative fiction, science fiction, fantasy, or other futuristic and/or supernatural themes), House of Bread (biblical and/or traditional foods; clean foods; fasting; feasts; and healthy, nutritious information presented in an educational and entertaining manner)

Guidelines: *www.oliviakimbrellpress.com/submission.html*

Tip: "Must meet our stated editorial standards. Follow our submission guidelines. Fiction series preferred over standalone titles. Complete manuscripts only."

OUR DAILY BREAD PUBLISHING

3000 Kraft Ave. S.E., Grand Rapids, MI 49512 | 800-653-8333
submissions@dhp.org | www.ourdailybreadpublishing.org
Dawn Anderson, senior editor

Joyce Dinkins, acquisitions editor

Parent company: Our Daily Bread Ministries

Mission statement: to publish resources that feed the soul with the Word of God

Submissions: Publishes forty-five titles per year; receives 1,000 submissions annually. First-time authors: 10-20%. Accepts manuscripts only through agents. Send proposal with sample chapters by email. Responds in six to eight weeks. Length: 50,000 words for nonfiction. Bible: NIV.

Types of books: offset paperback, hardcover, POD, ebook

Royalty: 12% on net, advance $2,500-7,500; flat fee for Bible reference and children's books

Types and topics: Christian living, popular Bible reference, children's, African-American

Imprint: Voices (for African-Americans)

Tip: "Ask yourself, 'How does my book feed the soul with the Word of God?'"

OUR SUNDAY VISITOR, INC.

200 Noll Plaza, Huntington, IN 46750-4303 | 260-356-8400, 800-348-2440

www.osv.com

Greg Willits, editorial director

Denomination: Catholic

Mission statement: to assist Catholics to be more aware and secure in their faith and capable of relating their faith to others

Submissions: Submit proposal through the website. Publishes thirty to forty titles per year; receives more than 500 submissions annually. First-time authors: 10%. Prefers not to work through agents. Responds in six to eight weeks.

Royalty: 10-12% of net, average advance $1,500

Also does: pamphlets and booklets

Types and topics: prayer—books and devotionals that help readers draw nearer to God; Scripture—books about how to read, understand, pray, and apply Scripture; family and marriage—books that reflect on the nature of marriage and practical books on family life; saints and heritage—informative and inspiring stories about Mary, the saints, and Catholic identity; faith and culture—books about the intersection of faith and contemporary culture; service—practical application of the call to serve the needy and love our neighbor; evangelization, apologetics, and catechetics—books that help readers explain, defend, and share their faith with others; worship—books about understanding and experiencing the graces of the sacraments, especially the eucharist; parish—books that help pastors, leaders, and parishioners conduct parish life more effectively

Guidelines: *osv.submittable.com/submit*

Tip: "All books published must relate to the Catholic Church; unique books aimed at our audience. Give as much background information as possible on author qualification, why the topic was chosen, and unique aspects of the project. Follow our guidelines. We are expanding our religious education product line and programs."

P&R PUBLISHING

1102 Marble Hill Rd., Phillipsburg, NJ 08865 | 908-454-0505
submissions@prpbooks.com | *www.prpbooks.com*
David Almack, acquisitions director
Amanda Martin, editorial director
Melissa Craig, children's editor

Mission statement: to serve Christ and his church by producing clear, engaging, fresh and insightful applications of Reformed theology to life

Submissions: Devoted to stating, defending, and furthering the gospel in the modern world. Download the submission form from the website, and email it with a proposal and two or three chapters. Publishes forty titles per year; receives 300-400 submissions annually. First-time authors: 10%. Length: 35,000-50,000 words. Responds in three months.

Types of books: hardcover, offset and POD paperback, ebook

Royalty: 12-16% net, advance

Types and topics: Christian living, marriage, family, parenting, counseling, children and teens, theology, women's, youth resources, books for African-Americans

Guidelines: *www.prpbooks.com/manuscript-submissions*

Tip: "We are looking for content from authors who have a theological commitment to Reformed theology."

PACIFIC PRESS

PO Box 5353, Nampa, ID 83653-5353 | 208-465-2531
booksubmissions@pacificpress.com | *www.pacificpress.com*
Scott Cady, acquisitions editor

Denomination: Seventh-day Adventist

Submissions: Books of interest and importance to Seventh-day Adventists and other Christians of all ages. Publishes thirty-five to forty titles per year; receives 500 submissions annually. First-time authors: 5%. Email or mail query. Accepts manuscripts directly from authors. Length: 40-90,000 words, 128-320 pages. Responds in one to three weeks. Requires requested proposal with three chapters by email or mail, manuscript by email.

Royalty: 12-16% net, advance $1,500

Also does: booklets

Types and topics: adults: inspiration/Christian life, prayer, doctrine and Bible study, church history, Ellen White, topics and issues, biographies and true stories, story collections, cookbooks, health and nutrition, marriage and parenting, books for sharing and gospel outreach; children: picture books illustrating a distinctive Adventist belief for ages 1-3; true or based-on-truth, contemporary or historical stories with Christian themes (usually in a series) for ages 6-8 and 9-12; sets of Bible stories for ages 8-108

Guidelines: *www.pacificpress.com/authors_artists/submission-guidelines*

Tip: "Most open to spirituality, inspirational, and Christian living. Our website has the most up-to-date information, including samples of recent publications. Do not send full manuscript unless we request it after reviewing your proposal."

PARACLETE PRESS

PO Box 1568, Orleans, MA 02653 | 508-255-4685
submissions@paracletepress | *www.paracletepress.com*
Jon Sweeney, publisher and editor-in-chief

Denomination: Catholic and Protestant

Submissions: Email proposal and two or three sample chapters as single, attached Word file. Responds in one month.

Types and topics: prayer, faith formation, spirituality, grief, Advent/Christmas or Lent/Easter picture books; poetry by invitation only

Guidelines: *www.paracletepress.com/pages/submission-guidelines*

PARSONS PUBLISHING HOUSE

PO Box 410063, Melbourne, FL 32941 | 850-867-3061
diane@parsonspublishinghouse.com | *www.parsonspublishinghouse.com*
Diane Parsons, chief editor

Mission statement: empowering Christians to walk with God in a deeper way on a daily basis

Submissions: Email query. No agents. Responds in four to six weeks. Publishes four to six titles per year; receives forty submissions annually. First-time authors: 50%. Length: 40,000+ words. No agents. Bible: NKJV, NLT.

Types of books: offset and POD paperback, ebook

Royalty: 10%, no advance

Types and topics: Christian living, spiritual growth

Tip: "Positive presentation of the Good News; uplifting, informative, and inspiring."

PAULINE BOOKS & MEDIA

50 Saint Paul's Ave., Boston, MA 02130-3491 | 617-522-8911
editorial@paulinemedia.com | *www.pauline.org*
Sean Mayer, FSP, acquisitions editor, adults
Marilyn Monge, FSP, and Jaymie Stuart Wolfe, editors, children and teens

Denomination: Catholic/Daughters of St. Paul

Submissions: Publishes twenty titles per year; receives more than

300 submissions annually. First-time authors: 10%. Accepts manuscripts directly from authors. Length: 10-60,000 words. Email proposal as an attachment, or mail it. Responds in two months. Bible: NRSV.

Royalty: 5-10% net, advance

Types and topics: adults: spirituality, prayer, lives of saints, faith formation, theology, family life; children: prayer books, lives of saints, Bible stories, activity books, easy reader and middle-grade fiction, board books, picture books; YA: fiction and nonfiction

Guidelines: *www.pauline.org/Publishing/Submit-a-Manuscript*

Tip: Looking for well-documented historical fiction and graphic novels for middle grade and YA.

PAULIST PRESS

997 Macarthur Blvd., Mahwah, NJ 07430-9990
submissions@paulistpress.com | www.paulistpress.com
Trace Murphy, editorial director

Denomination: Catholic

Submissions: Email proposal and sample chapters, pages for children's chapter books, or full manuscript for other children's books. Responds in two months.

Types and topics: academic, children's, popular, and professional or clergy books

Guidelines: *www.paulistpress.com/Pages/Center/auth_res_0.aspx*

PELICAN BOOK GROUP

See Harbourlight Books, Prism Book Group, Pure Amore, Watershed Books, and White Rose Publishing.

PRAYERSHOP PUBLISHING

2800 Poplar St., Ste. 43-L, Terre Haute, IN 47803 | 812-238-5504
jon@prayershop.org | www.prayershop.org
Jonathan Graf, publisher

Parent company: Harvest Prayer Ministries, Church Prayer Leaders Network

Mission statement: to help churches become houses of prayer by discipling and equipping individuals in the aspects of prayer since a praying believer is a kingdom believer who will be an asset to his or her local church

Submissions: We only do resources that will move an individual or church deeper in prayer. Publishes eight to ten titles per year; receives twenty submissions annually. First-time authors: 35%.

Accepts manuscripts directly from authors. Length: 20,000-30,000 words, 128-144 pages. Email or mail proposal with sample chapters or full manuscript. Reports in six to twelve weeks. Bible: NIV, ESV.

Types of books: offset paperback, hardcover, POD, ebook; first print run 3,500-5,000

Royalty: 10% net, no advance

Types and topics: prayer, revival, Christian living

Guidelines: *www.prayerleader.com/prayershop-publishing/submissions*

Also does: booklets and brochure-formatted prayer guides

Tip: "We are looking for authors who understand prayer and can encourage their readers to desire a deeper prayer life and can equip them to pray more effectively."

PRISM BOOK GROUP

PO Box 1738, Aztec, NM 87410

customer@prismbookgroup.com | www.prismbookgroup.com

Jacqueline Hopper, acquisitions editor, jhopper@prismbookgroup.com

Paula Mowery, acquisitions editor, pmowery@prismbookgroup.com

Parent company: Pelican Book Group

Mission statement: Our primary ministry is to publish quality books that reflect the salvation and love offered by Jesus Christ. Our titles adhere to mainline Christianity but are enjoyed by Christians and non-Christians alike.

Submissions: Novels 25,000-80,000 words. Submit proposal through the website form. Responds in three to four months. Accepts unagented submissions. Bible: NIV, NAB. Considers books for all ethnicities.

Types of books: offset and POD paperback, hardcover, ebook, audiobook

Royalty: 40% on download, 7% on print, advance sometimes

Types and topics: fiction: romance, Christian romance, Christian fiction, young adult

Imprints: Prism Lux (Christian), Prism CW (clean and wholesome)

Guidelines: *pelicanbookgroup.com/ec/index.php?main_page=page&id=76*

Tip: "Our books offer clean and compelling reads for the discerning reader. We will not publish graphic language or content and look for well-written, emotionally charged stories, intense plots, and captivating characters."

PURE AMORE

PO Box 1738, Aztec, NM 87410
customer@pelicanbookgroup.com | pelicanbookgroup.com
Nicola Martinez, editor-in-chief

Parent company: Pelican Book Group

Mission statement: Our primary ministry is to publish quality books that reflect the salvation and love offered by Jesus Christ. Our titles adhere to mainline Christianity but are enjoyed by Christians and non-Christians alike.

Submissions: Length: 40-45,000 words. Accepts unagented submissions. Responds to queries in one month, full manuscripts in four months. Email submissions only through the website.

Types of books: offset and POD paperback, hardcover, ebook, audiobook

Royalty: 40% on download, 7% on print, advance sometimes

Types and topics: only contemporary Christian romance, sweet in tone and in conflict, emotionally driven tales of youthful Christians between the ages of 21 and 33 who are striving to live their faith in a world where Christ-centered choices may not fully be understood

Guidelines: *pelicanbookgroup.com/ec/index.php?main_page=page&id=69*

Tip: "Pure Amore romances emphasize the beauty in chastity, so physical interactions, such as kissing or hugging, should focus on the characters' emotions, rather than heightened sexual desire; and scenes of physical intimacy should be integral to the plot and/or emotional development of the character or relationship."

RANDALL HOUSE PUBLICATIONS

114 Bush Rd., Nashville, TN 37217 | 615-361-1221
danny.conn@randallhouse.com | www.randallhouse.com
Danny Conn, acquisitions editor

Denomination: Free Will Baptist

Mission statement: to emphasize generational discipleship with creative excellence, communicating the Word of God with absolute integrity

Submissions: Email or mail proposal with sample chapters. Responds in ten to twelve weeks. Publishes twelve to fifteen titles per year; receives 300 submissions annually. First-time authors: 35%. Accepts manuscripts directly from authors. Length: 128-180 pages. Bible: ESV.

Types of books: offset paperback, ebook; first print run 5,000-10,000

Royalty: 14-18%, advance sometimes

Types and topics: Christian living, parenting, family ministry, small-group studies, church leadership, theology, academic, commentaries, marriage, counseling

Guidelines: *www.randallhouse.com/contact*

Tip: "Review the categories we publish, and do not submit other categories."

RESOURCE PUBLICATIONS

199 W. 8th Ave., Ste. 3, Eugene, OR 97401 | 541-344-1528
www.wipfandstock.com/imprint/resource-2

Parent company: Wipf and Stock

Types of books: POD, ebook

Types and topics: personal growth, textbooks, novels, poetry, sermon collections, biographies

Guidelines: *wipfandstock.com/submitting-a-proposal*

RESURRECTION PRESS

77 West End Rd., Totowa, NJ 07572 | 973-890-2400
info@catholicbookpublishing.com | *www.catholicbookpublishing.com*
Anthony Buono, editor

Denomination: Catholic

Parent company: Catholic Book Publishing Corp.

Submissions: Mail proposal and two chapters. Responds in four to six weeks.

Royalty: negotiable

Types and topics: prayer, healing, spirituality, pastoral and liturgical resources

Guidelines: *www.catholicbookpublishing.com/page/faq#manuscript*

REVELL BOOKS

6030 E. Fulton Rd., Ada, MI 49301 | 616-676-9185
www.bakerpublishinggroup.com/revell
Andrea Doering, editorial director
Rachel McRae, acquisitions editor
Kelsey Bowen, acquisitions editor (fiction)
Vicki Crumpton, acquisitions editor

Parent company: Baker Publishing Group

Submissions: Publishes inspirational fiction and nonfiction for the broadest Christian market. Accepts proposals only through agents, meeting an editor at a writers conference, or *ChristianBookProposals.com*.

Types and topics: apologetics/world religions, Bible study, biography/

memoir, Christian living, Christianity and culture, church life, marriage and family, Spirit-filled, fiction, children and youth fiction and nonfiction

Guidelines: *bakerpublishinggroup.com/contact/submission-policy*

ROSE PUBLISHING

PO Box 3473, Peabody, MA 01961-3473 | 800-358-3111
info@hendricksonrose.com | www.hendricksonrose.com
Lynette Pennings, managing editor

Parent company: Hendrickson Publishers

Mission statement: publishes resources that help believers love God by deepening their understanding of who God is

Submissions: Submit through *ChristianBookProposals.com.*

Types and topics: reference products packed with charts, timelines, and simple summaries to make the Bible and its teachings easy to understand

Also does: pamphlets, wall charts

ROSEKIDZ

PO Box 3473, Peabody, MA 01961-3473 | 800-358-3111
info@hendricksonrose.com | www.hendricksonrose.com
Karen McGraw, managing editor

Parent company: Hendrickson Publishers

Submissions: Email samples of work first.

Types and topics: reproducible Bible lesson material for children, including age-appropriate Sunday-school activities, instant Bible lessons, girls and boys devotionals, fiction; nursery, toddler, preschool, kindergarten, elementary, and preteen

SALEM BOOKS

300 New Jersey Ave., N.W., Ste. 500, Washington, DC 20001
regnery.com/custom/salem-books
Tim Peterson, acquisitions

Parent company: Regnery Publishing, Salem Media Group

Mission statement: to enrich the lives of Christians and proclaim the gospel of Jesus to the world through the written word

Submissions: Only accepts manuscripts and proposals from agents.

Types and topics: Christian living

SCEPTER PUBLISHERS

PO Box 360694, Strongsville, OH 44136 | 800-322-8773, 212-354-0670
info@scepterpublishers.org | www.scepterpublishers.org

Denomination: Catholic

Mission statement: to publish Catholic books that help men and
women find God in ordinary life and realize sanctity in their work,
family life, and everyday activities

Submissions: Send a one- or two-page proposal with cover letter by
mail or email.

SCRIVENINGS PRESS

15 Lucky Ln., Morrilton, AR 72110 | 501-548-2736

stvauthor@yahoo.com | scriveningspress.com

Shannon Vannatter, acquisitions editor

Linda Fulkerson, publisher, scriveningspress@gmail.com (speculative only)

Mission statement: "Scrivenings Press is a traditional, royalty-paying
publisher of clean and Christian fiction. Our goal is to produce
great books for our readers and help our authors build their careers."

Submissions: Submit proposal with sample chapters by email or
website form. Replies in two to four weeks. First-time authors:
70%. Length: 60,000-85,000 words. Publishes 15 books per year.
Bible: KJV preferred.

Types and topics: only fiction: contemporary and historical romance,
romantic suspense, historical, fantasy, and dystopian; will look at
sci-fi, but not preferred

Types of books: POD, ebook

Imprint: Expanse Books (speculative)

Royalty: 12% print, 50% ebook, 40% on pages read for Kindle
Unlimited; no advance

Guidelines: *scriveningspress.com/submissions*

Tip: "We are a small publishing house, and we try to keep a family
feel among our staff and authors. We encourage all our authors to
encourage one another and to cross-promote books from other
authors within our company."

SLANT

199 W. 8th Ave., Ste. 3, Eugene, OR 97401 | 541-344-1528
www.wipfandstock.com/imprint/slant-7

Parent company: Wipf and Stock

Types of books: POD, ebook

Types and topics: literary fiction

Guidelines: *wipfandstock.com/submitting-a-proposal*

SMITTEN HISTORICAL ROMANCE

100 Missionary Ridge, Birmingham, AL 35252 | 866-266-8399
editor@smittenromance.com | shoplpc.com/smitten-historical-romance
Denise Weimer, managing editor

Parent company: Lighthouse Publishing of the Carolinas/Iron Stream Media

Mission statement: to engage the reader from the first paragraph to the last in a story that touches the mind, heart, and spirit

Submissions: Publishes eight books per year; receives fifty proposals. First-time authors: 30%. Length: 75-85,000 words. Only accepts proposals through agents, author referrals, and conference meetings. Responds in three to twelve weeks.

Types of books: POD, ebook, audiobook

Royalty: 40% net, no advance

Types and topics: historical romance

Guidelines: *shoplpc.com/smitten*

Tip: "Submit stories steeped in real history/places populated by fascinating characters and a happily-ever-after ending that satisfies the reader. The history and Christian content should be organic to the time period, never preachy, and not overshadow the story. Implied Christian content without overt evangelism is preferred."

SMYTH & HELWYS BOOKS

6316 Peake Rd., Macon, GA 31210-3960 | 478-757-0564
proposal@helwys.com | www.helwys.com

Submissions: Email or mail proposal and two or three sample chapters. Responds in several weeks.

Types and topics: Christian living, ministry/leadership, biblical studies

Guidelines: *www.helwys.com/submit-a-manuscript*

SONFIRE MEDIA PUBLISHING, LLC

120 W. Grayson St., Ste. 350, Galax, VA 24333 | 276-233-0276
info@sonfiremedia.com | www.sonfiremedia.com
Larry VanHoose, executive editor

Submissions: Publishes two to five titles per year. Receives fifty per year. First-time authors: 95%. Length: 40-80,000 for nonfiction, 70-100,000 for fiction. Email proposal and two or three sample chapters as an attached Word document. Replies in one to two months. Bible: prefers NIV but open to others.

Type of book: POD

Royalty: 10-20%

Types and topics: devotionals; Christian living; writing instruction;

YA and adult fantasy, science fiction, speculative; open to other types of fiction except romance

Imprints: Sonfire Media (nonfiction), Taberah Press (fiction)

Guidelines: *www.sonfiremedia.com/submit.html*

Tip: "We are open to new writers if they are serious about their craft, understand the need for author marketing, and have a 'message that matters.'"

SONRISE DEVOTIONALS

100 Missionary Ridge, Birmingham, AL 35252 | 866-266-8399
lpcnonfictionsubmissions@gmail.com | *shoplpc.com/sonrise-devotionals*
Cindy Sproles, managing editor

Parent company: Lighthouse Publishing of the Carolinas/Iron Stream Media

Mission statement: to present books that shine a light into a dark world

Submissions: Publishes five books per year; receives fifty proposals. First-time authors: 50%. Length: 30-70,000 words. Only accepts proposals from agents and writers conference meetings. Responds in six months. Bible: any. Welcomes submissions from ethnic writers.

Types of books: POD, ebook, audiobook

Royalty: 50% net, no advance

Types and topics: daily devotionals, Hispanic audiences

Guidelines: *shoplpc.com/sonrise*

Tip: "Looking for devotions that move away from niche audiences and return to devotions that address everyone at any season in their lives."

STONE TABLE BOOKS

PO Box 656, Noarlunga, SA 5168, Australia | +61410240513
editor@stonetablebooks.com | *stonetablebooks.com*

Mark Worthing, senior editor

Ben Morton, editor

Mission statement: to publish fantasy and science fiction for all ages

Submissions: Publishes ten books per year; receives twenty proposals annually. First-time book authors: 70%. Length: 40,000-75,000 words. Submit a proposal with sample chapters by email, mail, or website form. Looks for writers at writers conferences. Responds in one month.

Types of books: hardcover, POD, ebook

Types and topics: speculative fiction (fantasy and science fiction) and occasionally nonfiction on speculative-fiction related topics

Royalty: 10%, no advance

Guidelines: *stonetablebooks.com/about-stone-table-books*

Tip: "Make sure that some creative writers you respect have read your work and given you some brutally honest feedback, then edit well with their advice in mind."

STRAIGHT STREET BOOKS

100 Missionary Ridge, Birmingham, AL 35252 | 866-266-8399
lpcnonfictionproposals@gmail.com | *shoplpc.com/straight-street-books*
Cindy Sproles, managing editor

Parent company: Lighthouse Publishing of the Carolinas/Iron Steam Media

Mission statement: to provide wholesome reading, leaning to both general and Christian markets

Submissions: Publishes six books per year; receives fifty proposals. First-time authors: 85%. Length: 60-80,000 words. Only accepts proposals through agents and writers conference meetings. Responds in six months. Bible: any. Welcomes submissions from ethnic writers.

Types of books: POD, ebook, audiobook

Royalty: 40% net, no advance

Types and topics: Christian living, pastoral help, marriage, disabilities, Christian walk

Guidelines: *shoplpc.com/straight-street*

Tip: "Fresh and unique subjects. We do not accept memoirs."

THOMAS NELSON PUBLISHERS

PO Box 141000, Nashville, TN 37214-1000 | 615-889-9000
www.thomasnelson.com

Becky Monds, acquisitions editor, fiction
Kyle Oland, senior acquisitions, W Publishing
Jenny Baumgartner, editorial director, Nelson Books
Jennifer Gott, editorial director, Thomas Nelson Gift
Joel Kneedler, publisher, Emanate Books

Parent company: HarperCollins Christian Publishing

Submissions: Only accepts proposals through agents or direct contact with editors. Does not accept or review any unsolicited queries, proposals, or manuscripts. Publishes fewer than 100 titles per year.

Types and topics: Christian living, church and ministry resources, Bible reference, commentaries, Bible book studies, business and leadership, biography, women's devotionals, fiction for adults and YA, gift books

Imprints: Nelson Books (spiritual growth and practical living), W

Publishing Group (memoir, help and hope for doing life better, and leading pastoral voices, with select practical living), Tommy Nelson (children and teens; see separate entry), Emanate Books (Charismatic), Thomas Nelson Fiction, Thomas Nelson Gift

TOMMY NELSON

PO Box 141000, Nashville, TN 37214-1000 | 615-889-9000
www.tommynelson.com
Mackinzie Howard, children's acquisitions editor

Parent company: Thomas Nelson Publishers
Submissions: Only accepts proposals through agents or direct contact with editors. Does not accept or review any unsolicited queries, proposals, or manuscripts.
Types and topics: board books, picture books, Bible storybooks, devotionals for middle grade and teens

TRAILBLAZER WESTERN FICTION

100 Missionary Ridge, Birmingham, AL 35252 | 866-266-8399
trailblazerwesterns@gmail.com | *shoplpc.com/trailblazer-western-fiction*
Jennifer Uhlarik, managing editor

Parent company: Lighthouse Publishing of the Carolinas/Iron Stream Media
Mission statement: to recapture the glory days of the Western, but with an updated feel that will ignite the hearts and minds of a new generation of readers
Submissions: Publishes four books annually. Length to 90,000 words. Accepts proposals through agents, conference meetings, and directly from authors. Responds in three months. Bible: NIV.
Types of books: POD, ebook, audiobook
Royalty: 40% net, no advances
Types and topics: contemporary and historical westerns
Guidelines: *shoplpc.com/trailblazer*
Tip: "Trailblazer is looking for quality fiction in the style of past greats like Louis L'Amour and Zane Grey, as well as new twists on the genre."

THE TRINITY FOUNDATION

PO Box 68, Unicoi, TN 37692 | 423-743-0199
tjtrinityfound@aol.com | *www.trinityfoundation.org*
Thomas W. Juodaitis, president

Mission statement: to publish books based on the truth that the Bible alone is the Word of God

Submissions: Publishes one to three titles per year; receives four proposals. First-time authors: 5%. Length: 60-300 pages. Email or mail a proposal with sample chapters. Responds in two to four weeks. Bible version: KJV, NKJV.
Types of books: offset paperback, ebook; first print run 500-1,000
Royalty: none, no advance, $2,000 flat fee
Types and topics: theology, philosophy
Guidelines: by email
Tip: "Books must be in line with the theology and philosophy of The Trinity Foundation."

TULIP PUBLISHING

PO Box 3150, Lansvale, New South Wales 2166 | +61 2 9055 2195
submissions@tulippublishing.com.au | tulippublishing.com.au
Brett Lee-Price, general manager

Mission statement: Tulip Publishing is committed to a holistic approach in ensuring that the church is equipped with resources that will help stretch and grow readers in their spiritual formulation, development, and knowledge.
Submissions: Prefers working with agents. Email proposal with sample chapters. Responds in one month. Publishes four to six books per year; receives thirty proposals. First-time book authors: 50%. Length: 40,000 words. Bible: ESV.
Royalty: 40-60%, no advance
Types of books: POD, ebook, audiobook
Types and topics: theology, church history, Christian living
Imprint: Studies in Reformed Thought
Guidelines: via email
Tip: "Short and succinct emails outlining what your book is about, who it is written to, and why you think your book is helpful are advantageous to your submission."

TYNDALE HOUSE PUBLISHERS

351 Executive Dr., Carol Stream, IL 60188 | 630-668-8300
www.tyndale.com
Sarah Atkinson, senior acquisitions, nonfiction
Jon Farrar, acquisitions director, devotionals
Jan Stob, fiction acquisitions

Submissions: Publishes more than 100 titles per year. First-time authors: 5%. Only reviews manuscripts submitted by agents, Tyndale authors, authors known to them from other publishers, or other people in the publishing industry. Responds in three to six months. Bible: NLT. Fiction length: 75-100,000 words.

Types of books: offset paperback, hardcover, ebook

Types and topics: home and family, Christian beliefs, finance, leadership, career, parenting, marriage, memoir, biography, devotionals, counseling; fiction with evangelical message: biblical, contemporary, futuristic, historical, romance, suspense/thriller

Imprint: Tyndale Kids (see separate entry), Tyndale Español (Spanish)

Guidelines: *www.tyndale.com/faq*

TYNDALE KIDS

351 Executive Dr., Carol Stream, IL 60188 | 630-668-8300
kidsandwandersubmissions@tyndale.com | *www.tyndale.com*
Linda Howard, associate publisher and acquisitions

Mission: We believe these early years often determine the spiritual direction of a young person's life, so we seek to communicate God to this younger generation in ways that capture their hearts and minds forever.

Types of books: hardcover, offset and POD paperback, ebook, audiobook

Submissions: Publishes ten to fifteen books per year; receives 300-400 proposals annually. Prefers proposals from agents, but will consider them from unagented writers and writers met at conferences. Email proposal with sample chapters or full manuscript. Responds in two to three months. First-time book authors: 5%. Bible: NLT.

Royalty: 10-24%, according to genre; advance

Types and topics: board books, picture books, first-chapter books, early readers, middle grade, YA, Bible stories, fiction, nonfiction, devotionals; books for African-Americans, Hispanics, and Asians

Imprint: Wander (YA)

Guidelines: none

Tip: "Looking for a solid, well-written proposal; strong platform; excellent writing."

WARNER CHRISTIAN RESOURCES

2902 Enterprise Dr., Anderson, IN 46013 | 765-644-7721
editors@warnerpress.org | *www.warnerpress.org*
Robin Fogle, kids and family ministry editor

Denomination: Church of God (Anderson)

Mission statement: produces resources to equip the church, to advance the Kingdom, and to give hope to future generations

Submissions: Publishes three to five books annually; receives fifty-plus proposals. First-time authors: 50%. Email or mail proposal with sample chapters or full manuscript. Accepts manuscripts directly from authors. Responds in six to eight weeks. Bible: KJV, NIV.

Types of books: offset paperback, ebook

Royalty: based on the author and type of book, advance sometimes

Types and topics: Bible studies, small-group teaching resources, children's teaching resources; also see entry in "Miscellaneous."

Guidelines: *www.warnerpress.org/submission-guidelines*

Tip: "Do your research and visit our website to view what we already produce."

WATERBROOK MULTNOMAH

10807 New Allegiance Dr., Ste. 500, Colorado Springs, CO 80921 | 719-590-4999

info@waterbrookmultnomah.com | www.waterbrookmultnomah.com
Andrew Stoddard, editorial director
Sarah Rubio, executive editor
Becky Nesbitt, executive editor, WaterBrook acquisitions
Bunmi Ishola, children's editor
Porscha Burke, senior editor, gifts

Parent company: Penguin Random House

Submissions: Publishes sixty books annually; receives 300 proposals. First-time authors: 15%. Length: 208-400 pages. Proposals from agents only. Responds in one to two months. Bible: ESV.

Types of books: offset and POD paperback, hardcover, ebook, audiobook

Royalty: advance

Types and topics: fiction: Amish, romantic suspense, historical, period; children's; creative, interactive books and journals; Christian living; spiritual growth; relationships; personal growth; devotional; inspirational; motivational; home and lifestyle

Guidelines: *waterbrookmultnomah.com/submissions*

Tip: "We recommend working with an agent whose clientele aligns with your strengths as a writer."

WATERSHED BOOKS

PO Box 1738, Aztec, NM 87410
customer@pelicanbookgroup.com | www.pelicanbookgroup.com
Nicola Martinez, editor-in-chief

Parent company: Pelican Book Group

Mission: Our primary ministry is to publish quality books that reflect the salvation and love offered by Jesus Christ. Our titles adhere to mainline Christianity but are enjoyed by Christians and non-Christians alike.

Submissions: Submit only through the website. Length: 25-65,000 words. Accepts unagented submissions. Responds in three to four months. Bible: NIV, NAB. Considers books for all ethnicities.

Types of books: offset and POD paperback, hardcover, ebook, audiobook

Royalty: 40% on download, 7% on print, advance sometimes

Types and topics: young-adult fiction (ages 14-19) that features young-adult characters; action-adventure, mystery (amateur sleuth or other), romance, science fiction, fantasy, supernatural, suspense, crime drama, police procedural, teen angst, coming-of-age, westerns; interested in series ideas

Guidelines: *pelicanbookgroup.com/ec/index.php?main_page=page&id=60*

Tip: "We want to see something other than dystopian."

WESTMINSTER/JOHN KNOX PRESS

100 Witherspoon St., Louisville, KY 40202-1396

submissions@wjkbooks.com | *www.wjkbooks.com*

Jessica Miller Kelley, acquisitions editor

David Dobson, editorial director

Denomination: Presbyterian

Parent company: Presbyterian Publishing Corporation

Submissions: Publishes approximately sixty books and other resources each year. Prefers emailed proposals but will take them by mail. Responds in two to three months.

Types and topics: children, theology, biblical studies, preaching, worship, ethics, religion and culture, and other related fields for four main markets: scholars and students in colleges, universities, seminaries, and divinity schools; preachers, educators, and counselors working in churches; members of mainline Protestant congregations; and general readers

Imprints: Flyaway Books (children), Geneva Press (books specifically related to the Presbyterian Church USA)

Guidelines: *www.wjkbooks.com/Pages/Item/1345/Author-Relations.aspx*

WHITAKER HOUSE

1030 Hunt Valley Cir., New Kensington, PA 15068 | 724-334-7000

publisher@whitakerhouse.com | *www.whitakerhouse.com*

Christine Whitaker, aquisitions

Parent company: Whitaker Corporation

Denomination: Charismatic

Mission statement: Our goal is to advance God's kingdom by publishing biblically focused authors who proclaim the power of the gospel and minister to the spiritual needs of people around the world.

Submissions: Prefers proposals from agents. Email a proposal with sample chapters. Responds in one to two months. Publishes seventy-five to one hundred titles per year; receives 200 submissions annually. First-time authors: 30%. Length: 50,000-80,000 words, 96-336 pages. Bible: KJV.

Types of books: offset and POD paperback, hardcover, ebook, audiobook

Royalty: 15-18%, advance sometimes

Types and topics: Christian living, devotionals, spiritual growth, inspirational, Charismatic interest, fiction, children's

Imprints: Whitaker Playhouse (parents with young children)

Guidelines: *www.whitakerhouse.com/contact,* click View Guidelines link

Tip: "Follow the questions and suggestions on our submission guidelines."

WHITE ROSE PUBLISHING

PO Box 1738, Aztec, NM 87410
customer@pelicanbookgroup.com | *www.pelicanbookgroup.com*
Nicola Martinez, editor-in-chief

Parent company: Pelican Book Group

Mission statement: Our primary ministry is to publish quality books that reflect the salvation and love offered by Jesus Christ. Our titles adhere to mainline Christianity but are enjoyed by Christians and non-Christians alike.

Submissions: Email submissions only through the website. Length: short stories, 10-20,000 words (ebook); novelettes, 20-35,000 words (ebook); novellas, 35-60,000 words (ebook); novels, 60-80,000 words (ebook and print). Accepts unagented submissions. Responds in three to four months. Bible: NIV, NAB. Considers books for all ethnicities.

Types of books: offset and POD paperback, hardcover, ebook, audiobook

Royalty: 40% on download, 7% on print, advance sometimes

Types and topics: only romance, interested in series ideas

Guidelines: *pelicanbookgroup.com/ec/index.php?main_page=page&id=58*

Tip: "The setting for White Rose books can be contemporary, historical or futuristic. They can be straight romances or include other factors such as mystery, suspense or supernatural elements, etc; however, an element of faith must be present in all White Rose stories—without becoming overbearing or preachy. Please specify in your proposal if your story includes elements beyond simple romance."

WHITEFIRE PUBLISHING

13607 Bedford Rd. N.E., Cumberland, MD 21502 | 866-245-2211
r.white@whitefire-publishing.com | www.whitefire-publishing.com
Roseanna White, managing editor

Mission statement: We seek books that shine the Light of God into the darkness and embrace the motto of "Where Spirit Meets the Page."

Submissions: Publishes fifteen to twenty titles per year; receives 200 annually. First-time authors: 20%. Email query letter only. Replies in three months. Length: 60,000-100,000 words. Actively seeking growth in books for minority audiences.

Types of books: POD, ebook, audiobook

Royalty: 50% on ebooks, 10% on print, advance sometimes ($1,500-2,000)

Types and topics: nonfiction in all genres; fiction: general, romance, historical, historical romance, suspense, contemporary, women's fiction

Imprints: Ashberry Lane (romance in all subgenres, see separate listing); WhiteSpark (young readers, see separate listing), WhiteFire (nonfiction and fiction) Chrism Press (Catholic and Orthodox fiction, see separate listing)

Guidelines: *whitefire-publishing.com/submissions*

Tip: "Familiarize yourself with our titles and mission."

WHITESPARK PUBLISHING

13607 Bedford Rd. N.E., Cumberland, MD 21502 | 866-245-2211
r.white@whitefire-publishing.com | www.whitefire-publishing.com
Roseanna White, senior fiction editor

Parent company: WhiteFire Publishing

Mission statement: WhiteSpark aims to engender a love of reading in kids with faith-based books.

Submissions: Publishes five to ten books a year; receives 100 proposals annually. Length: varies, depending on target age. Email query only. Responds in three months. First-time book authors: 10%.

Types and topics: picture books, middle grade, and young adult in all fiction subgenres; open to all topics

Royalty: 50% for ebooks, 10% of retail for print, advance sometimes ($200-1,000)

Types of books: hardcover, POD, ebook, audiobook

Guidelines: *whitespark-publishing.com/submissions*

Tip: "Come with fresh ideas on how to reach the young readership."

WILD HEART BOOKS

733 Flamingo Rd., Clover, SC 29710 | 704-363-0360
submissions@wildheartbooks.org | *www.wildheartbooks.org*
Misty M. Beller, managing editor

Parent company: Misty M. Beller Books, Inc.

Mission statement: Wild Heart Books publishes exciting historical romance stories, complete with heroes to make readers swoon, strong heroines, and inspirational messages to encourage their faith. We publish to a very small niche, and that's part of what makes us successful.

Submissions: Publishes ten books per year; receives seventy-five proposals. First-time authors: 50%. Length: 55-75,000 words. Email proposal with sample chapters. Works with agents and directly with writers. Responds in two weeks. Bible: KJV.

Types of books: POD, ebook, audiobook

Royalty: 35-50%, advance sometimes

Types and topics: historical romance only

Guidelines: *wildheartbooks.org/submissions.html*

Tip: "A good strong story (that fits with what we publish) will always snag our attention."

WILLIAM CAREY LIBRARY

626-720-8210
submissions@WCLBooks.com | *www.missionbooks.org*

Mission statement: to publish resources that edify, equip, and empower disciples of Jesus to make disciples of Jesus

Submissions: Publishes scholarly and professional or educational books, all related to missions. "We especially seek to assist the work of the mission executive, field missionary, church leader, and the student of world mission." Responds in three to six months. Send a maximum two-page query letter initially. No unsolicited manuscripts.

Types and topics: ethnography, biography, educational, nonfiction, missions, missiology

Guidelines: *missionbooks.org/pages/submission-guidelines*

Tip: "Read our publishing focus carefully. We only publish literature promoting world missions, specifically among unreached and unengaged peoples."

WINGED PUBLICATIONS

PO Box 8047, Surprise, AZ 85374 | 623-910-4279
cynthiahickey@outlook.com | *www.wingedpublications.com*
Cynthia Hickey, editor

> **Mission statement:** Where Your Stories Take Flight
> **Submissions:** Publishes fifty books per year. First-time authors: 25%. Length: at least 50,000 words. Email proposal with sample chapters. Prefers agent submissions. Also open to writers met at conferences. Responds in two weeks. Bible: NIV.
> **Types of books:** POD, ebook
> **Royalty:** 60%, no advance
> **Types and topics:** contemporary romance, historical romance, fantasy, young adult, science fiction, mystery, thriller, romantic suspense, mystery, memoir, devotional
> **Imprints:** Soaring Beyond (stories of hope, devotionals, self-help), Aisling Books (fantasy, science fiction), Jurnee Books (young adult, juvenile fiction), Gordian Books (mystery, suspense, thriller), Forget Me Not Romances (contemporary and historical romances)
> **Guidelines:** *wingedpublications.com/what-were-looking-for*
> **Tip:** "Send the cleanest proposal you can."

WIPF AND STOCK PUBLISHERS

199 W. 8th Ave., Ste. 3, Eugene, OR 97401-2960 | 541-344-1528
proposal@wipfandstock.com | *www.wipfandstock.com*
Rodney Clapp, editor, rodney@wipfandstock.com
Dr. Chris Spinks, editor, chris@wipfandstock.com

> **Submissions:** Email proposal with proposal form from the website. Responds in eight weeks. It is your responsibility to submit a manuscript that has been fully copyedited by a professional copy editor. Publishes more than 400 books per year.
> **Types of books:** short-run, ebooks
> **Types and topics:** primarily academic
> **Guidelines:** *wipfandstock.com/submitting-a-proposal*

WORTHY KIDS

6100 Tower Cir., Ste. 210, Franklin, TN 37067 | 615-932-7600
www.hachettebookgroup.com/imprint/hachette-nashville/worthy-books/worthykids
Peggy Schaefer, publisher

> **Parent company:** Hachette Book Group
> **Mission statement:** helping kids experience the heart of God
> **Submissions:** Publishes forty titles per year; receives 500 annually. First-time authors: 1-5%. Length: 200 words for board books,

800 words for picture books. Mail proposal with full manuscript. Responds only to manuscripts of interest. Prefers submissions from agents. Bible: no preference.

Types of books: hardcover, board

Royalty: 5-7%, advance

Types and topics: fiction, nonfiction, holiday

Tip: "Carefully study the types of books we have published and submit manuscripts that complement our product line but do not duplicate."

WORTHY PUBLISHING GROUP

6100 Tower Cir., Ste. 210, Franklin, TN 37067 | 615-932-7600

www.hachettebookgroup.com/imprint/hachette-nashville/worthy-books

Parent company: Hachette Book Group

Submissions: Publishes thirty-six titles per year. Requires submission by agents; unsolicited manuscripts returned unopened.

Royalty: for Worthy Books, flat fee for some of Worthy Inspired, advance

Types and topics: broad spectrum of genres, including current events, pop culture, biography, fiction, spiritual growth, and Bibles; Worthy Inspired: felt-need personal growth, inspirational, devotional, for professional women

Imprints: Worthy Books, Worthy Kids (see separate listing), Ellie Claire Gifts (see separate listing in "**Greeting Cards and Gifts**"), Museum of the Bible Books (engagement with the Bible)

WRITE INTEGRITY PRESS, LLC

PO Box 702852, Dallas, TX 75370 | 214-676-9974

MarjiLaine@WriteIntegrity.com | *www.WriteIntegrity.com*

Marji Laine Clubine, senior editor

Mission statement: to provide clean, wholesome, uplifting fiction and inspirational nonfiction

Submissions: Publishes six to twelve titles per year; receives 100. First-time authors: 5%. Length: fiction, 40,000-80,000 words; nonfiction, 35,000-50,000 words. Email proposal with first three chapters. Responds in three months. Bible: ESV. No simultaneous submissions.

Types of books: POD, ebook

Royalty: 50%, no advance

Types and topics: Christian living; devotional; Bible studies; YA adventure, coming of age, fantasy, dystopian, allegory; fiction: contemporary romance, romantic suspense, cozy mystery

Imprints: Favored Books (heartwarming stories and clean romance), Pursued Books (cozy mystery and romantic suspense), Emerged

Books (YA), Entrusted Books (Christian living, devotional)
Guidelines: *www.writeintegrity.com/submissions*
Tip: "Be ready to share why you would like to be published by our house."

YWAM PUBLISHING

PO Box 55787, Seattle, WA 98155 | 800-922-2143
books@ywampublishing.com | *www.ywampublishing.com*
> **Parent company:** Youth With A Mission
> **Submissions:** Email or mail proposal, following the template on the website. Will not respond to submissions that deviate from proposal guidelines.
> **Types and topics:** evangelism, mission adventures, missions for kids, Bible studies, devotionals, leadership, relationships; no longer accepts fiction or children's literature
> **Guidelines:** *www.ywampublishing.com/topic.aspx?name=submission*

ZONDERKIDZ

3900 Sparks Dr. S.E., Grand Rapids, MI 49512 | 616-698-6900
ZonderkidzSubmissions@harpercollins.com | *www.zonderkidz.com*
Megan Dobson, publisher and aquisitions
> **Parent company:** HarperCollins Christian Publishing
> **Submissions:** Requires submissions only through agents.
> **Types and topics:** children's fiction and nonfiction, teen fiction and nonfiction, children's Bibles
> **Guidelines:** none
> **Tip:** "We are seeking fresh fiction and nonfiction for children ages 0-18. Under our Zonderkidz and Zondervan imprints, we look for engaging picture books and board books, timeless storybook Bibles, faith-centric fiction from established authors, and nonfiction from key voices in the Christian sphere."

ZONDERVAN

501 Nelson Pl., Nashville, TN 37214
www.zondervan.com
Mick Silva, senior aquisitions editor
Andrew Rogers, nonfiction acquisitions editor
> **Parent company:** HarperCollins Christian Publishing
> **Submissions:** Requires submissions only through agents. Publishes 120 trade titles per year. Bible version: NIV.
> **Types and topics:** spiritual growth, marriage, family, social issues, leadership, finance, biography, commentaries, church and ministry, fiction (contemporary, mystery, historical, romance, science

fiction, fantasy, suspense)

Imprints: Zonderkidz (see separate entry), Editorial Vida (Spanish), Zondervan Academic, Zondervan Thrive (personal development, health and wellness, self-care, marriage and family)

Guidelines: none

Christian Writers Institute Courses Publisher Bundle

Courses in this bundle:
- The Elements of an Effective Book Proposal
- How to Get Published
- How to Sell Everything You Write
- What Editors Won't Tell You
- The Power Book Proposal
- 12 Ways to Please an Editor

Normal price: $62
Savings: 52%
Market guide price: $29.76

https://cwmg.link/publisher2021

How to Scan QR Codes

Use the camera on your smartphone to focus on the above QR code to activate the discount. It will give you the option to visit the site, which you will want to accept. If you are using an older smartphone, you may need to download a QR-code scanning app. You can also visit the URL below the code to activate the discount on your computer.

PART 2

INDEPENDENT BOOK PUBLISHING

2

INDEPENDENT BOOK PUBLISHERS

PUBLISHING A BOOK YOURSELF NO LONGER CARRIES THE STIGMA self-publishing has had in the past—if you do it right. Even some well-published writers are now hybrid authors, with independently published books alongside their royalty books. Others have built their readerships with traditional publishers, then moved to independent publishing where it is possible to make more money per sale.

Independent book publishers require the author to pay for part of the publishing costs or to buy a certain number of books. They call themselves by a variety of names, such as book packager, cooperative publisher, self-publisher, custom publisher, subsidy publisher, or simply someone who helps authors get their books printed. Services vary from including different levels of editing and proofreading to printing your manuscript as is.

Whenever you pay for any part of the production of your book, you are entering into a nontraditional relationship. Some independent publishers also offer a form of royalty publishing, so be sure you understand the contract they give you before signing it.

Some independent publishers will publish any book, as long as the author is willing to pay for it. Others are as selective about what they publish as a royalty publisher is. Some independent publishers will do as much promotion as a royalty publisher—for a fee. Others do none at all.

If you are unsuccessful in placing your book with a royalty publisher but feel strongly about seeing it published, an independent publisher can make printing your book easier and often less expensive than doing it yourself. POD, as opposed to a print run of 1,000 books or more, could save you upfront money, although the price per copy is higher. Having your manuscript produced only as an ebook is also a less-expensive option.

Entries in this chapter are for information only, not an endorsement of publishers. For every complaint about a publisher, several other authors may sing the praises of it. Before you sign with any company, get more than one bid to determine whether the terms you are offered are competitive.

A legitimate independent publisher will provide a list of former clients as references. Also buy a couple of the publisher's previous books to check the quality of the work—covers, bindings, typesetting, etc. See if the books currently are available through any of the major online retailers.

Get answers before committing yourself. You may also want someone in the book-publishing industry to review your contract before you sign it. Some experts listed in the "**Editorial Services**" chapter review contracts.

If you decide not to use an independent publisher but do the work yourself, at least hire an editor, proofreader, cover designer, and interior typesetter-designer. The "**Editorial Services**" and "**Design and Production Services**" chapters will help you locate professionals with skills in these areas, as well as printing companies. Plus the "**Distribution Services**" and "**Publicity and Marketing Services**" chapters can help you solve one of the biggest problems of independent publishing: getting your books to readers.

ACW PRESS

PO Box 110390, Nashville, TN 37222 | 800-21-WRITE
acwriters@aol.com | *www.acwpress.com*
Reg A. Forder, publisher

> **Types:** hardcover, offset and POD paperback, gift book
> **Services:** design, substantive editing, copyediting, proofreading, packages of services
> **Production time:** two to four months
> **Books per year:** thirty
> **Tip:** "We offer a high-quality publishing alternative to help Christian authors get their material into print. High standards, high quality. If authors have a built-in audience, they have the best chance to make self-publishing a success."

ALTEN INK

1888 Montara Way, San Jacinto, CA 92583 | 951-327-3698
AltenInk3@gmail.com | *www.AltenInk.blogspot.com*
Deborah L. Alten

> **Types:** paperback, ebook, picture book
> **Services:** design, online bookstore, publishing packages of services, à la carte options
> **Production time:** six months
> **Tip:** "Email us. You will get a quicker response."

AMPELOS PRESS

951 Anders Rd., Lansdale, PA 19446 | 484-991-8581
mbagnull@aol.com | *writehisanswer.com/ampelospress*
Marlene Bagnull, publisher

> **Types:** ebook, POD, offset paperback
> **Services:** manuscript evaluation, design, substantive editing, copyediting, proofreading
> **Production time:** six months
> **Books per year:** two
> **Description:** "Especially interested in issues fiction and nonfiction, as well as books about missions and the needs of children. Author pays a one-time fee, maintains all rights, and receives a 100% royalty."

BK ROYSTON PUBLISHING, LLC

PO Box 4321, Jeffersonville, IN 47131 | 502-802-5385
bkroystonpublishing@gmail.com | *www.bkroystonpublishing.com*
Julia A. Royston, CEO

> **Types:** hardcover, offset and POD paperback, ebook, audiobook, picture book
> **Services:** manuscript evaluation, design, substantive editing, copyediting, proofreading, promotional materials, marketing, distribution, author websites, online bookstore, packages of services, à la carte options
> **Production time:** two to three months
> **Books per year:** twenty-five to thirty
> **Also does:** ghostwriting, coaching, royalty contracts
> **Production time:** one to four months
> **Tip:** "Visit *www.getstartedwithroyston.com* to get submission guidelines."

BOOKBABY

7905 N. Crescent Blvd., Pennsauken, NJ 08110 | 877-961-6878
info@bookbaby.com | *www.bookbaby.com*

> **Types:** hardcover, ebook, offset and POD paperback, gift book, picture book, cookbook, comic book, yearbook, many other formats
> **Services:** manuscript evaluation, design, substantive editing, copyediting, proofreading, social-media ads, distribution, author website, online bookstore
> **Production time:** as quick as five days
> **Tip:** Has ebook and printed book distribution network for self-published authors around the globe.

BROWN CHRISTIAN PRESS

16250 Knoll Trail Dr., Ste. 205, Dallas, TX 75248 | 972-381-0009
publishing@brownbooks.com | *www.brownbooks.com/brown-christian-press*

> **Types:** hardcover, paperback, gift book, ebook, audiobook
> **Services:** substantive editing, copyediting, proofreading, indexing, ghostwriting, design, marketing, distribution, author website
> **Publication time:** six months
> **Tip:** "We are a relationship publisher and work with our authors from beginning to end in the journey of publishing."

CALLED WRITERS CHRISTIAN PUBLISHING

1900 Rice Mine Rd. N. 401, Tuscaloosa, AL 35406 | 205-872-4509
shannon@calledwriters.com | *CalledWriters.com*
Shannon McKinney, relationship builder

> **Types:** offset paperback, POD
> **Services:** manuscript evaluation, design, substantive editing, copyediting, proofreading, marketing, packages of services, à la carte options
> **Also offers:** royalty contracts
> **Production time:** six months
> **Books per year:** two
> **Tip:** "God will open the right doors for you at the right time. Don't give up."

CARPENTER'S SON PUBLISHING

307 Verde Meadow Dr., Franklin, TN 37067 | 615-472-1128
larry@christianbookservices.com | *www.carpenterssonpublishing.com*
Larry Carpenter, president-CEO, editor

> **Types:** offset and POD paperback, hardcover, ebook, audiobook, gift book, picture book
> **Services:** manuscript evaluation, design, substantive editing, copyediting, proofreading, indexing, promotional materials, marketing, distribution, author website, à la carte options
> **Production time:** three to six months
> **Books per year:** 100
> **Tip:** "Make sure someone is selling your book to the bookstores."

CASTLE GATE PRESS

244 E. Glendale Rd., St. Louis, MO 63119 | 314-962-1940
p.wheeler@castlegatepress.com | *www.castlegatepress.com*
Phyllis Wheeler, owner

Types: POD, ebook, audiobook
Services: manuscript evaluation, design, substantive editing, copyediting, proofreading, à la carte options
Publication time: depends on manuscript editing needs
Books per year: one or two
Tip: "Castle Gate Press was a traditional publisher from 2013-2018. One of our books is an Amazon genre bestseller, and another won a Selah Award for Christian fiction in the speculative category. Yet another was a finalist for Selah and also for the Realm Award, and another a finalist for the Grace Award. In short, we provide award-winning editing."

CHRISTIAN FAITH PUBLISHING

832 Park Ave., Meadville, PA 16335 | 800-955-3794
contact@christianfaithpublishing.com | www.Christianfaithpublishing.com
Chris Rutherford, president; Jason Murray, executive vice president

Types: offset and POD paperback, hardcover, ebook
Services: manuscript evaluation, design, copyediting, indexing, marketing, distribution, book trailer, packages of services, à la carte options
Also offers: royalty contracts
Production time: eight to ten months
Books per year: 1,200
Tip: "Be mindful of the fact that it is quite challenging to publish a book and have commercial success."

CLM PUBLISHING

PO Box 1217, Grand Cayman, Cayman Islands KY-11108 | 345-926 2507
production@clmpublishing.com | www.clmpublishing.com
Karen E. Chin, managing editor

Types: hardcover, ebook, offset and POD paperback, gift book, picture book
Services: manuscript evaluation, design, substantive editing, copyediting, proofreading, promotional materials, marketing, distribution, author website, online bookstore, publishing packages of services, à la carte options
Production time: three months
Also does: royalty contracts
Tip: "Even after many rejection letters, never stop writing. There is always a publisher for you."

COLEMAN JONES PRESS

13155 Noel Rd. 9th floor, Dallas, TX 75240 | 866-375-2525
info@colemanjonespress.com | *www.colemanjonespress.com*
Tracee and Ross Jones, owners

> **Types:** POD, hardcover, ebook, audiobook, Sunday school and school curriculum, picture book
> **Services:** design, promotional materials, marketing, distribution, author websites, packages of services
> **Production time:** three to six months
> **Tip:** "Write for the sake of getting the gospel out, not for the money. When choosing a cover or illustrator, make sure your design looks like something that is in major retail stores."

COVENANT BOOKS, INC.

11661 Hwy. 707, Murrells Inlet, SC 29576 | 800-452-3515
contact@covenantbooks.com | *www.covenantbooks.com*
Denice Hunter, president
Kasha Foret, vice president

> **Types:** offset and POD paperback, hardcover, ebook
> **Services:** design, copyediting, marketing, distribution, online bookstore, promotional materials, author website, packages of services, à la carte options
> **Also does:** royalty contracts
> **Production time:** six months
> **Books per year:** 1,000
> **Tip:** "Publishing a book can be a fun and enlightening process. Take your time, and choose a publisher you feel comfortable with."

CREATIVE ENTERPRISES STUDIO

1507 Shirley Way, Ste. A, Bedford, TX 76022-6737 | 817-312-7393
AcreativeShop@aol.com | *CreativeEnterprisesStudio.com*
Mary Hollingsworth, publisher

> **Types:** offset and POD paperback, hardcover, ebook, audiobook, gift book, picture book
> **Services:** manuscript evaluation, design, substantive editing, copyediting, proofreading, indexing, promotional materials, distribution, author website, online bookstore, à la carte options, translations, copyright, photo research
> **Production time:** six months
> **Books per year:** ten
> **Tip:** "Contact us by email to set a phone conference to discuss your

work before proceeding otherwise."

CREDO HOUSE PUBLISHERS

2200 Boyd Ct. N.E., Grand Rapids, MI 49525-6714
publish@credocommunications.net | *www.credohousepublishers.com*
Timothy J. Beals, publisher

Types: offset and POD paperback, hardcover, ebook, audiobook, gift
book, picture book
Services: manuscript evaluation, design, substantive editing,
copyediting, proofreading, indexing, promotional materials,
marketing, distribution, author website, online bookstore,
packages of services, à la carte options
Also offers: royalty contracts
Production time: three months
Books per year: thirty
Tip: "Come prepared. Be persistent. Get published."

DCTS PUBLISHING

PO Box 40216, Santa Barbara, CA 93140 | 805-570-3168
dennis@dctspub.com | *www.dctspub.com*
Dennis Hamilton, publisher

Type: offset paperback
Services: manuscript evaluation, design, substantive editing, indexing,
proofreading, promotional materials, packages of services
Production time: two to three months
Books per year: five
Tip: "Edit, edit, and edit."

DEEP RIVER BOOKS

PO Box 310, Sisters, OR 97759 | 541-549-1139
submit@deepriverbooks.com | *www.deepriverbooks.com*
Andy Carmichael, publisher

Types: hardcover, offset and POD paperback, ebook, audiobook
Services: manuscript evaluation, design, substantive editing,
copyediting, proofreading, promotional materials, marketing,
distribution, packages of services
Production time: nine to twelve months
Books per year: thirty to thirty-five
Tip: "Deep River Books is a full-service partner publisher. Unlike
self/vanity publishers, we not only provide editing, cover design,
and all production, we also provide full marketing, sales, and

distribution. We have a sales team that makes face-to-face calls on bookstore buyers who represent more than 2,000 stores. We also provide up to two hours of one-on-one social-media coaching for every author we publish. We carefully select only the manuscripts we feel have a strong chance to see success in retail sales."

DEEPER REVELATION BOOKS

PO Box 4260, Cleveland, TN 37320-4260 | 423-478-2843
info@deeperrevelationbooks.org | www.deeperrevelationbooks.org
Mike Shreve, CEO

Types: offset and POD paperback, hardcover, ebook, gift book, picture book

Imprints: Pure Heart Publications (fiction), Children of Promise (children), Pivotal Publications (success)

Services: design, substantive editing, copyediting, proofreading, promotional materials, distribution, marketing, author website, online bookstore, à la carte options, indexing, mentoring

Production time: four to six months

Books per year: twelve to fifteen

Tip: "Read *10 Steps to Success in Writing a Christian Book*, which can be found under Author's Corner on our website."

DESTINY IMAGE

167 Walnut Bottom Rd., Shippensburg, PA 17257 | 717-532-3040
manuscripts@norimediagroup.com | norimediagroup.com/pages/submit-your-manuscript
Mykela Krieg, executive acquisitions director

Types: hardcover, paperback, ebook

Services: evaluation, editing (whatever level is necessary), proofreading, design, marketing

Production time: one year

Tip: Requires prepurchase of copies. Major topics include dreams/dream interpretation, supernatural God encounters, healing/deliverance, prophecy, gifts of the Holy Spirit, prayer.

EABOOKS PUBLISHING

2726 Christmas Palm Pl., Oviedo, FL 32765 | 407-712-3431
info@eabookspublishing.com | www.eabookspublishing.com
Cheri Cowell, publisher
Michelle Booth, managing editor

Types: POD, ebook, audiobook, gift book, children's books

Services: manuscript evaluation, design, substantive editing, copyediting, proofreading, marketing, distribution, author website, packages of services, promotional materials, illustrations

Also offers: royalty contracts

Production time: two months

Books per year: forty-five

Tip: "Email us, and we'll set up a time to discuss your project and needs."

EBOOK LISTING SERVICES

PO Box 57, Glenwood, MD 21738 | 443-280-5077

sales@taegais.com | *ebooklistingservices.com*

Amy Deardon, CEO

Types: POD, ebook, audiobook

Services: design, packages of services, à la carte options, promotional materials, marketing, distribution

Production time: one to three months

Books per year: twenty

Tip: "We empower independent authors to become successful. Unlike most other independent publishers, we set you up so *you* are the publisher, rather than publishing through the independent company. You can create your own publishing company name and logo, and we help you with that. You remain fully in charge of all decisions, rights, and profits from start to forever. Once your book is published, you can buy as few or as many books as you want at the lowest printer's price (a 200-page book costs less than $3.50); and books are delivered in a week or two through Amazon. We also have additional packages that can list your book with the Library of Congress and help you rank higher on Amazon's search engines so readers can actually find your book and buy it. We provide you with ownership of your book and work with you to make that succeed."

ELECTRIC MOON PUBLISHING, LLC

PO Box 466, Stromsburg, NE 68666 | 402-366-2033

laree@emoonpublishing.com | *www.emoonpublishing.com*

Laree Lindburg, owner-publisher

Types: offset and POD paperback, hardcover, ebook, audiobook, gift book, picture book

Services: manuscript evaluation, design, substantive editing, copyediting, proofreading, promotional materials, distribution, author website, packages of services, à la carte options

Production time: six to nine months

Books per year: fifteen to twenty

Also does: script consulting/page-to-screen; go to *www.eclipsescripts.com*

Tip: "Be open to feedback from peers and professionals. Seek out a writers group to focus your skills. And attend writers conferences when possible to make publishing connections and grow in the craft of writing."

ELM HILL

836 S. Western Dr., Bloomington, IN 47403 | 800-254-2735
email through website | elmhillbooks.com

Types: POD, hardcover, ebook

Services: manuscript evaluation, substantive editing, copyediting, design, marketing, promotional materials, author website, video trailer, distribution assistance, packages of services, à la carte options

Tip: Parent company is Harper-Collins Christian Publishing in collaboration with Accurance, a production services company.

ESSENCE PUBLISHING

20 Hanna Ct., Belleville, ON K8P 5J2, Canada | 800-238-6376, 613-962-2360
info@essence-publishing.com | www.essence-publishing.com
Sherrill Brunton, manager of publishing department

Types: offset and POD paperback, gift book, ebook, picture book

Services: manuscript evaluation, design, substantive editing, copyediting, proofreading, indexing, promotional materials, marketing, distribution, online bookstore

Production time: three months

Books per year: 100-150

Tip: "Submit a copy of your manuscript for your free evaluation."

FAIRWAY PRESS

5450 N. Dixie Hwy., Lima, OH 45807-9559 | 800-241-4056, 419-227-1818
david@csspub.com | www.fairwaypress.com
Missy Cotrell, acquisitions editor

Types: hardcover, offset and POD paperback, ebook

Services: mechanical edit (spelling, grammar, punctuation, etc.), formatting, proofreading, cover design, printing (average print run five hundred copies, minimum fifty), ISBN, bar coding, copyright filing

Production time: six to nine months

Books per year: ten to fifteen

Tip: This is the subsidy division of CSS Publishing Company. No longer does color illustrations or four-color books.

FAITH BOOKS & MORE

PO Box 1024, Athens, OH 45701 | 678-232-6156
publishing@faithbooksandmore.com | *www.faithbooksandmore.com*
Nicole Antoinette Smith, owner

Types: offset paperback, hardcover, POD

Services: manuscript evaluation, design, copyediting, proofreading

Production time: three months

Books per year: five

Tip: "Write, rewrite, write, and rewrite again until you're 100% satisfied with your manuscript."

FIESTA PUBLISHING

PO Box 44984, Phoenix, AZ 85064 | 602-795-5868
julie@fiestapublishing.com | *www.fiestapublishing.com*
Julie Castro, owner

Types: POD, ebook

Services: manuscript evaluation, design, substantive editing, copyediting, proofreading, marketing, distribution, online bookstore, à la carte options, indexing

Production time: six to nine months

Books per year: two to four

Tip: "You can't put a price on a book that helps a person in some way. That help is priceless."

FIRESIDE PRESS

PO Box 571, Gleneden Beach, OR 97388
contact@firesidepress.com | *www.FiresidePress.com*
Suzanne Parrott, president and lead designer

Types: offset and POD paperback, hardcover, ebook, audiobook, gift book, picture book

Services: manuscript evaluation, design, substantive editing, copyediting, proofreading, indexing, promotional materials, marketing, distribution, author websites, packages of services, à la carte options

Also does: royalty contracts

Production time: six months to two years

Tip: "Fireside Press offers professional, personal, and affordable services every author deserves."

FIRST STEPS PUBLISHING

PO Box 571, Gleneden Beach, OR 97388 | 541-961-7641
publish@firststepspublishing.com | www.FirstStepsPublishing.com
Suzanne Fyhrie Parrott, publisher

Types: POD, hardcover, ebook

Services: manuscript evaluation, design, substantive editing, copyediting, proofreading, promotional materials, marketing, online bookstore

Also does: royalty contracts

Production time: twelve to eighteen months

Books per year: four to five

Tip: "Our goal is to publish books of high quality, including those that may have trouble finding homes in traditional markets. We love working with authors who are passionate about their work and have a desire to publish to the world. Are you writing a book you would like to see published? We have years of publishing experience as well as being authors ourselves. We know the quality and service you want from a publisher; and as your publisher, we seek to work with undiscovered and talented authors with the desire and potential to grow to success, whose work is exciting and fresh."

FRUITBEARER PUBLISHING, LLC

PO Box 777, Georgetown, DE 19947 | 302-856-6649
info@fruitbearer.com | www.fruitbearer.com
Candy Abbott, owner and publisher

Types: offset and POD paperback, hardcover, ebook, gift book, picture book

Services: manuscript evaluation, design, substantive editing, copyediting, proofreading, promotional materials, marketing, distribution, online bookstore, à la carte options, packages of services

Also offers: royalty contracts

Production time: three months

Books per year: six to ten

Tip: "Submit your manuscript in its best form using MS Word, double-spaced."

HEALTHY LIFE PRESS

12838 Southampton Cir., Bristol, VA 24202
healthylifepress@gmail.com | www.HealthyLifePress.com
Dr. David Biebel, publisher

Types: hardcover, POD, ebook, gift book, picture book
Services: manuscript evaluation, design, substantive editing,
  copyediting, proofreading, promotional materials, marketing,
  online bookstore
Also does: royalty contracts
Production time: three to six months
Books per year: eight to twelve
Tip: "Healthy Life Press is a cooperative (author-subsidized)
  and collaborative company, sharing costs and net proceeds
  equitably. We welcome well-written, edited, and ready-for-design
  manuscripts on topics the author is passionate about and about
  which he or she is able to provide a new, different, unique, or
  original perspective. Submit book proposal plus three sample
  chapters; inquiries and manuscripts by email only. Do not inquire
  by phone, except for clarification."

HONEYCOMB HOUSE PUBLISHING LLC

New Cumberland, PA
dave@fessendens.net | davefessenden.com/honeycomb-house-publishing-llc
David E. Fessenden, publisher

Types: POD, ebook
Services: design, substantive editing, copyediting, proofreading,
  promotional materials, marketing, distribution, packages of
  services, à la carte options
Production time: three to six months
Tip: "Prepare a book proposal, even if you plan to self-publish, and use
  it as a guideline for your book project."

IMMORTALISE

PO Box 656, Noarlunga Centre, SA 5168, Australia
email through website | immortalise.com.au
Ben Morton, senior editor

Types: POD, ebook
Services: writing coaching, manuscript assessment, editing,
  proofreading, typesetting, illustration, cover design, à la carte options

INSCRIPT BOOKS

PO Box 611, Bladensburg, MD 20710 | 240-342-3293
inscript@dovechristianpublishers.com | *inscriptpublishing.com*
Raenita Wiggins, acquisitions editor

Types: offset and POD paperback, hardcover, ebook, picture book
Services: design, substantive editing, copyediting, proofreading, indexing, marketing, distribution, online bookstore, packages of services, a la carte options
Also offers: royalty contracts
Production time: one to two months
Books per year: ten
Tip: "We receive new proposals via our online form only. Carefully review publishing guidelines on website."

LOGOS PUBLICATIONS, LLC

Lampter, PA 17537 | 717-681-8452
customerservice@logospub.com | *www.logospub.com*
Lois Robinson, author support

Types: paperback, POD, hardcover, ebook, audiobook
Services: manuscript evaluation, substantive editing, proofreading, promotional materials, marketing, author website, online bookstore
Also offers: royalty contracts
Production time: six months
Books per year: one to three
Tip: "Present your story to readers who will give you honest feedback during the creation process."

MORGAN JAMES PUBLISHING

5 Penn Plaza, 23rd Floor, New York City, NY 10001 | 516-900-5711
terry@morganjamespublishing.com | *www.morganjamespublishing.com*
W. Terry Whalin, acquisitions editor, Morgan James Faith

Types: hardcover, offset and POD paperback, ebook, audiobook, picture book
Services: design, distribution, marketing, promotional materials, online bookstore
Also does: royalty contracts
Production time: three to six months
Books per year: 180-200, 25-30 in Faith imprint
Tip: "General-market publisher with a Christian division. Our books have been on *The New York Times* bestseller list more than twenty-

five times (broad distribution). For nonfiction, requires authors to purchase 2,500 copies at print costs plus $2 over lifetime of agreement. Pays 20-30% royalties on sales; pays small advance. Email proposal with sample chapters or full manuscript. Only 30% of authors have agents."

NORDSKOG PUBLISHING

4562 Westinghouse St., Ste. E, Ventura, CA 93003 | 805-642-2070
email through website | nordskogpublishing.com
Michelle Shelfer, editor

> **Types:** paperback, hardcover
> **Services:** editing, design, marketing
> **Tip:** "Looking for the best in sound theological and applied Christian faith books, both nonfiction and fiction."

PARSON PLACE PRESS

PO Box 8277, Mobile, AL 36689-0277 | 251-643-6985
info@parsonplacepress.com | www.parsonplacepress.com
Michael L. White, managing editor

> **Types:** POD, hardcover, ebook
> **Services:** substantive editing, proofreading, distribution, design, author websites, online bookstore, press release
> **Also offers:** royalty contracts
> **Production time:** three to four months
> **Books per year:** three to five
> **Tip:** "Carefully review author's guidelines and FAQ on publisher's site before submitting queries, proposals, or manuscripts."

REDEMPTION PRESS

1218 Griffin Ave., Enumclaw, WA 98022 | 360-226-3488
andrea@redemption-press.com | www.redemption-press.com
Andrea Tomassi, director of acquisitions

> **Types:** offset and POD paperback, hardcover, ebook, audiobook, gift book, picture book
> **Services:** manuscript evaluation, design, substantive editing, copyediting, proofreading, indexing, promotional materials, marketing, distribution, author website, online bookstore, à la carte options
> **Production time:** six to ten months
> **Books per year:** 125

Tip: "Commit to excellence, and don't skip developmental editing and content coaching. Professional coaching for improving your manuscript and launching it well is vital. If you're going to self-publish the last thing you want to do is *look* like you're self-published. Your finished product should look and read like a traditionally published book. We offer many opportunities for you to learn and grow in your craft, including our She Writes for Him Bootcamp: 21 Days from Idea to Manuscript Blueprint and other online initiatives."

SALVATION PUBLISHER AND MARKETING GROUP

PO Box 40860, Santa Barbara, CA 93140 | 805-252-9822
opalmaedailey@aol.com
Dr. Opal Mae Dailey, editor

Types: hardcover, offset paperback, ebook
Services: manuscript evaluation, design, substantive editing, copyediting, proofreading
Production time: six to nine months
Books per year: five to seven
Tip: "Turning taped messages into book form for pastors is a specialty of ours. We do not accept any manuscript we would be ashamed to put our name on."

SERMON TO BOOK

424 W. Bakerview Rd., Ste. 105 #215, Bellingham, WA 98226 | 360-223-1877
info@sermontobook.com | *www.sermontobook.com*
Caleb Breakey, lead book director

Types: offset and POD paperback, ebook, audiobook
Services: design, substantive editing, copyediting, proofreading, indexing, promotional materials, marketing, distribution, author website, online bookstore, packages of services, manuscript evaluation
Production time: seven to nine months
Books per year: sixty
Tip: "Check out our materials at SermonToBook.com."

SPLASHDOWN BOOKS

Auckland, New Zealand
grace@splashdownbooks.com | *www.splashdownbooks.com*
Grace Bridges, owner

Types: ebook, POD

Services: manuscript evaluation, substantive editing, copyediting, proofreading, à la carte options, hybrid publishing

Production time: as needed

Books per year: four to eight

Tip: "Be an excellent indie author with support. Steep discounts on editing for well-critiqued work. Use of Splashdown branding may be offered after edits to qualifying. mainstream-compatible science-fiction and fantasy works."

STONE OAK PUBLISHING

PO Box 2011, Friendswood, TX 77549 | 832-569-4282
stoneoakpublishing@gmail.com | *www.stoneoakpublishing.com*
Karen Porter, editor

Types of books: POD and offset paperback, hardcover, gift book

Services: manuscript evaluation, design, substantive editing, copyediting, proofreading, indexing, promotional materials, marketing, distribution, author website, online bookstore, packages of services, à la carte options

Production time: six to eight months

Books per year: ten

Tip: "Our goal is to give you the highest-quality book with the best service. We hope to make your experience with Stone Oak Publishers better than you expected. To work with our excellent editors, designers, artists, and marketers, begin by contacting us with your book idea; and we will help you take it to the highest level."

STRONG TOWER PUBLISHING

PO Box 973, Milesburg, PA 16863 | 814-206-6778
strongtowerpubs@aol.com | *www.strongtowerpublishing.com*
Heidi L. Nigro, publisher

Types: ebook, POD

Services: manuscript evaluation, copyediting, proofreading, substantive editing, design, online bookstore

Production time: three to four months

Books per year: one or two

Tip: Specializes in books on end-times topics from the prewrath rapture perspective.

TEACH SERVICES, INC.

11 Quartermaster Cir., Fort Oglethorpe, GA 30742-3886 |
706-504-9192
publishing@teachservices.com | *www.teachservices.com*
Timothy Hullquist, author advisor

Types: offset and POD paperback, hardcover, ebook, gift book,
picture book, landscape hardback, mechanical binding
Services: manuscript evaluation, design, substantive editing,
copyediting, proofreading, indexing, promotional materials,
marketing, distribution, author websites, online bookstore,
packages of services, à la carte options
Also does: royalty contracts
Production time: one to four months
Tip: "We specialize in marketing our titles to Seventh-day Adventists."

TMP BOOKS

3 Central Plaza, Ste. 307, Rome, GA 30161
info@tmpbooks.com | *www.TMPbooks.com*
Tracy Ruckman, publisher

Types: POD, ebook, picture book, hardcover, audiobook
Services: manuscript evaluation, substantive editing, copyediting,
proofreading, promotional materials, marketing, distribution,
packages of services, à la carte options, author websites
Production time: six months
Books per year: twelve to twenty-four
Tip: "Study published books aimed at your target market; know your
market."

TRACT PLANET

1155 Fountain Coin Loop, Orlando, FL 32828 | 877-778-7228
support@tractplanet.com | *www.tractplanet.com*
Andy Lawniczak

Type: Gospel tracts
Services: design, promotional materials
Production time: varies
Tip: "We focus on Gospel tracts that follow the Way of the Master
method of evangelism."

TRAIL MEDIA

PO Box 1285, Orange, CA 92856
admin@ChisholmTrailMedia.com | *www.chisholmtrailmedia.com*
Christine "CJ" Simpson, director of publishing

> **Types:** POD, ebook, gift book, picture book
> **Services:** manuscript evaluation, substantive editing, copyediting, proofreading, promotional materials, marketing, packages of services, à la carte options
> **Production time:** negotiable
> **Tip:** "Our goal is to help new authors publish their work by coordinating the services needed with experts in the field and publishing in a co-op fashion under the Trail Media imprint, so 100% of the revenue generated goes to ministry of the authors. In many cases, we find scholarships and grants to help missionaries and those in the persecuted church. Trail Media is a ministry of modified tentmaking models."

TULPEN PUBLISHING

11043 Depew St., Westminster, CO 80020 | 303-438-7276
tulpenpublishing@gmail.com | *TulpenPublishing.com*
Sandi Rog, acquisitions editor

> **Types:** ebook, POD
> **Services:** manuscript evaluation, design, substantive editing, copyediting, proofreading, distribution, online bookstore, marketing
> **Production time:** twelve to twenty months
> **Tip:** Only accepts submissions via email. See the website for submission guidelines.

VIDE PRESS

email through website | *videpress.com*
Tom Frieling, director

> **Services:** design, printing, royalties, distribution, publicity, marketing
> **Tip:** "We are always searching for new voices, articulate Christian writers who have the courage to confront the issues challenging today's culture and our faith."

WESTBOW PRESS

1663 Liberty Dr., Bloomington, IN 47403 | 844-714-3454
email through website | *www.westbowpress.com*

Types: hardcover, paperback, ebook, audiobook
Services: manuscript evaluation, substantive editing, copyediting, design, illustrations, indexing, Spanish translation, marketing, video trailer, distribution
Tip: Independent publishing division of Thomas Nelson and Zondervan.

WORD ALIVE PRESS

119 DeBoets St., Winnipeg, MB R2J 3R9, Canada | 866-967-3782
publishing@wordalivepress.ca | *www.wordalivepress.ca*

Types: hardcover, offset and POD paperback, ebook, gift book
Services: packages of services, editing, design, marketing, distribution, online bookstore
Production time: four to five months

XULON PRESS

2301 Lucien Way, Ste. 415, Maitland, FL 32751 | 407-339-4217, 866-381-2665
email through website | *www.xulonpress.com*
Donald Newman, director of sales

Types: hardcover, offset and POD paperback, ebook
Services: manuscript review, editorial critique, developmental editing, copyediting, design, packages of services, à la carte options, color illustrations, back-cover copy, ghostwriting, translation, marketing, promotional materials, publicity, video trailer, 100% net royalty, online bookstore
Production time: three to six months

YO PRODUCTIONS, LLC

PO Box 1543, Reynoldsburg, OH 43068 | 614-452-4920
info_4u@yoproductions.net | *www.yoproductions.net*
Yolonda Sanders, CEO and senior editor

Types: POD, ebook, offset paperback, hardcover
Services: manuscript evaluation, design, substantive editing, copyediting, proofreading, à la carte options, promotional materials
Production time: two months
Books per year: six to twelve

Tip: "Believe in the value of what you are doing. Your attitude about your work will affect the value that others place on it. Know your worth, your personal value, and the value in that which God has gifted you."

ZOË LIFE PUBLISHING

PO Box 871066, Canton, MI 48187 | 888-400-4922
info@zoelifepub.com | www.zoelifepub.com
Sabrina Adams, publisher

Types: hardcover, paperback, ebook

Services: packages of services, editing, design, rights and registrations, warehousing, promotion, distribution and fulfillment, online bookstore

Production time: one year

Christian Writers Institute Courses
Indie Publishing Bundle

Courses in this bundle:
- How to Get Published
- Independent Publishing Basics
- Indie Publishing Technical How-To's
- How to Find Your Readers as an Indie Author
- Independent Publishing Subsidiary Rights
- Newsletter Marketing for Independent Authors
- SMART Copywriting for Independent Authors

Normal price: $140
Savings: 72%
Market guide price: $39.20

https://cwmg.link/indie2021

How to Scan QR Codes
Use the camera on your smartphone to focus on the above QR code to activate the discount. It will give you the option to visit the site, which you will want to accept. If you are using an older smartphone, you may need to download a QR-code scanning app. You can also visit the URL below the code to activate the discount on your computer.

3

DESIGN AND **PRODUCTION SERVICES**

AUTHOR SUPPORT SERVICES | RUSSELL SHERRARD
Carmichael, CA | 916-967-7251
russellsherrard@reagan.com | *www.sherrardsebookresellers.com/WordPress/ author-support-services-the-authors-place-to-get-help*
> **Contact:** email
> **Services:** Kindle ebook formatting, ebook linked table of contents, PDF creation, book-cover design
> **Charges:** flat fee
> **Credentials/experience:** Writing and editing since 2009; currently providing freelance services for multiple clients.

BACK•DOOR DESIGN
backdoordesign99@gmail.com | *backdoordesign99.wixsite.com/info*
> **Contact:** email, website form
> **Services:** book-cover design, book-interior design, typesetting, ebook conversion, illustrations
> **Charges:** flat fee, custom
> **Credentials/experience:** "At back•door DESIGN, our mission is to create high-quality book designs at DIY prices. We are all about book design, from front cover to back cover and everything in between. Adobe Certified Associate in Print & Digital Publication Using Adobe InDesign."

BETHANY PRESS INTERNATIONAL
6820 W. 115th St., Bloomington, MN 55438 | 888-717-7400
info@bethanypress.com | *www.bethanypress.com*
> **Contact:** email, phone, website form
> **Services:** short-run digital printing and long-run (minimum 500 copies) printing, only with files created by a professional book designer
> **Charges:** flat fee

Credentials/experience: Printer for the majority of Christian publishing houses since 1997. "We partner with publishers and ministries to create, produce, and distribute millions of life-changing Christian books each year. We invest our proceeds in training and sending missionaries through Bethany International."

BLUE LEAF BOOK SCANNING

618 Crowsnest Dr., Ballwin, MO 63021 | 314-606-9322
blue.leaf.it@gmail.com | www.blueleaf-book-scanning.com

Contact: email, phone, website form
Services: book and document scanning to multiple formats, ebook and audio conversions
Charges: flat fee
Credentials/experience: The first book-scanning service for consumers. Accurate optical character recognition (more than 99.6% accurate on ideal conditions) with excellent format retention. Can scan nearly 200 languages.

BOOK WHISPERS

Capalaba QLD 4157, Australia | +61 07 3167 6513
info@bookwhispers.com.au | www.bookwhispers.com.au

Contact: website form, phone
Services: cover design; interior design; typesetting; preparing print-ready files; promotional materials, including bookmarks, banners, and flyers

BREADBOX CREATIVE | ERYN LYNUM

1437 N. Denver Ave. #167, Loveland, CO 80538 | 970-308-3654
eryn@breadboxcreative.com | www.breadboxcreative.com/creators

Contact: website form
Services: website design, social-media assistance
Charges: flat fee
Credentials/experience: "At Breadbox Creative, we have more than twenty years of experience in web design. The owner, Eryn Lynum, is an author herself and marries her passion for writing with her passion for web design to come alongside writers and speakers and help them further spread the messages God has laid on their hearts. Breadbox Creative works with businesses, writers, and speakers by creating professional WordPress websites, as well as assisting with SEO and social-media platforms. We also offer assistance with preparing book proposals and writing consulting."

BROOKSTONE CREATIVE GROUP | SUZANNE KUHN

PO Box 211, Evington, VA 24550 | 302-514-7899
www.brookstonecreativegroup.com

Contact: website form

Services: book-cover design, book-interior design, offset and POD printing, distribution, website design, promotional materials

Charges: flat fee

Credentials/experience: Suzanne has more than thirty years of book-specific experience. Brookstone is an expansion of her business, SuzyQ, with a team of almost two dozen professionals who bring a wide range of knowledge and experience to help you get published.

BUTTERFIELD EDITORIAL SERVICES | DEBRA L. BUTTERFIELD

4810 Gene Field Rd. #2, St. Joseph, MO 64506 | 816-752-2171
deb@debralbutterfield.com | *TheMotivationalEditor.com*

Contact: website form

Services: book-cover design, book-interior design, ebook conversion

Charges: custom rate

Credentials/experience: "Five years of experience in interior book design, using Adobe InDesign; three years of book-cover design."

ByBRENDA | BRENDA WILBEE

4631 Quinn Ct., #202 | Bellingham, WA 98226 | 360-389-6895
brenda@brendawilbee.com | *brendawilbee.com*

Contact: email

Services: book-cover design, book-interior design, typesetting, printing, marketing and promotional products

Charges: hourly rate with estimate

Credentials/experience: "A writer and editor for thirty years and book designer for ten, I bring to your project an understanding of how books work and what makes them better. I particularly enjoy combining narrative and imagery—a synergistic alchemy. I hold an AA in Visual Communications, a BA in Creative Writing and Art, and an MA in Professional Writing. Examples of my work can be found on my website."

CASTELANE, INC. | KIM MCDOUGALL

Whitehall, PA | 647-281-1554
kimm@castelane.com | *www.castelane.com*

Contact: email

Services: book-cover design, ebook conversion, book video trailers

Charges: flat fee

Credentials/experience: "I have made more than five hundred book video trailers and three hundred book covers since 2009. Samples and references are available on the website."

CELEBRATION WEB DESIGN | BRUCE SHANK

PO Box 471068, Celebration, FL 34747 | 610-989-0400

info@celebrationwebdesign.com | *CelebrationWebDesign.com*

Contact: email, phone, website form

Service: website design

Charges: flat fee, hourly rate, custom rate

Credentials/experience: "Celebration Web Design offers tailor-made websites. If you can dream it, we can build it. Our vision is to work with you in creating a high-quality, visually engaging, full-featured website that exceeds your every expectation. Partnering with our team will revolutionize your web presence. Our goal is to take care of all the tech stuff, so you can focus on what you do best. We are committed to providing the best possible service at the lowest possible price. Our staff is dedicated to furthering the Kingdom of God by partnering with authors, ministries, missionaries, and churches to create websites with purpose."

CHRISTIANPRINT.COM

6820 W. 115th St., Bloomington, MN 55438 | 888-201-1322

www.christianprint.com

Contact: phone, website form

Services: prints ancillary products, such as business cards, brochures, booklets, banners, postcards, posters, and signs

Charges: flat fee

Credentials/experience: A division of Bethany Press, founded in 1997.

DESIGN CORPS | JOHN WOLLINKA

Colorado Springs, CO | 719-260-0500

john@designcorps.us | *designcorps.us*

Contact: email

Services: book-cover design, book-interior design, typesetting, ebook conversion, illustrations, website design, printing, marketing

Charges: flat fee

Credentials/experience: Design Corps has been serving Christian publishers, denominations, ministries, and organizations for more than twenty years.

DIGGYPOD | KEVIN OSWORTH

301 Industrial Dr., Tecumseh, MI 49286 | 877-944-7844
kosworth@diggypod.com | *www.diggypod.com*

> **Contact:** email, website form, phone
> **Services:** book-cover design, printing
> **Charges:** based on the number of books/pages being printed; website
> has an active quote calculator that provides 100% accurate pricing
> **Credentials/experience:** DiggyPOD has been printing books since
> 2001. All facets of the book printing take place in its facility.

EDENBROOKE PRODUCTIONS | MARTY KEITH

Franklin, TN | 615-415-1942
johnmartinkeith@gmail.com | *www.edenbrookemusic.com/booktrailers*

> **Contact:** email
> **Service:** book trailers with custom music
> **Charges:** flat fee
> **Credentials/experience:** Has produced music for everyone from CBS
> TV to Discovery Channel.

829 DESIGN | LINNE GARRETT

8749 Cortina Cir., Roseville, CA 95678 | 408-410-8072
linne@829design.com | *www.829design.com*

> **Contact:** email, phone, website form
> **Service:** book-cover design, book-interior design, typesetting, ebook
> conversion, website design
> **Charges:** flat fee, custom
> **Credentials/experience:** "As the owner and creative brand director of
> 829 Design, I have well over 25 years of experience in the graphic-
> design industry. I started my career in editorial design, working as
> art director for monthly magazines, weekly magazines, periodicals,
> and books for a variety of clients nationwide. Over the course of
> my career, I have excelled in both print and digital mediums. We
> are now a virtual agency that focuses on branding and custom web
> development in addition to our print side."

FINDLEY FAMILY VIDEO PRODUCTIONS | MARY C. FINDLEY

Tulsa, OK | 918-805-0669
mjmcfindley@gmail.com | *findleyfamilyvideoproductions.com*

> **Contact:** email, website form
> **Services:** book-cover design, book-interior design, ebook conversion,
> illustrations
> **Charges:** flat fee

Credentials/experience: "10 years video and graphic design experience, book covers, formatting, and trailers."

FISTBUMP MEDIA, LLC | DAN KING

5761 Old Summerwood Blvd., Sarasota, FL 34232 | 941-681-8015
sales@fistbumpmedia.com | *fistbumpmedia.com*
   Contact: email, phone
   Services: book-cover design, book-interior design, ebook conversion, website design
   Charges: flat fee, hourly rate
   Credentials/experience: "Our experience in online publishing and digital media goes back over 13 years, and we've been helping writers at all levels for over 8 years. We work with start-up writers trying to publish their first work, and we work with best-sellers who need some extra technical support."

FIVE J'S DESIGN | JOY A. MILLER

info@fivejsdesign.com | *fivejsdesign.com*
   Contact: email, website form
   Services: book-cover design, book-interior design, typesetting
   Charges: hourly rate, flat fee, custom rate
   Credentials/experience: "We have been designing and typesetting books since 2008, including the cover design and interior layout for *The Christian Writers Market Guide.*"

THE FOREWORD COLLECTIVE, LLC | MOLLY HODGIN

1726 Charity Dr., Brentwood, TN 37027 | 615-497-4322
info@theforewordcollective.com | *www.theforewordcollective.com*
   Contact: email
   Service: book-cover design
   Charges: flat fee, hourly rate
   Credentials/experience: "The Foreword Collective was founded by Molly Hodgin, a publishing professional with two decades of experience. Most recently, she served as the Associate Publisher for the Specialty Division of HarperCollins Christian Publishing working to acquire and create gift books, children's books, and new media products with authors and brands."

GRACE BRIDGES

New Zealand
gracebridges1@gmail.com | *www.gracebridges.com/hire-me*
   Contact: website form

Services: book-cover design, book-interior design, typesetting, ebook conversion

Charges: flat fee

Credentials/experience: "Interior print and ebook formatting on dozens of published books. My cover design is a basic service only, best suited to selected genres: picture + text (see website for examples)."

IMMORTALISE | BEN MORTON

Australia

info@immortalise.com.au | www.immortalise.com.au

Contact: email

Services: typesetting, illustrations, cover design

Credentials/experience: Published author, creative-writing teacher, experienced editor and publisher, MA fiction writing supervisor.

INKSMITH EDITORIAL SERVICES | LIZ SMITH

Mebane, NC | 336-514-2331

liz@inksmithediting.com | inksmithediting.com

Contact: email

Services: book-interior design, typesetting, ebook conversion

Charges: hourly rate

Credentials/experience: "In addition to editing and indexing services, Liz Smith offers interior book design (formatting, typesetting) and ebook conversion. She has helped dozens of self-publishing authors go from raw manuscript to polished and published book. Her portfolio and client testimonials can be found on her website."

JAMIE FOLEY

Bastrop, TX

jamie@jamiesfoley.com | jamiefoley.com

Contact: email

Service: typesetting

Charges: flat fee, hourly rate

Credentials/experience: "Twelve years of experience in the Christian publishing industry. BA in Arts & Technology. Worked for Thomas Nelson, Author Media, The Christian Writers Institute, Enclave Publishing, and many bestselling authors. Typesetter for *The Christian Writers Market Guide*."

KELLIE BOOK DESIGN | KELLIE PARSONS

Perth, WA, Australia | 0412 591 687

hello@kelliemaree.com | *business.facebook.com/kelliebookdesign*

Contact: email

Services: book-cover design, book-interior design, typesetting, ebook conversion, print liaison

Charges: flat fee

Credentials/experience: "Kellie Book Design has been doing graphic design for churches, ministries, and nonprofit organizations for over 10 years and has specialized in book design since 2015."

LAURA PACE GRAPHIC DESIGN | LAURA PACE

1287 Gambel Oaks Pl., Elizabeth, CO 80107 | 303-906-8850

pacelauradesign@gmail.com | *Laurapacedesign.com*

Contact: email, phone

Services: book-cover design, full-cover layouts, business cards, bookmarks, table tents, postcards, fliers

Charges: flat fee

Credentials/experience: "Freelance designer specializing in book-cover and full-cover layouts, as well as a large variety of print material for promotional and advertising purposes. I enjoy working directly with both authors and publishing companies."

MADISON BOOK COVER DESIGNS | RUTH DERBY

220 W. Elm St., Hanford, CA 93230 | 559-772-2489

rmadison_1@hotmail.com | *www.ruthiemadison.com*

Contact: email, website form

Service: book-cover design

Charges: flat fee

Credentials/experience: More than three years of experience and has had mentors in this field.

MARTIN PUBLISHING SERVICES | MELINDA MARTIN

Palestine, TX | 903-948-4893

martinpublishingservices@gmail.com | *melindamartin.me*

Contact: email, phone, website form

Services: book-cover design, book-interior design, typesetting, ebook conversion

Charges: flat fee

Credentials/experience: Five years of working with clients' manuscripts to achieve a design that is best for their platforms.

MCLENNAN CREATIVE | ALISON MCLENNAN

1933 Geraldson Dr., Lancaster, PA 17601 | 717-572-2585
alison@mclennancreative.com | www.mclennancreative.com

Contact: website form
Service: website design
Charges: customized packages
Credentials/experience: More than twenty years of experience in the publishing industry.

MEADE AGENCY | KRIS MEADE

460 King St. #200, Charleston, SC 29403 | 843-714-0090
hello@meadeagency.cc | www.meadeagency.cc

Contact: email, phone
Service: video production
Charges: custom fee
Credentials/experience: "Meade Agency is a professional video production company specializing in book trailers, branding videos, and online course creation. We have mastered the production of web-based, on-demand video education. Online courses are a powerful way to monetize a platform, and we've got you covered from filming lessons to the web development of your course. We have worked with a variety of leaders in the industry, such as Proverbs 31 Ministries, HarperCollins, Thomas Nelson, and David C. Cook Publishing."

MISSION AND MEDIA | MICHELLE RAYBURN

11510 County Highway M, New Auburn, WI 54757 | 715-382-6030
info@missionandmedia.com | www.missionandmedia.com

Contact: email, website form
Services: book-cover design, book-interior design, typesetting, ebook conversion
Charges: flat fee, hourly rate, free consultation
Credentials/experience: "Michelle works with indie and self-published authors to design a quality book cover and interior. She also coaches those who want to create their own imprint with full control of their own publishing process. Her area of specialty is with Amazon KDP. Michelle worked for a marketing and advertising agency for 3 years, and also has 19 years of experience on the writing and editing side of publishing. Portfolio and additional information are available on the website."

RANEY DAY CREATIVE | KEN RANEY

1848 Georgia St., Cape Girardeau, MO 63701 | 316-737-9724
kenraney@mac.com | *kenraney.design.blogspot.com*

Contact: email, phone
Services: book-cover design, book-interior design, ebook conversion,
illustrations, typesetting
Charges: flat fee, hourly rate
Credentials/experience: "Over 40 years' experience as an illustrator
and graphic designer."

RICK STEELE EDITORIAL SERVICES | RICK STEELE

26 Dean Rd., Ringgold, GA 30736 | 706-937-8121
email through website | *steeleeditorialservices.myportfolio.com*

Contact: email, website form
Services: book-interior design, typesetting
Charges: flat fee based on page count and complexity of layout
Credentials/experience: "More than twenty years of working
for Christian publishing houses has led me to wear many hats,
including typesetting and page-layout duties. I have more than two
decades of experience using page-layout software programs, such as
Adobe InDesign and QuarkXPress. I've performed layout duties
for countless trade fiction and nonfiction books, workbook Bible
studies, devotionals, and prayer journals."

ROSEANNA WHITE DESIGNS | ROSEANNA WHITE

roseannamwhite@gmail.com | *www.RoseannaWhiteDesigns.com*

Contact: email, website form
Services: book-cover design, book-interior design, typesetting, ebook
conversion, illustrations
Charges: flat fee, hourly rate, custom fee
Credentials/experience: "Roseanna has been designing and
typesetting books for nearly ten years, combining her keen eye and
artistic skills with her insider knowledge of the industry. As an
author herself, she knows how important it is for the appearance
of a book to match the words and strives to bring your story to
life at a single glance. She has worked for publishing houses and
independently for some of Christian fiction's top authors."

SCREE, LLC | LANDON OTIS

Sandpoint, ID | 208-290-4624
landon@scree.it | *scree.it*

Contact: website form

Services: website design, website development

Charges: hourly rate

Credentials/experience: Professional, full-time web developer at a local design and marketing firm. Websites include *veritasincorporated.com* and *mineralchurch.org*.

STARCHER DESIGNS | KARA STARCHER

Chloe, WV | 330-705-3399

info@starcherdesigns.com | *www.starcherdesigns.com*

Contact: website form

Services: book-interior design, typesetting

Charges: custom fee

Credentials/experience: BA in publishing, professional designer with more than fifteen years of experience.

SUZANNE FYHRIE PARROTT

PO Box 571, Gleneden Beach, OR 97388

author@suzannefyhrieparrott.com | *www.SuzanneFyhrieParrott.com*

Contact: website form

Services: book-cover design, book-interior design, ebook conversion, illustrations

Also does: publication and marketing

Charges: flat fee, hourly rate, custom fee

Credentials/experience: "Suzanne graduated from the University of Washington in 1981 and has earned several Montana Addy Awards for design excellence, working with such clients as Yellowstone Park, Old West Trail, Columbia Paint, Winston Fly Rod Company, and Montana Power Company. She is currently the lead designer for First Steps Publishing, Fireside Press, Penman Productions, and several other publishing companies. Her primary design focus is book design and publication, producing original layouts/designs in print and digital (ebook/audio), as well as creating a complete marketing plan for your publication success."

TLC BOOK DESIGN | TAMARA DEVER

Austin, TX

tamara@tlcbookdesign.com | *www.TLCBookDesign.com*

Contact: email

Services: book-cover design, book-interior design, typesetting, ebook conversion, printing, website design

Charges: custom rate

Credentials/experience: "TLC provides award-winning book design, editorial, printing, and guidance with a personal touch that takes the stress out of book creation and gives serious authors and publishers high-quality books they are proud to represent. The recipients of over 200 industry awards, we've been joyfully serving the publishing industry for twenty-five years."

TRILION STUDIOS | BRIAN WHITE
Lawrence, KS | 785-841-5500
hello@TriLionStudios.com | www.TriLionStudios.com

Contact: email, phone
Services: book-cover design, illustrations, web design, branding and logo design, video
Charges: flat fee, hourly rate
Credentials/experience: Twenty years in the design/web design/branding industry. Has worked with nonprofits and churches for more than fifteen years.

URIAH FRACASSI CREATIVE, LLC | URIAH FRACASSI
3660 E. Barbara Ct. #12, Oak Creek, WI 53154 | 224-545-6681
uriah@uriahfracassi.com | uriahfracassi.com

Contact: email
Services: book-cover design, book-interior design, typesetting, ebook conversion, illustrations, website design, author platform branding and strategic messaging
Charges: custom
Credentials/experience: "I help Christian leaders maximize their message, so they can focus on building a legacy of life change. I specialize in strategic messaging, visual branding and cover-to-cover book design. I have been a trusted art director and brand strategist at Artspeak Creative for several years."

VIVID GRAPHICS | LARRY VANHOOSE
2273 Snow Hill Rd., Galax, VA 24333 | 276-233-0276
larry@vivid-graphics.com | www.vivid-graphics.com

Contact: email, phone, website form
Services: book-cover design, book-interior design, ebook conversion, printing
Charges: hourly rate, flat fee, custom fee
Credentials/experience: "Publish and design magazines, literature, ads, websites, billboards; client consultant developing effective marketing and advertising programs; write and edit copy for literature, videos, ads, and training materials."

WRITER'S TABLET AGENCY | TERRI WHITEMORE

4371 Roswell Rd. #315, Marietta, GA 30062 | 770-648-4101

WritersTablet@gmail.com | www.WritersTablet.org

Contact: email

Services: book-cover design, book-interior design, typesetting, ebook conversion

Charges: flat fee

Credentials/experience: "Becoming a published author requires a lot more than a knack for writing and a great story. Partnering with the Writer's Tablet Agency will put you on the fast-track to seeing your name in print. Learn how to navigate the complex world of publishing alongside passionate published authors with years of experience. From polishing your final manuscript to launching your book, Writer's Tablet simplifies the Road to Publication."

YO PRODUCTIONS, LLC | YOLONDA SANDERS

PO Box 1543, Reynoldsburg, OH 43068 | 614-452-4920

info_4u@yoproductions.net | www.yoproductions.net

Contact: email

Services: book-interior design, typesetting, book-cover design

Charges: custom fee

Credentials/experience: "We work side-by-side with our clients to understand your needs and then to produce a quality product that meets them, using the most up-to-date software versions available. Don't have a solid design idea? Don't worry! We will help you brainstorm as well, if needed. We treat every project as if it were our own, and give the time and attention needed to make it a masterpiece."

Note: See **"Editorial Services"** and **"Publicity and Marketing Services"** for help with these needs.

Christian Publishing Show
Featured Episode

Podcast episode: How to Avoid the #1 Cause of Bad Book Covers:
  Design by Committee
Market guide price: FREE

https://cwmg.link/design2021

How to Scan QR Codes
Use the camera on your smartphone to focus on the above QR code to activate the discount. It will give you the option to visit the site, which you will want to accept. If you are using an older smartphone, you may need to download a QR-code scanning app. You can also visit the URL below the code to activate the discount on your computer.

4

DISTRIBUTION SERVICES

AMAZON ADVANTAGE
www.amazon.com/gp/seller-account/mm-product-page.html?topic=200329770
Advantage is a simple way to sell your books on one of the world's leading online retail websites even if you don't publish your books through Amazon or another company that will list them on this site. Advantage provides marketing and vendor support to maximize your sales. Titles enrolled in Advantage are eligible for Search Inside, customer service, order fulfillment services, and more. Annual fee for unlimited titles is $99, plus 55% commission.

CHRISTIANBOOK
PO Box 7000, Peabody, MA 01961-7000 | 800-247-4784
email through the website | www.christianbook.com
Sometimes distributes independently published books.

NOVELLA DISTRIBUTION
Unit 3, 5 Currumbin Ct., Capalaba, QLD 4157 Australia | +61 07 3167 6519
sales@novelladistribution.com.au | bookstores.novelladistribution.com.au
Provides warehousing and distribution to trade bookstores (Christian and general market), as well as library and educational suppliers and major online retailers. Also operates a specialist division that is the supplier of choice for many Christian schools in Australia.

PATHWAY BOOK SERVICE
34 Production Ave., Keene, NH 03431 | 800-345-6665
pbs@pathwaybook.com | www.pathwaybook.com
Provides warehousing, order fulfillment, and trade distribution. It is a longtime distributor to Ingram and Baker & Taylor, the vendors of choice for most bookstores. Pathway uploads new-title spreadsheets

to Ingram and Baker & Taylor, as well as to *Amazon.com*, Barnes & Noble, and Books-A-Million on a weekly basis. Distribution outside of North America is available through Gazelle Book Services in the United Kingdom. Also provides the option of having Pathway add titles to its Amazon Advantage account, which is at a lower discount and often a lower shipping cost per book than individual accounts.

STONEWATER BOOKS

info@stonewaterbooks.com | www.stonewaterbooks.com

Provides warehousing, fulfillment, and distribution of print books, through various channels. Books can be placed into the retail distribution chain to be orderable by independent bookstores, wholesalers, other distributors, and online retailers like Amazon, Christianbook.com, and Barnes & Noble. Stonewater also fulfills orders placed on the author's website, ships into the Amazon Advantage program, and can ship crowdfunded books to backers.

PART 3

PERIODICAL PUBLISHERS

5

TOPICS AND TYPES

This chapter is not an exhaustive list of types of manuscripts and topics editors are looking for, but it is a starting place for some of the more popular ones. For instance, almost all periodicals take manuscripts in categories like Christian living, so they are not listed here. Plus writers guidelines tend to outline general areas, not every specific type and topic an editor will buy.

CONTEMPORARY ISSUES
Brio
Catholic Sentinel
Christian Herald
Christianity Today
City Light News
The Covenant Companion
Faith Today
Focus on the Family
Holiness Today
Influence
Light + Life Magazine
Light Magazine
Ministry
New Frontier Chronicle
Now What?
Our Sunday Visitor Newsweekly
Presbyterians Today
St. Anthony Messenger
War Cry

DEVOTIONS
Focus on the Family
The Gem

Gems of Truth
Girlz 4 Christ Magazine
Keys to Living
ParentLife
Presbyterians Today

ESSAY
America
The Canadian Lutheran
The Christian Century
The Christian Librarian
Commonweal
The Cresset
CrossCurrents
Faith Today
Fathom
Image
Liguorian
Love Is Moving
The Lutheran Witness
Our Sunday Visitor Newsweekly
Poets & Writers
Relief Journal
Sharing

Story Embers
U.S. Catholic
The Writer
The Writer's Chronicle
Writer's Digest

EVANGELISM

Blue Ridge Christian News
The Christian Journal
Christian Research Journal
CommonCall
Evangelical Missions Quarterly
Facts & Trends
Faith on Every Corner
Just Between Us
Love Is Moving
The Lutheran Witness
Net Results
New Identity Magazine
On Mission
Outreach
War Cry

FAMILY

Boundless
Celebrate Life Magazine
Columbia
CommonCall
Evangelical Missions Quarterly
Faith & Friends
Faith on Every Corner
Focus on the Family
HomeLife
Influence
Joyful Living Magazine
Light Magazine
Ministry
The Mother's Heart
ParentLife
Power for Living

St. Anthony Messenger
Southwest Kansas Faith
and Family

FICTION

See **Short Story**.

FILLERS

Angels on Earth
Bible Advocate
Blue Ridge Christian News
Christian Herald
Christian Living in
the Mature Years
Creation Illustrated
Eternal Ink
FellowScript
Focus on the Family Clubhouse
Focus on the Family Clubhouse Jr.
Freelance Writer's Report
Girlz 4 Christ Magazine
Guideposts
LIVE
The Mother's Heart
War Cry
Words for the Way

FINANCES/MONEY

Boundless
Christian Living in
the Mature Years
Christian Standard
Columbia
Joyful Living Magazine
Just Between Us
Net Results
WritersWeekly.com

HOW-TO

Blue Ridge Christian News
Canada Lutheran
Celebrate Life Magazine

Charisma Leader
Christian Herald
Christian Living in
the Mature Years
Christian Standard
CommonCall
Creation Illustrated
Evangelical Missions Quarterly
Facts & Trends
Faith Today
Focus on the Family
Focus on the Family Clubhouse
Girlz 4 Christ Magazine
HomeLife
Homeschooling Today
InSite
The Journal of Adventist
Education
Joyful Living Magazine
Just Between Us
Leading Hearts
Light Magazine
LIVE
The Lutheran Witness
Ministry
The Mother's Heart
Mutuality
Net Results
New Identity Magazine
Outreach
ParentLife
Parish Liturgy
Poets & Writers
Prayer Connect
SAConnects
Story Embers
Teachers of Vision
Vibrant Life

The Writer
The Writer's Chronicle
Writer's Digest
Writing Corner

INTERVIEW/PROFILE

The Arlington Catholic Herald
Brio
byFaith
Cadet Quest
Canada Lutheran
Catholic Sentinel
Celebrate Life Magazine
Charisma
Charisma Leader
Christ Is Our Hope
The Christian Century
Christian Herald
The Christian Journal
Christianity Today
City Light News
Columbia
CommonCall
Converge
The Covenant Companion
Creation
The Cresset
DTS Magazine
Eternal Ink
Evangelical Missions Quarterly
Faith & Friends
Faith on Every Corner
Faith Today
Focus on the Family Clubhouse
Focus on the Family Clubhouse Jr.
Friends Journal
Gems of Truth
Girlz 4 Christ Magazine
History's Women

Homeschooling Today
Image
InSite
*International Journal
of Frontier Missiology*
Joyful Living Magazine
Kansas City Metro Voice
Leading Hearts
LEAVES
Leben
Light + Life Magazine
Liguorian
Love Is Moving
The Lutheran Witness
The Mother's Heart
Our Sunday Visitor Newsweekly
Outreach
Parish Liturgy
Peer
Poets & Writers
Point
Power for Living
St. Anthony Messenger
Story Embers
Testimony/Enrich
Today's Christian Living
U.S. Catholic
Vibrant Life
War Cry
The Writer's Chronicle
Writer's Digest

LEADERSHIP/MINISTRY

Charisma Leader
Christian Standard
CommonCall
Facts & Trends
Holiness Today
Just Between Us

Ministry
Mutuality
Net Results
Outreach

MARRIAGE

Boundless
Converge Magazine
Faith & Friends
Focus on the Family
HomeLife
Joyful Living Magazine
The Mother's Heart
St. Anthony Messenger

NEWSPAPER

The Anglican Journal
The Arlington Catholic Herald
Blue Ridge Christian News
Catholic New York
Catholic Sentinel
Christian Courier
Christian Herald
Christian News Northwest
City Light News
The Good News Journal
Kansas City Metro Voice
The Messianic Times
New Frontier Chronicle
Our Sunday Visitor Newsweekly
Prairie Messenger
The Southeast Outlook
*Southwest Kansas Faith
and Family*

PARENTING

The Christian Journal
City Light News
Columbia
Focus on the Family
HomeLife

Just Between Us
Light Magazine
The Light Magazine
The Mother's Heart
Parenting Teens
ParentLife
War Cry

PERSONAL EXPERIENCE

Angels on Earth
The Anglican Journal
Bible Advocate
Blue Ridge Christian News
The Breakthrough Intercessor
Canada Lutheran
Catholic New York
Catholic Sentinel
Celebrate Life Magazine
Chicken Soup for the
Soul Book Series
Christ Is Our Hope
The Christian Journal
Christian Living in
the Mature Years
Christian Standard
Christianity Today
Converge Magazine
Creation Illustrated
Divine Moments Book Series
DTS Magazine
Facts & Trends
Faith & Friends
Faith on Every Corner
Friends Journal
The Gem
Guideposts
Highway News
Holiness Today
The Journal of Adventist

Education
Joyful Living Magazine
Just Between Us
Keys to Living
Leading Hearts
LEAVES
LIVE
The Lutheran Witness
The Mother's Heart
Mutuality
Mysterious Ways
New Identity Magazine
Now What?
Point
Power for Living
Prayer Connect
SAConnects
Sharing
Shattered Magazine
Standard
Story Embers
Teachers of Vision
Testimony/Enrich
Today's Christian Living
Vibrant Life
Victorious Women in Christ
Words for the Way

POETRY

America
Bible Advocate
Chicken Soup for the
Soul Book Series
The Christian Century
Christian Courier
The Christian Journal
Commonweal
Creation Illustrated
The Cresset

CrossCurrents
Eternal Ink
Faith on Every Corner
Fathom
Focus on the Family Clubhouse Jr.
Friends Journal
The Gem
Gems of Truth
Girlz 4 Christ Magazine
Image
Keys to Living
LEAVES
LIVE
The Lutheran Journal
The Lutheran Witness
The Messenger
Mutuality
Poets & Writers
Power for Living
Relief Journal
St. Anthony Messenger
Sharing
Sojourners
Story Embers
Teachers of Vision
Time Of Singing
U.S. Catholic
Victorious Women in Christ
Words for the Way

PROFILE

See **Interview**.

REVIEWS

The Anglican Journal
byFaith
The Canadian Lutheran
Canadian Mennonite
Charisma
The Christian Century

Christian Courier
Christian Herald
The Christian Journal
Christian Librarian
Christian Retailing
Christianity Today
Converge
The Covenant Companion
Creation Research Journal
Faith on Every Corner
Faith Today
FellowScript
Girlz 4 Christ Magazine
The Good News (New York)
The Journal of Adventist Education
Kansas City Metro Voice
Leading Hearts
LEAVES
Light Magazine
The Living Church
Love Is Moving
The Messianic Times
Ministry
Mutuality
New Frontier Chronicle
On Mission
Sojourners
Story Embers
Time Of Singing
U.S. Catholic

SCIENCE

Creation
Nature Friend

SEASONAL

The Anglican Journal
Brio

Canadian Lutheran
Catholic New York
Celebrate Life Magazine
Charisma
The Christian Century
Christian Courier
Christian Living in
the Mature Years
Christian Standard
Columbia
Divine Moments Book Series
DTS Magazine
EFCA Today
Eternal Ink
Faith Today
Focus on the Family Clubhouse
Focus on the Family Clubhouse Jr.
Freelance Writer's Report
The Gem
Gems of Truth
Girlz 4 Christ Magazine
Guide
Insight
InSite
Keys to Living
Liguorian
LIVE
The Messenger
The Mother's Heart
Nature Friend
Our Little Friend
Outreach
Poets & Writers
Presbyterians Today
Primary Treasure
St. Anthony Messenger
Testimony/Enrich
Time Of Singing

U.S. Catholic
War Cry
Words for the Way
Writer's Digest
WritersWeekly.com

SHORT STORY/ FICTION

The Anglican Journal
Blue Ridge Christian News
Brio
Cadet Quest
The Christian Journal
CrossCurrents
Faith on Every Corner
Fathom
Focus on the Family Clubhouse
Focus on the Family Clubhouse Jr.
The Gem
Gems of Truth
Girlz 4 Christ Magazine
Image
Liguorian
LIVE
Nature Friend
Relief Journal
St. Anthony Messenger
Story Embers
Teachers of Vision
U.S. Catholic
Victorious Women in Christ
War Cry

TAKE-HOME PAPER

The Gem
Gems of Truth
Guide
LIVE
Our Little Friend
Power for Living
Primary Treasure

Standard

THEOLOGY

byFaith

The Canadian Lutheran

Christianity Today

Faith & Friends

The Lutheran Witness

Mature Living

The Messenger

Presbyterians Today

6

ADULT MARKETS

AMERICA

106 W. 56th St., New York, NY 10019-3803 | 212-581-4640
articles@americamagazine.org | www.americamagazine.org
Kevin Clarke, senior editor
Joseph Hoover, S.J., poetry editor, jhoover@americamagazine.org

Denomination: Catholic
Parent company: America Media, Jesuit Conference of the United States and Canada
Type: weekly print magazine plus online content, circulation 46,000
Audience: primarily Catholic; two-thirds are laypeople, college educated
Purpose: to provide a smart Catholic take on faith and culture
Submissions: Only accepts complete manuscripts submitted through the website. Unsolicited freelance: 100%. Responds in two weeks.
Types: Articles, 2,500 words maximum. "Faith in Focus," personal essays, 800 to 1500 words. "Short Take" opinion essays, 500-600 words. Poetry, 30 lines maximum.
Topics: Catholic take on a political, social, cultural, economic, or ecclesial news event or historical/cultural trend; essays on joys and challenges of living out one's faith in the midst of real life
Rights: first, electronic
Payment: competitive rates, on acceptance
Guidelines: *americamedia.submittable.com/submit*
Sample: download from the website
Tip: "We are known across the Catholic world for our unique brand of excellent, relevant, and accessible coverage. From theology and spirituality to politics, international relations, arts and letters, and the economy and social justice, our coverage spans the globe."

ANGELS ON EARTH

110 William St., Ste. 901, New York, NY 10038 | 212-251-8100
www.guideposts.org/our-magazines/angels-on-earth-magazine

Colleen Hughes, editor-in-chief
> **Parent company:** Guideposts
> **Type:** bimonthly print and digital magazine, circulation 550,000
> **Purpose:** to tell true stories of heavenly angels and earthly ones who find themselves on a mission of comfort, kindness, or reassurance
> **Submissions:** Submit complete manuscript through the website at *guideposts.org/tell-us-your-story*. Responds in two months or isn't interested. Unsolicited freelance: 90%. Articles to 1,500 words, 40-60 per year; short anecdotes similar to full-length articles, 50-250 words. All stories must be true.
> **Types of manuscripts:** personal experience, recipes, fillers
> **Topics:** true stories about God's angels and humans who have played angelic roles on earth; "Angel Sightings," pictures of angels
> **Rights:** all
> **Payment:** $25-500, on publication, 20% kill fee on assignments
> **Guidelines:** *www.guideposts.org/writers-guidelines*
> **Sample:** 7x10 SASE with four stamps
> **Tip:** "We are not limited to stories about heavenly angels. We also accept stories about human beings doing heavenly duties."

THE ANGLICAN JOURNAL

80 Hayden St., Toronto, ON M4Y 3G2, Canada | 416-924-9199
editor@national.anglican.ca | *www.anglicanjournal.com*
Matthew Townsend, editor
> **Denomination:** Anglican
> **Parent company:** Anglican Church of Canada
> **Type:** monthly (except July and August) print and digital newspaper, circulation 123,000, takes ads
> **Audience:** denomination
> **Purpose:** to share compelling news and features about the Anglican Church of Canada and the Anglican Communion and religion in general
> **Submissions:** No unsolicited manuscripts; email query as attachment. Length: 500-600 words. Freelance: 5%. Seasonal at least two months in advance. Responds in two weeks. Bible: NRSV.
> **Types of manuscripts:** personal experience, short stories, news, reviews
> **Topics:** Christian life, spiritual issues
> **Rights:** first
> **Payment:** $75-100, on acceptance
> **Guidelines:** *www.anglicanjournal.com/about-us/writers-guidelines*
> **Sample:** on website
> **Tip:** Looking for "local church/parish news stories, book reviews, spiritual reflection."

THE ARLINGTON CATHOLIC HERALD

200 N. Glebe Rd., Ste. 600, Arlington, VA 22203 | 703-841-2590
editorial@catholicherald.com | www.catholicherald.com
Ann M. Augherton, managing editor

Denomination: Catholic
Parent company: Arlington, Virginia, Diocese
Type: weekly print and digital newspaper, circulation 70,000, takes ads
Audience: denomination
Purpose: to support the Church's mission to evangelize by providing news from a Catholic perspective
Submissions: Email a query with a story idea.
Types of manuscripts: news, feature articles, profiles
Sample: on the website

BIBLE ADVOCATE

PO Box 33677, Denver, CO 80233
bibleadvocate@cog7.org | baonline.org
Sherri Langton, associate editor

Denomination: Church of God (Seventh Day)
Type: bimonthly print and digital magazine, circulation 13,000
Audience: denomination, general
Purpose: to advocate the Bible and represent the Church of God
Submissions: Email complete manuscript as attachment or in body of message. Unsolicited freelance: 25-30%. Buys ten to twenty manuscripts per year. Length: 600-1,300 words. Responds in four to ten weeks. No Christmas or Easter manuscripts. Bible: NKJV, NIV.
Types: teaching, poetry, personal experience, fillers, testimony
Topics: theme related, Christian life
Rights: first, reprint (tell when/where appeared), onetime, electronic
Payment: articles, $25-65; poems and fillers, $20; on publication
Guidelines and theme list: *baonline.org/write-for-us*
Sample: 9x12 envelope with three stamps
Tip: "Please read past issues of the magazine before you submit and become familiar with our style. No snail mail submissions or PDFs. No Christmas or Easter manuscripts."

BLUE RIDGE CHRISTIAN NEWS

261 Oak Ave., Spruce Pine, NC 28777 | 828-413-0506
brianb@brcnews.com | blueridgechristiannews.com
Brian Barrier, president
Cathy Pritchard, editor, cathyp@brcnews.com

Parent company: The Ninevah Productions, Inc.

Type: monthly print and digital newspaper; circulation: 16,000 print, 3,000 digital; ads

Purpose: to share the good news of Jesus and other positive, uplifting, and good news from around the world

Audience: people seeking to know more about God

Submissions: Email submission. Unsolicited freelance: 10%. Buys 100 manuscripts per year. Length: 1,000 words. Seasonal: one month in advance. Responds in one week. Bible: KJV, NKJV, NASB.

Types of manuscripts: personal experience, how-to, short stories, columns, fillers

Topics: Christian life, evangelism

Rights: first, reprint (tell where and when published), all, electronic

Payment: none

Guidelines: none

Sample: $3.00, send request to *cathyp@brcnews.com*

Tip: "Looking for positive, uplifting, good news."

THE BREAKTHROUGH INTERCESSOR

PO Box 121, Lincoln, VA 20160-0121 | 540-338-4131
breakthrough@intercessors.org | *www.intercessors.org*
Claudette Ammons, managing editor

Parent company: Breakthrough

Type: quarterly print magazine, circulation 4,000

Audience: adults interested in growing their prayer lives

Purpose: to encourage people to pray and to equip them to do so more effectively

Submissions: Email complete manuscript. Length: articles, 600-1,000 words.

Types of manuscripts: personal experience, teaching

Topic: prayer

Rights: first, onetime, nonexclusive electronic

Payment: none

Guidelines: *www.intercessors.org/media/downloads/Guidelines%20 &%20PermissionForm.pdf*

Sample: download from the website

byFAITH

1700 N. Brown Rd., Ste. 105, Lawrenceville, GA 30043 | 678-825-1005
editor@byfaithonline.com | *byfaithonline.com*
Dick Doster, editor, ddoster@byfaithonline.com

Denomination: Presbyterian Church in America (PCA)

Type: online magazine
Audience: denomination
Purpose: to provide news of the PCA, to equip readers to become a more active part of God's redemptive plan for the world, and to help them respond biblically and intelligently to the questions our culture is asking
Submissions: Email complete manuscripts. Articles 500-3,000 words.
Types: profiles, teaching, reviews, news
Topics: true stories of people living out their faith, practical theology, biblical perspective on arts and culture, reviews of current books and movies, Christian living, PCA news
Guidelines: *byfaithonline.com/about*
Tip: "Theologically, the writers are Reformed and believe the faith is practical and applicable to every part of life. Most of our writers (though not all) come from the PCA."

CANADA LUTHERAN

600-177 Lombard Ave., Winnipeg, MB R3B 0W5, Canada | 888-786-6707
www.elcic.ca
British Columbia Synod, Jude Whaley, editor, deacjudy09@yahoo.ca
Synod of Alberta and the Territories, Colleen McGinnis, editor,
  mail@caelinartworks.com
Saskatchewan Synod, sksynod@elcic.ca
Manitoba/Northwestern Ontario Synod, Rick Scherger, editor,
  rscherger@elcic.ca
Eastern Synod, Beverley Cunningham, editor,
  beverley@cunninghamcommunications.ca

Denomination: Evangelical Lutheran Church in Canada
Type: monthly print magazine (8x), circulation 14,000
Audience: denomination
Purpose: to engage the Evangelical Lutheran Church in Canada in a dynamic dialogue in which information, inspiration, and ideas are shared in a thoughtful and stimulating way
Submissions: Especially looking for articles for "Practising Our Faith," stories and ideas about how you or the people around you handle life's challenges and opportunities through faith. Length: 700-1,200 words. Also takes documentary articles and profiles of people of interest to readers (normally ELCIC members), seasonal, advice in how-to lists, and articles highlighting ministry in the synods. Email submissions.
Types of manuscripts: personal experience, profile, documentary,

how-to
Topics: seasonal, Christian living, ELCIC ministries
Rights: onetime
Guidelines: *www.elcic.ca/clweb/contributing.html*
Tip: "As much as is possible, the content of the magazine is chosen from the work of Canadian writers. The content strives to reflect the Evangelical Lutheran Church in Canada in the context of our Canadian society."

THE CANADIAN LUTHERAN

3074 Portage Ave., Winnipeg, MB R3K 0Y2, Canada | 800-588-4226, 204-895-3433
editor@lutheranchurch.ca | *www.canadianlutheran.ca*
Matthew Block, editor

Denomination: Lutheran Church—Canada
Type: bimonthly print magazine, circulation 20,000
Audience: denomination
Purpose: to inspire, motivate, and inform
Submissions: Email complete manuscript with "Canadian Lutheran article" in the subject line. Looking for Christian reflections on current events, teaching articles about our theology, discussions of contemporary culture in the light of faith, and more.
Types of manuscripts: news, teaching, essay
Topics: theology, contemporary culture, congregational and district news (submit to appropriate district editor and include photo)
Rights: first (but reserves the right to reprint)
Payment: none for unsolicited manuscripts
Guidelines: *canadianlutheran.ca/editors-and-submissions*
Sample: download from the website
Tip: "All feature articles with doctrinal content must go through doctrinal review to ensure fidelity to the Scriptures. As a result, authors may occasionally be asked to rewrite some sections of their article before publication."

CANADIAN MENNONITE

490 Dutton Dr., Unit C5, Waterloo, ON N2L 6H7, Canada | 519-884-3810
submit@canadianmennonite.org | *www.canadianmennonite.org*
Ross W. Muir, managing editor

Parent company: Canadian Mennonite Publishing Service
Denomination: Mennonite Church Canada
Type: biweekly print and digital magazine; 9,500 subscribers; ads

Audience: denomination

Purpose: to educate, inspire, inform, and foster dialogue on issues facing Mennonites in Canada as they share the good news of Jesus Christ from an Anabaptist perspective

Submissions: Email or mail query first. Unsolicited freelance: 5%. Length: 200-1,500 words. Responds in one week. Seasonal six months in advance. Bible: NRSV.

Types: personal reflections, reviews (books, music, movies), news, how-to

Topics: theme-related, must relate to Mennonites in Canada

Rights: onetime, reprint (tell when and where published)

Payment: varies, on publication

Guidelines and theme list: *www.canadianmennonite.org/submissions*

Sample: download from *canadianmennonite.org/pastissues*

Tip: "Please read the magazine online to see what types of content we use before submitting a query."

CATHOLIC NEW YORK

1011 First Ave., Ste. 1721, New York, NY 10022 | 212-688-2399
jwoods@cny.org | www.cny.org
John Woods, editor-in-chief

Denomination: Catholic

Parent company: Ecclesiastical Communications Corp.

Type: biweekly print and digital newspaper, circulation 127,000, takes ads

Audience: denomination

Purpose: to publish news and information of interest to Catholics in the Archdiocese of New York

Submissions: Email query or complete manuscript as attachment. Unsolicited freelance: 2%. Accepts five to ten manuscripts per year. Length: 600 words. Responds in one month. Seasonal two weeks in advance. Bible: NAB.

Types of manuscripts: news reports, personal experience, teaching

Topics: state news, Christian living, moral issues

Rights: onetime

Payment: $125, on publication

Guidelines: none

Sample: on website

Tip: "We use freelancers from New York to cover evening and weekend events."

CATHOLIC SENTINEL

2838 E. Burnside, Portland, OR 97214 | 503-281-1191
edl@CatholicSentinel.org | www.CatholicSentinel.org
Ed Langlois, managing editor

> **Denomination:** Catholic
> **Parent company:** Archdiocese of Portland
> **Type:** bimonthly print newspaper
> **Audience:** Catholics who live in Oregon
> **Purpose:** to feature Oregon people and Oregon issues that relate to Catholics
> **Submissions:** Articles 600-1,500 words. Query first. Feature stories about Catholics living out their faith. Columns about local, national, or international issues of interest with a local connection.
> **Types of manuscripts:** profiles, personal experience
> **Topics:** Christian living, issues
> **Payment:** variable rates for articles, none for columns
> **Guidelines:** *catholicsentinel.org/Content/About-Us/About-Us/Article/Article-Submission/15/60/11770*

CELEBRATE LIFE MAGAZINE

PO Box 1350, Stafford, VA 22555 | 540-659-4171
clmag@all.org | www.clmagazine.org
Susan Ciancio, editor

> **Denomination:** Catholic
> **Parent company:** American Life League
> **Type:** quarterly print and digital magazine, circulation 7,500, takes ads
> **Audience:** pro-life
> **Purpose:** to inspire, encourage, and educate pro-life activists
> **Submissions:** Email complete manuscript as an attachment. Freelance: 25%. Accepts six manuscripts per year. Length: 800-1,800 words. Seasonal six months ahead. Responds in one to two months. Bible: *Jerusalem Bible.*
> **Types of manuscripts:** personal experience, interviews, how-to, teaching
> **Topics:** matters concerning the sanctity of life and human personhood in harmony with the teachings of the Catholic Church; see specific list in guidelines
> **Rights:** first
> **Payment:** 10-25¢/word, on publication, sometimes kill fee
> **Guidelines:** *www.clmagazine.org/submission-guidelines*
> **Sample:** email for copy
> **Tip:** "Most in need of timely investigative reports and personal experiences."

CHARISMA

600 Rinehart Rd., Lake Mary, FL 32746 | 407-333-0600
charisma@charismamedia.com | *www.charismamag.com*
Christine D. Johnson, managing editor

Denomination: Pentecostal/Charismatic
Parent company: Charisma Media
Type: monthly print and digital magazine, circulation 90,000
Audience: passionate, Spirit-filled Christians
Purpose: to empower believers for life in the Spirit
Submissions: Query only through the online form. If accepted, prefers email submission. Responds in two to three months. Seasonal five months ahead. Assigned: 80%. Needs articles that reflect on the work of a particular ministry, Christian author, or artist, 700 words maximum; product reviews of newly released books, music, and movies/DVDs (assigned); in-depth feature stories to 2,600 words. Bible: MEV. Prefers third-person.
Types: profiles, interviews, reviews, feature stories
Topics: prayer, healing, spiritual warfare, end times, the prophetic and Israel, Christmas, Easter
Rights: all
Payment: on publication
Guidelines: *www.charismamag.com/about/write-for-us*
Sample: on the website
Tip: "Please take time to read—even study—at least one or two of our recent issues before submitting a query. Sometimes people submit their writing without ever having read or understood our magazine or its readers, and sometimes people will have read our magazine years ago and think it's the same as it has always been; but magazines undergo many changes through the years."

CHARISMA LEADER

600 Rinehart Rd., Lake Mary, FL 32746 | 407-333-0600
chris.johnson@charismamedia.com | *www.ministrytodaymag.com*
Christine D. Johnson, managing editor

Denomination: Pentecostal/Charismatic
Parent company: Charisma Media
Type: quarterly print and digital magazine, circulation 30,000
Audience: pastors, ministry leaders, business leaders
Purpose: to inspire and assist ministry leaders
Submissions: Email query through the online submission form. If no response in two weeks, assume not interested. Email (preferred) or mail manuscript after query if requested. Bible version: MEV. Most

open to departments: "Ministry Life," "Leadership," "Outreach," and "Facilities." Length: to 700 words. Also buys more in-depth features; length to 2,500 words.

Types of manuscripts: how-to, interviews, teaching
Topics: anything related to church ministry and leadership
Rights: all
Payment: unspecified, on publication
Guidelines: *ministrytodaymag.com/write-for-us*
Tip: "Most open to departments. Please take time to read—even study—at least one or two of our recent issues before submitting a query."

CHICKEN SOUP FOR THE SOUL BOOK SERIES

PO Box 700, Cos Cob, CT 06807
www.chickensoup.com
Amy Newmark, editor-in-chief

Parent company: Chicken Soup for the Soul Publishing, LLC
Type: trade paperback books, about a dozen yearly
Purpose: to share happiness, inspiration, and hope
Submissions: Submit complete manuscript only through the website. Unsolicited freelance: 98%. Length: 1,200 words maximum. "A Chicken Soup for the Soul story is an inspirational, true story about ordinary people having extraordinary experiences. . . . These stories are personal and often filled with emotion and drama." Poems tell a story; no rhyming. Accepts submissions from children and teens for some books. No reprints.
Types: personal experiences, poetry
Topics: *www.chickensoup.com/story-submissions/possible-book-topics*
Payment: $200, one month after publication, plus ten copies of the book
Tip: "The most powerful stories are about people extending themselves or performing an act of love, service, or courage for another person."

CHRIST IS OUR HOPE

16555 Weber Rd., Crest Hill, IL 60403 | 815-221-6100
magazine@dioceseofjoliet.org |
www.dioceseofjoliet.org/magazine/sectioncontent.php?secid=1
Carlos Briceño, editor

Denomination: Catholic
Parent company: Diocese of Joliet, Illinois
Purpose: to tell inspiring stories of faith and share information with the goal of educating and evangelizing others
Type: monthly print magazine
Submissions: Query by email.

Types: news, personal experiences, profiles
Topics: Catholic life, local news
Payment: none
Sample: on the website

THE CHRISTIAN CENTURY

104 S. Michigan Ave., Ste. 1100, Chicago, IL 60603-5901 |
312-263-7510
submissions@christiancentury.org | *www.christiancentury.org*
Steve Thorngate, managing editor
Jill Peláez Baumgaertner, poetry editor, poetry@christiancentury.org

Type: biweekly print magazine, takes ads
Audience: ecumenical, mainline ministers, educators, and church leaders
Purpose: to explore what it means to believe and live out the
Christian faith in our time
Submissions: Email query first. Responds in four to six weeks.
Unsolicited freelance: 90%. Seasonal four months in advance.
Articles 1,500-3,000 words, buys 150 per year; poetry (free verse,
traditional) to twenty lines. Bible version: NRSV.
Types of manuscripts: essays, humor, interviews, opinion, book
reviews (assigned), poetry
Topics: poverty, human rights, economic justice, international
relations, national priorities, popular culture, critiques of
individual religious communities
Rights: all, reprint (tell where/when published)
Payment: articles $100-300, poems $50, reviews to $75, on
publication
Guidelines and theme list: *www.christiancentury.org/submission-guidelines*
Sample: $3.50
Tip: "Keep in mind our audience of sophisticated readers, eager for
analysis and critical perspective that goes beyond the obvious. We are
open to all topics if written with appropriate style for our readers."

CHRISTIAN COURIER

2 Aiken St., St. Catherines, ON L2N 1V8, Canada | 800-969-4838,
905-937-3314
editor@christiancourier.ca | *www.christiancourier.ca*
Angela Reitsma Bick, editor-in-chief, editor@christiancourier.ca
Amy MacLachlan, features editor, features@christiancourier.ca
Brian Bork, review editor, bbork41@gmail.com

Denomination: Christian Reformed
Type: biweekly print newspaper, circulation 2,500, takes ads

Purpose: to connect Christians with a network of culturally savvy partners in faith for the purpose of inspiring all to participate in God's renewing work with His creation

Submissions: Email queries and manuscripts to the appropriate editor. Articles 700-1,200 words, book and movie reviews 750 words. Responds in one to two weeks, only if accepted. Seasonal three months ahead. Accepts simultaneous submissions. Uses some sidebars. Prefers NIV.

Types of manuscripts: editorials, reviews, columns, features, news, poetry

Rights: onetime, reprint (tell when/where appeared)

Payment: $45-$70, 30 days after publication; no pay for reprints

Guidelines: *christiancourier.ca/about/category/write-for-us*

Tip: "Suggest an aspect of the theme which you believe you could cover well, have insight into, could treat humorously, etc. Show that you think clearly, write clearly, and have something to say that we should want to read. Have a strong biblical worldview and avoid moralism and sentimentality."

CHRISTIAN HERALD

PO Box 68526, Brampton, ON L6R 0J8, Canada | 905-874-1731
info@christianherald.ca | *www.christianherald.ca*
Fazal Karim, Jr., editor-in-chief, publisher

Type: monthly (11x) print and digital newspaper, circulation 27,000, takes ads

Purpose: to keep Southern Ontario's Christian community informed of news and events

Audience: Southern Ontario's Christian community

Submissions: Email query letter with clips or manuscript as attachment. Gives assignments. To get an assignment, email résumé with subjects/categories of interest. Unsolicited freelance: 10%. Buys six articles per year. Length: 300-900 words. Seasonal two months in advance. Simultaneous OK. Responds in two weeks.

Types of manuscripts: how-to, interview, book/music/movie review, personal experience, event coverage (pre and post)

Topics: variety

Rights: first, reprint (tell when/where published), onetime, electronic, all

Payment: 10-30¢/per word on publication or acceptance, kill fee sometimes

Guidelines: by email

Sample: on website

Tip: "Book/music/movie reviews are a great place to start and build a relationship."

THE CHRISTIAN JOURNAL

1032 W. Main, Medford, OR 97501 | 541-773-4004 x2500
info@thechristianjournal.org | *www.TheChristianJournal.org*
Chad McComas, senior editor

Parent company: Set Free Christian Fellowship
Type: monthly print and digital journal; circulation 1,200 print
Audience: both Christians and non-Christians
Purpose: to provide inspiration and encouragement with the body of Christ in the Rogue Valley, Oregon
Submissions: Each article needs to inspire the reader to reconnect with God and his or her faith. Length: 500 words max. Seasonal one month in advance. Email manuscript. Buys 250 articles per year. Responds in two weeks. Bible: NIV.
Types of manuscripts: personal experience, review, short story, poetry
Topics: Christian life (themed), parenting, evangelism/witnessing, no controversial topics like politics or obvious doctrinal themes
Themes: *thechristianjournal.org/themes-and-deadlines-for-2021*
Rights: onetime
Payment: none
Guidelines: *thechristianjournal.org/writers-information-guidelines-for-writers*, email, mail with SASE
Sample: Call or email
Tip: "Call or email with your idea."

THE CHRISTIAN LIBRARIAN

PO Box 4, Cedarville, OH 45314 | 937-766-2255
tcl@acl.org | *www.acl.org*
Garrett Trott, editor-in-chief

Parent organization: Association of Christian Librarians
Type: biannual print journal
Audience: primarily Christian librarians in institutions of higher learning
Purpose: to publish articles, provide a membership forum, and encourage writing
Submissions: Mail or email manuscripts. Shorter articles, 1,000-3,000 words, are generally preferable for practical and nonresearch papers; scholarly articles to 5,000 words, some longer. Include a 100-word abstract.
Types of manuscripts: teaching, reviews, bibliographies
Topics: Christian interpretation of librarianship, theory and practice of library science, bibliographic essays, reviews, and human-interest articles relating to books and libraries

Rights: first, with signed grant of license
Payment: none
Guidelines: *www.acl.org/index.cfm/publications/the-christian-librarian/tcl-author-guidelines-4-24-18*

CHRISTIAN LIVING IN THE MATURE YEARS

2222 Rosa L Parks Blvd., Nashville, TN 37228
matureyears@umpublishing.org | matureyears.submittable.com/submit
Rachel Mullen, features and acquisitions editor

> **Denomination:** United Methodist
> **Parent company:** United Methodist Publishing House
> **Type:** quarterly print magazine
> **Audience:** ages 50 and older
> **Purpose:** to help older adults with opportunities and challenges related to aging
> **Submissions:** Submit through the website. Responds in two to four months. Seasonal one year in advance. Length: 250-2,000 words. Buys fifty manuscripts per year. Unsolicited freelance: 100%. Bible: CEB.
> **Types of manuscripts:** how-to, short memoir, personal experience, recipe, religious reflection/meditation, filler, puzzle
> **Topics:** grandparenting, Christian life, general interest, health, money, retirement, aging, Bible lessons
> **Rights:** onetime
> **Payment:** 7¢/word, on acceptance
> **Guidelines:** *matureyears.submittable.com/submit*
> **Sample:** email for a PDF
> **Tip:** "Our 'Fragments of Life' section always needs new writers. It is a short memoir section; four pieces needed each quarter. We do not accept articles about 'the good old days' or pieces that focus on negativity and death over health, wellness, and life."

CHRISTIAN NEWS NORTHWEST

PO Box 974, Newberg, OR 97132 | 503-537-9220
cnnw@cnnw.com | www.cnnw.com
John Fortmeyer, publisher and editor

> **Parent company:** Christian News Northwest Ministries Inc.
> **Type:** monthly print newspaper, circulation 26,000, ads
> **Audience:** evangelical Christians in western and central Oregon and southwest Washington
> **Purpose:** to inform and encourage the evangelical Christian community in our part of the Pacific Northwest

Submissions: Email (as attachment or in body of message) or mail complete manuscript, or use the website form. Unsolicited freelance: 10%. Length: 700 words. Responds in several days. Bible: NIV.

Types of manuscripts: news

Topics: all focused on church and ministry

Rights: onetime

Payment: none

Guidelines: by email

Sample: via email

Tip: "Our strongest focus is on ministry news in the Northwest."

CHRISTIAN RESEARCH JOURNAL

PO Box 8500, Charlotte, NC 28271-8500 | 704-887-8200
response@equip.org | *www.equip.org/christian-research-journal*
Melanie Cogdill, managing editor

Parent company: Christian Research Institute

Type: quarterly print journal

Audience: thoughtful laypeople, academics, scholars

Purpose: to equip Christians with the information they need to discern doctrinal errors; to evangelize people of other faiths; to present a strong defense of Christian beliefs and ethics; and to provide comprehensive, definitive responses to contemporary apologetic concerns

Submissions: Email query or a manuscript that follows formatting guidelines. Responds in four months. Articles should reflect a command of the subject at hand, including its history, the key personalities involved, the beliefs and/or practices surrounding the controversy, and the criticisms that have been made concerning the subject. Feature articles 2,200 or 3,500 words as assigned; include 250-300-word synopsis with main facts and arguments. Summary critique review 1,700 words, effective evangelism 1,700 words, viewpoint 1,700 words. All articles must be within 25 words of these word counts.

Types of manuscripts: feature articles, news stories, viewpoint, summary critiques

Topics: apologetics, evangelism, cults and new religions, the occult, New Age movement, aberrant Christian movements and teachings

Rights: first, reprint

Payment: $175-325, kill fee 50%

Guidelines: *www.equip.org/wp-content/uploads/2019/09/Writers-Guidelines.SEPT-2019.PDF*

Tip: "Almost nothing can better prepare you to write for the *Christian Research Journal* than familiarity with the journal itself. If you are not a regular reader of the journal, you should read all the articles in recent issues that correspond to the type of article you wish to write."

CHRISTIAN RETAILING

600 Rinehart Rd., Lake Mary, FL 32746 | 407-333-0600
retailing@charismamedia.com | *www.christianretailing.com*
Christine D. Johnson, editor, chris.johnson@charismamedia.com

Parent company: Charisma Media
Type: bimonthly print and digital trade journal
Audience: retailers, church bookstores, publishers, music labels, distributors, and others working and volunteering in the Christian products industry
Purpose: to champion the world of Christian resources and to provide critical information and insight to advance business and ministry
Submissions: Query only. Prefers third-person point of view. Bible: MEV.
Types of manuscripts: features, news stories, columns, reviews
Topics: all aspects of running a bookstore, trends in publishing, new-product reviews
Payment: varies by assignment
Guidelines: *christianretailing.com/index.php/general/28335-writers-guidelines-christian-retailing*

CHRISTIAN STANDARD

16965 Pine Ln., Ste. 202, Parker, CO 80134 | 800-543-1353
CS@christianstandardmedia.com | *www.christianstandard.com*
Michael C. Mack, editor
Jim Nieman, managing editor

Denomination: Christian Churches, Churches of Christ
Parent company: Christian Standard Media
Type: monthly print and digital magazine, circulation 13,000
Audience: Christian leaders
Purpose: to resource Christian leaders
Submissions: Email queries and manuscripts as attachments. Length: 500-1,800 words. Freelance: 5-10%. Buys fifteen manuscripts per year. Seasonal six to eight months in advance. Responds in one to three months. Bible: NIV.
Types of manuscripts: how-to, meditations, sidebars
Topics: theme-related, church and ministry leadership, church finances, intergenerational ministry, urban and rural ministry, international ministry and missions, Communion meditations
Rights: first, reprint (tell when/where published)
Payment: $50-250, on acceptance, kill fee sometimes

Guidelines: *www.christianstandard.com/contact-us/submit-articles*
Theme list: click link on guidelines page
Sample: by email
Tip: "We are looking for well-written articles especially by and about independent Christian churches (Restoration Movement churches). Success stories are great, of course, but we want real stories about real people who rely on God's grace and power to overcome adversity and grow in Christlikeness. How is the church/ministry/leader living out and carrying out the mission?"

CHRISTIANITY TODAY

465 Gundersen Dr., Carol Stream, IL 60188-2498 | 630-260-6200
editor@christianitytoday.com | *www.christianitytoday.com*
Daniel Harrell, editor in chief
Matt Reynolds, books editor, mreynolds@christianitytoday.com

Type: monthly (10x) print and digital magazine, 4.3 million page views per month, takes ads
Audience: Christian leaders throughout North America
Purpose: equipping Christians to renew their minds, serve the church, and create culture to the glory of God
Submissions: Submit query through link on guidelines page. Unsolicited freelance: small percentage. Length: 300-1,800 words. Bible: NIV.
Types of manuscripts: profiles, interviews, feature stories, book reviews, opinion pieces
Topics: see the website
Rights: first
Payment: varies on acceptance, kill fee sometimes
Guidelines: *help.christianitytoday.com/hc/en-us/articles/360047411253-How-do-I-write-for-CT-*
Sample: articles are on the website
Tip: "The most successful pitches combine Christian formation and credible information. We seek pieces that offer not just new ideas and opinions, but research, reporting, and biblical analysis to back them up."

THE CHURCH HERALD & HOLINESS BANNER

PO Box 4060, Overland Park, KS 66212
editor@heraldandbanner.com | *www.heraldandbanner.com*
Dr. Gordon L. Snider, editor

Denomination: Church of God (Holiness)
Parent company: Herald and Banner Press
Type: monthly print and digital magazine
Audience: denomination

Submissions: Email through the website for current needs. Includes various teaching articles each month that will inspire you in your Christian walk, help you understand more about a biblical topic, etc. Also featured are various articles promoting Christian ideals, such as the importance to live with gratitude.

Types of manuscripts: teaching

Topics: biblical teaching, Christian living from a holiness perspective

CITY LIGHT NEWS

20218 Fraser Highway, #200, Langley, BC V3A 4E6, Canada | 604-510-5070

editor@lightmagazine.ca | *alberta.lightmagazine.ca*

Steve Almond, editor

Parent company: Light Christian Media

Type: monthly print and digital newspaper, circulation 10,000, takes ads

Audience: Christians in Calgary, Red Deer, and Southern Alberta

Purpose: inspiring faith for everyday life

Submissions: Email in body of message. Freelance: 10%. Contact editor to get assignments. Buys twenty-four manuscripts per year. Seasonal two months in advance. Responds in one week. Length: 800 words maximum. Bible: no preference.

Types of manuscripts: lifestyle, news, testimony

Topics: parenting, senior life, Christian living, travel

Rights: first, reprint

Payment: 10¢/word on publication, kill fee sometimes

Guidelines: *alberta.lightmagazine.ca/about-us*

Sample: by email

Tip: "Looking for Christian lifestyle, local news; Canadian experience helpful."

COLUMBIA

1 Columbus Plaza, New Haven, CT 06510-3326 | 203-752-4398

columbia@kofc.org | *www.kofc.org/Columbia*

Alton J. Pelowski, editor-in-chief

Denomination: Catholic

Parent company: Knights of Columbus

Type: monthly print and digital magazine, circulation 1.7 million

Audience: general Catholic family

Submissions: Query first by email or mail. Length: 700-1,500 words. Seasonal six months in advance. No simultaneous.

Types of manuscripts: feature articles, profiles

Topics: current events, social trends, family life, parenting, social problems, health and nutrition, finances, Catholic practice and

teaching, church programs, institutions, personalities
Rights: first, electronic
Payment: varies, on acceptance
Guidelines: *www.kofc.org/en/news-room/columbia/guidelines.html*
Sample: click link on website

COMMONCALL: THE BAPTIST STANDARD MAGAZINE

PO Box 259019, Plano, TX 75025 | 214-630-4571 x1012
kencamp@baptiststandard.com | *www.baptiststandard.com*
Ken Camp, managing editor

Denomination: Baptist
Type: quarterly print magazine
Purpose: to aid and support the denomination
Submissions: Looking for stories about everyday Christians who are putting their faith into action.
Types of manuscripts: profiles, how-to
Topics: missions, evangelism, family life, leadership, effective church ministry, Texas Baptist history

COMMONWEAL

475 Riverside Dr., Rm. 405, New York, NY 10115 | 212-662-4200
editors@commonwealmagazine.org | *www.commonwealmagazine.org*
Paul Baumann, editor

Denomination: Catholic
Type: biweekly (20x) print and digital magazine
Audience: educated, committed Catholics, as well as readers from other faith traditions
Purpose: to provide a forum for civil, reasoned debate on the interaction of faith with contemporary politics and culture
Submissions: Submit through the website. Mail poetry; buys thirty per year. Articles fall into these categories: (1) "Upfronts," 1,000-1,500 words, brief, newsy, and reportorial, giving facts, information, and some interpretation behind the headlines of the day. (2) Longer articles, 2,000-3,000 words, reflective and detailed, bringing new information or a different point of view to a subject, raising questions, and/or proposing solutions to the dilemmas facing the world, nation, church, or individual. (3) "Last Word" column, a 750-word reflection, usually of a personal nature, on some aspect of the human condition: spiritual, individual, political, or social.
Types of manuscripts: essays, features, news with interpretation, poetry
Topics: public affairs, religion, literature, the arts
Rights: all

Payment: on publication
Guidelines: *www.commonwealmagazine.org/contact-us*
Sample: email request
Tip: "Articles should be written for a general but well-educated audience. While religious articles are always topical, we are less interested in devotional and churchy pieces than in articles which examine the links between 'worldly' concerns and religious beliefs."

CONVERGE MAGAZINE

4676 Main St. #201, Vancouver, BC V5V 3R7, Canada | 604-558-1982
editor@convergemedia.org | *www.convergemedia.org*
Leanne Janzen, editor

Type: quarterly print and digital magazine
Audience: millennials
Purpose: to influence a growing number of people through daily content that is intelligent, is authentic, and stimulates hope in God
Submissions: Email manuscripts with bio and photo. Articles 500-1,000 words. If no response in six weeks, assume no interest.
Types of manuscripts: personal experience, review, interview, commentary
Topics: life, relationships, experiences, work, culture, faith
Guidelines: *convergemagazine.com/write*
Sample: see link at *convergemagazine.com/magazine*
Tip: "We write for those in transition: between school and work, singleness and marriage, freedom and responsibility, doubt and faith. We write as friends on the journey together, rather than one coaching another down the path. We share what we've learned through experience, rather than what we've heard or been taught. Our stories, like our lives, don't need to be tidy, with all the right answers."

THE COVENANT COMPANION

8303 W. Higgins Rd., Chicago, IL 60631 | 773-907-3328
cathy.normanpeterson@covchurch.org | *covenantcompanion.com*
Cathy Norman Peterson, editor

Denomination: Evangelical Covenant Church
Type: monthly (10x) print magazine
Audience: denomination
Purpose: to inform, stimulate thought, and encourage dialogue on issues that impact the church and its members
Submissions: Email or mail. Length: 1,200-1,800 words.
Types of manuscripts: news, profiles, book reviews

Topics: Christian life, the church (local, denominational, and universal), spirituality, contemporary issues, social justice, outreach ministry

Rights: onetime

Payment: $35-100, two months after publication

Guidelines: *covenantcompanion.com/submit-story*

Tip: "We are interested in what is happening in local churches, conferences, and other Covenant institutions and associations, as well as reports from missionaries and other staff serving around the world. Human interest stories are also welcome."

CREATION

PO Box 4545, Eight Mile Plains, QLD 4113, Australia | 073-340-9888
m.wieland@creation.info | *creation.com*
Margaret Wieland, magazine coordinator

Parent company: Creation Ministries International

Type: quarterly print and digital magazine, circulation 40,000

Audience: families, homeschoolers, age 9 to adulthood

Purpose: to provide the young Earth creationist perspective for origins of everything

Submissions: Email manuscript as an attachment; cover letter required. Length: maximum 1,500 words. Buys more than 100 manuscripts per year. Seasonal: six months in advance. Responds in a week. Bible: ESV. Accepts manuscripts from teens. Unsolicited freelance: 20%.

Types of manuscripts: interviews with creationists, teaching

Topics: creation science, evolution's errors

Rights: will be requested

Payment: none

Theme list: via email

Guidelines: *creation.com/creation-magazine-writing-guidelines*

Sample: on the website

Tip: "Looking for articles on creation/evolution debate."

CREATION ILLUSTRATED

PO Box 141103, Spokane Valley, WA 99214-1103 | 800-360-2732
Jennifer@creationillustrated.com | *www.creationillustrated.com*
Jennifer Ish, associate editor

Type: quarterly print and digital magazine, circulation 10,000, takes ads

Audience: families

Purpose: to share the wonders of God's creation

Submissions: Email queries. Length: 700-1,500 words; children's stories 1,000-1,500 words. Bible: KJV, NKJV. Unsolicited freelance: 75%. Buys thirty-two manuscripts per year. Seasonal two to three months in advance. Response time varies.

Types of manuscripts: teaching, personal experience, children's stories, profile, how-to

Topics: nature, outdoor adventures, creatures, a creation day from Genesis; each story needs to be able to support strong, visual illustrations as we place many high-end photos with each story

Rights: all

Payment: articles $75-100, poetry $15; 30 days after publication; kill fee sometimes

Guidelines and theme list: *www.creationillustrated.com/writer--photographer-guidelines*

Sample: sign up for free digital issue

Tip: "All the stories are freelance submissions."

THE CRESSET

Lindwood House, Valparaiso University, 1320 S. Campus Dr., Valparaiso, IN 46383
cresset@valpo.edu| thecresset.org
Marci Rae Johnson, poetry editor

Parent company: Valparaiso University

Type: print journal, 5-6x per year

Audience: general readers interested in religious matters, mostly college teachers

Purpose: to comment on literature, the arts, and public affairs and explore ideas and trends in contemporary culture from a perspective grounded in the Lutheran tradition of scholarship, freedom, and faith while informed by the wisdom of the broader Christian community

Submissions: Email query first. Prefers submissions through the website but also takes them by email or mail.

Types of manuscripts: essays, poetry, interviews

Guidelines: *thecresset.org/submissions.html*

Sample: on the website

Tip: "The Cresset is not a theological journal, but a journal addressing matters of import to those with some degree of theological interest and commitment. Authors are encouraged to reflect upon the religious implications of their subject."

CROSSCURRENTS

475 Riverside Dr., Ste. 1945, New York, NY 10115 | 212-864-5439
splate@crosscurrents.org | onlinelibrary.wiley.com/journal/19393881
Brent Rodriguez-Plate, editor

Parent company: The Association for Religion and Intellectual Life

Type: quarterly print magazine

Audience: thoughtful activists for social justice and church reform
Submissions: Accepts emailed and mailed submissions with SASE. Responds in four to eight weeks. No unsolicited book reviews, reprints. Articles 3,000-5,000 words.
Types of manuscripts: essays, poetry, fiction
Payment: none
Guidelines: *onlinelibrary.wiley.com/page/journal/19393881/ homepage/forauthors.html*
Sample: on the website

CRW MAGAZINE

PO Box 300, Pasadena, CA 91129 | 800-309-4466
managing.editor@ptm.org | *www.ptm.org/magazine*
Greg Albrecht, senior editor

Parent company: Plain Truth Ministries
Type: bimonthly print and digital magazine
Audience: general
Purpose: to combat legalism and give hope, inspiration, and encouragement to those burned out by religion
Submissions: Queries only.
Types of manuscripts: teaching
Guidelines: by email
Sample: on the website

DIVINE MOMENTS BOOK SERIES

102 Corbett Ln., Black Mountain, NC 28711 | 828-231-1963
yvonnelehman3@gmail.com | *www.yvonnelehman.com/moments*
Yvonne Lehman, compiler and editor

Parent company: Grace Publishing
Purpose: to show how faith works in everyday life experiences
Audience: general and Christian
Type: two books per year
Submissions: Accepts fifty articles per book. Email complete manuscript as attachment. Length: 500-2,000. Seasonal six months in advance. Responds in one day. Bible: no preference.
Types of manuscripts: personal experience
Topics: theme-related, Christmas, romance, brokenness, questioning
Rights: onetime
Payment: none, royalties donated to Samaritan's Purse
Guidelines and theme list: *www.yvonnelehman.com/?page_id=171*
Tip: Needs stories for these books: *Grandma's Cookie Jar Moments, Broken Moments, Lost Moments, Can, Sir! Moments.*

DTS MAGAZINE

3909 Swiss Ave., Dallas, TX 75204
eherrelko@dts.edu | *www.dts.edu/magazine*
Ed Herrelko, executive director

> **Parent company:** Dallas Theological Seminary (DTS)
> **Type:** quarterly print and digital magazine
> **Audience:** evangelical laypeople, students, alumni, donors, and friends
> **Purpose:** to offer articles rich in biblical and theological exposition, tell stories of how God is working through students and alumni, and update friends on God's work at DTS
> **Submissions:** Email query first. Responds in six to eight weeks. Seasonal six months in advance. Articles: alumni profiles; exposition, usually authored by DTS faculty or similarly qualified individuals; Christian living, personal experience that encourages average Christians in how to live out their faith in the world and includes some exposition that ends with application of truth. Length: 1,500-2,000 words.
> **Types:** profiles, teaching, personal experience
> **Rights:** first, reprint
> **Payment:** up to $500 for first, $150 for reprints
> **Guidelines:** *dts.edu/magazine/editorial-policies*
> **Sample:** see the link on the website
> **Tip:** "DTS Magazine is a ministry of Dallas Theological Seminary. We prefer articles written by our alumni, faculty, students, staff, board members, donors and their families."

ETERNAL INK

4706 Fantasy Ln., Alton, IL 62002
sonsong@charter.net
Mary-Ellen Grisham, editor
Gary James Smith, poetry editor, garyjamessmith2005@yahoo.ca

> **Type:** biweekly print newsletter, circulation 400
> **Audience:** general
> **Purpose:** to share Christian inspiration
> **Submissions:** Email manuscript in the body of the message. Email editor for assignments. Unsolicited freelance: 10%. Accepts twenty-five manuscripts per year. Length: 400-600 words. Seasonal two months in advance. Responds in two weeks. Bible: NIV. Some themes that follow the Christian year.
> **Types of manuscripts:** devotions, meditations, feature articles, poetry, fillers, humor, reviews, columns
> **Topics:** Christian life, Christian witness, profile or character sketch
> **Rights:** all

Payment: none
Guidelines and theme list: by email
Sample: by email
Tip: Looking for features and brief devotions.

EVANGELICAL MISSIONS QUARTERLY

PO Box 398, Wheaton, IL 60187 | 770-457-6677
emq@missionexus.org | missionexus.org/emq
Peggy E. Newell, managing editor

Parent company: Missio Nexus
Type: quarterly digital journal
Audience: missionaries; mission executives, scholars, professors, students, pastors, and supporters; missionary candidates; lay leaders
Purpose: to increase the effectiveness of the evangelical missionary enterprise
Submissions: Email manuscript as attachment. Articles 2,000-3,000 words.
Types of manuscripts: reports, profiles, how-to
Topics: world missions, evangelism, missionary family life
Rights: first
Guidelines: *missionexus.org/emq/submit-an-article-to-emq*

FACTS & TRENDS

1 Lifeway Plaza, Nashville, TN 37234 | 615-251-2000
factsandtrends@lifeway.com | www.factsandtrends.net
Joy Allmond, managing editor
Aaron Earls, online editor

Denomination: Southern Baptist
Parent company: LifeWay Christian Resources
Type: daily digital magazine, 200,000 hits per month, takes ads
Audience: church leaders
Purpose: to help pastors and other Christian leaders navigate the issues and trends impacting the church by providing information, insights, and resources for effective ministry
Submissions: Email query as attachment. Gives assignments; to get one, email introduction, ask for writers guidelines, and pitch an idea. Unsolicited freelance: 40%. Length: 800-1,000 words. Seasonal three months in advance. Responds in one week. Bible: CSB.
Types of manuscripts: personal experience, research analysis, practical/how-to, columns
Topics: culture, leadership, discipleship, evangelism, ministry trends, missions, outreach, worship, church health, preaching, stewardship
Rights: commissioned text with nonexclusive license to writer
Payment: varies, on acceptance, kill fee sometimes

Guidelines: by email
Sample: on the website
Tip: "Become a devoted reader of *Facts & Trends*, so you can better understand our audience and our mission for the publication."

FAITH & FRIENDS

The Salvation Army, 2 Overlea Blvd., Toronto, ON M4H 1P4, Canada | 416-422-6226
faithandfriends@can.salvationarmy.org | *salvationist.ca/editorial/faith-and-friends*
Ken Ramstead, editor

Denomination: Salvation Army
Type: monthly print and digital magazine
Audience: general
Purpose: to show Jesus Christ at work in the lives of real people and to provide spiritual resources for those who are new to the Christian faith
Submissions: Email query or manuscript as attached file. Looking for stories about people whose lives have been changed through an encounter with Jesus: conversion, miracles, healing, faith in the midst of crisis, forgiveness, reconciliation, answered prayers, and more. Profiles of people who have found hope and healing through their ministries, including prisoners, hospital patients, nursing-home residents, single parents in distress, addicts, the unemployed, or homeless. Length: 750-1,200 words. Ten departments with 750-word narratives. Bible: TNIV.
Types of manuscripts: testimonies, personal experience, profiles
Topics: changed lives, marriage, family relationships, missionaries, theology
Payment: none
Guidelines: *salvationist.ca/files/salvationarmy/Magazines/FAITH-FRIENDS.pdf*
Sample: on the website

FAITH ON EVERY CORNER

159 Hudson Cajah Mountain Rd., Hudson, NC 28638 | 828-305-8571
faithoneverycorner@gmail.com | *www.faithoneverycorner.com/magazine*
Craig Ruhl, editor and general manager

Type: monthly digital magazine; circulation: 2,000 hits per month
Denomination: Baptist
Audience: families
Purpose: "Spreading the good news of Jesus Christ through articles, stories,

and photography that encourages, educates, and blesses our readers."

Submissions: Unsolicited freelance: 50%. Buys fifty manuscripts per year. Length: 750-1,500 words. Email query letter as attachment. Accepts teen writers. Responds in one to two days. Bible: NLT, NIV, CSB.

Types of manuscripts: testimonies, personal stories, short stories, poetry, reviews

Topics: Christian life, family, single mother/father, encouragement, evangelism

Rights: onetime

Payment: none

Guidelines: *www.faithoneverycorner.com/submissionguidelines.html,* also via email

Theme list: on the website

Sample: on the website

Tip: "Read a few past issues and send us suggestions for submission."

FAITH TODAY

9821 Leslie St., Ste. 103, Richmond Hill, ON L4B 3Y4, Canada
editor@faithtoday.ca | *www.faithtoday.ca*
Bill Fledderus, senior editor
Karen Stiller, senior editor

Parent company: The Evangelical Fellowship of Canada

Type: bimonthly print and digital magazine, print circulation 12,000, 5,000 online, takes ads

Audience: Canadian evangelicals

Purpose: to connect, equip, and inform Canada's four million evangelical Christians from Anglican and Baptist to Pentecostal and Salvation Army

Submissions: Email query with clips first. Responds in one week. Seasonal four months in advance. Length: 300-1,800. Freelance: 10%. Buys 100 manuscripts per year.

Types of manuscripts: analysis of trends in church and society, news, profiles, reviews of books and music, tips for lay ministry, how-to, journalistic features, essays

Topics: societal issues and trends, church issues and trends

Rights: first, onetime, electronic, reprint (tell when/where published)

Payment: 15-25¢ per word CAD, on acceptance, kill fee sometimes

Guidelines: *www.faithtoday.ca/writers*

Sample: *www.faithtoday.ca/digital*

Tip: "What is the Canadian angle? How does your approach include diverse Canadian voices from different churches, regions, generations, etc.?"

FATHOM

submissions@fathommag.com | fathommag.com
Kelsey Hency, editor in chief
Jonathan Minnema, managing editor

Type: digital magazine

Purpose: to stir reader's curiosity, believing indulging our curiosity acts like a weight to pull us beyond the surface of our faith

Submissions: Email query or manuscript. Length: 300-1,000 words. Drifts: three to five pieces of notes on culture, 100-200 words.

Topics: "Our content covers everything from specific Bible texts, theology, and doctrine to art, literature, and life experience."

Types of manuscripts: blog-like content, short essays, recurring series, short stories, profiles, poetry

Guidelines: *drive.google.com/file/d/ 0B7YGzKkpoxIfakFaWjBHRS0yRHc/view*

Tip: "Persuade; don't dictate. If we just tell people what to think we aren't helping create autonomous thinkers. Fight the temptation to present your conclusion and instead look to lead people through your argument. Invite them into your thought process. We want to make *Fathom* readers great conversationalists. Giving them something to contemplate is an excellent start."

FOCUS ON THE FAMILY

8605 Explorer Dr., Colorado Springs, CO 80920
focusmagsubmissions@family.org | www.focusonthefamily.com/magazine
Michael Ridgeway, editorial director

Parent company: Focus on the Family

Type: bimonthly print magazine

Audience: parents, primarily of ages 4-12

Purpose: to encourage, teach, and celebrate God's design for the family

Submissions: Email or mail to submissions editor. Responds in eight weeks or not interested. Departments: "Family Stages," 50-200 words, practical applications for parents of preschoolers, school-aged children, tweens, and teens; send complete manuscript. "Family Faith," 150 words, devotionals that explore how a biblical principle applies to marriage; 1,200-word articles that show how to help kids understand important biblical truths; send complete manuscript. Features, 1,200-1,500 words; send complete manuscript. "Family Living," 450 words on marriage and parenting; query.

Types of manuscripts: how-to, devotional, teaching

Topics: marriage, parenting

Rights: first
Payment: 25¢/word, $50 for "Family Stages," on acceptance
Guidelines: *www.focusonthefamily.com/magazine/call-for-submissions*
Tip: "Looking for stories about how parents have dealt with challenges and come up with active, practical ways (beyond explaining or talking) of solving those problems."

FRIENDS JOURNAL

1216 Arch St., Ste. 2A, Philadelphia, PA 19107 | 215-563-8629
martink@friendsjournal.org | www.friendsjournal.org
Martin Kelly, senior editor

Denomination: Religious Society of Friends
Type: monthly (11x) print and downloadable journal
Audience: denomination
Purpose: to communicate Quaker experience in order to connect and deepen spiritual lives
Submissions: Submit poetry through the website, maximum three. Feature articles 1,200-2,500 words, related to themes. Departments, around 1,500 words or fewer: "Celebration," "Earthcare," "Faith and Practice," "First-day School," "Friends in Business," "History," "Humor," "Life in the Meeting," "Lives of Friends," "Pastoral Care," "Q&A," "Reflection," "Religious Education," "Remembrance," "Service," "Witness."
Types of manuscripts: poetry, testimonies, teaching, profiles, personal experience
Topics: most issues are themed
Rights: first
Payment: none
Guidelines: *www.friendsjournal.org/submissions*
Theme list: on the website

THE GEM

PO Box 926, Findlay, OH 45839-0926 | 419-424-1961
gem@cggc.org | www.cggc.org
Rachel Foreman, managing editor, rachelf@cggc.org
Jenn Schlumbohm, assistant editor, jenns@cggc.org

Denomination: Churches of God, General Conference
Type: weekly take-home paper, circulation 3,000
Audience: denomination
Purpose: to encourage readers with inspiring stories
Submissions: Articles 200-1,200 words. Seasonal four months in advance. For fiction, it is important that characters are true to life and solutions to problems are genuine. Email complete manuscript

as Word attachment or in body of message. Responds in one month. Simultaneous OK. Accepts manuscripts from children and teens too. Freelance: 95%. Buys 100 manuscripts per year. Bible: NIV.

Types of manuscripts: personal experiences, devotionals, short stories, poetry, fillers
Topics: see themes on website
Rights: all
Payment: $10-30 on publication
Guidelines and theme list: *www.cggc.org/ministries/denominational-communications/the-gem*
Sample: #10 envelope with first-class postage
Tip: "We prefer true-to-life stories."

GEMS OF TRUTH

7407 Metcalf Ave., Overland Park, KS 66204 | 913-432-0331
email through website | www.heraldandbanner.com/product/gems-of-truth
Gordon L. Snider, editor of publications

Denomination: Church of God (Holiness)
Type: weekly take-home paper
Audience: denomination
Submissions: Send complete manuscript or query. Email through the website. Fiction 1,000-2,000 words. Seasonal six to eight months in advance. Bible: KJV.
Types of manuscripts: biography, profile, short story, devotional, poetry, teaching
Sample: download from website

THE GOOD NEWS (FLORIDA)

PO Box 670368, Coral Springs, FL 33067 | 954-564-5378
ShellyP@goodnewsfl.org | www.goodnewsfl.org
Shelly Pond, editor

Parent company: Good News Media Group, LLC
Type: monthly print and digital magazine
Audience: Dade, Broward, and Palm Beach, Florida areas
Submissions: Query through the website. Articles 500-800 words.
Payment: 10¢/word
Sample: on the website

THE GOOD NEWS (NEW YORK)

PO Box 18204, Rochester, NY 14618 | 585-271-4464
info@TheGoodNewsNewYork.com | www.thegoodnewsnewyork.com
Alexandre V. Boutakov, editor

Type: bimonthly print magazine, circulation 10,000
Audience: New York state
Submissions: Email query.
Types: articles, reviews
Sample: on the website

THE GOOD NEWS JOURNAL

9701 Copper Creek, Austin, TX 78729 | 512-269-6535
goodnewsjournal10@gmail.com | *www.thegoodnewsjournal.net*
Bill Myers, editor

    Type: bimonthly print and digital newspaper
    Audience: Capital MetroPlex and Central Texas areas
    Purpose: to provide leadership to individuals and corporations with a positive, patriotic, godly perspective
    Submissions: Articles 350 words. Email query first.
    Payment: none
    Sample: on the website

GRACECONNECT

PO Box 544, Winona Lake, IN 46590 | 574-268-1122
lcgates@bmhbooks.com | *www.graceconnect.us*
Liz Cutler Gates, executive director

    Denomination: Grace Brethren
    Type: quarterly print and digital magazine
    Audience: pastors, elders, and other leaders
    Purpose: to build bridges of communication between the people and churches of the denomination
    Submissions: Email through the website. Feature stories should have a Grace Brethren connection. Length: 1,000-1,500 words, sometimes 600-800 words or up to 2,000 words.
    Topics: theme-related
    Guidelines: *graceconnect.us/grace-stories/submit-a-story-idea*
    Sample: on the website

GUIDEPOSTS

110 William St., Ste. 901, New York, NY 10038 | 212-251-8100
www.guideposts.org/our-magazines/guideposts-magazine
Edward Grinnan, editor

    Type: bimonthly print and digital magazine
    Audience: general
    Purpose: to help readers find peace of mind, solve tough personal

problems, and build satisfying relationships

Submissions: Publishes true, first-person stories about people who have attained a goal, surmounted an obstacle, or learned a helpful lesson through their faith. A typical story is a first-person narrative with a spiritual point the reader can apply to his or her own life. Buys forty to sixty per year. Length: 1,500 words. Submit queries and manuscripts through the online form at *guideposts.org/tell-us-your-story*. If no answer in two months, not interested. Freelance: 40%. Short anecdotes similar to full-length articles, 50-250 words, for departments: "Someone Cares," stories of kindness and caring, *sc@guideposts.com*; "Mysterious Ways," "Family Room," "What Prayer Can Do." Also takes inspiring quotes for "The Up Side," *upside@guideposts.com*.

Types of manuscripts: personal experiences

Rights: all

Payment: $100-500, on acceptance, kill fee: 20% but not to first-time freelancers

Guidelines: *www.guideposts.org/writers-guidelines*

Tip: "Be able to tell a good story with drama, suspense, description, and dialog. The point of the story should be some practical spiritual help that the subject learns through his or her experience. Use unique spiritual insights, strong and unusual dramatic details."

HEARTBEAT

PO Box 9, Hatfield, AR 71945 | 870-389-6196
heartbeat@cmausa.org | *www.cmausa.org/cma_national/heartbeat.asp*
Misty Bradley, editor

Parent company: Christian Motorcyclists Association
Type: monthly print and digital magazine
Purpose: to inspire leaders and members to be the most organized, advanced, equipped, financially stable organization, full of integrity in the motorcycling industry and the Kingdom of God
Submissions: Email manuscript.
Topics: related to motocycling
Sample: sign up on website

HIGHWAY NEWS

PO Box 117, Marietta, PA 17547-0117 | 717-426-9977
editor@tfcglobal.org | *tfcglobal.org/highway-news/current-issue*
Inge Koenig, managing editor

Parent company: Transport for Christ, International
Type: monthly print and digital magazine, circulation 18-20,000
Audience: truck drivers and their families

Purpose: to lead truck drivers, as well as the trucking community, to Jesus Christ and help them grow in their faith

Submissions: Email manuscript as attachment or in the body of the message, or mail it. Simultaneous OK. Unsolicited freelance: 10-20%. Only responds if interested. Length: 800-1,000 words. Seasonal six months in advance. Bible: prefers ESV.

Types of manuscripts: personal experience, reports, short features

Topics: anything related to trucking life

Rights: first, reprint

Payment: none

Guidelines: by email

Sample: download from website

Tip: "Articles submitted for publication do not have to be religious in nature; however, they should not conflict with or oppose guidelines and principles presented in the Bible."

HISTORY'S WOMEN

22 Williams St., Batavia, NY 14020 | 585-297-3009
patty.chadwick@juno.com | *www.historyswomen.com*
Patti Chadwick, editor

Type: monthly print newsletter, circulation 21,000

Audience: women

Purpose: to make history come alive for women from a Christian worldview

Submissions: Looking for articles highlighting the extraordinary achievements of women throughout history that have made life better for their families and the societies in which they lived. Articles 400-1,200 words. Requires email submissions with no attachments; put "Article Submission" in the subject line.

Types of manuscripts: profiles, interviews

Topics: women of faith, social reformers, the Arts, early America, women rulers, life lessons for women, amazing moms, women in sports

Payment: none but offers alternative compensation

Guidelines: *historyswomen.com/writers-guidelines*

Tip: "Interviews or features about women who are making a difference in their world today are also welcomed and probably the most sought after."

HOLINESS TODAY

17001 Prairie Star Pkwy., Lenexa, KS 66220 | 913-577-0500
holinesstoday@nazarene.org | *www.holinesstoday.org*
Dr. Frank Moore, editor in chief

Jordan Eigsti, assistant editor

Denomination: Nazarene

Type: bimonthly print and digital magazine, circulation 11,000, takes ads

Audience: Nazarene laity

Purpose: to connect Nazarenes with their heritage, vision, and mission through stories of God at work in the world

Submissions: Email manuscript as attachment. Also accepts submissions from children and teens. Freelance: 30%. Buys six to eight manuscripts per year. Length: 700-1,100 words. Responds in one day. Bible: NIV.

Types of manuscripts: personal experience, sidebars, columns

Topics: Christian ministry, theological teaching, denominational insights on real-world issues

Rights: first, reprint (tell when/where published)

Payment: $135, on publication, pays kill fee

Guidelines and theme list: by email

Sample: self-addressed 9x12 envelope with two stamps

Tip: "We are always interested in hearing from Nazarene pastors, lay leaders, and experts in their fields. We are a Nazarene publication that wants our articles to be relevant and applicable to real-life scenarios and the world we live in."

HOMELIFE

1 Lifeway Plaza, Nashville, TN 37234-0172 | 615-251-2000
homelife@lifeway.com | www.lifeway.com/en/product-family/homelife-magazine?intcmp=SRDR-homelife
David Bennett, managing editor

Parent company: LifeWay Christian Resources

Denomination: Southern Baptist

Type: monthly print magazine; circulation 250,000

Audience: parents

Purpose: to address all things faith, family, and life

Submissions: Email manuscript as attachment. Unsolicited freelance: 10%. Buys twenty manuscripts per year. Length; 1,500 and 7,500 words. Seasonal four months in advance. Responds in several weeks. Bible: CSB.

Types of manuscripts: narrative, how-to, column

Topics: personal faith, marriage, parenting, living on mission

Rights: first

Payment: $100-400 on publication, kill fee sometimes

Guidelines: by email

Sample: on the website

Tip: "Include full bio, church name, and denomination with submission."

HOMESCHOOLING TODAY

PO Box 1092, Somerset, KY 42502 | 606-485-4105
ashley@homeschoolingtoday.com | *homeschoolingtoday.com*
Ashley Wiggers and Kay Chance, co-executive editors

Type: quarterly print and digital magazine, circulation 5-6,000, takes ads
Audience: homeschooling parents
Purpose: to encourage the hearts of homeschoolers and give them tools to instill a love of learning in their children
Submissions: Does not accept queries; email full manuscript as an attachment with "Article Submission" in the subject line. Responds in six months or not interested. Feature articles include information about a topic, unit study, encouragement, challenge, or an interview, 900-1,200 words. Departments: "Faces of Homeschooling," true stories about real homeschooling families, 600-900 words; "The Home Team," physical education, 600-900 words; "Homeschooling around the World," 600-900 words; "Language Learning," foreign languages, 600-900 words; "Thinking," logic, critical thinking, 600-900 words; "Unit Study," 800-1500 words; "Family Math," 600-900 words.
Types of manuscripts: how-to, unit studies, profiles, interviews
Topics: education, homeschooling
Rights: first, nonexclusive electronic
Payment: 10¢/published word
Guidelines: *homeschoolingtoday.com/write-for-us*
Sample: on the website

IMAGE

3307 Third Ave. W., Seattle, WA 98119 | 206-281-2988
mkenagy@imagejournal.org | *imagejournal.org*
Mary Kenagy Mitchell, managing editor
Lauren F. Winner, creative nonfiction editor
Nick Ripatrazone, culture editor

Type: quarterly print literary journal
Purpose: to demonstrate the continued vitality and diversity of contemporary art and literature that engage with the religious traditions of Western culture
Submissions: Email queries. Submit manuscripts through the website. Responds in three months. Accepts simultaneous submissions. Poetry: no more than five poems or ten pages total. Fiction, essays, and other nonfiction: 3,000-6,000 words.
Types of manuscripts: poetry, fiction, essays, interviews, artist profiles

Topics: related to art and literature

Rights: first

Payment: $25/published page, $3/line of poetry, maxiumum $400

Guidelines: *imagejournal.org/journal/submit*

Tip: "All the work we publish reflects what we see as a sustained engagement with one of the western faiths—Judaism, Christianity, or Islam. That engagement can include unease, grappling, or ambivalence as well as orthodoxy; the approach can be indirect or allusive, but for a piece to be a fit for *Image*, some connection to faith must be there."

INFLUENCE

1445 N. Boonville Ave., Springfield, MO 65802 | 417-862-2781

editor@influencemagazine.com | *influencemagazine.com*

George Paul Wood, executive editor

John Davidson, senior editor

Denomination: Assemblies of God

Type: bimonthly print and digital magazine

Audience: pastors and other leaders

Purpose: to provide a Christ-centered, Spirit-empowered perspective that propels people to engage their faith—as individuals, in community, and with the global Church

Submissions: Email query or manuscript; tell what section it fits. Follow-up emails are discouraged.

Topics: cultural and current events, family, daily life, career, community

Rights: first, occasional reprint

Guidelines: *influencemagazine.com/submission-guidelines*

Sample: *influencemagazine.com/en/issues*

Tip: "Both online and in print, we aim to unite and edify the Church through content marked by integrity and creativity. Our approach to the Christian life is holistic, offering a faith-based context for cultural and current events, as well as providing practical insight for your family, daily life, career and community."

INSITE

PO Box 62189, Colorado Springs, CO 80962-2189 | 719-260-9400

editor@ccca.org | *www.ccca.org/ccca/Publications.asp*

Parent company: Christian Camp and Conference Association

Type: bimonthly print and digital magazine, circulation 8,500

Audience: camp leaders

Purpose: to help our members maximize their ministries by learning and staying inspired while serving God's people

Submissions: Email query first. Responds within one week. Seasonal six months ahead. Profiles and features, 1,200-1,500 words; how-to articles, 1,000-1,200 words; sidebars, 250-500 words. Unsolicited freelance: 1-2%; email for assignment. Bible: NIV.
Types of manuscripts: profiles, interviews, how-to, sidebars
Topics: Christian camping, leadership, children and teen discipleship and development, legal, facilities, business operations
Rights: all
Payment: $300 on publication, sometimes pays kill fee
Guidelines and theme list: download from website
Sample: via email
Tip: "All articles must be applicable to camps and conference centers."

INTERNATIONAL JOURNAL OF FRONTIER MISSIOLOGY

1605 E. Elizabeth St., Pasadena, CA 91104 | 734-765-0368
editors@ijfm.org | www.ijfm.org
Brad Gill, editor

Parent company: International Society for Frontier Missiology
Type: quarterly print journal
Audience: mission professors, executives, and researchers; missionaries; young-adult mission mobilizers
Purpose: to cultivate an international fraternity of thought in the development of frontier missiology
Submissions: Query first. Articles 2,000-6,000 words.
Types: profiles, teaching
Topics: missiological perspective and principles, calls to commitment and involvement in frontier missions
Payment: none
Guidelines: *www.ijfm.org/author_info.htm*
Sample: download from website

THE JOURNAL OF ADVENTIST EDUCATION

12501 Old Columbia Pike, Silver Spring, MD 20904 | 301-680-5069
mcgarrellf@gc.adventist.org | jae.adventist.org
Faith-Ann McGarrell, editor

Denomination: Seventh-day Adventist
Parent company: General Conference of Seventh-day Adventists
Type: quarterly print and digital journal, circulation 10-16,000, takes ads
Audience: educators and administrators
Purpose: to aid professional teachers and educational administrators worldwide, kindergarten to higher education
Submissions: Submit complete manuscript through the website form. Unsolicited: 10%. Buys thirty-two articles per year. Length: 1,500-

2,500 words. Seasonal six months in advance. Responds in four to six weeks. Bible: NIV.

Types of manuscripts: how-to, personal experience, sidebars, reviews

Topics: pedagogy, educational administration, integration of faith and learning, philosophy of education

Rights: first, reprint (tell where/when published)

Payment: $100-250, on publication

Guidelines: *jae.adventist.org/en/for-authors*

Sample: on the website

Tip: Wants "articles on best practices for teaching and pedagogy that can be applied in education settings both nationally and internationally."

JOYFUL LIVING MAGAZINE

PO Box 311, Palo Cedro, CA 97073 | 530-247-7500
joyfullivingmagazineredding@gmail.com | *joyfullivingmagazine.com*
Cathy Jansen, editor-in-chief

Type: quarterly print and digital magazine, takes ads

Audience: general

Purpose: to share encouragement and hope, to help readers grow spiritually and emotionally, and to help them in their everyday lives with practical issues

Submissions: Email articles as attachments. Length: 200-700 words.

Types of manuscripts: profiles, personal experience, recipes, how-to

Topics: making dreams come true, family, marriage, work, singleness, recovery, finances, health, dealing with loss, depression, aging, physical fitness, overcoming obstacles, healthy eating, and more

Payment: none

Guidelines: *www.joyfullivingmagazine.com/writers-info*

Sample: download from website

JUST BETWEEN US

777 S. Barker Rd., Brookfield, WI 53045 | 262-786-6478
submissions@justbetweenus.org | *www.justbetweenus.org*
Shelly Esser, executive editor

Parent organization: Elmbrook Church

Type: quarterly print magazine, circulation 8,000

Audience: women

Purpose: to encourage and equip women for a life of faith and service

Submissions: Prefers emailed manuscripts as attachments but also takes them by mail. Responds in six to eight weeks only if accepts article. Articles, 500-1,500 words; testimonies, 450 words. Bible version: NIV.

Types of manuscripts: how-to, testimony, personal experience

Topics: balance, intimacy with Christ, handling criticism, friendship, conflict, faith, church life, prayer, evangelism, change, Spirit-filled living, finances, forgiveness, God's will, spiritual warfare, staying committed to Christ no matter what, parenting, pain, fighting weariness, church wounds, ministry helps

Payment: none
Guidelines: *justbetweenus.org/writers-guidelines*
Sample: *justbetweenus.org/sample-issue*
Tip: "Articles should be personal in tone, full of real-life anecdotes as well as quotes/advice from noted Christian professionals, and be biblically based. Articles need to be practical and have a distinct Christian and serving perspective throughout."

KANSAS CITY METRO VOICE

PO Box 1114, Lee's Summit, MO 64063 | 816-524-4522
dwight@metrovoicenews.com | *www.metrovoicenews.com*
Dwight Widaman, editor

Type: monthly print and digital newspaper, takes ads
Audience: Kansas City metropolitan area and Topeka/Northeast Kansas
Purpose: to inform and encourage the evangelical community in the area
Submissions: Email for current needs. Takes articles and reviews.
Types of manuscripts: profiles, reviews, opinion pieces, news reports
Sample: download from the website

KEYS TO LIVING

253 Steffens Rd., Danville, PA 17821
owcam@verizon.net
Connie Mertz, editor and publisher
Collesce Beck, associate editor

Type: quarterly print newsletter
Audience: nature enthusiasts
Purpose: to glorify God through nature and present inspirational writing for Christians
Submissions: Email complete manuscript in body of message. Accepts simultaneous submissions. Unsolicited freelance: 30%. Buys twelve manuscripts per year. Length: 500 words maximum. Also considers high-quality photos to accompany devotionals. Responds in one month. Bible: NIV. Accepts manuscripts from teens.
Type of manuscripts: devotions, personal experience, poetry
Topics: Christian living
Rights: reprint
Payment: none
Guidelines: by email
Sample: by email

Tip: "Poetry is welcome but limited to one page maximum. Should have a religious slant."

LEADING HEARTS

PO Box 6421, Longmont, CO 80501 | 303-835-8473
amber@leadinghearts.com | *leadinghearts.com*
Amber Weigland-Buckley, editor

Parent company: Right to the Heart Ministries
Type: bimonthly digital magazine, circulation 60,000, takes ads
Audience: women who lead hearts at home, church, work, and community; ages 35-50
Submissions: Articles on assignment only. To audition for an assignment, email an article of 1,200 words maximum and a short résumé. Gives preferred consideration to members of AWSA. Articles 800 words maximum. Columns 250-500 words. Bible version: NIV.
Types of manuscripts: personal experience, how-to, profiles, reviews
Topics: based on theme list
Rights: first, reprint
Payment: none
Guidelines: *leadinghearts.com/writers-guidelines*
Sample: download from the website

LEAVES

PO Box 87, Dearborn, MI 48121-0087 | 313-561-2330
editor.leaves@mariannhill.us | *www.mariannhill.us/leaves.html*
Rev. Thomas Heier, editor-in-chief

Parent company: Marianhill Mission Society
Denomination: Catholic
Type: bimonthly print magazine , circulation 10,000
Audience: Catholics, primarily in the Detroit, Michigan, area
Purpose: to promote devotion to God and testimony of His blessings
Submissions: Email or mail complete manuscript. Responds in one week. Accepts forty manuscripts per year. Length: 250 words. Unsolicited freelance: 50%. Bible: RSV Catholic edition.
Types of manuscripts: personal experience, testimonies, reviews, poetry
Topics: Christian life, pursuit of holiness
Rights: first, reprint
Payment: none
Sample: write, email, or call for a copy
Tip: Greatest need is for personal testimonies.

LEBEN

2150 River Plaza Dr., Ste. 150, Sacramento, CA 95833 | 916-473-8866
email through website | *www.leben.us*
Wayne C. Johnson, editor

Parent company: City Seminary of Sacramento, California
Type: quarterly print journal
Audience: general
Purpose: to tell the stories of the people and events that make up the Reformation tradition
Submissions: We are a popular history publication that aims at a general readership. Query first. Length: 500-2500 words.
Types of manuscripts: profiles
Topics: Protestant Reformers and those who have followed in their footsteps
Payment: not specified
Guidelines: *leben.us/write-for-leben*
Tip: "Focus on lesser-known events and people. We have no shortage of submissions about Luther, Calvin, Zwingli, etc."

LIGHT + LIFE MAGAZINE

770 N. High School Rd., Indianapolis, IN 46214 | 317-244-3660
jeff.finley@fmcusa.org | *lightandlifemagazine.com*
Jeff Finley, executive editor

Denomination: Free Methodist
Type: monthly print and digital magazine, circulation 14,000
Audience: general
Purpose: to offer encouragement, provide resources, deal with contemporary issues, share denominational news, and offer faith to unbelievers
Submissions: Articles: main article that provides a more detailed examination of the issue's theme, approximately 2,100 words, primarily in third person; action article that shares the story of someone living out the theme and sometimes serves as an instructional piece detailing how to take action, 1,000 words; discipleship, for use by a weekly small group or for individual study, 800 words, reflecting the theme plus two or three group discussion questions. Query first. Responds in two months. Unsolicited freelance: 50%. Bible: NIV.
Types of manuscripts: teaching, profile, Bible study
Topics: theme-related
Rights: first, onetime, occasional reprint (tell when/where appeared)

Payment: $100 for feature articles, $50 for others, on publication
Guidelines: *lightandlifemagazine.com/writers*
Themes: email the editor
Sample: download from website
Tip: "We search for authors who write competently, provide clear information, and employ contemporary style and illustrations."

LIGHT MAGAZINE

901 Commerce St., Ste. 550, Nashville, TN 37203 | 615-244-2495
lnicolet@erlc.com | *erlc.com/light*
Lindsay Nicolet, managing editor

    Parent company: The Ethics and Religious Liberty Commission
    Denomination: Southern Baptist
    Type: biannual print and digital magazine, circulation 10,000 ads
    Audience: church and ministry leaders
    Purpose: to bear witness to the gospel by speaking to congregations and consciences with a thoroughly Christian moral witness
    Submissions: Email manuscript as attachment. Unsolicited freelance: 10%. Buys ten manuscripts per year. Length: 1,500 words. Responds in one week. Bible: CSB.
    Types of manuscripts: how-to, column, review, news report
    Topics: parenting, family, religious liberty, technology, human dignity, pro-life, news, culture, politics, justice, ethics
    Rights: all
    Payment: depends on article and writer
    Guidelines: none
    Sample: email request
    Tip: "Looking for articles tied to current events and focus on local church ministry."

THE LIGHT MAGAZINE

20218 Fraser Highway, #200, Langley, BC V3A 4E6, Canada | 604-510-5070
editor@lightmagazine.ca | *www.lightmagazine.ca*
Steve Almond, editor

    Parent company: Light Christian Media
    Type: monthly print and digital magazine, circulation 18,000, takes ads
    Audience: greater Vancouver Christian community
    Purpose: to inspire faith for everyday life
    Submissions: Email in body of message. Freelance: 10%. Contact editor to get assignments. Buys twenty-four manuscripts per year.

Seasonal two months in advance. Length: 800 words maximum. Responds in one week. Bible: no preference.

Types of manuscripts: lifestyle, news, testimony

Topics: parenting, senior life, Christian living, travel

Rights: first, reprint

Payment: 10¢/word on publication, kill fee sometimes

Guidelines: *lightmagazine.ca/about-us*

Sample: by email

Tip: "Canadian experience is helpful; otherwise all areas are open to freelancers."

LIGUORIAN

1 Liguori Dr., Liguori, MO 63057 | 636-223-1538
liguorianeditor@liguori.org | *www.liguorian.org*
Elizabeth Herzing, editor

Denomination: Catholic

Type: monthly print and digital magazine

Audience: denomination

Purpose: to reinforce spiritual beliefs with inspiration and insight

Submissions: Currently not taking submissions. Check website for updates. Articles must not exceed 2,200 words. Personal essays should be limited to 1,000. Fiction submissions should be approximately 2,000 words. Seasonal articles and stories must be received eight months in advance. Email query. Email manuscripts as attachments. Responds in two to three months.

Types of manuscripts: essay, feature, short stories, interviews

Topics: explanations of Church teachings, theological insights, Christian living

Rights: first

Payment: 12-15¢/published word, on acceptance

Guidelines: *www.liguorian.org/submissions-and-rights-and-permissions*

Sample: 9x12 SASE with three stamps

LIVE

1445 N. Boonville Ave., Springfield, MO 65802-1894 | 417-862-2781
wquick@ag.org
Wade Quick, editor

Denomination: Assemblies of God

Type: weekly take-home paper, circulation 12,000

Audience: denomination

Purpose: to encourage Christians in their faith and to apply biblical principles to everyday problems

Submissions: Email submissions as attachments. Stories should be encouraging, challenging, and/or humorous. Even problem-centered stories should be upbeat. Stories should not be preachy, critical, or moralizing. They should not present pat, trite, or simplistic answers to problems. No Bible fiction or sci-fi. Length: maximum 1,200 words; inside stories, 200-600 words; poetry, 12-25 lines. Seasonal eighteen months in advance. Unsolicited freelance: 100%. Receives 100 manuscripts per year. Bible: NLT.

Types of manuscripts: personal experiences, short stories, how-to from first-person point of view, poetry, fillers

Topics: Christian life/testimony

Rights: first, reprint, electronic

Payment: 10¢/word for first, 7¢/word for reprint, $42-60 for poetry; on acceptance

Guidelines: *myhealthychurch.com/store/startcat.cfm?cat=tWRITGUID*

Samples: 5x8 SASE with $2.20 postage

Tip: "Make sure the stories have a strong Christian element, are written well, have strong takeaways, but do not preach."

THE LIVING CHURCH

PO Box 510705, Milwaukee, WI 53203-0121 | 414-292-1240
mmichael@livingchurch.org | *www.livingchurch.org*
Mark Michael, editor

Denomination: Episcopal

Type: biweekly print magazine

Audience: denomination

Purpose: to seek and serve the Catholic and evangelical faith of the one Church, to the end of visible Christian unity throughout the world

Submissions: Email for current needs.

Types: articles, reviews

LUTHERAN FORUM

PO Box 327, Delhi, NY 13753-0327 | 607-746-7511
email through website at alpb.org/e-mail-paul-r-sauer | *lutheranforum.com*
Paul R. Sauer, interim editor

Denomination: Lutheran

Parent company: American Lutheran Publicity Bureau

Type: quarterly print journal

Submissions: Articles 2,000-3,000 words. Submit manuscript by email or mail. Responds in three months.

Rights: first

Payment: none
Guidelines: *alpb.org/writers-guidelines*
Sample: download from the website
Tip: "Prospective writers are encouraged to reflect on what moves them most, intellectually and spiritually, and then, armed with adequate research and forethought, put their ideas to paper."

THE LUTHERAN JOURNAL

PO Box 28158, Oakdale, MN 55128 | 651-702-0176
christianad2@msn.com | *thelutheranjournal.com*
Roger Jensen, editor

Denomination: Lutheran
Type: annual print magazine
Audience: families
Purpose: to provide wholesome and inspirational reading for the enjoyment and enrichment of Lutherans
Submissions: Email for current needs.
Types of manuscripts: articles, poetry, prayers
Payment: none
Sample: download from the website

THE LUTHERAN WITNESS

1333 S. Kirkwood Rd., St. Louis, MO 63122-7226 | 800-248-1930
witness@lcms.org | *witness.lcms.org*
Roy S. Askins, editor

Denomination: Luthern Church Missouri Synod (LCMS)
Type: monthly (11x) print and digital magazine, circulation 120,000
Audience: denomination
Purpose: to provide Missouri Synod laypeople with stories and information that complement congregational life, foster personal growth in faith, and help interpret the contemporary world from a Lutheran Christian perspective
Submissions: Prefers query but will take full manuscript. Submit through the website. Length: 500, 1,000, or 1,500 words. Bible: ESV.
Types of manuscripts: profiles, how-to, teaching, humor, personal experience, Bible studies, essays, poetry
Topics: current events; theology; LCMS missions, ministries, members, history; evangelism, outreach, spiritual growth
Rights: first, electronic
Guidelines and themes: *witness.lcms.org/contribute*
Sample: on the website
Tip: "Because of the magazine's long lead time and because main

features are planned at least six months in advance of the publication date, your story should have a long-term perspective that keeps it relevant several months from the time you submit it."

MATURE LIVING

1 Lifeway Plaza, MSN 136, Nashville, TN 37234-0175 | 615-251-2000
matureliving@lifeway.com |
www.lifeway.com/en/product-family/mature-living-magazine
Debbie Dickerson, managing editor

Parent company: LifeWay Christian Resources
Denomination: Southern Baptist
Type: monthly print magazine
Audience: ages 55 and older
Purpose: to equip mature adults as they live a legacy of leadership, stewardship, and discipleship
Submissions: Email for possible assignment. Not accepting unsolicited manuscripts or queries. Open for "Kicks and Grins," fun stories of your grandkids, 25-125 words; challenging biblical word search puzzles; and crossword puzzles.
Types of manuscripts: personal experience, how-to, teaching, devotional, short stories, recipes
Topics: marriage, caregiving, evangelism, theology, relationship with adult children, grandchildren
Payment: varies
Sample: on the website

THE MESSENGER

440 Main St., Steinbach, MB R5G 1Z5, Canada | 204-326-6401
messenger@emconf.ca | *emcmessenger.ca*
Terry Smith, editor, tsmith@emconference.ca
Andrew Walker, assistant editor

Denomination: Evangelical Mennonite Conference (EMC)
Type: monthly print and digital magazine, circulation 2,300
Audience: denomination
Purpose: to inform concerning events and activities in the denomination, instruct in godliness and victorious living, and inspire to earnestly contend for the faith
Submissions: Email as attachment or mail query or complete manuscript. Simultaneous submissions OK. Unsolicited freelance: 25%. Buys thirty manuscripts per year. Also accepts manuscripts from children and teens. Length: 1,200 words maximum. Seasonal two months in advance. Responds in one week. Bible: modern translation.

Types of manuscripts: articles, poetry
Topics: theology, Christian life
Rights: first
Payment: $150 CAD for 1,200 words, on publication, kill fee always
Guidelines: *emcmessenger.ca/submission-guidelines*
Theme list: not available but follow the church year
Sample: *issuu.com/emcmessenger*
Tip: Looking for evangelical Anabaptist perspectives.

THE MESSIANIC TIMES

50 Alberta Dr., Amherst, NY 14226 | 866-612-7770
editor@messianictimes.com | *www.messianictimes.com*
Sheila Fisher, editorial coordinator

Parent company: Times of the Messiah Ministries
Denomination: Messianic
Type: bimonthly print and digital newspaper
Audience: Messianic community
Purpose: to provide accurate, authoritative, and current information to unite the international Messianic Jewish community, teach Christians the Jewish roots of their faith, and proclaim that Yeshua is the Jewish Messiah
Submissions: Query preferred. Email for current needs.
Types of manuscripts: analysis; opinion pieces; book, music, and film reviews; news

METHODIST HISTORY JOURNAL

36 Madison Ave., Madison, NJ 07940 | 973-408-3189
atday@gcah.org | *www.gcah.org/research/methodist-history-journal*
Alfred T. Day, III, general secretary

Denomination: United Methodist
Type: quarterly print and PDF journal
Audience: denomination
Submissions: Only email manuscripts as attachments. Articles on the history of other denominations and subjects will be considered when there are strong ties to events and persons significant to the history of the United Methodist tradition. Manuscripts pertaining to strictly local, as opposed to national or international interest, are not accepted. Length: maximum 5,000 words.
Topics: United Methodist history
Payment: none
Guidelines: *www.gcah.org/resources/guidelines-for-publication*

MINISTRY

12501 Old Columbia Pike, Silver Spring, MD 20904 | 301-680-6518
ministrymagazine@gc.adventist.org | *www.ministrymagazine.org*
Pavel Goia, editor

Denomination: Seventh-day Adventist

Type: monthly print and digital magazine, circulation 18,000

Audience: pastors, professors, administrators, chaplains, pastoral
students, lay leaders of all denominations

Purpose: to deepen spiritual life, develop intellectual strength, and
increase pastoral and evangelistic effectiveness of all ministers in
the context of the three angels' messages of Revelation 14:6-12

Submissions: For all submissions, include completed biographical
information form. Send all submissions as email attachments.
Articles to 2,500 words, book and resources reviews to 500 words.

Types of manuscripts: biblical studies, how-to, teaching, reviews

Topics: personal needs of the minister (spiritual, physical, emotional),
pastor-spouse team and ministry relationships, pastoral family
needs, pastoral skills, biblical studies for sermon preparation,
theological studies, worship, current issues

Rights: all

Payment: not specified, on acceptance

Guidelines: *www.ministrymagazine.org/article-submissions*

Sample: click Archives page on the website

Tip: "Writers should ask themselves: What do I expect the reader to
do with my manuscript?"

THE MOTHER'S HEART

PO Box 275, Tobaccoville, NC 27050 | 336-775-8519
Marilla@alwrightpublishing.com | *www.the-mothers-heart.com*
Kym Wright, editor and publisher

Parent company: alWright! Publishing

Type: bimonthly digital magazine, monthly hits under 100,000

Audience: mothers, homeschool moms, moms at home

Purpose: to encourage mothers in their enormous and fulfilling calling

Submissions: Email query or full manuscript. Seasonal six months
ahead. Unsolicited freelance: 20-30%. Buys twenty manuscripts
per year. Length: 750-1,000 and 1,500-2,500 words. Responds in
three months. Bible: any. Seasonal six months in advance

Types of manuscripts: personal experience, how-to, sidebar, filler,
columns

Topics: mothering, homeschooling, parenting, marriage, organization, family life, adoption

Rights: first, reprint (tell when/where published), on publication

Payment: $10-100 on publication

Guidelines: *the-mothers-heart.com/Writers%20Guidelines%202016-2019.pdf*

Sample: *the-mothers-heart.com/subscribe.htm*

Tip: "Looking for adoption stories, organization topics, and encouragement for moms and homeschooling moms."

MUTUALITY

122 W. Franklin Ave., Ste. 218, Minneapolis, MN 55404 | 612-872-6898
mutuality@cbeinternational.org |
www.cbeinternational.org/publication/mutuality-blog-magazine/print-archives
Ellen Josburg, editor

Parent company: Christians for Biblical Equality

Type: quarterly print and digital magazine

Audience: evangelicals in professional and volunteer ministry, seminary faculty and students, male and female leaders, and laypeople interested in egalitarian theory (Bible and theology) and practice (application in churches and homes)

Purpose: to provide inspiration, encouragement, and information on topics related to a biblical view of mutuality between men and women in the home, church, and world

Submissions: Email articles as attachments in Word. Responds in one month or more. Length: first-person narratives and feature articles, 800-1,800 words; book, movie, or music reviews, 500-800 words. Bible: NIV.

Types of manuscripts: personal experience, how-to, biblical reflection, poetry, reviews

Topics: theme-related

Rights: first with electronic

Payment: one-year CBE membership ($49–$59 value) or up to three CBE recordings (up to $30 value)

Guidelines: *www.cbeinternational.org/content/write-mutuality*

Theme list: *www.cbeinternational.org/content/upcoming-mutuality-themes*

Sample: *www.cbeinternational.org/content/mutuality-sample-issue*

MYSTERIOUS WAYS

110 William St., Ste. 901, New York, NY 10038 | 212-251-8100
www.guideposts.org/our-magazines/mysterious-ways-magazine
Diana Aydin, editor

Parent company: Guideposts

Type: bimonthly print and digital magazine

Audience: general

Purpose: to encourage through true stories of extraordinary moments and everyday miracles that reveal a spiritual force at work in our lives

Submissions: Submit complete manuscript through the online form. Looking for true stories of unexpected and wondrous experiences that reveal a hidden hand at work in our lives. The best stories are those that present a credible, well-detailed account that can even leave skeptics in awe and wonder. Length: 750-1,500 words. Also buys news stories and short material, 50-350 words, for recurring features like "Wonderful World," "His Humorous Ways," and "Dreams & Premonitions."

Types of manuscripts: personal experiences

Payment: varies, after scheduled for publication

Guidelines: *www.guideposts.org/write-for-mysterious-ways*

Tip: "A typical *Mysterious Ways* story is written in dramatic style, with an unforeseen twist that inspires the reader to look for miracles in his or her own life. It may be told from a 1st-person or 3rd-person perspective, and can be your own experience or someone else's story. We are also on the lookout for recent experiences."

NET RESULTS

308 West Blvd. N., Columbia, MO 65203 | 888-470-2456
submissions@netresults.org | *netresults.org*
Bill Tenny-Brittian, managing editor

Parent company: The Effective Church Group

Type: bimonthly print and digital magazine

Audience: pastors, church volunteers, and Christian organizations

Purpose: to share great ideas for vital ministry among leaders

Submissions: Email query first; email manuscripts as attached file. Responds in eight weeks. Practical and relevant articles on innovative ways to do mission and ministry, 1,750 words. Bible: TNIV. Takes reprints from noncompetitive periodicals with letter of release from original publication.

Types of manuscripts: how-to, teaching

Topics: evangelism, service, planning, trust-building, leadership and organizational development, worship, preaching, hospitality, Christian education, faith formation, mentoring, training, partnerships, property and technology development, fund-raising, financial planning, stewardship, communications, marketing

Rights: all print and electronic

Payment: on publication

Guidelines: *netresults.org/writers*

Theme list: *netresults.org/writers/upcoming-themes*
Sample: on the website
Tip: "We look for practical, hands-on ministry ideas that an individual can put into practice. The best ideas are those the author has actually used successfully."

NEW FRONTIER CHRONICLE

30840 Hawthorne Blvd., Rancho Palos Verde, CA 90275 | 562-491-8343
new.frontier@usw.salvationarmy.org | *www.newfrontierchronicle.org*
Christin Davis Thieme, editor-in-chief

Parent company: The Salvation Army Western Territory
Type: monthly print newspaper
Audience: denomination in the territory
Purpose: to empower Salvationists to communicate and engage with the Army's mission
Submissions: Query first. Shares information from across The Salvation Army world, reports that analyze effective programs to identify the unique features and trends for what works, tips to help local congregations better engage in the issues of today, and influential voices on relevant (and sometimes controversial) matters.
Types: articles, reviews
Guidelines: *www.newfrontierchronicle.org/submit*

NEW IDENTITY MAGAZINE

PO Box 1002, Mount Shasta, CA 96067 | 310-947-8707
submissions@newidentitymagazine.com | *www.newidentitymagazine.com*
Cailin Briody Henson, editor-in-chief

Type: quarterly print and digital magazine
Audience: new believers, ages 18-34
Purpose: to provide diverse, Bible-centered content to help lead new believers and seekers to a fuller understanding of the Christian faith
Submissions: Submit articles through online form. Responds in two weeks. Length: 500-3,500 words. Departments: "Grow," teaching new believers and seekers about different Christian perspectives on topics, understanding Christian concepts, jargon, disciplines, practical application of Scripture, etc.; "Connect," encouraging new believers and seekers with testimonies, articles about relationships, fellowship, church, community, discussions and expressions of faith; "Live," engaging new believers and seekers to live out their faith in the real world, with stories of people actively pursuing God and their passions, organizations and resources to apply one's gifts, talents and desires to serve God and others, sharing the love of Christ in everyday arenas.

Types of manuscripts: personal experience, teaching, testimonies, how-to, opinion

Topics: spiritual growth, applying Scripture, relationships, salvation, church, service, evangelism

Rights: first, electronic, sometimes reprint (tell when/where appeared)

Payment: none

Guidelines: *www.newidentitymagazine.com/write/writers-guidelines*

Sample: on the website

Tip: "Articles need creative, well-thought-out ideas that offer new insight. We value well researched, factually and biblically supported content."

NOW WHAT?

PO Box 33677, Denver, CO 80233
nowwhat@cog7.org | nowwhat.cog7.org
Sherri Langton, associate editor

Denomination: Church of God (Seventh Day)

Type: monthly digital magazine

Audience: seekers

Purpose: to address felt needs of the unchurched

Submissions: Each issue is built around a personal experience, with articles related to the topic. Personal experiences show a person's struggle that either led him to faith in Christ or deepened his walk with God. Unsolicited freelance: 100%. Buys ten to twelve per year. Email manuscripts and queries; query not necessary. Responds in four to ten weeks. Length: 1,000-1,500 words. Bible: prefers NIV. Avoid unnecessary jargon or technical terms. No Christmas or Easter pieces or fiction. No snail mail submissions or PDFs.

Types of manuscripts: personal experience

Topics: salvation, issues

Rights: first, electronic, reprint (tell when/where appeared), onetime

Payment: $25-65, on publication

Guidelines: *nowwhat.cog7.org/send_us_your_story*

Tip: "Think how you can explain your faith, or how you overcame a problem, to a non-Christian. Use storytelling techniques, like dialogue, scenes, etc., with the conflict clearly stated."

ON MISSION

4200 N. Point Pkwy., Alpharetta, GA 30022-4176 | 770-410-6000
fmorgan@namb.net | www.namb.net/on-mission-magazine-new
K. Faith Morgan Wroten, editor

Denomination: Southern Baptist

Parent company: North American Mission Board

Type: quarterly magazine

Audience: Christians who are impacting their world for Christ

Purpose: to highlight the work of missionaries and help readers be on mission where they work and live

Submissions: Open to freelance articles and reviews. Email for current needs.

Topics: missions, evangelism

Sample: download from website

OUR SUNDAY VISITOR NEWSWEEKLY

200 Noll Plaza, Huntington, IN 46750 | 800-348-2440, 260-356-8400
oursunvis@osv.com | *www.osvnews.com*
Gretchen R. Crowe, editorial director

Denomination: Catholic

Type: weekly print and digital newspaper

Audience: denomination

Purpose: to provide timely coverage of important national and international religious events reported from a Catholic perspective

Submissions: Query and send manuscript only through the online form. Responds in four to six weeks. Articles: news analysis, 950-1,100 words, including sidebars, but occasionally as short as 500 words or as long as 2,000 words; "In Focus," a package of articles totaling 3,000-4,000 words by one or more authors, query first; features linked to current events and trends of the day, 1,350 words; essays on relevant issues of the day, 500-750 words; profiles, 500-750 words; Q&A interviews, 1,200 words. Bible: RSV.

Types of manuscripts: news, essays, interviews, profiles

Topics: Catholic perspective on issues and news

Payment: unspecified, within four to six weeks of acceptance

Guidelines: *osv.submittable.com/submit*

Tip: "Our mission is to examine the news, culture, and trends of the day from a faithful and sound Catholic perspective—to see the world through the eyes of faith. Especially interested in writers able to do news analysis (with a minimum of three sources) or news features."

OUTREACH

Story Ideas, 5550 Tech Center, Colorado Springs, CO 80919
tellus@outreachmagazine.com | *www.outreachmagazine.com*
James P. Long, editor

Type: bimonthly magazine

Audience: senior pastors and church leadership, as well as laypeople who are passionate about outreach

Purpose: to be the gathering place of ideas, insights, and stories for churches focused on reaching out to their community—locally and globally—with the love of Christ

Submissions: Email or mail query or complete manuscript with cover letter and published clips. Seasonal six months ahead. Responds in eight weeks. Articles, 1,200-2,500 words; features, 1,500-2,500 words; "Pulse" stories of what churches and individuals are doing, 200-300 words; ideas for outreach events, 300 words; and "Soulfires" profiles of people who are passionate about reaching others for Christ, 600 words.

Types of manuscripts: profiles, how-to

Topics: what's new in ministry, evangelism training, focus on retention, small groups, keeping visitors engaged

Rights: first, reprint (tell when/where published)

Payment: $700-1,000 for feature articles

Guidelines: *www.outreachmagazine.com/magazine/3160-writers-guidelines.html*

Tip: "While most articles are assigned, we do accept queries and manuscripts on speculation. Please don't query us until you've studied at least one issue of *Outreach*."

PARENTING TEENS

1 Lifeway Plaza, Nashville, TN 37234-0172 | 615-251-2196
scott.latta@lifeway.com | *www.lifeway.com/en/product-family/parenting-teens*
Scott Latta, editor

Parent company: LifeWay Christian Resources
Denomination: Southern Baptist
Type: monthly print magazine
Audience: parents of teens
Purpose: to give parents encouragement and challenge them in their relationship with Christ, so they, in turn, can guide their teens
Submissions: Manuscripts by assignment. Email résumé, bio, and clips to get an assignment. Offers timely information, encouragement, expert insight, and practical advice to parents of teens. Bible: CSB.
Payment: unspecified
Guidelines: by email
Sample: on the website

PARENTLIFE

1 Lifeway Plaza, Nashville, TN 37234-0172 | 615-251-2196
parentlife@lifeway.com |
www.lifeway.com/en/product-familiy/parentlife-magazine

Nancy Cornwell, content editor

Parent company: LifeWay Christian Resources
Denomination: Southern Baptist
Type: monthly print magazine
Audience: parents of children birth to preteen
Purpose: to encourage and equip parents with biblical solutions that will transform families
Submissions: Serves as a springboard for parents who may feel exasperated or overwhelmed with information by offering a biblical approach to raising healthy, productive children. Offers practical ideas and information for individual parents and couples. Query first by email. Email requested manuscript as an attachment. Include one to three sidebars. Responds in six to twelve months. Length: 500-1,500 words. Bible: CSB.
Types of manuscripts: how-to, teaching, family devotional, sidebars
Topics: parenting, health, development, education, discipline, spiritual growth
Payment: unspecified
Guidelines: by email

PARISH LITURGY

16565 S. State St., South Holland, IL 60473 | 708-331-5485
acp@acpress.org | www.americancatholicpress.org/parLit.html
Rev. Michael Gilligan, executive director

Denomination: Catholic
Parent company: American Catholic Press
Type: quarterly print magazine, circulation 1,500
Audience: parish priests, music directors, litergy planners
Purpose: to provide material for each Sunday: themes, comments, petitions, and music suggestions
Submissions: Mail manuscript. Responds in eight weeks. Unsolicited freelance: 50%. Buys one manuscript per year. Articles 300 words. Bible: CR. Seasonal three months in advance. Responds in one month.
Types of manuscripts: teaching, how-to
Topics: liturgy, theology of liturgy, pastoral music
Rights: all
Payment: variable, on publication, pays kill fee
Guidelines: none
Sample: 9x12 envelope with $2 postage
Tip: "We use articles on the liturgy only—period. Do not send poetry or nonliturgical articles."

THE PLAIN TRUTH

1710 Evergreen St., Duarte, CA 91010 | 800-309-4466
managing.editor@ptm.org | www.ptm.org/pt-magazine
Brad Jersak, editor

> **Parent company:** Plain Truth Ministries
> **Type:** bimonthly digital and print magazine
> **Audience:** general
> **Purpose:** to discover authentic Christianity without all the religious "stuff"
> **Submissions:** Queries only.
> **Types of manuscripts:** teaching
> **Guidelines:** by email
> **Sample:** on the website

POINT

11002 Lake Hart Dr., Orlando, FL 32832 | 407-563-6083
mickey.seward@converge.org | www.converge.org/point-magazine
Mickey Seward, editor

> **Denomination:** Baptist General Conference
> **Type:** triannual digital magazine
> **Audience:** denomination
> **Purpose:** to increase movement awareness, ownership, and involvement by publishing captivating God-stories of Converge people and regional ministries
> **Submissions:** Open to freelance submissions. Email query with clips. Articles 300-1,400 words.
> **Types:** personal experiences, profiles, reports
> **Rights:** first, reprint, electronic
> **Payment:** $60-280, on publication
> **Sample:** on the website

POWER FOR LIVING

4050 Lee Vance Dr., Colorado Springs, CO 80918 | 800-708-5550, 719-536-0100
Powerforliving@davidccook.com | davidccook.org/power-for-living
Karen Bouchard, managing editor

> **Parent company:** David C. Cook
> **Type:** weekly take-home paper
> **Audience:** general, ages 50 and older
> **Purpose:** to connect God's truth to real life
> **Submissions:** Looking for inspiring stories and articles about famous

and ordinary people whose experiences and insights show the power of Christ at work in their lives. Length: 1,200-1,500 words. Buys twenty per year. Poetry related to matters of faith and biblically based, twenty lines; buys six to twelve per year. Columns 750 words; buys five to eight per year. Accepts reprints but prefers original work. Bible: NIV, KJV.

Types of manuscripts: personal experiences, interviews, poetry, columns

Topics: diverse range of subjects, from world missions to simple, relatable experiences with family and life

Rights: first, onetime, reprint

Payment: $375 for articles, $50 for poems, $150 for columns, on acceptance

Guidelines: download from website

PRAYER CONNECT

2800 Poplar St., Ste. 43-L, Terre Haute, IN 47803 | 812 238-5504
editor@prayerconnect.net | prayerconnect.net
Carol Madison, editor

Parent company: Church Prayer Leaders Network

Type: quarterly print and digital magazine; circulation 3,000 print; 10,000+ web; ads

Audience: prayer leaders, pastors, intercessors

Purpose: to resource prayer leaders and pastors with tools to help them motivate and mobilize believers in church to pray the purposes of God

Submissions: Email as an attachment manuscript or query letter. Unsolicited freelance: 30%. Buys ten manuscripts per year. Length: nontheme articles, 1,200-1,500 words; "Tips and Tools," 300-500 words; columns, 850 words. Responds in four weeks. Bible: NIV. Simultaneous OK.

Types of manuscripts: how-to with practical application (we like bullet points), along with personal illustrations that demonstrate you are a "prayer practitioner"

Topics: intercession, prayer teaching, prayer leading, unique prayer ideas or themes

Rights: first, reprint

Payment: 10¢/word, on publication; sometimes pays kill fee

Guidelines: *www.prayerleader.com/about-us/write-for-us*

Theme list: by email

Sample: on website

Tip: "Give us prayer ideas that you have used to increase the intercession in your personal life, family, church, or city. Don't write an article on the Lord's Prayer; we've seen dozens of those. Write something about how you have established prayer in your family or mobilized your congregation to pray for issues like sex trafficking, for example."

PRESBYTERIANS TODAY

100 Witherspoon St., Louisville, KY 40202-1396 | 800-728-7228
editor@pcusa.org | *www.presbyterianmission.org/ministries/today*
Donna Frischknecht Jackson, editor

Denomination: Presbyterian Church (USA)
Type: bimonthly print and digital magazine
Audience: denomination
Purpose: to explore practical issues of faith and life, tell stories of Presbyterians who are living their faith, and cover a wide range of church news and activities
Submissions: Query first. Responds in two weeks. Prefers to work with published writers. Length: 1,000-1,800 words. Seasonal three months in advance. Freelance: 25%. Bible: NRSV.
Topics: features about Presbyterians, theology, Bible study, devotional helps, church's role in society
Payment: $75-300, on acceptance
Guidelines: click on Writer's Guidelines
Sample: click on Digital

RELEVANT

55 W. Church St., Ste. 211, Orlando, FL 32801 | 407-660-1411
submissions@relevantmediagroup.com | *relevantmagazine.com*
Tyler Huckabee, senior editor

Type: bimonthly digital and annual print magazine
Audience: millennials
Purpose: to challenge people to go further in their spiritual journey; live selflessly and intentionally; care about positively impacting the world around them; and find the unexpected places God is speaking in life, music, and culture
Submissions: Email query and complete manuscript as attachment. Responds in two weeks or not interested. Length: 750-1,000 words.
Topics: faith, culture, and intentional living
Payment: $100-400
Guidelines: *www.relevantmagazine.com/write*
Sample: on the website

RELIEF: A JOURNAL OF ART & FAITH

Reade Center 122, Taylor University, 236 W. Reade Ave., Upland, IN 46989
email through website | www.reliefjournal.com
Daniel Bowman, Jr., editor in chief

Type: biannual print literary journal
Audience: general
Purpose: to promote full human flourishing in faith and art
Submissions: Looking for poetry and stories that reflect reality as honestly as Scripture reflects reality. Submit manuscript through the website only during October 1 to March 31. Costs $2 to submit a manuscript. Length: stories, 8,000 words maximum; poetry, 1,000 words maximum; creative nonfiction, exploratory essays with an emotional arc that may or may not be narrative, 5,000 words maximum
Types of manuscripts: short stories, creative nonfiction, poetry
Rights: first, electronic
Payment: none
Guidelines: *www.reliefjournal.com/print-submit*

SACONNECTS

440 W. Nyack Rd., West Nyack, NY 10994-1739 | 845-620-7200
saconnects.org
Robert Mitchell, managing editor

Denomination: Salvation Army
Type: monthly print and digital magazine
Audience: denomination in the eastern territory
Submissions: Manuscripts only from people who live in the eastern territory. Email manuscripts as attachments through the website.
Types of manuscripts: news, how-to, personal experience
Guidelines: *saconnects.org/submission-guidelines-magazine*
Sample: on the website

ST. ANTHONY MESSENGER

28 W. Liberty St., Cincinnati, OH 45202-6498 | 513-241-5615
MagazineEditors@Franciscanmedia.org |
FranciscanMedia.org/st-anthony-messenger
Christopher Heffron, executive editor

Denomination: Catholic
Type: monthly print and digital magazine
Audience: family-oriented, majority are women ages 40-70
Purpose: to offer readers inspiration from the heart of Catholicism—

the Gospels and the experience of God's people

Submissions: Query only by email. Responds in eight weeks. Email manuscripts as attachments. Seasonal one year in advance. Length: about 2,000 words or shorter pieces. Fiction 2,000-2,500 words; buys twelve per year. Stories should be about family relationships and about people struggling and coping with problems, triumphing in adversity, persevering in faith, overcoming doubt, or coming to spiritual insights. Poetry 20 lines maximum. Bible: NAB.

Types of manuscripts: profiles, biblical teaching, short stories, poetry

Topics: church, sacraments, education, spiritual growth, family, marriage, social issues

Rights: first, electronic

Payment: 20¢/word, $2/line for poetry with minimum of $20, on acceptance

Guidelines: *www.franciscanmedia.org/writers-guidelines*

Sample: on website

SHARING

PO Box 780909, San Antonio, TX 78278-0909 | 877-992-5222
sharing@OSLToday.org | osltoday.org/sharing-magazine
Jamie Henry, editor

Parent company: International Order of St. Luke the Physician

Type: bimonthly print magazine

Audience: general

Purpose: to inspire, educate, and inform about Christian healing of body, soul, and spirit

Submissions: Share your stories, experiences, thoughts, insights, inspirational poems, and testimonies of God's amazing power to heal. Length: articles 200-1,500 words, poetry 30-50 words. Prefers emailed submissions as attachments but will take them by mail.

Types of manuscripts: personal experience, testimonies, teaching, essays, poetry

Topics: theme-related

Rights: onetime

Payment: none

SHATTERED MAGAZINE

PO Box 134, Huntsville, AL 35804
256-783-8350
submissions@shatteredmagazine.net | shatteredmagazine.net

Type: quarterly digital magazine, takes ads

Audience: general

Purpose: to celebrate our unique, God-given stories

Submission: Looking for testimonies of encountering Jesus to use in the features, life, community, and mission sections. "Where did He meet you? Where does He continue to meet you? How has He used what others intended for evil in your life for good? How has He taken what you have screwed up and redeemed for His glory? How has He used community to be a part of your story? Or, how has your community been a part of a larger story? Has God moved you to share Him with others? What has that looked like?" Query through the website. Length: 750-1,000 words.

Types of manuscripts: personal experience

Payment: $50

Guidelines: *shatteredmagazine.net/legal/submission-guidelines*

SOJOURNERS

408 C St. N.E., Washington, DC 20002 | 202-328-8842
submissions@sojo.net, queries@sojo.net, poetry@sojo.net, reviews@sojo.net |
www.sojo.net
Jim Rice, editor

Type: monthly print and digital magazine

Audience: community influencers

Purpose: to explore the intersections of faith, politics, and culture; uncover in depth the hidden injustices in the world around us; and tell the stories of hope that keep us grounded, inspired, and moving forward

Submissions: Query only with no attachments. Responds in six to eight weeks. Feature articles are typically 1,800-2,000 words. Email poetry. Length: 25-40 lines. Often tries to use poetry geared toward particular seasons.

Types of manuscripts: feature articles, reviews, poetry

Topics: social justice, popular culture, spirituality

Rights: all

Payment: unspecified, $50 per poem, on publication

Guidelines: *sojo.net/magazine/write*

THE SOUTHEAST OUTLOOK

920 Blankenbaker Pkwy., Louisville, KY 40243 | 502-253-8600
www.southeastoutlook.org
Jacob Glassner, editor

Parent company: Southeast Christian Church

Type: weekly print newspaper; circulation 25,000; ads

Audience: Louisville, Kentucky, and surrounding communities

Purpose: to connect people to Jesus and one another

Submissions: Assignments only; no unsolicited freelance. Length: 600-800 words. Seasonal: one month in advance. Responds in one week.

Types of manuscripts: articles

Topics: Christian life

Rights: onetime

Payment: none

Guidelines: none

Sample: rack locations in Louisville

Tip: "We do not pay for unsolicited work."

SOUTHWEST KANSAS FAITH AND FAMILY

PO Box 1454, Dodge City, KS 67801 | 620-225-4677

info@swkfaithandfamily.org | www.swkfaithandfamily.org

Stan Wilson, publisher

Type: monthly print newspaper

Audience: residents of the area

Purpose: to share the Word of God and news and information that honors Christian beliefs, family traditions, and values that are the cornerstone of our nation

Submissions: Email query or complete manuscript.

Topics: any Christian or family issue

Guidelines: *www.swkfaithandfamily.org/submitarticle.html*

SPORTS SPECTRUM MAGAZINE

640 Plaza Dr., Ste. 110, Highlands Ranch, CO 80129 | 866-821-2971

jon@sportsspectrum.com | sportsspectrum.com/magazine

Jon Ackerman, managing editor

Parent company: Pro Athletes Outreach

Type: quarterly to bimonthly print and digital magazine, circulation 3,000

Audience: sports fans, predominantly male, ages 20-55

Purpose: to be a resource for sports fans who are followers of Jesus, telling stories of athletes of all levels displaying an athletic lifestyle pleasing to God

Submissions: Email query with clips. Unsolicited freelance: 10%. Buys four articles per year. Length: 1,500-2,000 words. Responds in one week. Bible: NIV.

Types of manuscripts: feature stories

Topic: sports

Rights: all

Payment: 15-20¢/word, on acceptance

Guidelines: none

Sample: call

Tip: "Looking for stories of prominent athletes living out their faith in Christ and a plan for obtaining original quotes."

STANDARD

PO Box 843336, Kansas City, MO 64184-3336 | 816-931-1900
standard.foundry@gmail.com | *www.thefoundrypublishing.com/catalog/ product/view/id/6623/s/standard-st-son20/category/19*
Jeanette Gardner Littleton, editor

Denomination: Nazarene

Parent company: The Foundry Publishing

Type: weekly take-home paper, circulation 40,000

Audience: denomination

Purpose: to encourage and inspire our audience and to reinforce curriculum

Submissions: Primarily assignment only. To get an assignment, send clips of personal-experience articles. Buys 104 manuscripts per year. Length: 400 and 800-900 words. Seasonal one year in advance. Response time varies. Bible: NIV.

Types of manuscripts: personal experience

Topics: theme-related

Rights: first, reprint, all

Payment: $35 and $50, on acceptance

Guidelines and theme list: by email

Sample: email for PDF

Tip: "Writers should know basics of Wesleyan-Arminian theological perspective. Write to the theme list; please indicate which theme you're proposing it for. Nonfiction cannot be preachy. Put full contact information in the body of the manuscript, not only in the email. It helps to know if you're Nazarene or another Wesleyan/ holiness denomination."

TEACHERS OF VISION

PO Box 45610, Westlake, OH 44145 | 888-798-1124
tov@ceai.org | *ceai.org/teachers-of-vision-magazine*
Dawn Molnar, managing editor

Parent organization: Christian Educators Association International

Type: triannual print and digital magazine, circulation 4,000, takes ads

Audience: Christian educators in public schools

Purpose: to provide biblically principled resources that encourage, equip, and empower Christian educators

Submissions: Email submission or query with clips as attached file. Minifeatures, 400-800 words; theme-based features, 800-1,200 words; personal interest, 400-1,000 words; methodology and inspirational, 400-800 words. Unsolicited freelance: 8%. Buys more than forty manuscripts per year. Seasonal nine months in advance. Responds in two weeks during the school year. Bible: NIV. Simultaneous OK. Accepts submissions from children and teens. Gives assignments to their regularly published writers.

Types of manuscripts: personal experience, how-to, poetry, trends

Topics: theme-based, educational success story, teaching techniques, inspirational

Rights: first, reprint, electronic

Payment: $50-75, on publication, always pays kill fee

Guidelines: *ceai.org/tov-writers-guidelines*

Sample: download from website

Tip: "Our published writers are able to integrate secular and spiritual insights; faithful to the teachings of Scripture; mindful of our audience (Christian educators); up-to-date on trends in contemporary education; positive, encouraging, and inspiring; focused on education in general or how the issue's theme relates to education; clear, concise, and creative."

TESTIMONY/ENRICH

2450 Milltower Ct., Mississauga, ON L5N 5Z6, Canada | 905-542-7400
testimony@paoc.org | *www.testimony.paoc.org*
Stacey McKenzie, editor

Parent company: Pentecostal Assemblies of Canada

Type: bimonthly print magazine

Audience: general

Purpose: to celebrate what God is doing in and through the Fellowship, while offering encouragement to believers by providing a window into the struggles that everyday Christians often encounter

Submissions: Query first by email. Length: 800-1,000 words. Responds in six to eight weeks. Seasonal four months ahead. Bible: NIV.

Types of manuscripts: personal experience, interviews, sidebars

Rights: first

Payment: unspecified

Guidelines: *testimony.paoc.org/submit*

Tip: "Our readership is 98% Canadian. We prefer Canadian writers or at least writers who understand that Canadians are not Americans in long underwear. We also give preference to members of this denomination, since this is related to issues concerning our fellowship."

TIME OF SINGING: A JOURNAL OF CHRISTIAN POETRY

PO Box 5276, Conneaut Lake, PA 16316
timesing@zoominternet.net | *www.timeofsinging.com*
Lora Homan Zill, editor

Parent organization: Wind & Water Press
Type: quarterly print journal, circulation 250
Audience: general
Purpose: to reflect on our walk with God through the art and craft of poetry, to create a community of creative people who loves both the written and living Word and shares a Christian worldview
Submissions: Prefers poems without religious jargon, that show and don't tell, and take creative chances with faith and our walk with God. Unsolicited freelance: 95%. Length: 40 lines maximum. Send complete manuscript by mail or email. Responds in three months. Seasonal six months ahead. Accepts simultaneous submissions. Buys 150 per year.
Types of manuscripts: poetry, assigned reviews of poetry books published by *Time Of Singing* poets
Topics: our walk with God, nature, the human condition, any topic
Rights: first, reprint (tell when/where published)
Payment: none
Guidelines: *www.timeofsinging.com/guidelines.html*
Sample: $4 each or 2/$7 (checks, money orders payable to Wind & Water Press)
Tip: "Study the craft of poetry. If you don't read poetry, you can't write it. I don't publish sermons that rhyme or greeting-card type poetry. *Time Of Singing* is a literary poetry journal. I love poets who think outside the theological box and challenge my assumptions. We don't write or read poetry to find answers but to wrestle with the questions."

TODAY'S CHRISTIAN LIVING

PO Box 5000, Iola, WI 54945 | 800-223-3161, 715-445-5000
dan@jpmediallc.com | *www.todayschristianliving.org*
Dan Brownell, editor

Type: bimonthly print and digital magazine
Audience: general
Purpose: to challenge Christians in their faith, so they may be strengthened to fulfill the call of God in their lives
Submissions: Prefers complete manuscripts; discourages queries. Personality and ministry profiles, 1,400-1,600 words plus sidebar of 150-250 words. Personal story/anecdote 670-700 words. "Grace Notes," how important biblical principles and attributes are illustrated in everyday life, 650-700 words. Hospitality,

inspirational story plus recipe, 700-1,500 words. Humorous anecdotes, 50-200 words.

Types of manuscripts: personal experience, profiles, recipes, humor
Rights: all
Payment: $25-150, after publication
Guidelines: *todayschristianliving.org/writers-guidelines*
Sample: on the website

TRUTH ALIVE

truthalive@sathyam.org | sathyam.org/truth-alive
Dr. C. V. Vadavana, chief editor

Parent company: Truth Ministries/Sathyam Publications in India
Type: monthly print and online magazine; circulation 6,000 print, 22,000 online
Submissions: Open to a series.
Types of manuscripts: feature, news, teaching with national and international perspective
Sample: online

U.S. CATHOLIC

205 W. Monroe St., Chicago, IL 60606 | 312-544-8169
submissions@uscatholics.org | www.uscatholic.org
Emily Sanna, managing editor

Denomination: Catholic
Type: monthly print magazine
Audience: denomination
Submissions: Email manuscripts. Responds in six to eight weeks. Seasonal six months in advance. Features that go beyond basic reporting by offering analysis and interpretation of the issues, 2,500-3,500 words. Essays, 800 to 1,600 words, present thoughtful reflections or opinions on concerns Catholics face in everyday life. "Practicing Catholic," 1,100 words with short sidebar, reflects on the meaning of a particular prayer practice. "Sounding Board" opinion piece, 1,400 words. Profiles, 800 words; reviews, 315 words; fiction, 1,500 words.
Types of manuscripts: essays, profiles, features, short stories, poetry, reviews
Payment: $75-500
Guidelines: *www.uscatholic.org/writers-guide*

VIBRANT LIFE

PO Box 5353, Nampa, ID 83653-5353 | 208-465-2584
email through website | www.vibrantlife.com

Heather Quintana, editor

Parent company: Pacific Press Publishing Association
Denomination: Seventh-day Adventist
Type: bimonthly print magazine
Audience: general
Purpose: to promote physical health, mental clarity, and spiritual balance from a practical, Christian perspective
Submissions: Send complete manuscript by email as attachment or by mail. Short articles, 450-650 words; feature articles, to 1,000 words plus a sidebar if informational.
Types of manuscripts: teaching, interviews, profiles, personal experiences, how-to, sidebar
Topics: health, exercise, nutrition
Rights: first, reprint
Payment: $100-300, on acceptance
Guidelines: *www.vibrantlife.com/writers-guidelines-2*
Tip: "Information must be reliable—no faddism. Articles should represent the latest findings on the subject, and if scientific in nature, should be properly documented. (References to other lay journals are generally not acceptable.)"

VICTORIOUS WOMEN IN CHRIST MAGAZINE

2310 S. Green Bay Rd., Ste. C #503, Racine, WI 53406
contactvwmag@gmail.com | www.victoriouswomenmag.org
Semone Love, executive director

Type: quarterly print and digital magazine
Submissions: Length: maximum 500 words. Email as attachment in Microsoft Word.
Types of manuscripts: short stories, articles, poetry, personal experience
Topics: looking for women who have a faith-based story of victory
Rights: onetime
Payment: none

WAR CRY

615 Slaters Ln., PO Box 269, Alexandria, VA 22314 | 703-684-5500
thewarcry.org
Jeff McDonald, editorial director

Denomination: Salvation Army
Type: monthly print and digital magazine plus special Christmas and Easter issues; circulation 185,000 in general, 1.7 million at

Christmas, 1 million at Easter; takes ads

Audience: denomination plus general

Purpose: to represent the Army's mission of preaching the gospel of Jesus Christ and meeting human needs in His name without discrimination

Submissions: Length: 500-1,500 words. Seasonal six months in advance. Unsolicited freelance: 25%. Buys eighty per year. Email complete manuscript through online form. Responds in one month. Simultaneous OK. Seasonal six months ahead. Bible: NLT.

Types of manuscripts: features, short stories, fillers, sidebars, testimony

Topics: parenting, Christian life, evangelism, profiles, Christ and culture, contemporary issues, apologetics from Wesleyan perspective

Rights: first, reprint (tell when/where published), electronic

Payment: 35¢/word, 15¢/word for reprints, on acceptance

Guidelines and theme list: *thewarcry.org/submission-guidelines*

Sample: *thewarcry.org/magazines*

Tip: Needs Thanksgiving and other seasonal articles.

WORD&WAY

PO Box 1771, Jefferson City, MO 65102-1771 | 573-635-5939
bkaylor@wordandway.org | *wordandway.org*
Brian Kaylor, editor

Denomination: Baptist

Type: monthly print magazine

Audience: denomination, general

Purpose: to accurately inform Baptists and others of relevant news, promote the work of Christ, and encourage inspirational living

Submissions: Email for needs.

Sample: click link on *www.wordandway.org/advertise*

7

TEEN/YOUNG ADULT MARKETS

BOUNDLESS

8605 Explorer Dr., Colorado Springs, CO 80920 | 719-531-3400
editor@boundless.org | *www.boundless.org*
Lisa Anderson, director

Parent company: Focus on the Family
Type: website and articles; circulation 300,000 visitors per month
Audience: single adults in 20s and 30s
Purpose: to help Christian young adults grow up, own their faith, date with purpose, and prepare for marriage and family
Submissions: Rarely accepts unsolicited articles but open to considering new writers. To get an assignment, send a sample or two of your writing, a link to your blog, and a proposal of what you're interested in writing about. Length: 1,200 words. Accepts unsolicited blog posts 500-800 words; email manuscript.
Bible: prefers ESV
Types of manuscripts: articles and blog posts
Topics: fit in these three categories: (1) adulthood: being single, career, family, money; (2) faith: spiritual growth, ministry; (3) relationships: dating, marriage, sexuality, community
Rights: all
Guidelines: *www.boundless.org/write-for-us*
Tip: "Aim to engage our readers' hearts, as we're primarily in the business of affecting lives, not changing society. Use personal stories as illustrations and to spark our readers' imaginations."

THE BRINK

See entry in "**Daily Devotional Booklets and Websites.**"

BRIO

8605 Explorer Dr., Colorado Springs, CO 80920 | 719-531-3400
submissions@briomagazine.com | *focusonthefamily.com/parenting/*
   brio-magazine
Pam Woody, editorial director, editor@briomagazine.com

   Parent company: Focus on the Family
   Type: bimonthly magazine, circulation 60,000
   Audience: teen girls
   Purpose: to provide inspiring stories, fashion insights, fun profiles,
   and practical tips, all from a biblical worldview
   Submissions: Email as Word attachment. Fiction must be complete
   mansuscript. Length: 200-1,400 words.
   Types of manuscripts: fiction, articles, profiles
   Topics: seasonal, girl-like-me profile (1,200-1,400 words), character
   trait (650-750 words), entertainment/social media (800-900
   words), prayer (200-300 words), relationships (800-900 words)
   Rights: first
   Payment: minimum 30¢/word, on acceptance
   Guidelines: *media.focusonthefamily.com/brio/pdf/brio-writers-*
   guidelines-2019.pdf
   Sample: *www.focusonthefamily.com/parenting/brio-magazine*
   Tip: "We are looking for unique and interesting nonfiction articles,
   especially stories about real-life teen girls. Every article should
   have a Christian emphasis, though it shouldn't be preachy or
   overbearing. The topics, concepts, and vocabulary should be
   appropriate for our teen audience."

GIRLZ 4 CHRIST

Medford, OR

G4Csubmissions@gmail.com | *Girlz4Christ.org*
Jessica Lippe, editor/publisher, Girlz4christ@yahoo.com

   Type: quarterly print and digital magazine, circulation 2,000, takes ads
   Audience: teen girls
   Purpose: to provide uplifting, quality media options to girls around
   the world
   Submissions: Email complete manuscript as attachment. Accepts
   submissions from teens. Freelance: 100%. Accepts fifty
   manuscripts per year. Length: 100-1,000 words. Seasonal: two to
   three months in advance.
   Types of manuscripts: devotions, interviews, games, how-to, short
   stories, sidebars, columns, fillers, reviews

Topics: fit one of these sections: "Godly Girlz," "Girlz in Action," "Beautiful Girlz," "Fun 4 Girlz"; beauty, health, fashion
Rights: all
Payment: free product
Guidelines: *girlz4christ.org/submissions*
Theme list: "Girlz 4 Christ Contributors" Facebook group
Sample: Join "Girlz 4 Christ Contributors" on Facebook, or order from *girlz4christ.org/print-copies*
Tip: "Read our magazines and books."

LOVE IS MOVING

9821 Leslie St., Ste. 103, Richmond Hill, ON L4B 3Y4, Canada | 905-479-5885
Ilana@loveismoving.ca | *www.loveismoving.ca*
Ilana Reimer, editor

Parent company: The Evangelical Fellowship of Canada
Type: bimonthly print and digital magazine; circulation 8,000 print, 2,000 online; takes ads
Audience: teens and young adults
Purpose: to encourage young adults to express their faith creatively to increase their passion for Jesus and compassion for people
Submissions: Email query letter as attachment. Unsolicited freelance: 30%. Buys 115 manuscripts per year. Length: 700-1,500 words. Seasonal four months in advance. Responds in five days. Bible: NIV.
Types of manuscripts: personal experience, opinion pieces, music/book review
Topic: Christian living, biblical and cultural literacy, evangelism, artist spotlight, ministry stories
Rights: first, reprint (tell when/where published), electronic
Payment: none
Guidelines: *loveismoving.ca/about/contribute*
Theme list: email *Katie@loveismoving.ca*
Sample: *faithtoday.ca/Subscribe-LIM*
Tip: "Best to have a Canadian angle or Canadian content."

PEER

615 Sisters Ln., Alexandria, VA 22314 | 703-684-5500
peer@usn.salvationarmy.org | *peermag.org*
Captain Jamie Satterlee, editor

Denomination: The Salvation Army

Type: monthly print and digital magazine; circulation 30,000, 1400 digital

Audience: 16-22 years old

Purpose: to ignite a faith conversation that will deepen biblical perspective, faith, and holy living by addressing topics related to faith, community, and culture

Submissions: Email complete manuscript, or submit it through the website. To get an assignment, have a website/portfolio. Length: 800-1,200 words. Responds in one day. Submit at least three months in advance of theme issue. Bible: NLT.

Types of manuscripts: articles, profile

Topics: faith, current events, Christian living, culture

Rights: first, reprint (tell when and where published)

Payment: 35¢/word, 15¢/word for reprints

Guidelines and theme list: *peermag.org/contribute*

TAKE 5 PLUS

See entry in "**Daily Devotional Booklets and Websites.**"

UNLOCKED

See entry in "**Daily Devotional Booklets and Websites.**"

8

CHILDREN'S MARKETS

CADET QUEST

1333 Alger St. S.E., Grand Rapids, MI 49507 | 616-241-5616
submissions@CalvinistCadets.org |
www.CalvinistCadets.org/cadet-quest-magazine
Steve Bootsma, editor

Parent company: Calvinist Cadet Corps
Type: print magazine, 7x/year; 24 pages; circulation 6,000
Audience: boys ages 9-14
Purpose: to help boys grow more Christlike in all areas of life
Submissions: Unsolicited freelance: 5-10%. Buys 20 manuscripts per year. Mail complete manuscript, or email it in body of message. Accepts manuscripts from kids and teens. Length: 1,000-1,500 words. Bible: NIV. Responds four months before publication.
Types of manuscripts: short stories, projects, puzzles, profiles
Topics: theme-related, profiles of Christian athletes, sports, camping, nature
Rights: first, reprint, all
Payment: at least 5¢/word
Guidelines and theme list: download from website
Sample: download from website
Tip: "Looking for fun fiction, without being preachy, for preteen boys. It needs to have some action, and don't be cliché with a Jesus-always-wins type of ending."

DEVOKIDS

See entry in "**Daily Devotional Booklets and Websites.**"

FOCUS ON THE FAMILY CLUBHOUSE

8605 Explorer Dr., Colorado Springs, CO 80920 | 719-531-3400
Rachel.Pfeiffer@fotf.org | *focusonthefamily.com/clubhouse-magazine*
Rachel Pfeiffer, assistant editor

Parent company: Focus on the Family
Type: monthly print magazine with online extras, 32 pages, circulation 80,000, takes ads
Audience: children ages 8-12
Purpose: to inspire, entertain, and teach Christian values to children
Submissions: Unsolicited freelance: 15%. Length: 500-2,000 words. Buys eighty manuscripts per year. Mail complete manuscript. Responds in three months. Seasonal eight months ahead. Accepts submissions from children and teens. Bible: HCSB. Once an author publishes with us three or more times, we often begin to give assignments. We also give assignments to writers whom we meet at Christian writers conferences.
Types of manuscripts: nonfiction, short stories, crafts, recipes, quizzes, interviews
Topics: personality stories of ordinary kids doing something extraordinary, Christian living, apologetics
Rights: first
Payment: 15-25¢ per word, on acceptance, kill fee sometimes
Guidelines: *focusonthefamily.com/clubhouse-magazine/about/ submission-guidelines*
Sample: 9x12 SASE with check for $3.99 made out to Focus on the Family
Tip: "Study the magazine to learn the voice and style. Best way to break in is through nonfiction, especially 'Truth Pursuer' and kid-profile articles."

FOCUS ON THE FAMILY CLUBHOUSE JR.

8605 Explorer Dr., Colorado Springs, CO 80920 | 719-531-3400
Kate.Jameson@fotf.org | focusonthefamily.com/clubhouse-jr-magazine
Kate Jameson, assistant editor

Parent company: Focus on the Family
Type: monthly print magazine with online extras, 32 pages, circulation 50,000, ads
Audience: children ages 3-7
Purpose: to inspire, entertain, and teach Christian values to children
Submissions: Unsolicited freelance: 15%. Buys fifty manuscripts per year. Length: 400-1,000 words. Mail complete manuscript. Responds in three months. Seasonal eight months ahead. Bible: NIrV. Accepts submissions from children and teens. Once an author publishes with us three or more times, we often begin to give assignments. We also give assignments to writers whom we meet at Christian writers conferences.

Types of manuscripts: Bible stories, kid profiles, nature/animal stories, recipes, crafts, short stories, poetry, activities, rebus, interviews, biographies

Topics: ordinary kids doing something extraordinary, Christian life

Rights: first

Payment: 15-25¢ per word, on acceptance

Guidelines: *focusonthefamily.com/clubhouse-jr-magazine/about/ submission-guidelines*

Theme list: by email

Sample: 9x12 SASE with check for $3.99 made out to Focus on the Family

Tip: "Read the magazine to learn our style and reading level. Aim at early and beginning readers. Rebus and Bible stories are a great way to break in."

GUIDE

PO Box 5353, Nampa, ID 83653-5353
guide.magazine@pacificpress.com | *www.guidemagazine.org*
Lori Futcher, editor

Denomination: Seventh-day Adventist

Parent company: Pacific Press Publishing Association

Type: weekly take-home paper, circulation 26,000

Audience: ages 10-14

Purpose: to show readers, through stories that illustrate Bible truth, how to walk with God now and forever

Submissions: Prefers complete manuscript. Submit online or by mail with SASE. Responds in four to six weeks. Seasonal eight months in advance. Accepts submissions from teens 14 and older. Bible: NKJV.

Types of manuscripts: true stories 1,000-1,200 words (some shorter pieces 450 words and up), sometimes accepts quizzes and other unique nonstory formats; must include a clear spiritual element

Topics: adventure, personal growth, humor, inspiration (answers to prayer, biblical narratives, mission stories, and examples of young people living out their Christian beliefs), biography, nature

Rights: first, reprint (tell when and where published)

Payment: 7-10¢ per word, $25-40 for games and puzzles, on acceptance

Guidelines: *www.guidemagazine.org/writers-guidelines*

Sample: download from guidelines page

Tip: "Use your best short-story techniques (dialogue, scenes, a sense of plot) to tell a true story starring a kid age 10-14. Bring out a clear spiritual/biblical message. We publish multipart true stories regularly, two to twelve parts, 1,200 words each. All topics indicated need to be addressed within the context of a true story."

KEYS FOR KIDS
See entry in "**Daily Devotional Booklets and Websites.**"

LIVING FAITH FOR KIDS
See entry in "**Daily Devotional Booklets and Websites.**"

NATURE FRIEND
4253 Woodcock Ln., Dayton, VA 22821 | 540-867-0764
editor@naturefriendmagazine.com | *www.naturefriendmagazine.com*
Kevin Shank, editor

> **Parent company:** Dogwood Ridge Outdoors
> **Type:** monthly print magazine, 28 pages, circulation 10,000
> **Audience:** ages 6-14, 80% are ages 8-12
> **Purpose:** to increase awareness of God and appreciation for God's works and gifts, to teach accountability toward God's works, and to teach natural truths and facts
> **Submissions:** Freelance: 55%. Mail complete manuscript with SASE, or email as attachment. Length: 500-800 words. Buys forty to fifty per year. Seasonal four months in advance. Accepts simultaneous submissions. Bible: KJV only.
> **Rights:** first, reprint
> **Payment:** 5¢/edited word, 3¢/word for reprints, on publication
> **Types:** crafts, projects, experiments, fiction, articles, photo features
> **Topics:** nature-related, science experiments, stories about people interacting with nature or about an animal, nature-friendly gardening, nature photography lessons, survival/wilderness first-aid, weather, astronomy, flowers, marine life
> **Guidelines:** *naturefriendmagazine.com/index.pl?linkid=12;class=gen*
> **Sample:** *www.naturefriendmagazine.com/index.pl?linkid=4;class=gen*
> **Tip:** "While talking animals can be interesting and teach worthwhile lessons, we have chosen to not use them in *Nature Friend*. Excluded are puzzle-type submissions such as 'Who Am I?'"

OUR LITTLE FRIEND
PO Box 5353, Nampa, ID 83653
anita.seymour@pacificpress.com | *primarytreasure.com*
Anita Seymour, managing editor

Denomination: Seventh-day Adventist
Parent company: Pacific Press Publishing Association
Type: weekly take-home paper, circulation 16,000
Audience: ages 1-5
Purpose: to teach about Jesus and the Christian life
Submissions: Length: one to two double-spaced pages. Email complete manuscript as attached file. Seasonal eight to nine months ahead. Responds in four weeks. Buys fifty-two per year. Bible: ICB or NIrV.
Payment: $25-50, on acceptance
Rights: onetime, electronic
Type of manuscripts: true stories
Topics: Christian life, God's love, seasonal, nature; see list in guidelines
Guidelines: *primarytreasure.com/for-writers*
Theme list: by mail with SASE
Sample: for 9x12 SAE
Tip: "We need true, age-appropriate stories that teach about the Christian life."

PRIMARY TREASURE
PO Box 5353, Nampa, ID 83653
anita.seymour@pacificpress.com | www.primarytreasure.com
Anita Seymour, managing editor
    Denomination: Seventh-day Adventist
Parent company: Pacific Press Publishing Association
Type: weekly take-home paper, circulation 14,000
Audience: ages 6-9
Purpose: to teach children about the love of God and the Christian life through true stories
Submissions: Freelance: 80%. Buys 104 per year. Email complete manuscript as attached file. Length: three to five double-spaced pages. Seasonal eight months ahead. Responds in four weeks.
Type of manuscripts: true stories
Topics: Christian life, seasonal, nature; see list in guidelines
Rights: onetime, electronic
Payment: $25-50, on acceptance
Guidelines: *primarytreasure.com/for-writers*
Theme list: by mail with SASE
Sample: for 9x12 SAE
Tip: "We need age-appropriate stories that teach about Jesus and the Christian life."

Christian Writers Institute
Featured Course

Writing Children's Short Stories by Lurlene McDaniel

Normal price: $4
Savings: 100%
Market guide price: FREE

https://cwmg.link/children2021

How to Scan QR Codes
Use the camera on your smartphone to focus on the above QR code to activate the discount. It will give you the option to visit the site, which you will want to accept. If you are using an older smartphone, you may need to download a QR-code scanning app. You can also visit the URL below the code to activate the discount on your computer.

9

WRITERS MARKETS

FELLOWSCRIPT

PO Box 99509, Edmonton, AB T5B 0E1, Canada
fseditor@gmail.com | www.inscribe.org/fellowscript
Nina Morey, editor-in-chief

Parent company: InScribe Christian Writers' Fellowship
Type: quarterly PDF and print magazine; circulation 200;
subscription free with InScribe membership; ads
Audience: members of InScribe Christian Writers' Fellowship
Purpose: to provide support, inspiration, and instruction and provide
members with an opportunity to submit work
Submissions: Submit complete manuscript by email. Pays 3¢ per
word (Canadian funds) for onetime rights, 1.5¢ per word for
reprint rights, extra .5¢ for publication with author's permission
on the website for no more than three months. Pays by PayPal on
publication.
Types of manuscripts: Feature articles, 750 words; columns, 300-
600 words; reviews, 150-300 words; fillers/tips, 25-500 words;
general articles, 700 words. Responds in four weeks. Submission
deadlines are February 1, May 1, August 1, and November 1. Plans
six months ahead.
Guidelines: *inscribe.org/fellowscript/submission-guidelines*
Tip: "We always prefer material specifically slanted toward the needs
and interests of Canadian Christian writers. We give preference to
members and to Canadian writers."

FREELANCE WRITER'S REPORT

PO Box A, North Stratford, NH 03590 | 603-922-8338
info@writers-editors.com | www.writers-editors.com
Dana K. Cassell, editor

Parent company: Writers-Editor Network
Type: monthly online and print newsletter; subscription $39-49

Audience: established writers

Purpose: to help serious, professional freelance writers—whether full-time or part-time—improve their earnings and profits from their editorial businesses

Submissions: Freelance: 25%. Complete manuscript by email as attachment or copied into message. Pays 10¢ per edited word on publication for onetime rights. Responds within one week. Seasonal two months ahead. Accepts simultaneous submissions and reprints (tell when/where appeared).

Types of manuscripts: The bulk of the content is market news and marketing information—how to build a writing/editing business, how to maximize income. Articles to 900 words, fifty per year. Prose fillers to 400 words. Likes bulleted lists.

Guidelines: *www.writers-editors.com/Writers/Membership/Writer_Guidelines/writer_guidelines.htm*

Sample: *freelancekeys.com/samplecopy*

Tip: "No articles on the basics of freelancing since readers are established freelancers. Looking for marketing and business-building for freelance writers, editors, and book authors."

POETS & WRITERS

90 Broad St., Ste. 2100, New York, NY 10004-2272 | 212-226-3586

editor@pw.org | *www.pw.org*

Melissa Faliveno, senior editor

Parent company: Poets & Writers, Inc.

Type: bimonthly print magazine; circulation 100,000; subscription $12.00; ads

Audience: emerging to established literary writers

Purpose: to provide practical guidance for getting published and pursuing writing careers

Submissions: Query with clips via email or mail. Pays $150-500 for exclusive worldwide, periodical publication and syndication rights in all languages and nonexclusive reprint rights shared 50/50 thereafter. Pays when scheduled for production. Responds in four to six weeks.

Types of manuscripts: "News & Trends," 500-1,200 words; "The Literary Life," essays, 1,500-2,500 words; "The Practical Writer," how-to and advice, 1,500-2,500 words; profiles and interviews, 2,000-3,000 words (35 per year)

Guidelines: *www.pw.org/about-us/submission_guidelines*

Sample: sold at large bookstores and online

Tip: Most open to "News & Trends," "The Literary Life," and "The Practical Writer."

STORY EMBERS

140 Churchill Ln., Mount Airy, NC 27030 | 724-290-8099

submissions@storyembers.org | *storyembers.org*

Josiah DeGraaf, editor-in-chief, josiah@storyembers.org

Brianna Storm Hilvety, managing editor, brianna@storyembers.org

Daeus Lamb, poetry editor, daeus@storyembers.org

> **Type:** digital magazine updated two times a week, 30,000 page views per month; ads
>
> **Audience:** Christian writers
>
> **Purpose:** to help Christian writers enthrall readers through honest storytelling that fearlessly grapples with hard issues
>
> **Submissions:** Email as attachment. Rights: first. No payment. Unsolicited freelance: 40%. Buys 100 manuscripts per year. Length: articles, 750-3,000 words; fiction, 1,000-5,000 words; poetry, 100-500 words. Responds in three weeks.
>
> **Types of manuscripts:** how-to on writing, especially fiction; also takes fiction and poetry
>
> **Guidelines:** *storyembers.org/submissions*
>
> **Sample:** see the website
>
> **Tip:** "In our fiction, we're looking for stories that honestly depict the human experience as it is and that grapple with Christian themes without being simplistic or heavy-handed. In our nonfiction, we're looking for articles that delve into specific writing subjects in-depth in a practical way."

WORDS FOR THE WAY

5042 E. Cherry Hills Blvd., Springfield, MO 65809 | 417-812-5232

OzarksACW@yahoo.com | *www.ozarksacw.org*

Renee Srch, managing editor

Jeanetta Chrystie, acquisitions editor

> **Parent company:** Ozarks Chapter of American Christian Writers
>
> **Type:** bimonthly (5x) print and digital newsletter; circulation 60; subscription $10; ads
>
> **Audience:** writers at all levels
>
> **Purpose:** to encourage and educate Christians to follow their call to write and learn to write well
>
> **Submissions:** Freelance: 95%. Buys forty-five manuscripts per year.

Seasonal two months in advance. Responds in one month. Email query or complete manuscript as attachment with brief bio and photo. No payment for reprint and electronic rights. Responds in three weeks. Seasonal two months ahead.

Types of manuscripts: Length: 500-1,000 words. All submissions must speak to writing, the writing life, how to write better, etc., including any poetry or fillers. Personal experience: writing stories that teach something about the writing life. Encouragement to follow God's call to write. Poetry, sidebars, columns, fillers. Stories only from spring contest. Any Bible version.

Guidelines: *www.OzarksACW.org/guidelines.php*

Sample: request by email

Tip: "Write clearly about writing. Focus on a single topic per submission. Think 'What would help or encourage Christian writers and want-to-be writers?' and write your piece to help them."

THE WRITER

Editorial, Madavor Media, 25 Braintree Hill Office Park, Ste. 404, Braintree, MA 02184
tweditorial@madavor.com | *www.writermag.com*
Nicki Porter, senior editor

Parent company: Madavor Media

Type: monthly print and digital magazine; circulation 30,000; subscription $32.95; ads

Audience: writers at all levels

Purpose: to expand and support the work of professional and aspiring writers with a straightforward presentation of industry information, writing instruction, and professional and personal motivation

Submissions: Unsolicited freelance: 80%. Query first with short bio. Query for features six months ahead. No reprints. Pay varies by type and department on acceptance for first rights. If no response in two weeks, probably not interested.

Types of manuscripts: Primarily looking for how-to articles on the craft of writing. Also has a variety of columns and departments: "Breakthrough," first-person articles about a writer's experience in breaking through to publication, 1,000 words; "Writing Essentials," basics of the craft of writing, 1,000 words plus a short sidebar of resources; "Market Focus," reports on specific market areas, 1,000 words; "Off the Cuff," essays on a particular aspect of writing or the writing life, 1,000 words; "Poet to Poet," how-to on writing poetry, 500-750 words; "Take Note," topical items of literary interest, 200-500 words; "Writer at Work," specific writing problem and how it was successfully overcome on the way to publication, 750-1,500 words. Uses some sidebars.

Guidelines: *www.writermag.com/the-magazine/submission-guidelines*
Sample: sold at large bookstores
Tips: "Personal essays must provide takeaway advice and benefits for writers. Include plenty of how-to, advice, and tips on techniques. Be specific. All topics must relate to writing."

THE WRITER'S CHRONICLE

5245 Greenbelt Rd, Box #246, College Park, MD 20740 | 301-226-9710
chronicle@awpwriter.org | *www.awpwriter.org/magazine_media/writers_
chronicle_overview*
Supriya Bhatnagar, editor

Parent company: Association of Writers & Writing Programs
Type: bimonthly print and digital magazine during academic year; circulation 35,000; subscription $20; ads
Audience: serious writers, writing students and teachers
Purpose: to provide diverse insights into the art of writing that are accessible, pragmatic, and idealistic for serious writers
Submissions: Unsolicited freelance: 90%. Submit via website portal. Pays $18 per 100 words for first and electronic rights on publication. Responds in three months.
Types of manuscripts: Interviews, 3,000-5,000 words; profiles and appreciations of contemporary writers, 2,000-5,000 words; essays on the craft of writing, 2,500-5,000 words. Uses some sidebars. Also buys blog posts year round for *The Writer's Notebook*, 500-1,500 words, $100 per post.
Guidelines: *www.awpwriter.org/magazine_media/submission_
guidelines*
Tip: "Keep in mind that 18,000 of our 35,000 readers are students or just-emerging writers."

WRITER'S DIGEST

4445 Lake Forest Dr., Ste. 407, Blue Ash, OH 45242
wdsubmissions@aimmedia.com | *www.writersdigest.com*
Amy Jones, editor-in-chief

Parent company: Active Interest Media
Type: print magazine, eight issues/year; circulation 60,000;

subscription $19.96; ads

Audience: aspiring and professional writers

Purpose: to celebrate the writing life and what it means to be a writer in today's publishing environment

Submissions: Unsolicited freelance, 20%; assigned, 60%. Email query or manuscript in the message; no attachments. Responds in two to four months. Pays 30-50¢ per word on acceptance for first and electronic rights. No reprints.

Types of manuscripts: "Inkwell," opinion pieces, 800-900 words and short how-to pieces, trends, humor, 300-600 words; "5-Minute Memoir," 600-word essay reflections on the writing life; author profiles, 800-2,000 words; articles on writing techniques, 1,000-2,400 words; market reports. Seasonal eight months ahead. Requires requested manuscript by email, copied into message. Kill fee 25%. Regularly uses sidebars.

Guidelines: *www.writersdigest.com/submission-guidelines*; theme list: *www.writersdigest.com/advertise/editorialcalendar*

Sample: available at newsstands and through *www.writersdigestshop.com*

Tip: "Although we welcome the work of new writers, we believe the established writer can better instruct our readers. Please include your publishing credentials related to your topic with your submission."

WRITERSWEEKLY.COM

200 2nd Avenue S. #526, St. Petersburg, FL 33710 | 305-768-0261
Brian@booklocker.com | *www.writersweekly.com*
Brian Whiddon, managing editor
Angela Hoy, publisher

Parent company: BookLocker.com, Inc.

Type: weekly digital newsletter; circulation 30,000; free

Audience: writers seeking to make more money from their writing

Purpose: to feature paying markets (making more money through writing), as well as give publishing advice

Submissions: Freelance: 75%. Buys 200 per year. Length: 600 words. Email query letter in body of the message; don't send manuscript until requested. Seasonal two months in advance. Responds in one week. Simultaneous OK. Pays $60 on acceptance and only via PayPal for first or reprint nonexclusive rights. Pays kill fee.

Types of manuscripts: feature articles on how to make more money writing, articles on paying Christian markets for writers, features that teach book-marketing techniques, book and author backstories

Guidelines: *writersweekly.com/writersweekly-com-writers-guidelines*

Sample: on website

Tip: "Please review our guidelines and website before querying us. We require specific queries targeting our readership. Please do not send a message simply asking if you can write for us. Send an idea for an article."

WRITING CORNER

410-536-4610

writingcorner@bizconcepts.com | writingcorner.com

Type: website

Audience: writers at all levels

Purpose: to provide concrete, useful advice from those who have been in the trenches and made a successful journey with their writing

Submissions: Responds in two days. Send queries and manuscripts via email only. Accepts reprints. No payment for nonexclusive rights; regular contributors get free sidebar ads on the site. Length: 600-900 words.

Types of manuscripts: Open to how-to articles on writing fiction and nonfiction, writing life, tips and tricks, basic and advance writing techniques.

Guidelines: *writingcorner.com/main-pages/submission-guidelines*

Tip: "Our site visitors are from all areas of writing, so keep that audience in mind when writing for us."

PART 4

SPECIALTY MARKETS

10

DAILY DEVOTIONAL BOOKLETS AND WEBSITES

Note that most of these markets assign all manuscripts. If there is no information listed on getting an assignment, request a sample copy and writers guidelines if they are not on the website. Then write two or three sample devotions to fit that particular format, and send them to the editor with a request for an assignment.

THE BRINK

114 Bush Rd., Nashville, TN 37217 | 800-877-7030, 615-361-1221
thebrink@randallhouse.com | *www.thebrinkonline.com*
David Jones, young adult editor

Denomination: Free Will Baptist
Parent company: Randall House
Audience: college students and young adults
Type: quarterly print
Details: Devotions are by assignment only to coordinate with the curriculum. For feature articles, such as interviews, stories, and opinion pieces, email query with 100-200-word excerpt if available. Does not respond unless interested. Rights: all.
Guidelines: *thebrinkonline.com/contact*

CHRIST IN OUR HOME

PO Box 1209, Minneapolis, MN 55440-1209 | 800-328-4648
afsubmissions@1517.media | *www.augsburgfortress.org*
Denomination: Evangelical Lutheran Church in America

Audience: adults
Type: quarterly print, email, audio
Details: Assignment only. Submit sample devotions as explained in the guidelines. Length: 1190 characters, including spaces, maximum. Rights: all. Bible version: NRSV.
Guidelines: download from *ms.augsburgfortress.org/downloads/ Submission%20Guidelines.pdf?redirected=true*
Tip: "*Christ in Our Home* is read by people in many nations, so avoid thinking only in terms of those who live in the U.S."

CHRISTIANDEVOTIONS.US

PO Box 6494, Kingsport, TN 37663 | 423-384-4821
christiandevotionsministries@gmail.com | *www.ChristianDevotions.us*
Martin Wiles, managing editor
Cindy Sproles, executive editor

Parent company: Christian Devotions Ministries
Audience: adults, teens
Type: daily website
Details: Accepts freelance submissions. Length: 300-400 words. Email as attached Word document. Payment: none. Rights: onetime, reprint. Bible version: author's choice, must be referenced.
Guidelines: *www.christiandevotions.us/writeforus*
Tip: "Follow our guidelines."

DEVOKIDS

sandramillerhart@gmail.com | *devokids.com*
Sandra Miller Hart, executive editor

Parent company: Christian Devotions Ministries
Audience: kids ages 6-12
Type: website
Details: Takes freelance submissions. Length: 75-250 words. Email as an attached Word document. Payment: none. Rights: onetime.
Also accepts: submissions from kids
Guidelines: *devokids.com/write-for-us*

DEVOTIONS

www.standardlesson.com/standard-lesson-resources
See *The Quiet Hour* for details.

FORWARD DAY BY DAY

412 Sycamore St., Cincinnati, OH 45202-4110 | 800-543-1813
editorial@forwardmovement.org | *www.forwardmovement.org*
Richelle Thompson, managing editor

Denomination: Episcopal
Audience: adults
Type: quarterly print and online, daily podcast and email
Details: Devotions are written on assignment. To get an assignment, send three sample meditations based on three of the following Bible verses: Psalm 139:21; Mark 8:31; Acts 4:12; Revelation 1:10. Likes author to complete an entire month's worth of devotions. Length: 220 words, including Scripture. Pays $300 for a month of devotions.
Guidelines: *www.forwardmovement.org/Pages/About/Writers-Guidelines.aspx*
Tip: "*Forward Day by Day* is not the place to score points on controversial topics. Occasionally, when the scripture passage pertains to it, an author chooses to say something about such a topic. If you write about a hotbutton issue, do so with humility and make certain your comment shows respect for persons who hold a different view."

FRUIT OF THE VINE

211 N. Meridian St., Ste. 101, Newberg, OR 97132 | 503-538-9775
admin@barclaypress.com | *www.barclaypress.com*
Cleta Crisman, editor

Denomination: Quakers
Parent company: Barclay Press
Audience: adults
Type: quarterly print
Details: Accepts freelance submissions, one week at a time. Length: 250 words. Payment: contributor copies and subscription. Rights: onetime. Bible version: NIV.
Guidelines: *tinyurl.com/y8vwx5gj*
Tip: "We ask writers to submit devotional readings for seven days, starting with Sunday. Writers have the freedom to choose their own themes and Bible readings. It helps to follow a general theme throughout the week. Indicate references for Bible quotations in parentheses in the body of the devotional. If you use a translation other than the New International Version, please indicate the translation for each quotation."

GOD'S WORD FOR TODAY

1445 N. Boonville Ave., Springfield, MO 65802 | 417-862-2781
DDawson@ag.org | *ag.org/Resources/Devotionals/Gods-Word-for-Today*
Dilla Dawson, editor

Denomination: Assemblies of God
Audience: adults
Type: quarterly print, online
Details: Request writers guidelines and sample assignment (unpaid).
After samples are approved, writers will be added to the list for
assignments. Length: 210 words. Payment: $25/devotion. Rights:
all. Bible version: NIV.
Tip: "Writers will receive detailed guidelines upon inquiry."

KEYS FOR KIDS

PO Box 1001, Grand Rapids, MI 49501-1001 | 616-647-4500
editorial@keysforkids.org | *www.keysforkids.org*
Courtney Lasater, editor

Parent company: Keys for Kids Ministries
Audience: children ages 8-12, often used for family devotions
Type: quarterly print, daily online, phone app
Details: Takes only freelance submissions. Submit through the
website. Payment: $30 on acceptance. Rights: all. Length: 375
words. Seasonal four to five months ahead. Bible version: NKJV.
Guidelines: *www.keysforkids.org/writersguidelines*
Tip: "Most of our stories use real-world illustrations to help kids
understand spiritual truth."

LIGHT FROM THE WORD

PO Box 50434, Indianapolis, IN 46250-0434 | 317-774-7900
submissions@wesleyan.org | *www.wesleyan.org/wph*
Susan LeBaron, project communications manager

Denomination: Wesleyan
Audience: adults
Type: quarterly print, daily online
Details: Must be affiliated with The Wesleyan Church. Email three
sample devotions to fit the format and request an assignment. Write
"Devotion Samples" in the subject line. Length: 200-240 words.
Payment: $200 for seven devotions. Rights: all. Bible version: NIV.
Guidelines: *wesleyan.org/wph/writers-guidelines*
Tip: Wesleyan-Armenian doctrine.

LIVING FAITH

PO Box 292824, Kettering, OH 45429 | 800-246-7390
info@livingfaith.com | *livingfaith.com*
Terence Hegarty, editor

- **Denomination:** Catholic
- **Audience:** adults
- **Type:** quarterly print
- **Details:** Assignments only; email one or two samples and credentials to request an assignment.
- **Guidelines:** Click FAQ.
- **Tip:** "*Living Faith* provides daily reflections based on a Scripture passage from the daily Mass. With readings for daily Mass listed at the bottom of each devotion, this booklet helps Catholics pray and meditate in spirit with the seasons of the Church Year."

LIVING FAITH FOR KIDS

PO Box 292824, Kettering, OH 45429 | 800-246-7390
editor@livingfaithkids.com | *livingfaithkids.com*
Connie Clark, editor

- **Denomination:** Catholic
- **Audience:** ages 8-12
- **Type:** quarterly print
- **Details:** Assignments only; email samples and credentials to request an assignment.
- **Guidelines:** *www.livingfaithkids.com/faq.php*
- **Tip:** "*Living Faith for Kids* features daily devotions based on the daily Scripture readings from the Catholic Mass. Each quarterly issue helps children 8-12 develop the habit of daily prayer and build their relationship with Jesus and the Church."

LOVE LINES FROM GOD

128 Leyland Ct., Greenwood, SC 29649 | 864-554-3204
mandmwiles@gmail.com | *www.lovelinesfromgod.com*
Martin Wiles, managing editor

- **Audience:** adults
- **Type:** daily website
- **Details:** Accepts freelance submissions. Length: 400 words. Payment: none. Rights: first. Bible version: NIV.
- **Guidelines:** *lovelinesfromgod.blogspot.com/p/write-for-us_3.html*
- **Tip:** "We are looking for devotions that encourage, not preach.

221

Following the submission guidelines will result in a better chance of having the submission accepted."

PATHWAYS—MOMENTS WITH GOD

2902 Enterprise Dr., Anderson, IN 46013 | 800-741-7721
editors@warnerpress.org | *www.warnerpress.org/curriculum/adult-curriculum/pathways.html*
Kevin Stiffler, editor

Denomination: Church of God
Audience: adults
Type: quarterly print
Details: Written on assignment only. To be considered as a writer, submit a sample devotional. Length: 140-150 words. Should give readers living examples of what the Bible passage is about and how it can apply to life.
Guidelines: *www.warnerpress.org/submission-guidelines*

THE QUIET HOUR

4050 Lee Vance Dr., Colorado Springs, CO 80918
thequiethour@davidccook.com | *www.davidccook.org*
Scott Stewart, editor

Parent company: David C. Cook
Audience: adults
Type: quarterly print
Details: By assignment only. North America postal address is necessary to receive contract and payment. Length: 200 words. Payment: $140 for seven devotions. Rights: all. Bible version: NIV, KJV.
Guidelines: *davidccook.org/wp-content/uploads/2018/02/Devotion-Quiet-Hour-Spec-Devotional-Guidelines.pdf*
Tip: "Submit spec devotional on a key verse you select in a Scripture passage of your choice. Begin with anecdotal opening then transition to relevant biblical insight and encouragement for a life of faith rooted in the key verse."

REFLECTING GOD

PO Box 419527, Kansas City, MO 64141 | 816-931-1900
dcbrush@wordaction.com | *reflectinggod.com*
Duane Brush, editor

Denomination: Nazarene
Audience: adults

Type: daily online

Details: Send a couple of sample devotions to fit the format and request an assignment. Length: 180-200 words. Pays $115 for seven devotions.

Tip: "Our purpose is the pursuit to embrace holy living. We want to foster discussion about what it means to live a holy life in the 21st century."

THE SECRET PLACE

1075 First Ave., King of Prussia, PA 19406 | 610-768-2434
thesecretplace@judsonpress.com | www.judsonpress.com
Ingrid Dvirnak, editor

Denomination: American Baptist

Audience: adults

Type: quarterly print

Details: Accepts freelance submissions; does not give assignments. Length: 200 words. Payment: $20 per devotion. Rights: first, electronic. Bible version: no preference.

Guidelines: *www.judsonpress.com/Content/Site189/ BasicBlocks/10258GUIDELINES_00000128358.pdf*

Tip: "Use less-familiar Bible verses."

TAKE 5 PLUS

1445 N. Boonville Ave., Springfield, MO 65802 | 417-862-2781
rl-take5plus@ag.org | myhealthychurch.com
Wade Quick, wquick@ag.org

Denomination: Assemblies of God

Audience: teens

Type: quarterly print

Details: Assignment only. Request via email writers guidelines and sample assignment (unpaid). After samples are approved, writers will be added to the list for assignments. Length: 210-235 words. Payment: $25 per devotion on acceptance. Rights: all. Bible version: NIV.

Tip: "Study the publication before attempting the sample assignment."

THESE DAYS: DAILY DEVOTIONS FOR LIVING BY FAITH

100 Witherspoon St., Louisville, KY 40202 | 800-624-2412
mlindberg@presbypub.com | www.thethoughtfulchristian.com/Pages/Item/ 59264/These-Days.aspx
Mary Lindberg, editor

Denomination: Presbyterian Church (USA)
Audience: adults
Type: quarterly print
Details: Accepts freelance submissions. Length: 190 words. Payment: $100 or $150 worth of books for seven devotions. Rights: first. Bible version: NRSV.
Tip: "Write thoughtful entries based on a Scripture passage, use gender-inclusive language for God and humanity, and include a brief closing prayer."

UNLOCKED

PO Box 1001, Grand Rapids, MI 49501-1001 | 616-647-4500
editorial@unlocked.org | *www.unlocked.org*
Hannah Howe, editor

Parent company: Keys for Kids Ministries
Audience: teens
Type: quarterly print, online; daily podcast
Details: Accepts only freelance submissions. Payment: $30 on acceptance. Rights: all. Length: devotion, 200-315 words; fiction, 200-350 words; poetry, 16-23 lines. Takes teen writers. Bible version: CSB, NIV, NLT, WEB.
Guidelines: *unlocked.org/writers-guidelines*
Tip: "We are open to styles and genres not typically seen in teen devotionals as long as they fit the overall purpose outlined in our guidelines. We want our devotional pieces to challenge teens and help them wrestle with things they're dealing with, not talk down to them or shy away from deep topics."

THE UPPER ROOM

1908 Grand Ave., Nashville, TN 37212 | 615-340-7252
ureditorial@upperroom.org | *upperroom.org*
Andrew Garland Breeden, acquisitions editor

Denomination: United Methodist
Audience: adults
Type: bimonthly print, daily online
Details: Accepts freelance submissions. Length: 300 words, which include everything on the printed page. Payment: $30 on publication. Rights: first, exclusive for one year. Bible versions: NIV, NRSV, CEB, KJV. Prefers submissions through the website.
Guidelines: *submissions.upperroom.org/en/guidelines*

Tip: "A strong devotional will include three main elements: 1. A personal story or experience. 2. A connection to Scripture. 3. A way for the reader to apply the message to his or her own life."

THE WORD IN SEASON

PO Box 1209, Minneapolis, MN 55440-1209 | 414-963-1222
rochelle@writenowcoach.com | *www.augsburgfortress.org*
Rochelle Melander, managing editor

Denomination: Evangelical Lutheran Church in America
Audience: adults
Type: quarterly print
Details: Assignment only. Email three sample devotions from an ECLA perspective as explained in the guidelines to afsubmissions@1517.media. Length: 1190 characters. Payment: $30 per devotion. Rights: all. Bible version: NRSV.
Guidelines: download from *ms.augsburgfortress.org/downloads/ Submission%20Guidelines.pdf?redirected=true*
Tip: "Use concrete language, use the historical-critical tools to understand the biblical passage, and tell us how this passage applies to our daily lives."

Christian Writers Institute Courses
Devotional Bundle

Courses in this bundle:
- Prepare Your Heart to Be a Writer
- Deeper: Spiritual Formation for the Writer
- How to Write Devotionals
- The Four Cs of a Godly Writer
- The God Factor
- Five Marks of a Christian Writer

Normal price: $96
Savings: 50%
Market guide price: $48

https://cwmg.link/devo2021

How to Scan QR Codes
Use the camera on your smartphone to focus on the above QR code to activate the discount. It will give you the option to visit the site, which you will want to accept. If you are using an older smartphone, you may need to download a QR-code scanning app. You can also visit the URL below the code to activate the discount on your computer.

11

DRAMA

CHRISTIAN PUBLISHERS, LLC

PO Box 248, Cedar Rapids, Iowa 52406 | 319-368-8009
editor@christianpub.com | *www.christianpub.com*
Rhonda Wray, editor

Parent company: Brooklyn Publishers

Audiences: children, teens, adults

Submissions: Submit complete script, preferably through the website form or as an email attachment. Simultaneous submission is OK. Replies in at least three months. Publishes fifteen to thirty scripts per year; receives 250 submissions. Length: prefers 10-30 minutes, occasionally up to an hour.

Types: one-act and full-length plays and musicals, compilation of skits, monologues, readers theater, scripts for children and teens; most scripts are for Advent/Christmas or Lent/Easter

Also publishes: banners

Payment: 10% royalty, often to a fixed amount. No advance.

Guidelines: *www.christianpub.com/default.aspx?pg=ag*

Tip: "We like drama that is so enthralling it doesn't need elaborate productions with complicated sets and hard-to-obtain costumes and props. Scripts that meet a need in the life of a church are also welcome, such as mother-daughter event scripts. We embrace all styles, from humorous to solemn and worshipful. It would be most helpful to go to our website and familiarize yourself with the types of works we carry. Please include a cast list and production notes that share with would-be directors anything they need to know in order to stage your drama effectively."

CSS PUBLISHING GROUP, INC.

See entry in "**Book Publishers.**"

DRAMA MINISTRY

2814 Azalea Pl., Nashville, TN 37204 | 866-859-7622
service@dramaministry.com | *www.dramaministry.com*
Vince Wilcox, general manager

Audiences: children, teens, adults

Submissions: Open to all topics, including seasonal/holidays. Email or mail script. Buys all rights.

Types: only short skits of 2-10 minutes, comedy, drama, monologue, readers theater

ELDRIDGE CHRISTIAN PLAYS & MUSICALS

PO Box 4904, Lancaster, PA 17604 | 850-385-2463
newworks@histage.com | *www.95church.com*
Susan Shore, editor

Audiences: children, teens, adults

Submissions: Publishes fifteen to twenty scripts per year; receives three hundred submissions annually. Length: plays and musicals, minimum 30 minutes. Submit complete script via email. Simultaneous OK. Responds in three months.

Types: full-length plays, one-act plays, compilations of skits, musicals, readers theater, children, teens

Payment: 50% royalty plus 10% copy sales, no advance

Guidelines: *www.95church.com/submission-guidelines*

Tip: "We like all kinds of plays and are always open to new ideas. Generally speaking, our customers like plays with more female than male roles or flexible casting in which roles can be played by either men or women. This is not a hard-and-fast rule, however. We like easy costuming and scenery, if possible, as many church budgets are limited."

GROUP PUBLISHING

See entry in "**Book Publishers.**"

12

GREETING CARDS
AND **GIFTS**

BLUE MOUNTAIN ARTS, INC.

Editorial Dept., PO Box 1007, Boulder, CO 80306 | 303-449-0536
editorial@sps.com | *www.sps.com*

Audience: adults, teens

Products: general publisher with some inspirational greeting cards, calendars, gift books, bookmarks, magnets, wallet cards, miniature prints

Submissions: Looking for contemporary prose or poetry written from personal experience that reflects the thoughts and feelings people today want to communicate to one another but don't always know how to put into words. Have a loved one in mind as you write. Considers writings on special occasions (birthday, anniversary, congratulations, etc.), as well as the challenges and aspirations of life. Not looking for rhymed poetry, religious verse, humor, or one-liners. Length: 50 to 300 words. Buys all rights. Accepts freelance submissions by email, website form, or mail. Responds in two months or not interested. Holiday deadlines: Christmas and general holidays, July 15; Valentine's Day, September 12; Easter, November 8; Mother's Day and graduation, December 13; Father's Day, February 7.

Guidelines: *www.sps.com/greeting-card-guidelines-submissions*

Payment: $300 per poem for worldwide, exclusive rights to publish it on a greeting card and other products; $50 per poem for one-time use in a book

DICKSONS, INC.

709 B Ave. E, Seymour, IN 47274 | 812-522-1308
submissions@dicksonsgifts.com | *www.dicksonsgifts.com*

Audience: adults

Products: figurines, crosses, wall decor, mugs, flags

Submissions: Two to eight lines, maximum sixteen, suitable for plaques, bookmarks, etc. Email submission. Responds in three months. Subjects can cover any gift-giving occasion and Christian, inspirational, and everyday social-expression topics. Phrases or acrostics of one or two lines for bumper stickers are also considered. Buys reprint rights.

Payment: royalty, negotiable

Tip: Looking for religious verses.

ELLIE CLAIRE

6100 Tower Cir., Ste. 210, Franklin, TN 37013 | 615-932-7600
www.worthypublishing.com

Parent company: Hachette Book Group

Audience: adults

Products: gifts, journals, devotionals, gift books

Submissions: Email submissions. Also makes assignments. To be considered for an assignment, email letter, résumé, three full samples of devotional writing. Buys all rights.

Guidelines: by email

Payment: flat fee, royalty; $30-40 per devotion

Tips: "Please do not send unsolicited manuscripts or samples. Contact us first with an introduction and elevator pitch. If we are interested, we will ask for more. We operate in the gift market, and the writing will need to reflect that. We are not interested in Bible studies but in inspirational and encouraging devotions, funny stories with a spiritual component, and compilations from a Christian worldview."

WARNER CHRISTIAN RESOURCES

2902 Enterprise Dr., Anderson, IN 46013 | 800-741-7721
editors@warnerpress.org | *www.warnerpress.org*

Audience: children, adults

Products: boxed everyday and Christmas cards

Submissions: Most accepted verses average four lines in length. Themes include birthday, anniversary, baby congratulations, sympathy, get well, kid's birthday and get well, thinking of you, friendship, Christmas, praying for you, encouragement. Use a conversational tone with no lofty poetic language, such as *thee, thou, art*. Length: average of four lines. Responds in six to eight weeks. Email or mail with SASE. Buys all rights. Deadines: everyday, July 31; Christmas, October 1.

Guidelines: *www.warnerpress.org/submission-guidelines*

13

TRACTS

The following companies publish gospel tracts but do not have writers guidelines. If you are interested in writing for them, email or phone to find out if they currently are looking for submissions. Also check your denominational publishing house to see if it publishes tracts.

CHRISTIAN LIGHT PUBLICATIONS
PO Box 1212, Harrisonburg, VA 22803-1212 | 800-776-0478
info@clp.org | *www.clp.org*

FELLOWSHIP TRACT LEAGUE
PO Box 164, Lebanon, OH 45036 | 513-494-1075
mail@fellowshiptractleague.org | *www.fellowshiptractleague.org*

GOOD NEWS PUBLISHERS
1300 Crescent St., Wheaton, IL 60187 | 630-682-4300
info@crossway.org | *www.crossway.org*

GOSPEL PUBLISHING HOUSE
1445 N. Boonville Ave., Springfield, MO 65802 | 800-641-4310
newproducts@myhealthychurch.com | *gospelpublishing.com*

GOSPEL TRACT SOCIETY
PO Box 1118, Independence, MO 64051 | 816-461-6086
gospeltractsociety@gmail.com | *gospeltractsociety.org*

GRACE VISION PUBLISHERS
321-745-9966 (text only)
www.gracevision.com

MOMENTS WITH THE BOOK

PO Box 322, Bedford, PA 15522 | 814-623-8737
email through the website | *mwtb.org*

TRACT ASSOCIATION OF FRIENDS

1501 Cherry St., Philadelphia, PA 19102
info@tractassociation.org | *www.tractassociation.org*

14

BIBLE CURRICULUM

This list includes only the major, nondenominational curriculum publishers. If you are in a denominational church, also check its publishing house for curriculum products. Plus some organizations, like Awana Clubs International and Pioneer Clubs, also produce curriculum for their programs.

Since Bible curriculum is written on assignment only, you'll need to get samples for age groups you want to write for (from the company's website, large Christian bookstores, or your church) and study the formats and pieces. Look for editors' names on the copyright pages of teachers manuals, or call the publishing house for this information.

Then write query letters to specific editors. Tell why you're qualified to write curriculum for them, include a sample of curriculum you've written or other sample of your writing, and ask for a trial assignment. Since the need for writers varies widely, you may not get an assignment for a year or more.

Some of these companies also publish undated, elective curriculum books that are used in a variety of ministries. Plus some book publishers publish lines of Bible-study guides. (See "**Book Publishers.**") These are contracted like other books with a proposal and sample chapters.

ABEKA BOOKS
PO Box 17900, Pensacola, FL 32522-7900 | 877-356-9385
www.joyfullifesundayschool.com
   Type: Sunday school
   Imprint: Joyful Life

DAVID C . COOK
4050 Lee Vance Dr., Colorado Springs, CO 80918 | 800-708-5550
shop.davidccook.org

Type: Sunday school
Imprints: Accent, The Action Bible, Bible-in-Life, Echoes, Gospel
Light, HeartShaper, Scripture Press, SEEN, Standard Lesson,
Tru, and some denominational imprints

GROUP PUBLISHING

1515 Cascade Ave., Loveland, CO 80538 | 970-669-3836
submissions@group.com | *www.group.com*

Types: Sunday school, vacation Bible school, children's worship
Imprints: Be Bold, Dig In, FaithWeaver NOW, Fearless Conversation,
Hands-On Bible, LIVE, Simply Loved, KidsOwn Worship
Guidelines: *grouppublishingps.zendesk.com/hc/en-us/
articles/211878258-Submissions*

UNION GOSPEL PRESS

2000 Brookpark Rd., Cleveland, OH 44109 | 800-638-9988
editorial@uniongospelpress.com | *uniongospelpress.com*

Type: Sunday school
Guidelines: *uniongospelpress.com/ugp-prospective-writers*

URBAN MINISTRIES, INC.

1551 Regency Ct., Calumet City, IL 60409-5448 | 800-860-8642
urbanministries.com

Types: Sunday school, vacation Bible school

15

MISCELLANEOUS

These companies publish a variety of books and other products that fall into the specialty-markets category, such as puzzle books, game books, children's activity books, craft books, charts, church bulletins, and coloring books.

BARBOUR PUBLISHING
See entry in "**Book Publishers.**"

BROADSTREET PUBLISHING
See entry in "**Book Publishers.**"

CHRISTIAN FOCUS PUBLICATIONS
See entry in "**Book Publishers.**"

DAVID C . COOK
See entry in "**Book Publishers.**"

GROUP PUBLISHING
See entry in "**Book Publishers.**"

ROSE PUBLISHING
See entry in "**Book Publishers.**"

ROSEKIDZ
See entry in "**Book Publishers.**"

WARNER CHRISTIAN RESOURCES
2902 Enterprise Dr., Anderson, IN 46013 | 800-741-7721
editors@warnerpress.org | *www.warnerpress.org*

Church bulletins: Short devotions that tie into a visual image and incorporate a Bible verse. Especially interested in material for holidays and special Sundays, such as Christmas, New Year's Day, Palm Sunday, Easter, Pentecost, and Communion. General themes are also welcome. Length: 250 words maximum. Deadline: April 30. Buys all rights. Payment varies.

Children's coloring and activity books: Most activity books focus on a Bible story or biblical theme, such as love and forgiveness. Ages range from preschool (ages 2-5) to upper elementary (ages 8-10). Include activities and puzzles in every upper-elementary book. Coloring-book manuscripts should present a picture idea and a portion of the story for each page. Deadlines: May 1 and October 1. Payment varies.

Guidelines: *www.warnerpress.org/submission-guidelines*

PART 5

SUPPORT
FOR
WRITERS

16

LITERARY AGENTS

Asking editors and other writers is a great way to find a reliable agent. You may also want to visit *www.sfwa.org/other-resources/for-authors/writer-beware/agents* for tips on avoiding questionable agents and choosing reputable ones.

The general market has an Association of Authors' Representatives (*www.aaronline.org*), also known as *AAR*. To be a member, the agent must agree to a code of ethics. The website has a searchable list of agents. Some listings below indicate agents who belong to the AAR. Lack of such a designation, however, does not indicate the agent is unethical; most Christian agents are not members.

ALIVE LITERARY AGENCY

5001 Centennial Blvd. #50742, Colorado Springs, CO 80908
contact through website | *www.aliveliterary.com*

Agents: Bryan Norman (president), Lisa Jackson (vice president)
Agency: Established in 1989 by Rick Christian. Represents more than 125 clients. Member of Association of Authors' Representatives.
Types of books: adult novels, nonfiction, crossover, juvenile
New clients: Only taking proposals by referral or request. Contact by email. Responds in six to eight weeks to referrals only.
Commission: 15%

AMBASSADOR LITERARY AGENCY

PO Box 50358, Nashville, TN 37205 | 615-370-4700
info@AmbassadorAgency.com | *www.AmbassadorAgency.com*

Agent: Wes Yoder, *wes@AmbassadorSpeakers.com*
Agency: Established in 1997. Represents twenty-five to thirty clients.
New clients: Open to unpublished book authors. Contact by email with a short description of the manuscript and a request to submit it for review. Responds in four to six weeks.

Types of books: adult nonfiction and fiction, crossover books, no sci-fi or medical
Commission: 15%
Fees: none

APOKEDAK LITERARY AGENCY

113 Winn Ct., Waleska, GA 30183 | 678-744-7745
sallyapokedak@outlook.com | *sally-apokedak.com*

Agents: Sally Apokedak, Melissa Richeson
Agency: Established in 2018. Represents twenty-five clients.
Types of books: children's fiction and nonfiction: board books, picture books, middle grade, and young adult; adult Christian fiction and nonfiction
Specialty: children's
New clients: Open to writers who have not published a book, writers met at conferences, and members of Society of Children's Book Writers and Illustrators. Initial contact: email with full proposal or a cover letter, synopsis, comp books, and full manuscript; also by referral from current client. Accepts simultaneous submissions. Responds in three months.
Other services: freelance services and phone consults
Commission: 15%
Fees: none
Tip: "Stellar writing combined with fresh premise and a universal appeal is the key to gaining an offer from us."

AUTHORIZE ME®

PO Box 1816, South Gate, CA 90280 | 310-508-9860
AuthorizeMeNow@gmail.com | *lifethatmatters.net/authorizeme*

Agent: Sharon Norris Elliott
Agency: Established 2020. Represents four clients.
Types of books: adult nonfiction (books of hope and help for daily life as a believer), Bible study, devotionals, children's picture books, early readers, middle-grade chapter books, personal stories (memoirs of relatively unknown people whose stories offer hope and help)
New clients: Represents writers who have not published a book, well-established book writers needing a fresh wind, self-published writers, and writers met at conferences. Contact: email, phone, website form. Simultaneous OK. Responds in two to four weeks.

Commission: 15%

Fees: none

Tip: "If the author needs help to bring writing up to publishable standards, other services offered by the AuthorizeMe company can be acquired prior to signing as a client of the agent."

BANNER LITERARY

PO Box 1828, Winter Park, CO 80482

mike@mikeloomis.co | www.mikeloomis.co

Agent: Mike Loomis

Agency: Established in 2004. Represents forty-eight clients.

Types of books: nonfiction, self-help, business, inspiration, politics

New clients: Open to writers who have not published a book and self-published writers. Contact through email or website form. Responds in two weeks.

Commission: 15%

Fees: none

Other services: See listing in "Publicity and Marketing Services."

Tip: "Send your web address with query."

THE BINDERY

Colorado Springs, CO

Info@thebinderyagency.com | www.TheBinderyAgency.com

Agent: Alexander Field (principle and founder), Ingrid Beck (managing director)

Agency: Established in 2017. Represents more than fifty clients.

Types of books: fiction, spirituality, memoir, biography, sci-fi, fantasy, business and leadership, lifestyle, self-help, pop culture, and more

New clients: Represents well-established book writers, first-time book authors, self-published writers, and writers met at conferences. Initial contact: email, referral from current client. Query first or send full proposal. Accepts simultaneous submissions. Responds in eight to ten weeks.

Commission: 15%

Fees: none

Tip: "Query with a clear summary of your book concept, table of contents (for nonfiction), author biography, at least one sample chapter, relevant contact information, and your publishing history. You are welcome to attach a book proposal; and feel free to include a sample chapter in the body of the email, just following your query letter. We will review every submission. However, if you have not heard back from us after twelve weeks have passed, please consider our response to be a pass."

THE BLYTHE DANIEL AGENCY, INC.

PO Box 64197, Colorado Springs, CO 80962-4197 | 719-213-3427
blythe@theblythedanielagency.com | *www.theblythedanielagency.com*

Agents: Blythe Daniel; Stephanie Alton, *stephanie@ theblythedanielagency.com*

Agency: Established in 2005. Represents one hundred clients.

Types of books: Christian life, spiritual growth, current events, business/leadership, church resources, marriage, parenting, social issues, women's issues, men's issues, devotionals; gift books: seasonal, lifestyle, home and family; other specialty books

Specialty: nonfiction

New clients: Open to writers who have not published a book, well-established book writers, writers met at conferences. Contact: email with full proposal, referral from current client. Accepts simultaneous submissions. Responds in eight weeks.

Other services: Traditional publicity (media-driven); blog campaigns, launch teams, podcast interviews; writing, branding, social media, and email coaching. See listing in **"Publicity and Marketing Services."**

Commission: 15% of standard book royalties, other formats vary

Fees: none

Tip: "Visit our website to see the types of projects we represent and services we offer. We are happy to consider your project, coaching needs, or marketing you want to pursue. We have a projects manager who assists us with these (*rebecca@theblythedanielagency.com*)."

BOOKS & SUCH LITERARY MANAGEMENT

52 Mission Cir., Ste. 122, PMB 170, Santa Rosa, CA 95409-5370
representation@booksandsuch.com | *www.booksandsuch.com*

Agents: Janet Kobobel Grant (president), Wendy Lawton (vice president), Rachelle Gardner, Rachel Kent, Cynthia Ruchti, Barb Roose

Agency: Established in 1996. Represents 250 clients.

Types of books: adult fiction and nonfiction; some children's and YA; no poetry, academic books, or speculative adult fiction

New clients: Open to writers who have not published a book, well-established book writers, and self-published writers. Contact by email with query first. Accepts simultaneous submissions. Responds in six to eight weeks if interested.

Commission: 15%

Fees: none

Tip: "Provide clear and compelling details about your project in your query. We read each query we receive and forward it to the agent most likely to be interested in your project if it seems to be a good fit for our agency."

CHRISTIAN LITERARY AGENT

PO Box 428, Newburg, PA 17240 | 717-423-6621

keith@christianliteraryagent.com | www.christianliteraryagent.com

Agent: Keith Carroll

Agency: Established in 2010. Represents ten to fifteen new clients annually.

Types of books: faith-centered

New clients: Open to first-time book authors and self-published writers. Initial contact: email, website form. Responds in two to four weeks.

Commission: 10%

Fee: $90 application fee

Other service: writing coach

Tip: "I try to help you make your material more of an effective read."

THE CHRISTOPHER FEREBEE AGENCY

submissions@christopherferebee.com | christopherferebee.com

Agents: Christopher Ferebee, Angela Scheff, Jana Bruson

Agency: Established in 2011.

Types of books: variety of genres in nonfiction and fiction; no children's books, academic works, or poetry

New clients: Submit proposal as email attachment. Responds in four weeks.

Tip: "As a small agency, we focus our efforts on a very select group of authors. Our primary focus and attention is always on existing client relationships. But we are looking for the right authors with important ideas."

CREATIVE MEDIA AGENCY, INC.

212-812-1494

query@cmalit.com | cmalit.com.

Agent: Paige Wheeler, *page@cmalit.com*

Agency: Established in 1997. Represents more than thirty clients. Member of Association of Authors' Representatives.

Types of books: Fiction: All commercial fiction and upscale (think book club) fiction, as well as women's fiction, romance (all types), mystery, thrillers, inspirational/Christian, and psychological suspense. I enjoy both historical fiction as well as contemporary fiction, so do keep that in mind. Nonfiction: I'm looking for both narrative nonfiction and prescriptive nonfiction. I'm looking for books where the author has a huge platform and something new to say in a particular area. Some of the areas that I like are lifestyle, relationship, parenting, business/entrepreneurship, food-subsistence-homesteading topics, popular/trendy reference projects and women's issues. I'd like books that would be a good fit on the *TODAY* show.

New clients: Open to writers at all levels, including self-published and those who have not published a book. Query by email. Simultaneous queries OK. Responds in six to eight weeks.

Commission: 15%

Fees: none

Tip: "Please check out our website."

CURTIS BROWN, LTD.

10 Astor Pl., New York, NY 10003-6935 | 212-473-5400
info@cbltd.com | *www.curtisbrown.com*

Agent: Laura Blake Peterson, *lbp@cbltd.com*

Agency: Member of Association of Authors' Representatives. General agency that handles some religious/inspirational books.

Types of books: fiction, nonfiction, children's

New clients: Email query, and attach the first fifty pages of your manuscript. Include "lbpquery" in the subject line of your email. Responds in three to four weeks only if interested in your book.

CYLE YOUNG LITERARY ELITE, LLC

PO Box 1, Clarklake, MI 49230 | 330-651-1604
submissions@cyleyoung.com | *www.cyleyoung.com*

Agents: Cyle Young, Tessa Emily Hall, Caroline George, Hope Bolinger, Alyssa Roat, Kenzi Melody, Del Duduit, Chrysa Keenon, Megan Burkhart, Jori Hanna

Agency: Established in 2018. Represents eighty clients.

Types of books: children's, middle grade, YA, and adult; fiction and nonfiction

Specialty: children's and nonfiction

New clients: Currently closed to queries and proposals except when meeting one of the agents at a writers conference or an online writing event. Check the website for changes in this policy. Simultaneous submissions OK. Responds in three months or longer.

Commission: 15%

Tip: "We look for projects with great writing, big ideas, and great platform."

FINE PRINT LITERARY MANAGEMENT

115 W. 29th St., 3rd Fl., New York, NY 10001 | 212-279-1282
peter@fineprintlit.com | *www.fineprintlit.com*

Agent: Peter Rubie

Agency: General agency that handles some spirituality books.

Types: adult fiction and nonfiction, some middle grade and YA fiction

New clients: Open to unpublished authors. Email query.

Commission: 15%

FOUNDARY LITERARY + MEDIA

33 W. 17th St. PH, New York, NY 10011
cpsubmissions@foundrymedia.com | *foundrymedia.com*

Agent: Chris Park

Types of books: memoir, narrative nonfiction, sports

GARY D. FOSTER CONSULTING

733 Virginia Ave., Van Wert, OH 45891 | 419-238-4082
gary@garydfoster.com | *www.garydfoster.com*

Agent: Gary Foster

Agency: Established in 1989. Represents more than fifty clients.

Types of books: overtly Christian nonfiction

New clients: Open to unpublished book and well-established authors. Initial contact: email or mail full proposal or referral from current client. Accepts simultaneous submissions. Responds in one to three weeks.

Commission: 15%

Fee: nominal fee on signing representation agreement

Tip: "Think about how you will build your market-exposure platform."

THE GATES GROUP LITERARY AGENCY

sarah@the-gates-group.com | *www.gatesliterary.co*

Agent: Don Gates
Agency: Established in 2013. Represents more than thirty authors.
New clients: Works with pastors and ministry leaders.

GOLDEN WHEAT LITERARY

www.goldenwheatliterary.com

Agent: Jessica Schmeidler, *jessica@goldenwheatliterary.com*; Nicole Payne, *submissions@goldenwheatliterary.com*
Agency: Established in 2015.
Types of books: variety of fiction genres, nonfiction picture books, memoir, devotionals, middle-grade adventure stories and historical fiction, young adult; also sells to the general market
New clients: Email query letter and first three chapters, all in body of message; no attachments. If no response in six months, assume the agent is not interested.

HARTLINE LITERARY AGENCY

123 Queenston Dr., Pittsburgh, PA 15235 | 412 -829-2483
jim@hartlineliterary.com | *www.hartlineagency.com*

Agents: Jim Hart, *jim@hartlineliterary.com*; Joyce A. Hart, *joyce@hartlineliterary.com*; Cyle Young, *cyle@hartlineliterary.com*; Linda Glaz, *linda@hartlineliterary.com*; Patricia Riddle-Gaddis, *patricia@hartlineliterary.com*
Agency: Established in 1992. Represents 260 clients.
Types of books: Jim Hart: nonfiction: Christian living, church growth, leadership, business, social issues, ministry, parenting, self-help; fiction: suspense/thrillers, romance (contemporary, historical, suspense, Amish), women's fiction, literary, fantasy, sci-fi, and speculative; not looking at children's or middle-grade fiction at this time

Linda Glaz: fiction: romance, either contemporary, suspense, or historic; no children's books

Cyle Young: YA, middle grade, chapter books, easy readers, picture books, and board books; genre fiction, especially romance, speculative (sci-fi and fantasy); nonfiction: parenting, leadership, ministry, and self-help; screenplays

Patricia Riddle-Gaddis: fiction: sweet romance, cozy mysteries, and young-adult categories (think *The Princess Diaries* and a modern Nancy Drew); a range of nonfiction

New clients: Open to writers who have not published a book, well-established book writers, self-published writers, writers met at conferences. Initial contact: email with full proposal. Accepts simultaneous submissions. Responds in six to eight weeks.

Commission: 15%, foreign 20%, films 20-25%

Fees: none

Tips: "Please look at our website before submitting. Guidelines are listed, along with detailed information about each agent. Be sure to include your bio and publishing history with your proposal. The author-agent relationship is a team effort. Working together we can make sure your manuscript gets the exposure and attention it deserves."

HIDDEN VALUE GROUP, LLC

27758 Santa Margarita Pkwy. #361, Mission Viejo, CA 92691
njernigan@hiddenvaluegroup.com | *www.HiddenValueGroup.com*

Agent: Nancy Jernigan

Agency: Established in 2001. Member of Association of Authors' Representatives.

Type of books: women's nonfiction

New clients: Open to previously published authors only, not including self-published. Email proposal with two or three chapters. Responds in ten days.

Commission: 15%

Fees: none

Tip: "Include how you will help support the marketing of your project. Include all social-media numbers; social-media platforms; radio, print, and TV marketing."

ILLUMINATE LITERARY AGENCY (FORMERLY D. C. JACOBSON & ASSOCIATES)

Portland, OR
support@illuminateliterary.com | *www.illuminateliterary.com*

Agents: Jenni Burke, Tawny Johnson

Agency: Established in 2006. Represents thirty-two clients.

Types of books: spiritual growth, personal development, lifestyle (home, decor, travel, etc.), memoir, faith and culture, women's issues, business and leadership, church and ministry, family and relationships, Bible studies, devotionals, gift books

Specialty: adult nonfiction

New clients: Open to writers who are well-established or have not published a book and have a significant platform. Initial contact:

website form, referral from current client, full proposal. Responds in six weeks if proposal catches their interest.

Commission: 15%

Tip: "Please thoroughly review our website before submitting."

JEVON BOLDEN LITERARY SERVICES

PO Box 953607, Lake Mary, FL 32795

info@jevonbolden.com | jevonbolden.com/services

Agent: Jevon Bolden

Agency: Established in 2017. Represents twenty clients. Jevon has been in the publishing industry for almost twenty years.

Types of books: spiritual and personal growth, Christian living, children's nonfiction

New clients: Closed to queries until February 1. Check the website after that date for information on what she's looking for.

Tip: "I seek to place authors with innovative and well-established publishers who see the big picture when it comes to true author partnerships."

K J LITERARY SERVICES, LLC

1540 Margaret Ave., Grand Rapids, MI 49507 | 616-551-9797

kim@kjliteraryservices.com | www.kjliteraryservices.com

Agent: Kim Zeilstra

Agency: Established in 2006.

Also does: editing, proofreading, project management, permissions

New clients: Only taking new authors by referral at this time. Initial contact by email or phone.

Commission: 15%

KIRKLAND MEDIA MANAGEMENT

PO Box 1539, Liberty, TX 77575 | 936-581-3944

jessica@kirklandmediamanagment.com | jessiekirkland.com

Agent: Jessica Kirkland

Agency: Established in 2015. Sells to general market too.

Types of books: fiction, nonfiction, film contracts in the inspirational market; no children's, short stories, or poetry

New clients: Email query only. Guidelines on the website. If no response in three months, not interested.

Commission: 15%

Tip: "She is searching for powerful stories that encourage, equip, challenge, and change, but is most enthusiastic about inspirational true stories."

THE KNIGHT AGENCY

232 W. Washington St., Madison, GA 30650 | 706 473-0994
pamela.harty@knightagency.net | *knightagency.net*

Agent: Pamela Harty
Agency: Established in 1996. Member of Association of Authors' Representatives. Agency represents 330 authors.
Types of books: Christian living, fiction, children's
New clients: Open to writers who have not published a book, well-established book writers, and self-published writers. Initial contact by query via Query Manager on the website. All other queries will not be reviewed or returned. Responds in six weeks.
Commission: 15%
Fees: none
Tip: "Please visit our website for submission guidelines."

LITERARY MANAGEMENT GROUP, LLC

8530 Calistoga Way, Brentwood, TN 37027 | 615-812-4445
brucebarbour@literarymanagementgroup.com |
www.literarymanagementgroup.com

Agent: Bruce R. Barbour
Agency: Established in 1996. Represents more than 100 clients.
Also does: book packaging, publishing consulting
Type of books: adult nonfiction; no gift books, memoir, text/academic
New clients: No unpublished authors or self-published books. Email proposal. Accepts simultaneous submissions. Responds in three to four weeks.
Commission: 15%
Fees: none

MACGREGOR AND LUEDEKE

PO Box 1316, Manzanita, OR 97130 | 503-389-4803
submissions@macgregorliterary.com | *www.macgregorandluedeke.com*

Agents: Chip MacGregor (president), Amanda Luedeke (vice president)

Agency: Established in 2006. Member of Association of Authors' Representatives. Represents sixty clients.

Types of books: wide variety of nonfiction and select list of novelists

Specialty: memoir, Christian living

New clients: Open to writers with an established platform and a solid book idea. Initial contact: website form, referral from current client; query first. Not accepting unsolicited fiction manuscripts. Accepts simultaneous submissions. Responds in one month.

Commission: 15%

Fees: none

Tip: "A well-written proposal and sample chapters is the best way to gain our attention. We're always looking for fresh ideas expressed through great writing, from authors with a proven platform."

MARK SWEENEY & ASSOCIATES

302 Sherwood Dr., Carol Stream, IL 60188 | 615-403-1937
sweeney2@comcast.net

Agents: Mark Sweeney, Janet Sweeney

Agency: Established in 2003. Represents more than 75 clients.

Types of books: memoir, narrative nonfiction, Christian living, Bible study, apologetics

Specialty: popular apologetics

New clients: Looking for authors with a great book idea who have both the skill to communicate in writing and a platform from which to write. Open to well-established book writers, as well as those who have not published a book. Initial contact: email, referral from current client. Query first. Responds in one week.

Fees: none

Other services: publishing consulting for individuals and organizations

Tip: "Check with the agency's current author clients for a referral."

MARTIN LITERARY & MANAGEMENT

914 164th St. S.E., Ste. B12, #307, Mill Creek, WA 98102 | 206- 466-1773
adria@martinliterarymanagment.com | www.martinlit.com

Agent: Adria Goetz

Agency: General agency established in 2003. Adria has more than twenty-five clients.

Types of books: picture books, middle grade, young adult, adult fiction/nonfiction, devotionals, Christian living, lifestyle

Specialty: "I look for books that delight readers, that help inspire wonder and imagination, that foster deep empathy and compassion for our fellow human beings, that provide rich character representation of marginalized people groups, that take the reader on an adventure, that uncover fascinating stories from history's footnotes, that explore issues of faith and how to apply Christ's teachings to our own life, that celebrate women and the female experience, that ask nitty gritty questions and don't settle for easy answers, that make people disappointed when they have to close the book and go to bed, and books that add a touch of magic to readers' lives."

New clients: Open to writers who have not published a book, self-published writers, writers met at conferences. Contact by email. Accepts simultaneous submissions. Responds in two weeks. Be sure to read *www.martinlit.com/submission-policy*.

Commission: 15%, foreign 25%

Other services: film and TV adaptation

Tip: "Check out my full wish list, which is updated frequently, at *adriagoetz.com*."

METAMORPHOSIS LITERARY AGENCY

646-397-1640

info@metamorphosisliteraryagency.com | *www.metamorphosisliteraryagency.com*

Agents: Stephanie Hansen, *info@metamorphosisliteraryagency.com*; Amy Brewer, *abrewer@metamorphosisliteraryagency.com*; Lauren Miller, *lmiller@metamorphosisliteraryagency.com*

Agency: General agency established in 2016. Represents ninety Christian clients.

Types of books: picture books, adult fiction, some nonfiction

New clients: Open to writers who have not published a book, well-established book writers, writers met at conferences. Initial contact: website form. Responds in three months.

Commission: 15%

Fees: none

Tip: "Our mission is to help authors become traditionally published. We represent well-crafted commercial fiction and nonfiction. Metamorphosis Literary Agency works with authors to ensure that every book is in the best presentable form. Our publishing connections come from numerous conferences, hard work, and genuine care. We do not charge reading fees as we adhere to the Association of Authors' Representatives' Canon of Ethics."

NATASHA KERN LITERARY AGENCY, INC.

PO Box 1069, White Salmon, WA 98672
agent@natashakern.com | *www.natashakernliterary.com*

Agent: Natasha Kern
Agency: Established in 1987. Represents thirty-six religious clients.
Types of books: adult fiction
New clients: Closed to queries from unpublished writers. Open to meeting with writers at conferences and accepting referrals from current clients and editors. Cannot read unsolicited queries or proposals.

THE SEYMOUR AGENCY

475 Miner Street Rd., Canton, NY 13617 | 239-398-8209
nicole@theseymouragency.com | *www.theseymouragency.com*

Agents: Nichole Resciniti; Julie Gwinn, *julie@theseymouragency.com*; Tina Wainscott, *QueryMe.Online/TinaWainscottTSA*
Agency: Established in 1992. Member of Association of Authors' Representatives.
Types of books: inspirational, YA, middle grade, picture books, mysteries, thrillers, romance, science fiction, fantasy, women's fiction, literary fiction, historical fiction, speculative fiction, assorted nonfiction
New clients: Open to writers who have not published a book, well-established book writers, self-published writers, and writers met at conferences. Contact by email with one-page query first or referral from current client. Responds in two weeks to queries, three months to proposals.
Commission: 15%
Fees: none
Tip: "Hone your craft. Take advantage of writers groups, critique partners, etc., to polish your manuscript into the best shape it can be."

SPENCERHILL ASSOCIATES

8126 Lakewood Main St. #204, Lakewood Ranch, FL 34202 | 941-907-3700
submissions@spencerhillassociates.com | *www.spencerhillassociates.com*

Agent: Karen Solem
Agency: Member of Association of Authors' Representatives. Established in 2001. General agent who represents fifteen to twenty-five clients with religious books.
Types of books: adult fiction and nonfiction
New clients: Initial contact by querying through website form or

email. Responds in three months.
Commission: 15%

STANLEY O. WILLIFORD LITERARY AGENCY
9013 Buckles St., Downey, CA 90241 | 562-382-3516
query@thewillifordagency.com
> **Agent:** Stanley O. Williford
> **Agency:** Established in 2016. Represents fifteen clients.
> **Types of books:** any Christian
> **Specialty:** Charismatic authors
> **New clients:** Open to writers who have not published a book, well-established book writers, self-published writers, writers met at conferences. Initial contact: email with query, phone. Responds in two weeks.
> **Commission:** 15%
> **Fees:** none
> **Tip:** "I will represent any Christian writer as long as he or she adheres to Christian precepts."

THE STEVE LAUBE AGENCY
24 W. Camelback Rd. A-635, Phoenix, AZ 85013 | 602-336-8910
info@stevelaube.com | *www.stevelaube.com*
> **Agents:** Steve Laube, *krichards@stevelaube.com*; Tamela Hancock Murray, *ewilson@stevelaube.com*; Bob Hostetler, *rgwright@stevelaube.com*
> **Agency:** Established in 2004. Represents more than 300 clients.
> **Types of books:** adult fiction and nonfiction of all types and genres; see website blog post by each agent for what he or she is looking for
> **New clients:** Open to unpublished and published authors. Email proposal as attachment according to the guidelines on the website. Steve Laube also will take proposals by mail. Accepts simultaneous submissions. Responds in eight to twelve weeks.
> **Commission:** 15%
> **Fees:** none
> **Tip:** "Please follow the guidelines! Since your book proposal is like a job application, you want to present yourself in the most professional manner possible. Your proposal will be a simple vehicle to convey your idea to us and, ultimately, to a publisher."

SUSAN SCHULMAN LITERARY AGENCY LLC

454 W. 44, New York, NY 10036 | 917-488-0906

publishersmarketplace.com/members/Schulman

> **Agents:** Susan Schulman, *Susan@schulmanagency.com*; Christine LeBlond, *Cleblond@Schulmanagency.com*
>
> **Agency:** General agency established in 1990. Represents 150 clients. Member of Association of Authors' Representatives.
>
> **Types of books:** fiction, nonfiction
>
> **Specialty:** books for, by, and about women and women's issues and interests
>
> **New clients:** Open to writers at all levels, including self-published. Email (no attachments) or mail query. Accepts simultaneous submissions. Responds in two weeks.
>
> **Commission:** 15%
>
> **Fees:** none
>
> **Tip:** "Know your market for your project. Please do not submit first drafts or unedited or unfinished projects."

VAN DIEST LITERARY AGENCY

37950 S.E. Dodge Park Blvd., Boring, OR 97009 | 503-676-8009

david@christianliteraryagency.com | *www.ChristianLiteraryAgency.com*

> **Agents:** David Van Diest, Sarah Van Diest
>
> **Agency:** Established in 2003. Represents twenty-five clients.
>
> **Types of books:** nonfiction, select fiction, children's
>
> **New clients:** Open to unpublished authors. Contact by email through the website. Responds in one month or not interested.
>
> **Commission:** 15%
>
> **Fees:** none
>
> **Tip:** "We believe the best books are yet to be written! We're not talking about 'new truth' revealed, but God's timeless truth delivered to a new audience, in a way that is fresh, understandable, and applicable to them and their lives."

WENDY SHERMAN ASSOCIATES, INC.

27 W. 24th St., Ste. 700B, New York, NY 10110 | 212-279-9027

submissions@wsherman.com | *www.wsherman.com*

> **Agents:** Wendy Sherman, Cherise Fisher
>
> **Agency:** General agency that handles some religious books. Established in 1999.
>
> **Types of books:** adult spirituality and Christianity
>
> **New clients:** Open to unpublished authors. Contact by email query

only; no attachments. Guidelines on the website.

Commission: 15%

Tip: "We have infinite respect for those writers who craft compelling query letters and follow our guidelines. Remember, there is an art to creating a truly sensational query letter!"

WHEELHOUSE LITERARY

Nashville, TN | 615-738-6970

jonathan@wheelhouseliterary.com | *www.wheelhouseliterary.com*

Agent: Jonathan Clements

Agency: Established in 2010 after Jonathan worked for five years with authors and brands for another agency.

Types of books: inspirational, historical, contemporary, military fiction; biography/memoir, sports, current events, pop culture

New clients: Email or send through the website form. Responds in two months if interested in more information.

WILLIAM K. JENSEN LITERARY AGENCY

119 Bampton Ct., Eugene, OR 97404 | 541-688-1612

queries@wkjagency.com | *www.wkjagency.com*

Agents: William K. Jensen, Rachel MacMillan, Teresa Evenson

Agency: Established in 2005. Represents more than fifty clients.

Types of books: most types of Christian books, including Christian living, devotional, marriage, family life, apologetics, biography, gift books, cookbooks, prophecy, humor, health, inspirational, political, social issues, women's and men's issues, adult fiction; no science fiction, fantasy, or youth

New clients: Open to unpublished authors. Contact by email only; no attachments. See the website for complete query details. Accepts simultaneous submissions. Responds in one month or not interested.

Commission: 15%

Fees: none

WINTERS & KING, INC.

2448 E. 81st St., Ste. 5900, Tulsa, OK 74137-4259 | 918-494-6868

dboyd@wintersking.com |
wintersking.com/practice-areas/publishing-agent-services

Agent: Thomas J. Winters

Agency: Established in 1983. Represents 150 clients. Part of a law firm.

Types of books: fiction, nonfiction

New clients: Open to well-established book writers only. Contact by email. Responds in two weeks.

Commission: 15%

Fees: none

Other services: legal review of publishing contracts, drafting of work-for-hire agreements to contract writer/editor services, copyright/trademark filing

Tip: "Submissions should be carefully edited and free of typos. Accompanying manuscripts or sample chapters for presentation to publishers should be edited, typo-free, and basically print-ready."

WOLGEMUTH & ASSOCIATES

Aurora, CO

info@wolgemuthandassociates.com | *www.wolgemuthandassociates.com*

Agents: Robert Wolgemuth, Andrew Wolgemuth, Erik Wolgemuth, Austin Wilson

Agency: Established in 1992. Member of Association of Authors' Representatives.

Types of books: teen/YA and adult nonfiction

New clients: Only authors with at least one traditionally published book or by referral from current client or close contact. Query by email. Accepts simultaneous submissions.

Commission: 15%

Fees: none

WORDSERVE LITERARY GROUP

7500 E. Arapahoe Rd., Ste. 285, Centennial, CO 80112 | 303-471-6675

admin@wordserveliterary.com | *www.wordserveliterary.com*

Agents: Greg Johnson, *greg@wordserveliterary.com*; Sarah Freese, *sarah@wordserveliterary.com*; Nick Harrison, *nick@wordserveliterary.com*; Keely Boeving, *keely@wordserveliterary.com*

Agency: Established in 2003. Represents more than 180 clients.

Types of books: All genres in the Christian market. In the general market: history/military, health, business, YA, humor, sports, memoir.

New clients: Open to well-established book writers, writers who have not published a book yet, self-published writers, and writers met at conferences. Email query or full proposal. Accepts simultaneous submissions. Responds in two to four weeks.

Commission: 15%

Fees: none

Tip: "Follow instructions on how to query our agency on our website."

WORDWISE MEDIA SERVICES

4083 Avenue L, Ste. 255, Lancaster, CA 93536 | 661-382-8083
get.wisewords@gmail.com | *www.wordwisemedia.com*

Agents: Steven Hutson (owner), *steve@wordwisemedia.com*; David
Fessenden; Michelle S. Lazurek

Agency: Established in 2011. Represents sixty clients, half
with religious books. Member of Association of Authors'
Representatives.

Types of books: novels and nonfiction for adults and children, picture
books

New clients: Open to unpublished book authors. Prefers referrals or
conference meets. For all submissions, use the query form on the
website. For other inquiries, phone or email is OK; no postal mail.
Accepts simultaneous submissions. Responds in one month; OK
to nudge after then.

Commission: 15%

Fees: maybe for printing and postage at cost for a manuscript mailed
to a publisher

Tip: "For all submissions, please follow the instructions on the website
carefully. Specify the agent's name in the email subject line if you
have a preference."

YATES & YATES

1551 N. Tustin Ave., Ste. 710, Santa Ana, CA 92705 | 714-480-4000
email@yates2.com | *www.yates2.com*

Agents: Sealy Yates, Matt Yates, Curtis Yates, Mike Salisbury, Karen
Yates

Agency: Established in 1989. Represents fewer than fifty clients.

Types of books: adult nonfiction

New clients: No unpublished authors. Contact by email with full
proposal. Responds in one to two months.

Commission: negotiable

Other services: author coaching and ecourses available at
authorcoaching.com

Tip: "We serve passionate, articulate, gifted Christian communicators,
using our strengths to guide, counsel, and protect them, fiercely
advocate for them, and help them advance life- and culture-
transforming messages for the sake of the Kingdom."

Christian Writers Institute Courses
Literary Agent Bundle

Courses in this bundle:
- The Elements of an Effective Book Proposal
- The 10 Ks of a Good Book
- Do I Need an Agent?
- Mistakes New Writers Make
- How to Use *The Christian Writers Market Guide*
- How to Sell Everything You Write
- Redeeming Rejection
- The Publishing Process
- The Power Book Proposal
- The Ten Enemies of Good Writing

Normal price: $85
Savings: 53%
Market guide price: $39.95

https://cwmg.link/agents2021

How to Scan QR Codes
Use the camera on your smartphone to focus on the above QR code to activate the discount. It will give you the option to visit the site, which you will want to accept. If you are using an older smartphone, you may need to download a QR-code scanning app. You can also visit the URL below the code to activate the discount on your computer.

17

WRITERS CONFERENCES AND SEMINARS

Due to the fluid situation with COVID-19, many conference directors had not set dates yet when this book went to print. Also, some directors already decided to hold their conferences online in 2021; they are listed in the Online section at the end of this chapter.

ALABAMA

SOUTHERN CHRISTIAN WRITERS CONFERENCE

Tuscaloosa, Al | June | *www.southernchristianwriters.com*
> **Director:** Cheryl Wray, *scwritersconference@gmail.com*
> **Description:** The SCWC is a two-day conference for beginners or experienced writers that focuses on several genres: nonfiction books, magazines, fiction, grammar, business aspects, legal aspects, etc.
> **Faculty includes:** editors, agents, and publishers
> **Attendance:** 160-200

CALIFORNIA

MOUNT HERMON WRITERS

Mount Hermon, CA (near Santa Cruz)
> **Director:** Kathy Ide, *Kathy@ChristianEditor.com*
> **Description:** The 50-year Mount Hermon Christian Writers

Conference was cancelled due to COVID-19; but after pandemic concerns and restrictions are over, events for writers at this location will be planned. For details, email Kathy Ide or check the MH Writers Facebook page.

Attendance: 300

SoCAL CHRISTIAN WRITERS' CONFERENCE

Southern CA | *www.SoCalCWC.com*

Director: Kathy Ide, *KathyIde@SoCalCWC.com*

Description: Christian writers' conference with a strong focus on screenwriting.

Special track: screenwriting

Speakers: Bob Saenz, Jeff Willis

Attendance: 100

Contest: Promising Beginnings contest offers one full scholarship, including meals, lodging, and travel stipend.

COLORADO

COLORADO CHRISTIAN WRITERS CONFERENCE

Estes Park, CO | May 12-15 | *colorado.writehisanswer.com*

Director: Marlene Bagnull, 951 Anders Rd., Lansdale, PA 19446; 484-991-8581; *mbagnull@aol.com*

Description: To encourage and equip you to write about a God who is real, is reachable, and changes lives. Sharpen your writing and marketing skills from your choice of eight continuing sessions and more than fifty workshops. Seven keynotes, four or more one-on-one 15-minute appointments. Our 2020 conference was postponed until 2021 because of the pandemic. We will be featuring the same faculty and program. If COVID-19 makes it unsafe to meet in person, we will go virtual.

Special track: teens

Faculty includes: editors, agents, and publishers

Scholarships: partial

Attendance: 220

Contest: For registered conferees. Entries based on the conference theme. Prose (maximum 500 words) or poetry by published and not-yet-published authors. The winner in each of the four categories receives 50% off the registration fee for the following year. Entry fee $10.

WRITE IN THE SPRINGS CONFERENCE

Colorado Springs, CO | April 9-10 | *www.acfwcosprings.com*

> **Director:** Erin Kohler, PO Box 7862, Colorado Springs, CO 80933; *erin730kohler@gmail.com*
>
> **Description:** Experience an unforgettable weekend of teaching and inspired writing featuring *USA TODAY*'s best-selling author and founder of My Book Therapy and Novel Academy, Susan May Warren.
>
> **Faculty includes:** editors
> **Speaker:** Susan May Warren
> **Scholarships:** full, partial
> **Attendance:** 100

WRITERS ON THE ROCK

Denver, CO | February | *www.writersontherock.com*

> **Director:** David Rupert, 14473 W. 3rd, Golden, CO 80401; 720-237-7487; *conference@writersontherock.com*
>
> **Description:** A yearly gathering of Christian writers in our community who come from a variety of experience levels in order to write the words that will help change the world.
>
> **Attendance:** 300

CONNECTICUT

reNEW RETREAT FOR NEW ENGLAND WRITING & SPEAKING

West Hartford, CT | October 8-10 | *www.reNEWwriting.com*

> **Director:** Lucinda Secrest McDowell, reNEW Writing, PO Box 290707, Wethersfield, CT 06129; 860-402-9551; *info@reNEWwriting.com*
>
> **Description:** reNEW is a spiritual retreat open to all beginning and seasoned writers and speakers who desire to communicate the good news of Jesus through their written or spoken words. At reNEW, we believe the core of our calling as writers and speakers is faithfulness to Christ. And so, our emphasis is on the need to grow deep inwardly, so we can be effective in our outward reach.
>
> **Faculty includes:** editors, agents, publishers
> **Special track:** speaking
> **Scholarships:** partial
> **Attendance:** 50-70

DELAWARE

DELMARVA CHRISTIAN WRITERS CONFERENCE

Georgetown, DE | October 16 | *delmarvawriters.com/conference*

> **Director:** Candy Abbott, Crossroad Community Church, 20864 State Forest Rd., Georgetown, DE 19947; 302-542-8510; *info@ delmarvawriters.com*
> **Description:** Delmarva Christian Writers Conference is for writers who want to be obedient to God's call to write. It's your opportunity to be encouraged, equipped, and inspired.
> **Faculty includes:** editors, publishers
> **Attendance:** 60

FLORIDA

FLORIDA CHRISTIAN WRITERS CONFERENCE

Leesburg, FL | October 20-24 | *word-weavers.com/floridaevents*

> **Director:** Eva Marie Everson, PO Box 520224, Longwood, FL 32752; 407-615-4112; *FloridaCWC@aol.com*
> **Description:** If you have a book inside of you, if you have the dream to publish that book, and you don't know where to begin, come be encouraged and trained at the Florida Christian Writers Conference.
> **Special track:** speaking
> **Faculty includes:** editors, agents, and publishers
> **Speaker:** Bill Myers
> **Scholarships:** full, partial
> **Attendance:** 200
> **Contest:** See the website for details.

GEORGIA

WORD WEAVERS INTERNATIONAL KID'S LIT CONFERENCE

Toccoa, GA | March | *word-weavers.com/georgiaevents*

> **Director:** Eva Marie Everson, PO Box 520224, Longwood, FL 32752; 407-615-4112; *wordweaversinternational@aol.com*
> **Description:** Our spring conference is genre specific. This year we

will focus on Kid's Lit, bringing in the top agents, editors, and freelancers to encourage, meet with, instruct, and excite children's book writers. We will span from board books to young adult.
Faculty includes: editors, agents, and publishers
Speaker: Dandi Daley Mackall
Scholarships: partial, full
Attendance: 50
Contest: See website for details.

ILLINOIS

KARITOS ART AND WORSHIP CONFERENCE

Chicago, IL area | July | *karitosnation.org*

> **Director:** Bob Hay, PO Box 17218, Indianapolis, IN 46217; 847-925-8018; *info@karitos.com*
> **Description:** The mission of Karitos is to provide biblically based artistic and technical growth experiences to Christian artists, including writers.
> **Attendance:** 150

WRITE-TO-PUBLISH CONFERENCE

Wheaton, IL (Chicago area) | June 16-19 | *www.writetopublish.com*

> **Director:** Lin Johnson, 9118 W. Elmwood Dr., Ste. 1G, Niles, IL 60714-5820; 847-296-3964; *lin@writetopublish.com*
> **Description:** For 50 years, Write-to-Publish has been training writers and connecting them with editors who want to publish their work and with literary agents who want to represent them. You will hear what editors, publishers, and agents in the Christian market are looking for and meet with them one-on-one to discuss your ideas and manuscripts. You also will learn how to write a variety of publishable manuscripts, improve your writing skills, find appropriate markets for your ideas, and deal with the business side of writing. Plus you will have multiple opportunities to get feedback on your manuscripts.
> **Faculty includes:** editors, agents, and publishers
> **Plenary speaker:** Allie Pleiter
> **Scholarships:** full
> **Attendance:** 150-175
> **Contests:** Best New Writer and Writer of the Year awards, both for alumni who attend this year. Serious Writer contests in multiple genres for unpublished and published writers.

INDIANA

TAYLOR UNIVERSITY'S PROFESSIONAL WRITERS' CONFERENCE

Upland, IN | July | *taylorprofessionalwritersconference.weebly.com*

Director: Linda K. Taylor, 236 W. Reade Ave., Upland, IN 46989; 765-998-5591; *TaylorPRWConference@gmail.com*

Description: Hear from agents, editors, and authors who will inspire and encourage you.

Faculty includes: editors, agents, publishers

Special track: teens

Attendance: 120

KANSAS

CALLED TO WRITE

Pittsburg, KS | April | *calledtowriteconference.wordpress.com*

Director: Barbara Gordon, PO Box 33, Moundville, MO 64771; *calledtowriteconference@gmail.com*

Description: The Called to Write Conference is an annual conference sponsored by Christian Writers Fellowship, Girard, Kansas. Main sessions and workshops are designed for both beginning and seasoned writers.

Faculty includes: editors

Scholarships: partial

Attendance: 50

Contest: for fiction, nonfiction, poetry, devotionals, children's fiction, and children's nonfiction

KENTUCKY

KENTUCKY CHRISTIAN WRITERS CONFERENCE

Elizabethtown, KY | June 17-19 | *www.kychristianwriters.com*

Director: Jean Matthew Hall, 704-578-0858, *jean@jeanmatthewhall.com*

Description: The Kentucky Christian Writers Conference provides an annual, interdenominational event to equip and encourage Christian writers in their quest for publication.

Faculty includes: editors, agents, publishers

Special track: teens

Scholarships: partial, full
Attendance: 100

LOUISIANA

AMERICAN CHRISTIAN FICTION WRITERS (ACFW) CONFERENCE

New Orleans, LA | September 9-12 | *www.ACFW.com/conference*

Director: Robin Miller, PO Box 101066, Palm Bay, FL 32910-1066; *cd@ACFW.com*

Description: Continuing education sessions and workshop electives specifically geared for five levels of fiction-writing experience from beginner to advanced. New: Track for readers, ACFW Storyfest. Note: This conference changes locations every year.

Special track: advanced writers

Faculty includes: editors and agents

Scholarships: full

Attendance: 500

Contest: The Genesis Contest is for unpublished writers whose Christian fiction manuscript is completed. The Carol Awards honor the best of Christian fiction from the previous calendar year.

MICHIGAN

BREATHE CHRISTIAN WRITERS CONFERENCE

Grand Rapids, MI | October | *www.breatheconference.com*

Director: Ann Byle, 1765 3 Mile Rd. N.E., Grand Rapids, MI 49515; 616-389-4436; *register@breatheconference.com*

Description: Breathe offers thirty-six breakouts, two plenary breakouts, and two keynote addresses, with sessions for both advanced and beginning writers. We have a strong community feel and welcome all writers.

Faculty includes: editors, agents, and publishers

Scholarships: full

Attendance: 160

Contest: See website.

MARANATHA CHRISTIAN WRITERS' CONFERENCE

Norton Shores, MI | September 23-25 | *www.maranathachristianwriters.com*

Director: Sherry Hoppen, 4759 Lake Harbor Rd., Norton Shores, MI

49441; 231-798-2161; *info@maranathachristianwriters.com*
Description: A broad variety of publishers, agents, and editors. Up to five
one-to-one appointments with the experts at no additional charge.
Faculty includes: agents, editors, and publishers
Scholarships: partial
Attendance: 80

SPEAKUP CONFERENCE
Grand Rapids, MI | July | *www.speakupconference.com*
Director: *bonnie@speakupconference.com*
Description: Offers two tracks: writing and speaking. In the speakers
track, you have an opportunity to try out what you are learning
in small, interactive groups with a trained professional leading
the feedback. In the writers track, you may preselect up to four
15-minute appointments with writing professionals.
Faculty includes: editors, agents, publishers
Scholarships: partial

MINNESOTA

NORTHWESTERN CHRISTIAN WRITERS CONFERENCE
St. Paul, MN | July 16-17 | *www.northwesternchristianwritersconference.com*
Contact: Melissa Clutter, *ncwc@unwsp.edu*, 651-631-5315
Description: Northwestern Christian Writers Conference engages
the hearts and minds of writers who are Christians. We celebrate
and cultivate Christian writers whose work is inspirational and
accessible, artful and nuanced.
Special track: advanced writers
Speakers: Danielle Strickland, Andrew Peterson
Faculty includes: editors, agents, publishers
Scholarships: partial, full
Attendance: 500
Contests: Prizes: scholarships and awards

MISSOURI

HEART OF AMERICA CHRISTIAN WRITERS NETWORK
Kansas City, MO | October | *www.hacwn.org*
Director: Jeanette Littleton, 3706 N.E. Shady Lane Dr., Gladstone,
MO 64119; 816-459-8016; *jeanettedl@earthlink.net*

Description: We specialize in having faculty who are looking for new writers.
Faculty includes: editors, agents, and publishers
Attendance: 100
Contests: In eight categories. Prizes include critiques and consultations.

REALM MAKERS
St. Louis, MO | July 15-17| *www.realmmakers.com*

Director: Scott Minor, *scott@realmmakers.com*
Description: Realm Makers is the premier conference serving speculative fiction writers. This event offers multilevel education in writing craft, the business of being an author, and the spiritual journey writers face.
Special tracks: advanced writers, teens
Scholarships: full and partial
Faculty includes: agents, editors, and publishers from both CBA and general markets
Speaker: Frank Peretti
Attendance: 350
Contest: The Realm Awards are open to new speculative fiction books written by Christian authors, judged by hand-selected industry professionals. Books may win awards in genre-specific categories and contend for the honor of being named Book of the Year.

NORTH CAROLINA

ASHEVILLE CHRISTIAN WRITERS CONFERENCE
Asheville, NC | February 26-28 |
www.ashevillechristianwritersconference.com

Director: Cindy Sproles, PO Box 6494, Kingsport, TN 37663; 423-384-4821; *cindybootcamp@gmail.com*
Description: To train new and seasoned authors to write and honor God's call, one writer at a time.
Faculty includes: editors, agents, publishers
Speakers: Bob Hostetler, Eva Marie Everson
Scholarships: partial
Attendance: 140
Contests: Sparrow Book Award for a new manuscript and Advance His Kingdom Devotional Contest

BLUE RIDGE MOUNTAINS CHRISTIAN WRITERS CONFERENCE

Black Mountain, NC | May 30—June 3 | www.*BlueRidgeConference.com*

Director: Edie Melson, 604 S. Almond Dr., Simpsonville, SC 29681; 864-373-4232; *Edie@ediemelson.com*

Description: This conference began nearly four decades ago as a Spirit-filled environment where writers could move forward in their writing journey and publishing dreams. The legacy event is focused on God's path for each writer, and the conference is dedicated to meeting professional and spiritual needs.

Special tracks: advanced writers, teens, speaking

Faculty includes: editors, agents, publishers

Scholarships: full

Attendance: 450

Contests: Selah, open to published writers (traditional and self-published); Director's Choice, open to former conferees who have a published book (traditional or self-published); Foundation Awards, open to unpublished attendees

MOUNTAINSIDE MARKETING RETREAT

Black Mountain, NC | *www.blueridgeconference.com/mountainside-marketing-retreat*

Director: Edie Melson, 604 S. Almond Dr., Simpsonville, SC 29681; 864-373-4232; *Edie@ediemelson.com*

Description: Marketing is an integral part of the publishing journey. This hands-on retreat will help you learn the basics of marketing to ensure your work lands in the hands of your readers.

Speakers: Edie Melson, DiAnn Mills

Attendance: 30-50

MOUNTAINSIDE NONFICTION RETREAT

Black Mountain, NC | *www.blueridgeconference.com/mountainside-nonfiction-retreat*

Director: Edie Melson, 604 S. Almond Dr., Simponsville, SC 29681; 864-373-4232; *Edie@ediemelson.com*

Description: Nonfiction writing is one of the foundational skill sets every professional writer must have. Even a novelist's career will be enhanced by knowing how to write compelling articles, devotions, and essays.

Attendance: 30-50

MOUNTAINSIDE NOVELIST RETREAT

Black Mountain, NC | *www.blueridgeconference.com/mountainside-novelist-retreat*

> **Directors:** Edie Melson, 604 S. Almond Dr., Simpsonville, SC 29681; 864-373-4232; *edie@ediemelson.com*
>
> **Description:** Storytelling is the ancient art of entertaining others with a powerful story. What better way to learn the craft than at a novelist retreat in the mountains through small-group instruction and hands-on exercises from bestselling writers.
>
> **Speakers:** Edie Melson, DiAnn Mills
>
> **Attendance:** 30-50

MOUNTAINSIDE SPEAKING RETREAT

Black Mountain, NC | *www.blueridgeconference.com/mountainside-speaking-retreat*

> **Directors:** Edie Melson, 604 S. Almond Dr., Simponsville, SC 29681; 864-373-4232; *Edie@ediemelson.com*
>
> **Description:** Speaking is an art, but it's also a skill that can be learned. It's a gift to pair with writing or as a singular means of sharing God's Word as we teach and motivate others. Come expecting to learn the techniques that separate the professionals from the amateurs. Included will be techniques on enunciation, hooking the listener, voice inflection, content, poise, and dress.
>
> **Speakers:** DiAnn Mills, Edie Melson, Karen Porter
>
> **Attendance:** 30-50

NORTH CAROLINA CHRISTIAN WRITERS CONFERENCE

Liberty, NC | March 4-6 | *www.seriouswriter.com/nc*

> **Director:** Angie Duduit, 3572 W. Greensboro Chapel Hill Rd., Liberty, NC 27298; *support@seriouswriter.com*
>
> **Description:** The goal of the North Carolina Christian Writers Conference is to provide the most up-to-date information and strategies in marketing, social media, and platform-building, along with best practices and how-to's in the craft of nonfiction, fiction, and children's writing.
>
> **Special track:** marketing
>
> **Faculty includes:** editors, agents, publishers
>
> **Attendance:** 75

SHE SPEAKS CONFERENCE

Concord, NC | July | *shespeaksconference.com*

> **Director:** Lisa Allen, 630 Team Rd. #100, Matthews, NC 28105;

704-849-2270; *shespeaks@Proverbs31.org*
Description: Speaking and writing tracks.
Faculty includes: editors and agents
Attendance: 700

PENNSYLVANIA

EVANGELICAL PRESS ASSOCIATION ANNUAL CHRISTIAN MEDIA CONVENTION

Lancaster, PA | April 28-30 | *epaconvention.com*

Director: Lamar Keener, Executive Director, PO Box 1787, Queen
Creek, AZ 85142; 888-311-1732; *director@evangelicalpress.com*
Description: A convention for everyone involved in Christian
periodicals and content-based websites. Note: This conference
changes locations every year.
Faculty includes: editors, publishers
Attendance: 200
Contest: for members of the Evangelical Press Association, including
freelance writers who enter articles or blog posts

GREATER PHILADELPHIA CHRISTIAN WRITERS CONFERENCE

Lansdale, PA | end of July/early August | *philadelphia.writehisanswer.com*

Director: Marlene Bagnull, 951 Anders Rd., Lansdale, PA 19446;
484-991-8581; *mbagnull@aol.com*
Description: To encourage and equip you to write about a God who
is real, who is reachable, and who changes lives. Seven continuing
sessions, forty-two workshops, six keynotes, authors night, and book
signing. Our 2020 conference was postponed until 2021 because of
the pandemic. We will be featuring the same faculty and program. If
COVID-19 makes it unsafe to meet in person, we will go virtual.
Special track: teens
Faculty includes: editors, agents, and publishers
Keynote speaker: Liz Curtis Higgs
Scholarships: partial
Attendance: 200
Contest: For registered conferees. Entries based on the conference
theme. Prose (maximum 500 words) or poetry by published
and not-yet-published authors. The winner in each of the four
categories receives 50% off the registration fee for the following
year. Entry fee $10.

MONTROSE CHRISTIAN WRITERS CONFERENCE

Montrose, PA | July | *www.montrosebible.org/OurEvents.aspx*

Director: Marsha Hubler, 1833 Dock Hill Rd., Middleburg, PA
17842; 570-837-0002; *marshahubler@outlook.com*

Description: Over 50 workshops for beginners and published authors
presented by agents, editors, and best-selling authors. Almost all
genres covered, including how to begin, editing skills, marketing,
and self-publishing.

Faculty includes: editors, agents, publishers

Special tracks: advanced writers and teens

Scholarships: partial

Attendance: 75

Contest: $200 toward tuition awarded to an unpublished conferee
who submits the winning entry to the Shirley Brinkerhoff
Memorial Scholarship Contest

ST. DAVIDS CHRISTIAN WRITERS' CONFERENCE

Grove City, PA | June | *www.stdavidswriters.com/conference*

Director: Sue Boltz, *treasurer@stdavidswriters.com*

Description: Small Christian writers conference to learn, grow, and
connect in your writing journey.

Faculty includes: editors and agents

Scholarships: full and partial

Attendance: 45

Contests: See detailed list on the website.

SUPER SATURDAY

Lancaster, PA | April 24 | *lancasterchristianwriters.wordpress.com,
lancasterchristianwriterstoday.blogspot.com*

Director: JP Robinson, PO Box 271, Lampeter, PA 17537; 717-681-
8452; *lancasterwrites@gmail.com*

Description: Super Saturday allows writers to hone their craft and
discover publishing opportunities by collaborating with successful
authors and industry leaders.

Faculty includes: editors, agents, publishers

Attendance: 125

SOUTH CAROLINA

CAROLINA CHRISTIAN WRITERS CONFERENCE

Spartanburg, SC | March 12-13 | *www.fbs.org/writers*

> **Director:** Linda Gilden, 1288 Old Switzer Rd., Woodruff, SC 29388; 864-583-7245; *linda@lindagilden.com*
>
> **Description:** Carolina Christian Writers Conference is open to writers of all skill levels and offers opportunities to learn, network, meet with editors, enter the contest, worship, and build relationships with those in the industry. The small size allows writers to have lots of interaction with faculty and industry professionals who will encourage, enlighten, and equip them to meet their writing goals.
>
> **Faculty includes:** editors, agents, publishers
>
> **Scholarships:** full
>
> **Attendance:** 125
>
> **Contest:** Kudos Contest for new and published writers

WRITE2IGNITE MASTER CLASSES FOR CHRISTIAN WRITERS OF CHILDREN AND YOUNG ADULT LITERATURE

Tigerville, SC | September | *write2ignite.com*

> **Director:** Deborah S. DeCiantis, PO Box 41, Tigerville, SC 29688; 803-517-4143; *info.write2ignite@gmail.com*
>
> **Description:** Write2Ignite seeks to: (1) inspire and challenge novice to experienced writers, middle school through adult, to serve God and young readers through their writing; (2) facilitate Christian writers' development by providing instruction on writing craft and professional publishing, especially of children's and young-adult literature; and (3) connect authors with one another and with published authors, editors and literary agents, illustrators, and other writing and publishing professionals.
>
> **Faculty inludes:** editors, agents, and publishers
>
> **Special tracks:** teens, advanced writers
>
> **Scholarships:** full, partial
>
> **Attendance:** 55-80
>
> **Contest:** Unpublished Picture Book manuscript

TENNESSEE

ART OF WRITING CONFERENCE

Nashville, TN | October—November | *www.christyawards.com*

   Director: Cindy Carter, ECPA, 480-966-3998, *TheChristyAward@ ecpa.org*

   Description: A focused conference for writers, storytellers, and publishing curators. Held in conjunction with the Christy Awards.

   Faculty includes: editors, publishers, agents

   Attendance: 150-200

   Contest: Watch our social-media partners for contest opportunities.

TEXAS

COLLAB CONFERENCE

Waco, TX | April | *www.collab-conference.com*

   Director: Elizabeth Oates, 712 Austin Ave., Waco, TX 76712; 254-855-9429; *info@collab-conference.com*

   Description: Collab Conference is a distinct Christian women's conference for those longing to live out their God-given calling through writing, blogging, speaking, teaching, and leading.

   Faculty includes: agents

   Scholarships: full

   Attendance: 50

TEXAS CHRISTIAN WRITERS CONFERENCE

Houston, TX | August 7 | *www.centralhoustoniwa.com*

   Director: Martha Rogers, *marthalrogers@sbcglobal.net*

   Description: The Texas Christian Writers Conference brings first-class teaching and networking opportunities to both new and experienced writers through its one-on-one chats with professional writers and editors, and a variety of workshops aimed at developing the writing craft and marketability in our rapidly changing publication environment.

   Attendance: 50

   Contests: The Inspirational Writers Alive! Open Writing Competition offers small cash prizes in the following categories: adult/YA short story, children/teens short story, articles, poetry, devotionals and book proposals for adult nonfiction, adult novels, and children's books.

WASHINGTON

NORTHWEST CHRISTIAN WRITERS RENEWAL
Bellevue, WA | May 15-16 | *www.nwchristianwriters.org*
> **Directors:** Charles and Perry Harris, PO Box 2706, Woodinville, WA
> 98072; 206-250-6885; *renewal@nwchristianwriters.org*
> **Description:** This conference is where writers, editors, and publishers
> can connect, network, and collaborate. Conferees will sharpen
> their skills, learn strategies, and form connections to boost their
> success on the writing journey.
> **Faculty includes:** editors, agents, publishers
> **Scholarships:** full
> **Attendance:** 130

AUSTRALIA

OMEGA WRITERS CONFERENCE
Gold Coast, QLD | October 8-10 | *www.omegawriters.org/conference*
> **Director:** Raewyn Elsegood, *conference@omegawriters.org*
> **Description:** A conference for Australian and New Zealand Christian
> writers—a great time for networking with and learning from
> fellow Christian writers.
> **Faculty includes:** publishers, editors
> **Keynote speaker:** Susan May Warren
> **Scholarships:** full and partial
> **Attendance:** 100
> **Contest:** Caleb Awards

CANADA

InSCRIBE CHRISTIAN WRITERS' FELLOWSHIP ANNUAL FALL CONFERENCE
Edmonton, AB | September 30—October 2 | *inscribe.org/events/fall-conference*
> **Director:** Box 68025, Edmonton, AB T6C 4N6; *president@inscribe.org*
> **Description:** Intimate conference to encourage and inspire Canadian
> writers of Christian faith.
> **Special track:** advanced writers
> **Speaker:** D.S. Martin
> **Scholarships:** full, partial

Attendance: 50

Contest: multiple genres

WRITE! CANADA CONFERENCE

writecanada.org

> **Contact:** Box 77001, Markham, ON L3P 0C8; *info@thewordguild.com*
>
> **Description:** Write! Canada is an annual writers conference hosted by The Word Guild. Seasoned writers host workshops where writers of all experience levels and genres can meet and hone their skills.

NEW ZEALAND

NZ CHRISTIAN WRITERS RETREAT

Whitianga, New Zealand | April 29—May 2 | *www.nzchristianwriters.org/retreat-2020*

> **Director:** Justin St. Vincent, 179B St. Johns Road, St. Johns, Auckland, North Island 1072; *editor@xtrememusic.org*
>
> **Description:** Our seminar speakers will inspire, refresh, and upskill each of us on our writing journey.
>
> **Faculty includes:** editors, publishers
>
> **Attendance:** 40

ONLINE

THE BUSINESS OF BEING A SPIRITUAL WRITER

January 11-14 | *writingforyourlife.com/the-business-of-being-a-spiritual-writer-online-edition*

> **Director:** Brian Allain, PO Box 72, Adelphia, NJ 07710; *brian@writingforyourlife.com*
>
> **Description:** Not only do authors need a platform, they must enter the market strategically in order to make that platform, and that book, happen. They must operate like an entrepreneur—agile, flexible, and creative in their business.
>
> **Attendance:** 15

CHRISTIAN CHILDREN'S BOOK 2021 ONLINE CONFERENCE

May 10-14 | *writingforyourlife.com/conferences*

> **Director:** Brian Allain, PO Box 72, Adelphia, NJ 07710; *brian@writingforyourlife.com*

Description: The conference is geared toward Christian children's book readers and writers, including educators and librarians. Our speakers include authors, illustrators, educators, editors, and more.
Faculty includes: editors
Attendance: 100

MID-SOUTH CHRISTIAN WRITERS CONFERENCE

March 19-20 | *MidSouthChristianWriters.com*

Director: Beth Gooch, PO Box 823, Byhalia, MS 38611; 901-277-5525; *midsouthchristianwriters@gmail.com*
Description: The basic conference fee includes all-day Saturday with a well-known keynote speaker and break-out sessions led by a diverse faculty with expertise in fiction, nonfiction, and business. Optional Friday classes offer in-depth instruction in specific areas of interest; some include one-on-one coaching.
Faculty includes: editors, agents, publishers
Speaker: Rachel Hauck
Attendance: 100

OREGON CHRISTIAN WRITERS FALL CONFERENCE

October 16 or 23 | *www.oregonchristianwriters.org*

Contact: Tracie Heskett, *contact@oregonchristianwriters.org*
Description: Encouragement and instruction for fiction and nonfiction writers of all levels who want to improve their craft.
Speaker: Susy Flory
Attendance: 125

OREGON CHRISTIAN WRITERS SPRING CONFERENCE

May 15 | *www.oregonchristianwriters.org*

Contact: Tracie Heskett, *contact@oregonchristianwriters.org*
Description: Encouragement and instruction for fiction and nonfiction writers of all levels who want to improve their craft.
Speaker: Peter Leavell
Attendance: 100

OREGON CHRISTIAN WRITERS SUMMER CONFERENCE

August 16-19 | *www.oregonchristianwriters.org/summerconference*

Director: Lindy Jacobs, 1075 Willow Lake Rd. N., Kelzer, OR 97303; 541-408-6306; *summerconf@oregonchristianwriters.org*
Description: Includes seven hours of training under a specific coach for beginning writers to advanced in multiple genres; twenty one-hour workshops; intensive, four-hour, small-group critique via

Zoom; manuscript reviews; one-on-one appointments with editors and agents; mentor appointments

Special track: advanced writers

Faculty includes: editors, agents, publishers

Speakers: Rachel Hauck, Brett Lott

Scholarships: partial

Attendance: 300

Contest: Cascade Writing Contest (see "**Contests**") winners will be announced live August 18.

OREGON CHRISTIAN WRITERS WINTER CONFERENCE

February 20 | *www.oregonchristianwriters.org*

Contact: Tracie Heskett, *contact@oregonchristianwriters.org*

Description: Encouragement and instruction for fiction and nonfiction writers of all levels who want to improve their craft.

Speaker: Mesu Andrews

Attendance: 125

PENCON

May 12-14 | *penconeditors.com*

Director: Denise Loock, 699 Golf Course Rd., Waynesville, NC 28786; 908-868-5854; *director@penconeditors.com*

Description: Are you wondering if editing is right for you? Are you an established editor looking for face-to-face connections? Are you an in-house editor seeking an editing community or continuing education? Want to brush up on your editing skills or learn something new? Join us to learn from industry professionals and network with fellow editors from beginners to seasoned professionals. PENCON is the only annual conference for Christian proofreaders and editors in the industry.

Faculty includes: editors

Speaker: Robert Hudson

Special track: Establishing and maintaining a freelance editing business

Attendance: 50

PUBLISHING IN COLOR 2021 SPRING ONLINE CONFERENCE

April 19-23 | *publishingincolor.com*

Director: Brian Allain, PO Box 72, Adelphia, NJ 07710; *brian@writingforyourlife.com*

Description: Publishing in Color has only one objective: increase

the number of books published by spiritual writers of color. This includes such groups as African Americans, Asian Americans, Latinx Americans, and Native Americans, who have been under-represented in terms of the number of published books. The goals of these conferences are to: 1. Foster relationships between spiritual writers of color and representatives of spiritual book-publishing companies and magazines; 2. Provide networking and educational opportunities, so prospective writers can learn more about how to work with these publishers and magazines; 3. Result in an increased number of books and articles published by writers of color.
Faculty includes: editors, agents
Scholarships: full
Attendance: 100

WEST COAST CHRISTIAN WRITERS CONFERENCE
February 25-27 | *www.westcoastchristianwriters.com*
Director: Susy Flory, 1750 Prairie City Rd., Ste. 130 #689, Folsom, CA 95630; 510-828-5360; *westcoastchristianwriters@gmail.com*
Description: West Coast Christian Writers (WCCW) is a strong community of writers with writing events known for high value, expert speakers, and teachers, along with hands-on help and innovation. A legacy conference of nearly 30 years, WCCW is a place where writers thrive. Online version is temporary for 2021.
Special tracks: advanced writers, plus monthly mini-masterclass workshops where recognized experts go deep
Faculty includes: editors, agents, publishers
Speakers: Vivian Mabuni, Marlena Graves
Scholarships: partial, full
Attendance: 300
Contests: The Goldie Awards, named for the iconic Golden Gate Bridge, is an annual writing contest for fiction, nonfiction, poetry, and children's writing. We also give a Lifetime Achievement Award to a writer, editor, or literary agent with a body of work that has left a positive mark on the industry.

WRITING FOR YOUR LIFE 2021 SPRING ONLINE CONFERENCE
March 22-26 | *writingforyourlife.com/conferences*
Director: Brian Allain, PO Box 72, Adelphia, NJ 07710; *brian@writingforyourlife.com*

Description: If you write or read books that matter—books with substance and soul—then this is the place for you. Writing for Your Life produces writing conferences featuring leading authors and industry experts presenting on various topics in the areas of how to write, how to get published, and how to market. You do not need to be an experienced writer to attend. Our conferences have a reputation for high-quality speakers, collegiality, and a lack of competitiveness among attendees, so please do not be intimidated if you have not yet published much. Come join us, and enjoy the supportive environment.

Faculty includes: editors, agents

Speaker: Barbara Brown Taylor

Attendance: 100

CONFERENCES THAT CHANGE LOCATIONS

The following conferences change locations every year but are listed with their 2021 locations:

AMERICAN CHRISTIAN FICTION WRITERS CONFERENCE

EVANGELICAL PRESS ASSOCIATION ANNUAL CONVENTION

REALM MAKERS

Christian Publishing Show
Featured Episode

Podcast episode: How to Pitch Your Book at a Writers Conference with Bob Hostetler
Market guide price: FREE

https://cwmg.link/pitch2021

How to Scan QR Codes
Use the camera on your smartphone to focus on the above QR code to activate the discount. It will give you the option to visit the site, which you will want to accept. If you are using an older smartphone, you may need to download a QR-code scanning app. You can also visit the URL below the code to activate the discount on your computer.

18

WRITERS GROUPS

In addition to the groups listed here, check these websites for other groups in your area:

American Christian Writers chapters: *www.acwriters.com*
American Christian Fiction Writers chapters: *www.ACFW.com*
Word Weavers International chapters: *www.Word-Weavers.com*

NATIONAL AND ONLINE

ACFW BEYOND THE BORDERS
www.facebook.com/groups/ACFWBeyondtheBorders
> **Contact:** Iola Goulton, *beyondborders@acfwchapter.com*
> **Members:** 100
> **Affiliation:** American Christian Fiction Writers

AMERICAN CHRISTIAN FICTION WRITERS
ACFW.com
> **Contact:** Robin Miller, executive director, PO Box 101066, Palm Bay, FL 32910; *cd@ACFW.com*
> **Services:** Email loop, genre Facebook pages, online courses, critique groups, and local and regional chapters. Sponsors contests for published and unpublished writers and conducts the largest fiction writers conference annually.
> **Members:** 2600+

CHRISTIAN AUTHORS NETWORK
ChristianAuthorsNetwork.com
> **Meetings:** Online and at major writing-industry events, daily via private loop
> **Contact:** Angela Breidenbach, *contact@christianauthorsnetwork.com*
> **Members:** 115
> **Membership fee:** $50/year plus $50 one-time fee

CHRISTIAN INDIE AUTHOR NETWORK

www.christianindieauthors.com

> **Meetings:** 24/7 on Facebook and website
> **Contact:** Mary C. Findley, 918-805-0669, *mjmcfindley@gmail.com*
> **Members:** 400+

CHRISTIAN WOMEN WRITER'S GROUP

cwwriters.com

> **Meetings:** weekly and monthly communications
> **Contact:** Jen Gentry, 918-724-3996, *jennyokiern37@gmail.com*
> **Members:** 100+
> **Affiliation:** Christian Indie Author Network

EVERYTHING MEMOIR CRITIQUE GROUPS

www.facebook.com/groups/everythingmemoir

> **Meetings:** online
> **Contact:** Penelope Childers, director of critique groups
> **Members:** 35
> **Membership fee:** none; by application only and membership in the online Everything Memoir Private Group
> **Affiliation:** West Coast Christian Writers

INSPIRE CHRISTIAN WRITERS

www.inspirewriters.com

> **Meetings:** regional and online critique groups
> **Contact:** Robynne Miller, 530-217-8233, *inspiredirectors@gmail.com*
> **Members:** 150
> **Affiliation:** West Coast Christian Writers

PEN-SOULS

> **Meetings:** online and email; monthly reminders are emailed to members to pray for one another and share urgent, personal prayer requests and publishing announcements
> **Contact:** Janet Ann Collins, 530-272-4905, *jan@janetanncollins.com*
> **Members:** 10-12

REALM MAKERS

www.realmmakers.com

> **Meetings:** quarterly online
> **Contact:** Rebecca Minor, *members@realmmakers.com*
> **Membership:** 100
> **Membership fee:** varies from free to $24.99/month

WORD WEAVERS INTERNATIONAL, INC.
www.Word-Weavers.com
> **Contact:** Eva Marie Everson, president, PO Box 520224, Longwood, FL 32708; 407-615-4112; *WordWeaversInternational@aol.com*
> **Services:** Local chapters and Zoom for manuscript critiquing. Sponsors Florida Christian Writers Conference and North Georgia Christian Writers Conference.
> **Members:** 1,000+
> **Membership fee:** $45/year, adults; $35/year, students

ALABAMA

WORD WEAVERS NORTH ALABAMA
> **Meetings:** Hartsell; third Thursday of the month, 10:00 a.m.-noon
> **Contact:** Lisa Worthey Smith, *LisaWSmith75@gmail.com*
> **Members:** 10
> **Membership fee:** $45/year
> **Affiliation:** Word Weavers International

ARIZONA

ACFW ARIZONA
www.christianwritersofthewest.com
> **Meetings:** Denny's, 4400 N. Scottsdale Rd., Scottsdale; third Saturday of the month, 1:00-3:00 p.m.
> **Contact:** Ruth Douthitt, *Arizona@acfwchapter.com*
> **Members:** 30
> **Membership fee:** $10/year plus national fee
> **Affiliation:** American Christian Fiction Writers

CHANDLER WRITERS' GROUP
chandlerwriters.wordpress.com
> **Meetings:** member's home, near Gilbert and Ocotillo Roads; first Friday of the month, 9:00-11:30 a.m.
> **Contact:** Jenne Acevedo, 480-510-0419, *editor@jenneacevedo.com*
> **Members:** 10
> **Membership fee:** none

FOUNTAIN HILLS CHRISTIAN WRITERS' GROUP
> **Meetings:** Fountain Hills Presbyterian Church, 13001 N. Fountain

Hills Blvd.; second Friday of the month, 9:00 a.m. to noon
Contact: Jewell Johnson, 480-836-8968, *tykeJ@juno.com*
Members: 12
Membership fee: $10/year
Affiliation: American Christian Writers

WORD WEAVERS NORTHERN ARIZONA
Meetings: Verde Community Church, 102 S. Willard, Cottonwood; second Saturday of the month, 9:30-11:30 a.m.
Contact: Alice Klies, *Alice.Klies@Gmail.com*
Membership fee: $45/year
Affiliation: Word Weavers International

ARKANSAS

ACFW ARKANSAS
acfwarkansas.com
Meetings: Searcy Public Library, 113 E. Pleasure Ave., Searcy; second Saturday of the month, 1:00 p.m.
Contact: Tonya Ashley, *Arkansas@acfwchapter.com*
Members: 20
Membership fee: national fee
Affiliation: American Christian Fiction Writers

ACFW NW ARKANSAS
www.facebook.com/groups/127662834752320
Meetings: Robinson Avenue Church of Christ, 1506 W. Robinson Ave., Springdale; last Saturday of the month, 3:30 p.m.
Contact: Robyn Hook, *NWArkansas@acfwchapter.com*
Members: 12
Membership fee: $10 plus ACFW fee
Affiliation: American Christian Fiction Writers, American Christian Writers

CALIFORNIA

ACFW ORANGE COUNTY
acfwoc.com
Meetings: Marie Callendar's, 307 E. Katella Ave., Orange; second Thursday of the month, 6:30 p.m.
Contact: Susan K. Beatty, *orangecounty@acfwchapter.com*

Members: 15
Membership fee: $10 plus national dues
Affiliation: American Christian Fiction Writers

ACFW SAN FRANCISCO BAY AREA CHAPTER
acfwsfba.wordpress.com
> **Meetings:** Crosswalk Community Church, 445 S. Mary Ave.,
> Sunnyvale; third Saturday of odd months, 10 a.m. to noon
> **Contact:** Beth Worcester, *sanfranciscobay@acfwchapter.com*
> **Members:** 15
> **Membership fee:** $17/year plus national dues
> **Affiliation:** American Christian Fiction Writers, American Christian Writers

WORD WARRIORS
www.facebook.com/wordwarriorswriters
> **Meetings:** 3 Crosses Church, 20600 John Dr., Castro Valley; first
> Monday of the month September—June, 7:00 p.m.
> **Contact:** Debbie Jones Warren, 510-329-4141, *debbiencj@aim.com*
> **Members:** 15
> **Membership fee:** none

COLORADO

ACFW COLORADO SPRINGS
acfwcosprings.com
> **Meetings:** First Evangelical Free Church, 3022 W. Fontanero St.,
> Colorado Springs; first Saturday of the month, 10:00 a.m.-noon
> **Contact:** Erin Kohler, *coloradosprings@acfwchapter.com*
> **Members:** 45
> **Membership fee:** national fee
> **Affiliation:** American Christian Fiction Writers

SPRINGS WRITERS
springswriters.wordpress.com
> **Meetings:** Woodmen Valley Chapel, 250 E. Woodmen Rd., Colorado
> Springs; second Tuesday of each month except July, August, and
> December, 6:00-8:00 p.m.
> **Contact:** Scoti Springfield Domeij, 719-209-9066, *springswriters@gmail.com*
> **Members:** 350
> **Membership fee:** none

WORD WEAVERS PIKES PEAK

www.facebook.com/groups/415291469231448

> **Meetings:** 2650 Leoti Dr., Colorado Springs; third Saturday of each month, 9:30-11:30 a.m.
> **Contact:** Tez Brooks, *tezwrites@gmail.com*, 407-797-4408
> **Members:** 10-15
> **Membership fee:** $45 per year
> **Affiliation:** Word Weavers International

WORD WEAVERS WESTERN SLOPE

> **Meetings:** Grand Junction; fourth Saturday of the month, 10:00 a.m. to noon
> **Contact:** Darlia Sawyer, *darliadawn@gmail.com*
> **Membership fee:** $45 per year
> **Affiliation:** Word Weavers International

WRITERS ON THE ROCK

www.writersontherock.com/groups

> **Meetings:** multiple locations in Colorado, various meeting times; see the website for locations
> **Contact:** David Rupert, 720-237-7487, *david@writersontherock.com*
> **Members:** 580
> **Membership fee:** none

CONNECTICUT

WORD WEAVERS BERKSHIRES

wordweaversberkshires.org

> **Meetings:** Sherman Church, 6 Church Rd., Sherman; third Saturday of the month, 9:00 a.m. to noon
> **Contact:** Tara Alemany, *info@wordweaversberkshires.org*
> **Members:** 15
> **Membership fee:** $45/year
> **Affiliation:** Word Weavers International

DELAWARE

DELMARVA CHRISTIAN WRITERS' ASSOCIATION

www.delmarvawriters.com

> **Meetings:** Georgetown Presbyterian Church, Tunnell Hall, 203 N. Bedford St., Georgetown; third Saturday of the month, 9:00 a.m. to noon

Contact: Candy Abbott, 302-856-6649, *cfa@candyabbot.com*
Members: 20
Membership fee: none

KINGDOM WRITERS FELLOWSHIP

Meetings: Atlanta Road Alliance Church, 22625 Atlanta Rd.,
    Seaford; second Tuesday of the month, 6:00-9:00 p.m.
Contact: Teresa Marine, 302-841-2432, *tdm4Him@yahoo.com*
Members: 8
Affiliation: Delmarva Christian Writers' Fellowship

FLORIDA

ACFW CENTRAL FLORIDA

Meetings: Longwood; third Saturday of the month
Contact: Nancy Schalm, *centralflorida@acfwchapter.com*
Membership fee: national fee
Affiliation: American Christian Fiction Writers

SUNCOAST CHRISTIAN WRITERS GROUP

Meetings: Panera Bread, Largo Mall, 10500 Ulmerton Rd., Largo;
    third Thursday of the month, 10 a.m.
Contact: Elaine Creasman, 727-251-3756, *emcreasman@aol.com*
Members: 15
Membership fee: none

WORD WEAVERS CLAY COUNTY

Meetings: Panera Bread, 1510 County Rd. 220, Fleming Island;
    second Saturday of the month, 9:00-11:30 a.m.
Members: 7
Membership fee: $45/year
Affiliation: Word Weavers International

WORD WEAVERS DESTIN

Meetings: Village Baptist Church, 101 Matthew Dr.; second Saturday
    of the month, 9:30 a.m.-12:30 p.m.
Contact: Susan Neal, *susanneal@bellsouth.net*
Members: 18
Membership fee: $45/year
Affiliation: Word Weavers International

WORD WEAVERS GAINESVILLE
www.facebook.com/groups/277156498961942
> **Meetings:** various locations; fourth Sunday of the month, 2:00-4:30 p.m.
> **Contact:** Lorilyn Roberts, *authorLorilynRoberts@gmail.com*
> **Members:** 5
> **Membership fee:** $45/year
> **Affiliation:** Word Weavers International

WORD WEAVERS LAKE COUNTY
> **Meetings:** Leesburg Public Library, 100 E. Main St., Leesburg; second Saturday of the month, 10:00 a.m.-12:30 p.m.
> **Contact:** Frank Stanfield, *FrankEStanfield@gmail.com*
> **Members:** 7
> **Membership fee:** $45/year
> **Affiliation:** Word Weavers International

WORD WEAVERS MARIANNA
> **Meetings:** Eastside Baptist Church, 4785 Highway 90; third Saturday of the month, 9:30 a.m.-noon
> **Contact:** Sherri Stone, *sherristone62@hotmail.com*
> **Members:** 5
> **Membership fee:** $45
> **Affiliation:** Word Weavers International

WORD WEAVERS NAPLES
> **Meetings:** North Naples Baptist Church, 1811 Oakes Blvd.; third Tuesday of the month, 6:30-9:00 p.m.
> **Contact:** Julie Christian, *ugabuggy3@gmail.com*
> **Members:** 8
> **Membership fee:** $45
> **Affiliation:** Word Weavers International

WORD WEAVERS OCALA
> **Meetings:** Belleview Public Library, 13145 S.E. County Hwy. 484, Belleview; second Friday of the month, 10:00 a.m.-12:30 p.m.
> **Contact:** Jennifer Odom, *odomj@live.com*
> **Members:** 10+
> **Membership fee:** $45/year
> **Affiliation:** Word Weavers International

WORD WEAVERS ORLANDO
> **Meetings:** Calvary Chapel, 5015 Goddard Ave.; second Saturday of

the month, 10:00 a.m.-12:30 p.m.
Contact: Kim Clark, *kim@kimmclark.com*
Members: 40-45
Membership fee: $45/year
Affiliation: Word Weavers International

WORD WEAVERS PENSACOLA

Meetings: Hillcrest Baptist Church, 800 E. 9 Mile Rd.; second
    Tuesday of the month, 5:00-8:00 p.m.
Contact: Ginny Cruz, *gincru@gmail.com*
Members: 5
Membership fee: $45/year
Affiliation: Word Weavers International

WORD WEAVERS SARASOTA

Meetings: First United Methodist Church, 104 S. Pineapple Ave.;
    fourth Sunday of the month, 2:00-4:00 p.m.
Contact: Sam Wright, *drsamwright@comcast.net*
Members: 5
Membershiip fee: $45
Affiliation: Word Weavers International

WORD WEAVERS SOUTH FLORIDA

Meetings: Gracepoint Church, 5590 N.E. 6th Ave., Fort Lauderdale;
    second Saturday of the month, 9:00 a.m.-12:30 p.m.
Contact: Patricia Hartman, *patricia@patriciahartman.com*
Members: 15
Membership fee: $45/year
Affiliation: Word Weavers International

WORD WEAVERS TAMPA

Meetings: Jan Powell, 1901 S. Village Ave.; first Saturday of the
    month, 9:30 a.m.-12:30 p.m.
Contact: Sharron Cosby, *sharroncosby@gmail.com*
Members: 22
Membership fee: $45/year
Affiliation: Word Weavers International

WORD WEAVERS TREASURE COAST

Meetings: First Church of God, 1105 58th Ave., Vero Beach; first
    Saturday of the month or second Saturday if the first falls on a
    major holiday, 9:30 a.m. to noon

Contact: Del Bates, *handstoblessu_@hotmail.com*
Members: 17
Membership fee: $45/year
Affiliation: Word Weavers International

WORD WEAVERS VOLUSIA COUNTY
Meetings: Faith Church of United Brethren in Christ, 4700 S. Clyde
   Morris Blvd., Port Orange; first Monday of the month, 7:00 p.m.
Contact: Renee Hanson, *rlhhh2@gmail.com,* 386-341-7576
Members: 25
Membership fee: $45/year
Affiliation: Word Weavers International

GEORGIA

ACFW NORTH GEORGIA
acfwnga.com
Meetings: Atlanta; fourth Tuesday of the month
Contact: Hope Welborn, *northgeorgia@acfwchapter.com*
Membership fee: national fee
Affiliation: American Christian Fiction Writers

ACFW NORTHWEST GEORGIA
acfwnorthwestga.blogspot.com
Meetings: Marietta; second Tuesday of each month, 630-8:30 p.m.
Contact: Cindy Stewart, *nwgeorgia@acfwchapter.com*
Members: 14
Membership fee: $15 plus national dues
Affiliation: American Christian Fiction Writers

CHRISTIAN AUTHORS GUILD
www.christianauthorsguild.org
Meetings: Zoom; first Monday of the month, except holidays, 7:00 p.m. ˙
Contact: Cynthia Simmons, *cynthialsimmons@gmail.com*
Members: 25-30

WORD WEAVERS BROOKHAVEN
Meetings: Brookhaven; second Saturday of the month, 10:00 a.m.-12:30 p.m.
Contact: Debra Bryant, *dbryant2941@gmail.com*
Membership fee: $45/year
Affiliation: Word Weavers International

WORD WEAVERS COLUMBUS
Meetings: Cornerstone Church of God, 7701 Lloyd Rd.; third
Monday of the month, 6:30-7:30 p.m.
Contact: Susan Sloan, *SPSloan@Yahoo.com*
Membership fee: $45/year
Affiliation: Word Weavers International

WORD WEAVERS GREATER ATLANTA
Meetings: 4541 Vendome Pl. N.E., Roswell; first Saturday of the
month, 9:30 to noon
Contact: Barbara Fox, *barb@barbjfox.com*
Membership fee: $45/year
Affiliation: Word Weavers International

WORD WEAVERS MACON-BIB
Meetings: Central City Church, 621 Foster Rd., Macon; second
Sunday of the month, 3:00-5:30 p.m.
Contact: Robin Dance, *RobinDance.Me@Gmail.com*
Membership fee: $45/year
Affiliation: Word Weavers International

WORD WEAVERS MADISON
Meetings: Bethel Christian Church, 1930 Bethel Rd. N.E., Conyers;
second Saturday of the month, 10:00 a.m. to noon
Contact: Barbara Latta, *blatta146@gmail.com*
Membership fee: $45/year
Affiliation: Word Weavers International

WORD WEAVERS WOODSTOCK
Meetings: Prayer & Praise Christian Fellowship, 6409 Bells Ferry Rd.;
third Monday of the month, 6:30-9:00 p.m.
Contact: Frieda Dixon, *friedas@bellsouth.net*
Members: 20
Membership fee: $45/year
Affiliation: Word Weavers International, Christian Authors Guild

ILLINOIS

ACFW CHICAGO
www.ACFWchicago.com
Meetings: Schaumburg Public Library, 130 S. Roselle Rd.,

Schaumburg; second Friday of every month, 6:30-8:30 p.m.
Contact: Susan Miura, 847-714-4755, *chicago@acfwchapter.com*
Members: 25
Membership fee: $25/month
Affiliation: American Christian Fiction Writers

WORD WEAVERS AURORA

Meetings: email for location; second Saturday of each month, 1:00-3:00 p.m.
Contact: JoDee Starrick, *JoDee.Starrick@gmail.com*
Members: 18
Membership fee: $45/year
Affiliation: Word Weavers International

WORD WEAVERS LAND OF LINCOLN

Meetings: Lincoln Christian University, 100 Campus View Dr.,
Lincoln; second Saturday of every month, 10:00 a.m. to noon
Contact: Rita Klundt, *ritaklundt@ymail.com*
Members: 9
Membership fee: $45/year
Affiliation: Word Weavers International

WORD WEAVERS ON THE BORDER

Meetings: Fox Lake Library, 255 E. Grand Ave., Fox Lake; fourth
Thursday of the month, 7:00-9:00 p.m.
Contact: Fred Von Kamecke, 815-359-0439, *FVonKamecke@comcast.net*
Members: 3
Membership fee: $45/year
Affiliation: Word Weavers International

INDIANA

ACFW INDIANA

www.hoosierink.blogspot.com
Meetings: various places in Indiana, quarterly
Contact: Linda Samaritoni, *indiana@acfwchapter.com*
Members: 50
Membership fee: national fee
Affiliation: American Christian Fiction Writers

BLUFFTON CHRISTIAN WRITING CLUB

Facebook group: Bluffton IN Christian Writing Group

Meetings: Zoom; third Monday of the month, 6:30-8:30 p.m.
Contact: Kayleen Reusser, *KayleenReusser@gmail.com*
Members: 10
Membership fee: none

FORT WAYNE CHRISTIAN WRITERS GUILD

Facebook group: Fort Wayne Christian Writers Guild

Meetings: Zoom; fourth Tuesday of the month, 6:00-8:00 p.m.
Contact: Kayleen Reusser, *KayleenReusser@gmail.com*
Members: 10
Membership fee: none

HEARTLAND CHRISTIAN WRITERS

www.HeartlandChristianWriters.com

Meetings: Mount Pleasant Christian Church, 381 N. Bluff Rd.,
    Greenwood; third Monday of every month, 10:00 a.m. and 6:30 p.m.
Contact: John Matthew Walker, *admin@heartlandchristianwriters.com*
Members: 15
Membership fee: national fee
Affiliation: American Christian Fiction Writers

WORD WEAVERS FORT WAYNE

Meetings: The Chapel, 2505 W. Hamilton Rd. S.; second Saturday of
    the month, 10:00 a.m. to noon
Contact: Jo Massaro, *jmmassaro1@gmail.com*
Membership fee: $45/year
Affiliation: Word Weavers International

IOWA

WORD WEAVERS DES MOINES

Meetings: Union Park Baptist Church, 821 Arthur Ave.; last Monday
    of the month except holidays, 6:30-8:30 p.m.
Contact: Alex Long, *alexdavidlong@gmail.com*
Members: 10
Membership fee: $45
Affiliation: Word Weavers International

KANSAS

ACFW SOUTHCENTRAL KANSAS
www.facebook.com/groups/928780377178743
>**Meetings:** second Thursday of the month
>**Contact:** Karissa Fisher, *southcentralkansas@acfwchapter.com*
>**Membership fee:** national fee
>**Affiliation:** American Christian Fiction Writers

KENTUCKY

ACFW LOUISVILLE
acfwlouisville.com
>**Contact:** Betty Owens, *louisville@acfwchapter.com*
>**Membership fee:** national fee
>**Affiliation:** American Christian Fiction Writers

WORD WEAVERS BOONE COUNTY
www.facebook.com/groups/349709925923088
>**Meetings:** Boone County Public Library Scheben Branch, 8899 US 42, Union; first Saturday of the month, 10:30 a.m.-12:30 p.m.
>**Contact:** Karisa Moore, *karisam660@gmail.com*
>**Members:** 10
>**Membership fee:** $10
>**Affiliation:** Word Weavers International

LOUISIANA

ACFW LOUISIANA
>**Meetings:** Bossier City; last Saturday of the month
>**Contact:** Carole Lehr Johnson, *louisiana@acfwchapter.com*
>**Membership fee:** national fee
>**Affiliation:** American Christian Fiction Writers

SOUTHERN CHRISTIAN WRITERS
scwguild.com
>**Meetings:** Gospel Bookstore, Westside Shopping Center, 91 Westbank Expy., Gretna; third Saturday of the month,

January—October, 10:00 a.m.
Contact: Teena Myers, *scwg@cox.net*
Members: 30
Membership fee: $50/year (optional, other benefits)
Affiliation: Southern Christian Writers Guild—Northshore

MARYLAND

MOUNTAIN CHRISTIAN WRITER'S GROUP
Meetings: New Life Center, Room 26, 1824 Mountain Rd., Bel Air;
Sundays, 2:30-4:30 p.m.
Contact: Christy Struben, 410-259-3673, *cstruben711@gmail.com*
Members: 20-30
Membership fee: none

MICHIGAN

ACFW GREAT LAKES
greatlakeschapter.blogspot.com
Meetings: first Saturday of various months
Contact: Catherine Breakfield, *greatlakes@acfwchapter.com*
Membership fee: national fee
Affiliation: American Christian Fiction Writers

WORD WEAVERS WEST MICHIGAN—GRAND RAPIDS NORTH
www.facebook.com/groups/1010345115695535
Meetings: Russ' Restaurant, 3531 Alpine Ave. N.W., Walker; first and
third Tuesdays of the month, 6:00-8:00 p.m.
Contact: Kathy Bruins, *KBruins@ameritech.net*
Members: 6-8
Membership fee: $45/year
Affiliation: Word Weavers International

WORD WEAVERS WEST MICHIGAN—GRANDVILLE
www.facebook.com/groups/1010345115695535
Meetings: Russ' Restaurant, 4440 Chicago Dr., S.W., Grandville; first
and third Tuesdays, 6:30-8:30 p.m.
Contact: Kathy Bruins, *KBruins@ameritech.net*
Members: 5

Membership fee: $45/year
Affiliation: Word Weavers International

WORD WEAVERS WEST MICHIGAN—HOLLAND ZEELAND
www.facebook.com/groups/1010345115695535
Meetings: City on a Hill, 100 Pine St., Zeeland; first and third
Tuesdays of the month, 12:30-2:30 p.m.
Contact: Kathy Bruins, *KBruins@ameritech.net*
Members: 10
Affiliation: Word Weavers International

WORD WEAVERS WEST MICHIGAN—MUSKEGON/ NORTON SHORES
www.facebook.com/groups/1010345115695535
Meetings: Norton Shores Public Library, 705 Seminole Rd., Norton
Shores; first and third Tuesdays, 5:45-7:45 p.m.
Contact: Kathy Bruins, *KBruins@ameritech.net*
Members: 10
Membership fee: $45/year
Affiliation: Word Weavers International

MINNESOTA

ACFW MINNESOTA
www.facebook.com/ACFW.MN.NICE
Meetings: Minneapolis; fourth Sunday of the month
Contact: Michelle Aleckson, *minnesota@acfwchapter.com*
Membership fee: national fee
Affiliation: American Christian Fiction Writers

MINNESOTA CHRISTIAN WRITERS GUILD
www.mnchristianwriters.com
Meetings: Oak Knoll Lutheran Church, 600 Hopkins Crossroad,
Minnetonka; second Monday of the month, September—May,
7:00-8:30 p.m.
Contact: Pat vanderMerwe, *pdvdm@comcast.net*
Membership fee: $50/year

MISSISSIPPI

BYHALIA CHRISTIAN WRITERS
www.facebook.com/groups/129990696510
> **Meetings:** First United Methodist Church, 2511 Churst St. Byhalia; first Saturday of the month, 9:00-11:00 a.m.
> **Contact:** Beth Gooch, 901-277-5525, *gooch.beth@gmail.com*
> **Members:** 20
> **Membership fee:** none
> **Affiliation:** American Chrstian Writers

MISSOURI

ACFW MOZARKS
> **Meetings:** Springfield, MO; third Saturday of the month
> **Contact:** Savanna Kaiser, *mozarks@acfwchapter.com*
> **Membership fee:** national fee
> **Affiliation:** American Christian Fiction Writers

HEART OF AMERICA CHRISTIAN WRITERS NETWORK
www.hacwn.org
> **Meetings:** Colonial Presbyterian Church, 12501 W. 137th St., Overland; second Thursday of the month, 7:00 p.m.
> **Contact:** Jeanette Littleton, 816-459-8016, *HACWN@earthlink.net*
> **Members:** 150
> **Membership fee:** $3/meeting, members; $5/meeting, nonmembers

HEARTLAND CHRISTIAN COLLEGE WRITERS GUILD
www.facebook.com/groups/663817230321189
> **Meetings:** Heartland Community Church, 6434 Shelby Co. Rd. 150, Bethel; first Thursday of the month, 6:30 p.m.
> **Contact:** Kathy Nickerson, *Kathy@kathynick.com*
> **Members:** 25
> **Membership fee:** none

OZARKS CHAPTER OF AMERICAN CHRISTIAN WRITERS
www.OzarksACW.org
> **Meetings:** University Heights Baptist Church, 1010 S. National, Springfield; second Saturday, September—May, 10:00 a.m.-2:00 p.m.
> **Contact:** Dr. Jeanetta Chrystie, 417-832-8409, *OzarksACW@yahoo.com*

Members: 50
Membership fee: $20/year, $30 family, $10 newsletter
subscription only
Affiliation: American Christian Writers

NEBRASKA

MY THOUGHTS EXACTLY
mythoughtsexactlywriters.wordpress.com
Meetings: Keene Memorial Library, 1030 N. Broad St., Fremont; third
Monday of the month
Contact: Cheryl Paden, 402-727-6508, *cheryl@seekingbalancebycheryl.com*
Members: 9
Membership fee: none

NEW JERSEY

ACFW NY/NJ
www.facebook.com/groups/ 955365637934907
Meetings: South Ridge Community Church, 7 Pittstown Rd., Clinton,
NJ; first Saturday of the month, 10:00 a.m. to noon
Contact: Cher Gatto, *cherlyngatto@gmail.com*, 315-926-9277
Members: 20
Membership fee: $20/year
Affiliation: American Christian Fiction Writers

NORTH JERSEY CHRISTIAN WRITERS GROUP
www.njcwg.blogspot.com
Meetings: Cornerstone Christian Church, 495 Wyckoff Ave., Wyckoff;
first Saturday of each month, 10:00 a.m. to noon
Contact: Barbara Higby, 551-804-1014, *bhigby9323@gmail.com*
Members: 12
Membership fee: none

NEW YORK

SOUTHERN TIER CHRISTIAN WRITERS
Meetings: Olean First Baptist Church, 133 S. Union St., Olean; monthly
Contact: Deb Wuethrich, 716-379-8702, *deborahmarcein@gmail.com*

Members: 8
Membership fee: none
Affiliation: American Christian Writers

WORD WEAVERS NIAGRA

Meetings: Forestview Church of God, 1250 Saunders Settlement Rd., Niagara Falls; second Tuesday of the month, 1:00-3:00 p.m.
Contact: Rene Aube, 716-534-2910
Membership fee: $45/year
Affiliation: Word Weavers International

WORD WEAVERS WESTERN NEW YORK

Meetings: 2458 Rush Mendon Rd., Honeoye Falls; third Monday of the month, 6:30-9:00 p.m.
Contact: Karen Rode, *karen.a.rode@gmail.com*
Members: 10
Membership fee: $45/year
Affiliation: Word Weavers International

NORTH AND SOUTH DAKOTA

ACFW DAKOTAS

www.facebook.com/groups/ACFWDakotas

Meetings: location, day of week, and frequency varies by region
Contact: Shannon McNear, 843-327-0583, *dakotas@acfwchapter.com*
Members: 15
Membership fee: national fee
Affiliation: American Christian Fiction Writers

NORTH CAROLINA

ACFW NORTH CAROLINA

Meetings: Raleigh
Contact: Kyle Beale, *northcarolina@acfwchapter.com*
Membership fee: national fee
Affiliation: American Christian Fiction Writers

WORD WEAVERS CHAPEL HILL

www.facebook.com/groups/2514244742149516

Meetings: Zoom temporarily; 114 Wisteria Dr., Chapel Hill; second

Monday of the month, 10:00 a.m. to noon
Contact: Lynn Trogdon, *lynnwtrogdon@gmail.com*
Members: 5
Membership fee: $45/year
Affiliation: Word Weavers International

WORD WEAVERS CHARLOTTE

charlottewordweavers.com

Meetings: Waverly Whole Foods, Community Room, 7221 Waverly
Walk; first Saturday of the month, 9:45 a.m.-12:45 p.m.
Contact: Kim Dent, 330-904-5130, *kimberlyjamesdent@gmail.com*
Members: 20
Membership fee: $45
Affiliation: Word Weavers International

WORD WEAVERS PIEDMONT TRIAD

Meetings: Wellspring Community Church, 600 May Rd.,
Thomasville; third Saturday of the month, 10:00 a.m. to noon
Contact: Renee Leonard Kennedy, *ReneeLK3588@icloud.com*, 336-491-2040
Members: 10
Membership fee: $45
Affiliation: Word Weavers International

WORD WEAVERS WILMINGTON

Meetings: Calvary Baptist Church, 423 23rd St.; second Monday of
the month, 6:30-8:30 p.m.
Contact: Angie Mojica, *ms_a_2000@yahoo.com*
Membership fee: $45
Affiliation: Word Weavers International

OHIO

ACFW OHIO

www.facebook.com/groups/220166801456380

Meetings: Etna United Methodist Church, 500 Pike St., Etna; first
Saturday of the month, noon to 3:00 p.m.
Contact: Rebecca Waters, *ohio@acfwchapter.com*
Membership: 20
Membership fee: national fee
Affiliation: American Christian Fiction Writers

COLUMBUS CHRISTIAN WRITERS ASSOCIATION (CCWA)/POTTERS HOUSE SCRIBES

Meetings: Potters House Church of God, 3220 Lowell Dr., Columbus; second Saturday of every month
Contact: Mina R. Raulston, 614-507-7893, *m_raulston@hotmail.com*
Members: 20
Membership fee: none

DAYTON CHRISTIAN SCRIBES

facebook.com/DaytonChristianScribes

Meetings: Kettering Seventh-Day Adventist Church, 3939 Stonebridge Rd., Kettering; second Thursday of the month, 7:00-9:00 p.m.
Contact: Lois Pecce, 937-433-6470
Members: 35
Affiliations: Dayton Christian Writers Guild, Middletown Area Christian Writers

DAYTON CHRISTIAN WRITERS GUILD

www.facebook.com/ChristianAuthorToles

Meetings: Corinthian Baptist Church, 700 S. James McGhee Blvd.; second Saturday of the month, 2:00 p.m.
Contact: Tina Tole, through Facebook page

MAC WRITERS (MIDDLETOWN AREA CHRISTIAN WRITERS)

www.facebook.com/MACwriters

Meetings: Healing Word Assembly of God, 5303 S. Dixie Hwy., Middletown; second Tuesday of each month, 7:00-8:30 p.m.
Contact: Donna Shepherd, 513-423-1627, *donna.shepherd@gmail.com*
Members: 20
Membership fee: $30/year, $5/meeting

WORD WEAVERS HUDSON

Meetings: River of Life Community Church, 5649 Stow Rd.; second Tuesday of the month, 6:45-8:30 p.m.
Contact: Stephanie Pavlantos, *stephaniep.oh@netzero.net*
Members: 7
Membership fee: $45/year
Affiliation: Word Weavers International

WORD WEAVERS MINERVA

Meetings: Minerva Public Library, 677 Lynnwood Dr.; third Tuesday of the month, 6:00-7:50 p.m.
Contact: Lisa Kibler, *Lisa@LisaKibler.com*
Membership fee: $45/year
Affiliation: Word Weavers International

WORD WEAVERS NORTHEAST OHIO

Meetings: Ashland Church of the Brethren, 122 E. 3rd St., Ashland; first Thursday of each month, 6:30-8:30 p.m.
Contact: Cherie Martin, *kitties395@yahoo.com*
Members: 8
Membership fee: $45/year
Affiliation: Word Weavers International

OKLAHOMA

ACFW OKLAHOMA CITY

okchristianfictionwriters.com

Meetings: third Saturday of the month
Contact: Kat Lewis, *OklahomaCity@acfwchapter.com*
Membership fee: national fee
Affiliation: American Christian Fiction Writers

FELLOWSHIP OF CHRISTIAN WRITERS

fellowshipofchristianwriters.org

Meetings: Kirk of the Hills Presbyterian Church, 4102 E. 61st, Tulsa; second Tuesday of month, 6:30 p.m.
Contact: Rosemarie Saenz, *rosemariesaenz@gmail.com*, 480-200-6694
Members: 45
Membership fee: $25 and $35/year

OKLAHOMA CHRISTIAN FICTION WRITERS

okchristianfictionwriters.com

Meetings: Central Park Drive Office Building, 525 Central Park Dr., Oklahoma City; third Saturday of each month, 1:00-3:00 p.m.
Contact: Kat Lewis, *ocfwchapter@gmail.com*
Members: 35
Membership fee: $20 plus ACFW fee of $70
Affiliation: American Christian Fiction Writers

WORDWRIGHTS
www.wordwrights-okc.com
> **Meetings:** Catholic Pastoral Center, Room B13, 7501 N.W. Expressway, Oklahoma City; second Saturday of the month, 10:00 a.m. to noon
> **Contact:** Milton Smith, *hiswordmatters12@gmail.com*
> **Members:** 30

OREGON

OREGON CHRISTIAN WRITERS
www.oregonchristianwriters.org
> **Meetings:** Portland metro area, three all-day Saturday conferences, summer coaching conference
> **Contact:** *president@oregonchristianwriters.com,* 503-927-5701
> **Membership fee:** $60/year, $75 couples, $35 students and seniors

WORDWRIGHTS
> **Meetings:** Gresham/east Multnomah County; two times a month, Thursday afternoons
> **Contact:** Susan Thogerson Maas, 503-663-7834, *susan.maas@frontier.com*
> **Members:** 5
> **Membership fee:** none
> **Affiliation:** Oregon Christian Writers

PENNSYLVANIA

CHRISTIAN WRITERS GUILD
> **Meetings:** Perkins Restaurant, 505 Galleria Dr., Johnstown; last Tuesday of each month, 1:00 p.m.
> **Contact:** Betty Rosian, 814-255-4351, *wordsforall@hotmail.com*
> **Members:** 12
> **Membership fee:** $1/meeting

GREATER PHILLY CHRISTIAN WRITERS FELLOWSHIP
www.writehisanswer.com/cwfsmorningcritiquegroup
> **Meetings:** virtually; every other Thursday, 10 a.m. to noon
> **Contact:** Marlene Bagnull, 484-991-8581, *mbagnull@aol.com*
> **Members:** 10

Membership fee: none

LANCASTER CHRISTIAN WRITERS

Facebook.com/LancasterChristianWritersAssociation
   Meetings: place to be determined; third Saturday of each month, 9:30 a.m.
   Contact: JP Robinson, 717-341-8457, *lancasterwrites@gmail.com*
   Members: 400
   Membership fee: none

LANSDALE, PA WOMEN'S CRITIQUE GROUP

www.writehisanswer.com/cwfseveningcritiquegroup
   Meetings: virtually; every other Thursday, 7:30-10:00 p.m.
   Contact: Marlene Bagnull, 484-991-8581, *mbagnull@aol.com*
   Members: 12
   Membership fee: none

SOUTH CAROLINA

ACFW SOUTH CAROLINA

scwritersACFW.blogspot.com
   Meetings: North Anderson Baptist Church, 2308 N. Main St.,
      Anderson; fourth Saturday of the month except July and
      December, 2:00-5:00 p.m.
   Contact: Elva Cobb Martin, 864-226-7024, *southcarolina@
      acfwchapter.com*
   Members: 20+
   Membership fee: $21/year plus national dues
   Affiliation: American Christian Fiction Writers

ACFW SOUTH CAROLINA LOW COUNTRY

   Meetings: Mt. Pleasant; fourth Saturday of the month
   Contact: Laurie Larsen, *SCLowCountry@acfwchapter.com*
   Membership fee: national fee
   Affiliation: American Christian Fiction Writers

WORD WEAVERS AIKEN

aikenwordweavers.com
   Meetings: Trinity United Methodist Church, 2724 Whiskey Rd.;
      second Tuesday of the month, 7:00-9:00 p.m.
   Contact: Lee Allen-Russ, *LeeAllenRuss@gmail.com*, 864-608-5530
   Members: 10

Membership fee: $45
Affiliation: Word Weavers International

WORD WEAVERS CHARLESTON

www.facebook.com/groups/2112701302307131

> **Meetings:** Walton Hall, St. John's Parish Church, 3673 Maybank Hwy., John's Island; third Saturday of the month, 10:00 a.m. to noon
> **Contact:** Bonnie Anderson, *bonnieanderson0706@gmail.com*
> **Members:** 10
> **Membership fee:** $45/year
> **Affiliation:** Word Weavers International

WORD WEAVERS HARTSVILLE

> **Meetings:** Coker College Library, 300 E. College Ave.; first Monday of the month, 6:30-9:00 p.m.
> **Contact:** Barbara Arthur, *barbaraarthur@barbaraarthur.com*
> **Membership fee:** $45/year
> **Affiliation:** Word Weavers International

WORD WEAVERS LEXINGTON SC

www.LexingtonWordWeavers.com

> **Meetings:** Trinity Baptist Church, 2003 Charleston Hwy., Cayce; second Monday of every month, 6:45-9:00 p.m.
> **Contact:** Jean Wilund, *jwilund@me.com*
> **Members:** 33
> **Membership fee:** $45/year
> **Affiliation:** Word Weavers International

WORD WEAVERS SUMMERVILLE

> **Meetings:** Summerville Presbyterian Church, 407 S. Laurel St., Summerville; first Monday of each month, 7:00 p.m.
> **Contact:** Jeannine Brummett, *Summerville.lady@yahoo.com*
> **Members:** 9
> **Membership fee:** $45/year
> **Affiliation:** Word Weavers International

WORD WEAVERS UPSTATE SC

> **Meetings:** Fountain Inn First Baptist Church, 206 N. Weston St., Fountain Inn; second Thursday of the month, 9:30 a.m.-12:30 p.m.
> **Contact:** Tammy Karasek, *wwupstatesc@yahoo.com*
> **Members:** 34

Membership fee: $45/year
Affiliation: Word Weavers International

WRITING FOR HIM

Meetings: First Baptist Church, 250 E. Main St., Spartanburg; second Thursday of the month, 9:45-11:30 a.m.
Contact: Linda Gilden, *linda@lindagilden.com*
Members: 25
Membership fee: none

TENNESSEE

ACFW KNOXVILLE

Meetings: Parkway Baptist Church, 401 S. Peters Rd.; second Tuesday of the month
Contact: Debra Jenkins, *knoxville@acfwchapter.com*
Membership fee: national fee
Affiliation: American Christian Fiction Writers

ACFW MEMPHIS

Meetings: Compassion Church, 3505 S. Houston Levee, Germantown; third Saturday of the month except December, 10 a.m. to noon
Contact: Lynn Watson, *memphis@acfwchapter.com*
Members: 15
Membership fee: national fee
Affiliation: American Christian Fiction Writers

ACFW MID-TENNESSEE

www.acfwmidtn.org

Meetings: Woodmont Baptist Church, 2100 Woodmont Blvd., Nashville; every other month, 10 a.m. to noon
Contact: Sheila Stovall, *midtennessee@acfwchapter.com*
Members: 30
Membership fee: $24 plus national dues
Affiliation: American Christian Fiction Writers

WORD WEAVERS KNOXVILLE

Meetings: Rio Revolution Church, 3419 E. Lamar Alexander Pkwy., Maryville; third Saturday of the month, 9:30 a.m. to noon
Contact: Beth Boring, *boringb@bellsouth.net*

Membership fee: $45/year
Affiliation: Word Weavers International

WORD WEAVERS NASHVILLE
Meetings: Goodletsville Public Library, 205 Rivergate Pkwy.,
  Goodlettsville; second Saturday of the month, 10:00 a.m. to noon
Contact: Kim Aulich, *KAAfterGodsOwnHeart@gmail.com*
Members: 12
Membership fee: $45/year
Affiliation: Word Weavers International

WORD WEAVERS ROBERTSON COUNTY
Meetings: Stokes Brown Public Library, 405 White St., Springfield;
  fourth Thursday of the month
Contact: Callie Daruk, 615-308-5638
Membership fee: $45/year
Affiliation: Word Weavers International

TEXAS

ACFW ALAMO CITY
acfwalamocity.com
  Meetings: San Antonio; second Saturday of the month
  Contact: Jessica Alvarado, *alamocity@acfwchapter.com*
  Membership fee: national fee
  Affiliation: American Christian Fiction Writers

ACFW CENTRAL TEXAS
www.centexACFW.com
  Meetings: Georgetown Public Library, 402 W. 8th St., Georgetown;
  third Saturday of the month, 9:30-11:30 a.m.
  Contact: Teresa Lynn, *centraltexas@acfwchapter.com*
  Members: 20
  Membership fee: $20 plus national dues
  Affiliation: American Christian Fiction Writers

ACFW DFW CHAPTER (AKA READY WRITERS)
www.dfwreadywriters.blogspot.com
  Meetings: Arlington Community Church, 1715 W. Randol Mill Rd.,
  Arlington; second Saturday of every month, 10:00 a.m.
  Contact: Stacy Simmons, *dfw@acfwchapter.com*

Members: 25-30
Membership fee: national fee
Affiliation: American Christian Fiction Writers

ACFW EAST TEXAS

Meetings: Longview; third Saturday of the month
Contact: Joy K. Massenburge, *easttexas@acfwchapter.com*
Membership fee: national fee
Affiliation: American Christian Fiction Writers

ACFW THE WOODLANDS

wotsACFW.blogspot.com

Meetings: Lupe Tortilla, 19437 Interstate 45, Shenandoah; second
Saturday of every month except October and December, 11:00
a.m.-1:00 p.m.
Contact: Annette O'Hare, *thewoodlands@acfwchapter.com*
Members: 30
Membership fee: $30/year plus national dues
Affiliation: American Christian Fiction Writers

CENTRAL HOUSTON INSPIRATIONAL WRITERS ALIVE!

www.centralhoustoniwa.com

Meetings: Houston's First Baptist Church, 7474 Katy Fwy. (I-10);
second Thursday of each month, 7:00-9:00 p.m.
Contact: Martha Rogers, *martharogers@sbcglobal.net*
Members: 17
Membership fee: none

CHRISTIAN WRITERS WORKSHOP (CWW)

www.facebook.com/groups/374145049720167

Meetings: First Woodway Baptist Church, 101 Ritchie Rd., Waco;
beginning in January each year, we meet for eleven consecutive
Wednesday evenings; four critique groups meet year round once a
month
Contact: Reita Hawthorne, *reitahawthorne2@gmail.com*,
254-339-3060
Members: 50
Membership fee: none

CROSS REFERENCE WRITERS

sites.google.com/site/crossreferencewriters

Meetings: place and time varies

Contact: Tammy L. Hensel, *crossrefwriters@yahoo.com*
Members: 10
Membership fee: none

ROARING WRITERS
roaringwriters.org
> **Meetings:** various locations in Dallas/Fort Worth area; check the website
> **Contact:** Jan Johnson, email through website
> **Members:** 250

ROCKWALL CHRISTIAN WRITERS' GROUP
www.facebook.com/groups/rockwallchristianwritersgroup
> **Meetings:** second Monday of each month except December, 7:00 p.m.
> **Contact:** Leslie Wilson, 214-505-5336, *leslieporterwilson@gmail.com*
> **Members:** 20
> **Membership fee:** none

WORD WEAVERS NORTH TEXAS
> **Meetings:** 7209 Gerrard's Cross, Plano; second Thursday of the
> month, 7:00-9:00 p.m.
> **Contact:** Suzanne Reeves, *suzreeves@comcast.net*
> **Membership fee:** $45/year
> **Affiliation:** Word Weavers International

VIRGINIA

ACFW VIRGINIA
acfwvirginia.com
> **Meetings:** Woodbridge, fourth Saturday of the month, online second
> Thursday of the month
> **Contact:** Kelly Goshorn, *virginia@acfwchapter.com*
> **Membership fee:** national fee
> **Affiliation:** American Christian Fiction Writers

CAPITAL CHRISTIAN WRITERS FELLOWSHIP
ccwritersfellowship.org
> **Meetings:** 4207 Collier Rd., Fairfax; second Monday of odd months
> **Contact:** Sarah Haymaker, *president@ccwritersfellowship.org*
> **Members:** 50
> **Membership fee:** $40/year

WORD WEAVERS RICHMOND

weag.churchcenter.com/groups/interest-based-groups/word-weavers

Meetings: West End Assembly of God, 401 N. Parham Rd., Henrico; first Monday of the month, 7:00-9:00 p.m.

Contact: Sue Schlesman, 804-586-4078, *sueschlesman@gmail.com*

Members: 20

Membership fee: $45/year

Affiliation: Word Weavers International

WASHINGTON

VANCOUVER CHRISTIAN WRITERS

Meetings: Vancouver; first Monday of each month, 9:00 a.m.

Contact: Jon Drury, 510-909-0848, *jondrury2@yahoo.com*

Members: 9

Affiliation: Oregon Christian Writers

WALLA WALLA CHRISTIAN WRITERS

Meetings: SonBridge, 1200 S.E. 12th St., College Place; first and third Tuesday of each month, 3:00 p.m.

Contact: Helen Heavirland, 541-938-3838, *hlh@bmi.net*

Members: 5

WISCONSIN

ACFW WISE

www.facebook.com/wiseacfw

Meetings: Brookfield Public Library, Rotary Club room, 1900 N. Calhoun Rd., Brookfield; first Tuesday of the month, 6:30 p.m.

Contact: Susan Lindstrom, *wisconsinSE@acfwchapter.com*

Members: 12

Membership fee: $25/year plus national dues

Affiliation: American Christian Fiction Writers

PENS OF PRAISE CHRISTIAN WRITERS

Meetings: Manitowoc Public Library, 707 Quay St., Manitowoc; monthly, 6:00-8:00 p.m.

Contact: Susan Marlene Kinney, 920-242-3631, *susanmarlenekinney@gmail.com*

Members: 15

WESTERN WISCONSIN CHRISTIAN WRITER'S GUILD
sites.google.com/site/wwcwginfo
> **Meetings:** Bethesda Lutheran Church, 123 W. Hamilton, Eau Claire; second Tuesday of each month, September—May, 7:00-9:00 p.m.
> **Contact:** Sheila Wilkinson, 715-839-1207, *wwcwg.info@gmail.com*
> **Members:** 15
> **Membership fee:** $30

WORD AND PEN CHRISTIAN WRITERS
wordandpenchristianwriters.wordpress.com
> **Meetings:** St. Thomas Episcopal Church, 226 Washington St., Menasha; second Monday of the month except December, 6:30 p.m.
> **Contact:** Chris Stratton, 920-739-0752, *gcefsi@new.rr.com*
> **Members:** 20
> **Membership fee:** $10/year

AUSTRALIA AND NEW ZEALAND

AUSTRALASIAN CHRISTIAN WRITERS (ACW)
australasianchristianwriters.com,
www.facebook.com/groups/AustralasianChristianWriters
> **Meetings:** Tuesday book chats on website and in Facebook group
> **Contacts:** Narelle Atkins, Jenny Blake, and Iola Goulton, *australasianchristianwriters.com/contact*
> **Members:** 700
> **Affiliation:** Omega Writers

CHRISTIAN WRITERS DOWNUNDER (CWD)
christianwritersdownunder.blogspot.com,
www.facebook.com/groups/121373687949378
> **Meetings:** Facebook discussions, occasional physical meetings
> **Contact:** Jeanette O'Hagan, *cwdbloggers@gmail.com*
> **Members:** 1,100
> **Affiliation:** Omega Writers

NEW ZEALAND CHRISTIAN WRITERS
www.nzchristianwriters.org
> **Meetings:** for locations and leaders: *www.nzchristianwriters.org/groups*
> **Contact:** Justin St. Vincent, *president@nzchristianwriters.org*
> **Members:** 210+

OMEGA WRITERS
www.omegawriters.org
> **Contact:** Susan Barnes, *membership@omegawriters.org*
> **Service:** Australian group with chapters across the country. See the website for locations. Also sponsors an annual conference and the CALEB Award to recognize the best in Australasian Christian writing, published and unpublished.
> **Members:** 150
> **Membership fee:** $60 AUD

CANADA

InSCRIBE CHRISTIAN WRITERS' FELLOWSHIP
inscribe.org
> **Contact:** *president@inscribe.org*
> **Service:** Canadian group with chapters across the country. See the website for locations. Also sponsors workshops, a fall conference, and contests and produces the quarterly magazine *FellowScript* that is included with membership.
> **Membership:** 160
> **Membership fee:** varies, see website

MANITOBA CHRISTIAN WRITERS ASSOCIATION
> **Meetings:** Bleak House, 1637 Main St., Winnipeg; Saturdays once a month except July and August, 1:00 p.m.
> **Contact:** Frieda Martens, 204-770-8023, *friedamartens1910@gmail.com*
> **Membership:** 25
> **Membership fee:** $30/year
> **Affiliation:** InScribe Christian Writers' Fellowship

THE WORD GUILD
www.thewordguild.com
> **Contact:** Box 77001, Markham, ON L3P 0C8, Canada; 800-969-9010; *info@thewordguild.com*
> **Services:** Regional writers chapters across Canada. Sponsors contests and awards for Canadian Christian writers.
> **Members:** 325

19

EDITORIAL SERVICES

Entries in this chapter are for information only, not an endorsement of editing skills. Before hiring a freelance editor, ask for references if they are not posted on the website; and contact two or three to help determine if this editor is a good fit for you. You may also want to pay for an edit of a few pages or one chapter before hiring someone to edit your complete manuscript.

A LITTLE RED INK | BETHANY KACZMAREK
Jarrettsville, MD | 443-608-4013
editor@bethanykaczmarek.com | *www.bethanykaczmarek.com*
> **Contact:** email
> **Services:** manuscript evaluation, substantive editing/rewriting, copyediting, proofreading
> **Types of manuscripts:** short stories, novels, adult, teen/YA
> **Charges:** hourly rate
> **Credentials/experience:** "An ACFW Editor of the Year finalist (2015), Bethany enjoys working with both traditional and indie authors. Several of her clients are award-winning and best-selling authors, though she does work with aspiring authors as well. She has edited for speculative fiction publishing houses Enclave Publishing and Brimstone Fiction."

A LITTLE RED INK | ERYNNE NEWMAN
41 Barclay Dr., Travelers Rest, SC 29690
ErynneNewman@gmail.com | *www.ALittleRedInk.com*
> **Contact:** website form
> **Services:** manuscript evaluation, copyediting, proofreading, back-cover copy
> **Types of manuscripts:** short stories, novels, adult, teen/YA
> **Charges:** hourly rate

Credentials/experience: "I am a writer of Romantic Suspense and a researcher of things that probably have me on several government watch lists. I have been editing professionally since 2014 and, in addition to my own, I have seen over a hundred of my authors' stories published, even won a Rita Award and a few best seller ribbons. I love story, and I think that's what makes me a great editor. I can see the diamond in your rough and help make it sparkle while keeping your voice your voice. My specialty is characters. I want to help you deepen your point of view and make readers fall in love with your hero ... and maybe even your villain. I'm an unapologetic grammar nerd, and I hope we can laugh our way through learning the rules (and learning when and where to break them) together."

A WAY WITH WORDS WRITING AND
EDITORIAL SERVICES | RENEE GRAY-WILBURN

Colorado Springs, CO | 719-271-7076
waywords@earthlink.net | *awaywithwordswriting.wordpress.com*

Contact: email

Services: substantive editing/rewriting, copyediting, proofreading, ghostwriting, coauthoring, discussion questions for books, write from transcriptions, write children's books and other material, résumé design and writing, back-cover copy

Types of manuscripts: articles, nonfiction books, devotionals, short stories, novels, curriculum, gift books, technical material, adult, teen/YA, picture books, easy readers, middle grade, query letters, Bible studies

Charges: hourly rate, project fee

Credentials/experience: "More than twenty years of freelance writing and editing. Wrote five children's books for Capstone Press; extensive curriculum writing for David C. Cook and Group Publishing; wrote children's articles/activities and parenting articles for Focus on the Family; developed online study guides for Wallbuilders; extensive copyediting and proofreading for NavPress (including the Remix Message Bible), David C. Cook, WaterBrook, and major international ministries, as well as numerous independent authors. Coauthored nonfiction book and wrote dozens of articles and devotions. Writing and editing experience for both fiction and nonfiction manuscripts in children, YA, and adult markets."

AB WRITING SERVICES LLC | ANN BYLE

3149 Boyes Ave. N.E., Grand Rapids, MI 49525 | 616-389-4436

annbyle@gmail.com | www.annbylewriter.com

> **Contact:** email
>
> **Services:** manuscript evaluation, copyediting, ghostwriting, coauthoring, discussion questions for books, back-cover copy
>
> **Types of manuscripts:** articles, nonfiction books, devotions, novels, query letters, book proposals, adult
>
> **Charges:** hourly rate
>
> **Credentials/experience:** "Ann's experience includes years as a newspaper copy editor, freelance journalist for newspapers and magazines including *Publishers Weekly*, writing her own books including *Christian Publishing 101*, and co- and ghost-writing book projects."

ABOVE THE PAGES | PAM LAGOMARSINO

209-878-0245

abovethepages@gmail.com | www.abovethepages.com

> **Contact:** email
>
> **Services:** manuscript evaluation, copyediting, proofreading, discussion questions for books, back-cover copy
>
> **Types of manuscripts:** articles, nonfiction books, devotions, short stories, novels, curriculum, gift books, adult, teen/YA, picture books, easy readers, middle grade, query letters, book proposals, Bible studies, scripts
>
> **Charges:** flat fee, word rate, custom
>
> **Credentials/experience:** "Over five years of experience editing, proofreading, or beta-reading Christian nonfiction books, devotionals, sermons, Bible studies, homeschool curriculum, children's books, and Christian fiction. AA in English, as well as certificates in Children's Books, Essential Skills for Editing Nonfiction, Devotionals, Proofreading, and Young Adult Fiction from the Christian PEN, and Keys to Effective Editing from Sandhills Community College."

ACEVEDO WORD SOLUTIONS LLC | JENNE ACEVEDO

editor@jenneacevedo.com | www.jenneacevedo.com

> **Contact:** email
>
> **Services:** copyediting, proofreading, discussion questions for books, manuscript evaluation, back-cover copy, project management

Types of manuscripts: articles, nonfiction books, devotions, query letters, book proposals, curriculum, gift books, adult, teen/YA, short stories, novels, Bible studies, academic

Charges: hourly rate, word rate, flat rate

Credentials/experience: "Editor, project manager, and consultant for private and corporate clients. Works with a variety of editors and freelancers. Proofreader for publishers. Cofounder of Christian Editor Network LLC, former director of The Christian PEN: Proofreaders and Editors Network, former director of PENCON, member of Christian Editor Connection, editing/proofreading instructor for The PEN Institute, founder and director of the Chandler Writers' Group (AZ) since 2011."

ACW CRITIQUE SERVICE | REG A. FORDER

PO Box 110390, Nashville, TN 37222 | 800-21-WRITE
ACWriters@aol.com | *www.ACWriters.com*

Contact: email

Services: manuscript evaluation, substantive editing/rewriting, copyediting, proofreading

Types of manuscripts: articles, nonfiction books, devotions, poetry, short stories, novels, query letters, book proposals, curriculum, scripts, gift books, technical material, adult, teen/YA, picture books, easy readers, middle grade

Charges: flat fee, hourly rate, page rate, word rate

Credentials/experience: Established for 35 years. Staff of experienced editors.

AM EDITING AND FREELANCE WRITING |
ANGELA MCCLAIN

amediting35@gmail.com | *www.amediting.webs.com*

Contact: email

Services: manuscript evaluation, copyediting, proofreading, ghostwriting, coauthoring, writing coach, discussion questions for books, back-cover copy

Types of manuscripts: nonfiction books, devotions, poetry, short stories, novels, gift books, articles, Bible studies, teen/YA, adult, picture books, easy readers, middle grade

Charges: page rate

Credentials/experience: "As an editor, Angela is a communications professional who assists writers with writing tasks. Angela is an experienced editor and writer with thorough knowledge of grammar, composition, and other fields relating to the written word. Angela works as a freelance contractor who assists writers with the creation and presentation of written material. Angela works on written material in various capacities, from simple proofreading of internal documents to the creation, presentation, and sometimes even publication of mass-printed material. In addition to the general requirements of written language, she ensures the material conforms to the needs of the author. Angela pays close attention to detail. Angela possesses these traits as well as an overall talent for written communication."

AMBASSADOR COMMUNICATIONS |
CLAIRE GRACE HUTCHINSON

13733 W. Gunsight Dr., Sun City West, AZ 85375 | 812-390-7907
claire@clairehutchinson.net | www.clairehutchinson.net

> **Contact:** email
> **Services:** manuscript evaluation, script analysis, books into scripts
> **Types of manuscripts:** scripts
> **Charges:** flat fee, custom
> **Credentials/experience:** "M.A. English, Cert. Professional Program in Screenwriting, UCLA. Writer of the film *Lucky's Treasure*, distributed by Pureflix and Universal. 11 years copyediting an academic journal. 17 years as a script analyst and screenwriter."

AMI EDITING | ANNETTE IRBY

Tacoma, WA
editor@AMIediting.com | www.AMIediting.com

> **Contact:** email
> **Services:** manuscript evaluation, substantive editing/rewriting, copyediting, proofreading, critiquing
> **Types of manuscripts:** short stories, novels
> **Charges:** hourly rate
> **Credentials/experience:** "Annette spent five years working in acquisitions with a CBA publisher. She has almost twenty years of experience editing in the CBA marketplace and has worked with several well-known authors and publishers. She's an award-winning author and book reviewer. See her website for testimonials."

AMY BOEKE'S EDITING SERVICE | AMY BOEKE

3149 Sandy Hollow Rd., Rockford, IL 61109
abboeke@gmail.com

> **Contact:** email
> **Services:** copyediting, proofreading

Types of manuscripts: articles, nonfiction books, novels, adult, teen/
YA

Charges: word rate

Credentials/experience: "English degree, master's level secondary
English teaching degree, several years of experience freelance
editing for multiple book genres."

AMY DROWN

Kalispell, MT | 719-244-1743
editing@amydrown.com | *www.amydrown.com/editing*

Contact: email

Services: manuscript evaluation, substantive editing/rewriting,
copyediting, proofreading, back-cover copy

Types of manuscripts: novels, adult, teen/YA, back-cover copy, pitch
sheets

Charges: flat fee, word rate

Credentials/experience: "Internationally recognized freelance editor
specializing in inspirational fiction writing and editing since 2009.
I contract with publishers, as well as directly with authors, both
published and prepublished, and offer highly competitive rates."

ANDREA MERRELL

60 McKinney Rd., Travelers Rest, SC 29690 | 864-616-5889
AndreaMerrell7@gmail.com | *www.AndreaMerrell.com,*
www.TheWriteEditing.com

Contact: email, website form

Services: copyediting, proofreading, back-cover copy

Types of manuscripts: articles, nonfiction books, devotions, short
stories, novels, adult

Charges: hourly rate

Credentials/experience: "Professional freelance editor. Associate
editor for LPC Books and Christian Devotions Ministries. Member
of The Christian PEN: Proofreaders and Editors Network."

ANN KROEKER, WRITING COACH

ann@annkroeker.com | *annkroeker.com/writing-coach*

Contact: email, website form

Service: writing coach

Types of manuscripts: articles, nonfiction books, devotions, poetry,
query letters, book proposals, gift books, adult, Bible studies

Charges: hourly rate, package fees

Credentials/experience: "I leverage over 25 years of experience in the publishing industry to equip clients to reach their writing goals. A published author and coauthor, corporate and freelance writer, book editor, and poet, I've served on the editorial teams of two large online organizations and focused on serving others in my role as a writing coach. My clients have signed book contracts, won awards, been accepted into prestigious MFA programs, launched their own freelance writing businesses, and landed articles and essays in national publications. I stay up-to-date with best practices and refine skills through professional development that builds on a B.A. in English (Creative Writing emphasis), Indiana University."

ANNE RAUTH

3120 Karnes Blvd., Kansas City, MO 64111 | 913-710-8484
anne@annerauth.com

Contact: email
Services: newsletters, marketing and blog posts to promote your book and writing
Types of manuscripts: blog posts, websites
Charges: hourly rate
Credentials/experience: "Anne Rauth has been working in the marketing field for over twenty years at Fortune 500 Companies, nonprofit organizations as well as assisting individuals to promote their books."

ARMOR OF HOPE WRITING AND PUBLISHING SERVICES, LLC | DENISE WALKER

Covington, GA | 678-590-1596
armorofhope121@gmail.com | *www.armorofhopewritingservices.com*

Contact: email
Services: copyediting, proofreading, write discussion questions for books, writing coach, substantive editing
Types of manuscripts: nonfiction books, devotions, novels, teen/YA, picture books, easy readers, middle grade
Charges: fees are on the website
Credentials/experience: "Freelance editor (3½ years), Educator, English Instructor for 19 years, writing coach, and biblical literacy workshop host."

AUTHOR SUPPORT SERVICES | RUSSELL SHERRAD

Carmichael, CA | 916-967-7251

russellsherrard@reagan.com | www.sherrardsebookresellers.com/WordPress/ author-support-services-the-authors-place-to-get-help

Contact: email

Services: manuscript evaluation, substantive editing/rewriting, copyediting, proofreading, blog administration

Types of manuscripts: articles, nonfiction books, devotions, short stories, novels, teen/YA, picture books, easy readers, middle grade

Charges: flat fee

Credentials/experience: "Writing and editing ebooks since 2009, freelance services for multiple number of clients."

AUTHORIZE ME® | SHARON NORRIS ELLIOTT

PO Box 1816, South Gate, CA 90280 | 310-508-9860

AuthorizeMeNow@gmail.com | lifethatmatters.net/authorizeme

Contact: email

Services: manuscript evaluation, substantive/developmental editing, copyediting, proofreading, ghostwriting, coauthoring, book-contract evaluation, discussion questions for books, writing coach, back-cover copy

Types of manuscripts: articles, nonfiction books, devotions, children's poetry, book proposals, curriculum, Bible studies, gift books, academic, adult, teens/YA, board/picture books, easy readers, middle grade

Charges: page rate, word rate, custom

Credentials/experience: "Sharon's credentials/experience as an editor include her 35-year career as a high school English teacher, years as a managing editor of several magazines, functioning as a freelance editor for major publishing houses, and being a sought-after keynote and seminar instructor at major Christian writers' conferences nationwide. Sharon is a multi-published author herself, and is a member of ACE (Academy of Christian Editors), SCBWI (Society of Children's Book Writers and Illustrators), and AWSA (Advanced Writers and Speakers Association). Because of her growing positive reputation as an editor and book developer in the publishing arena, she started AuthorizeMe in 2008 to be able to help others enter the publishing world. Sharon's personal, hands-on assistance is what sets AuthorizeMe apart as special and unique."

AVODAH EDITORIAL SERVICES | CHRISTY DISTLER
Warminster, PA | 267-231-6723
email through website | www.avodaheditorialservices.com

Contact: email

Services: manuscript evaluation, substantive editing/rewriting, copyediting, proofreading

Types of manuscripts: nonfiction books, devotions, poetry, short stories, novels, adult, picture books, easy readers

Charges: word rate

Credentials/experience: "Educated at Temple University and University of California–Berkeley. Thirteen years of editorial experience, both as an employee and a freelancer. Currently works mostly for publishing houses but accepts freelance work as scheduling allows."

BANNER LITERARY | MIKE LOOMIS
Mike@MikeLoomis.co | www.MikeLoomis.co

Contact: email, website form

Services: manuscript evaluation, substantive editing/rewriting, copyediting, proofreading, ghostwriting, coauthoring, book-contract evaluation, newsletters, small group/Bible study guides, curriculum lesson plans, discussion questions for books, writing coach, back-cover copy

Types of manuscripts: articles, nonfiction books, devotions, query letters, book proposals

Charges: flat fee, custom

Credentials/experience: "I'm a book developer, ghostwriter, and editor. I also coach authors on planning the best book for their goals. Because of my twenty years of experience in publishing, I help authors refine their idea, polish their work, and reach their audience. I've worked with *New York Times* bestselling authors, publishers (Simon & Schuster, Multnomah, Zondervan, Random House, Nelson, NavPress, and Penguin) but am most energized by helping first-time authors."

BARBARA KOIS
1007 Cherry St., Wheaton, IL 60187 | 630-532-2941
barbara.kois@gmail.com | www.barbarakois.com

Contact: email

Services: manuscript evaluation, substantive editing/rewriting, copyediting, proofreading, ghostwriting, coauthoring, writing coach, back-cover copy

Types of manuscripts: nonfiction books, devotions, novels, Bible studies, gift books, adult, query letters, academic

Charges: word rate

Credentials/experience: "Barbara has worked as a writer, ghostwriter, editor, teacher, coach, corporate communication consultant and journalist. She has written or co-written ten books, published more than 600 articles in the *Chicago Tribune*, and edited more than 200 books for various publishers and authors. Barbara has helped dozens of writers prepare for the publication of their books, including both those who have published with traditional publishers and those who have chosen to self-publish, including teaching a six-video writing course for a publisher."

BLACK DOG EDITING | TORI MERKIEL

18508 Carnegie Overlook Blvd., Davidson, NC 28036 | 330-515-1857
blackdogeditor@gmail.com | *www.blackdogediting.com*

Contact: email

Services: manuscript evaluation, substantive editing, copyediting, proofing

Types of manuscripts: short stories, novels, query letters, adult, teen/YA, middle grade

Charges: flat fee, word rate, custom

Credentials/experience: "Tori is a #1 Amazon Bestselling author and previously acquired and edited novels for Curiosity Quills Press. She is a skilled editor with a keen eye for pacing and world-building, and she especially loves nit-picky grammar. If you're looking for quality editing or proofreading from someone who's been on both sides of the publishing industry, reach out to Tori ASAP."

BOOKOX | THOMAS WOMACK

165 S. Timber Creek Dr., Sisters, OR 97759 | 541-788-6503
Thomas@BookOx.com | *www.BookOx.com*

Contact: email

Services: manuscript evaluation, copyediting, writing coach, discussion questions for books

Types of manuscripts: nonfiction books, devotions, novels, Bible studies, adult, book proposals, picture books

Charges: word rate

Credentials/experience: "Four decades of full-time book editing experience."

BREAKOUT EDITING | DORI HARRELL
Yakima, WA | 509-910-2220
doriharrell@gmail.com | www.doriharrell.wixsite.com/breakoutediting

Contact: email

Services: substantive editing/rewriting, copyediting, proofreading, write website text

Types of manuscripts: articles, nonfiction books, devotions, short stories, novels, query letters, adult, teen/YA, picture books, middle grade

Charges: word rate

Credentials/experience: "Dori is a multiple-award-winning writer and a highly experienced editor who freelance edits full time and has edited more than 300 novels and nonfiction books. Breakout authors final in awards or win awards almost every year! She edits for publishers, including Gemma Halliday Publishing and Kregel Publications, and as an editor, she releases more than twenty books annually."

BRIANNA STORM HILVETY
brianna@theliterarycrusader.com | www.theliterarycrusader.com

Contact: email, website form

Services: copyediting, proofreading

Types of manuscripts: articles, nonfiction books, short stories, novels, devotions, adult, teen/YA, middle grade

Charges: word rate, custom

Credentials/experience: "Brianna has five years of experience working on a variety of projects for individual clients, publishers, and writers organizations, including Gilead Publishing, Castle Gate Press, and KingdomPen.org. She cofounded, co-owns, and codirects StoryEmbers.org, a website dedicated to guiding and inspiring Christian novelists. As managing editor, she oversees the entire publishing department and its personnel, ensuring that content is processed, scheduled, and posted on the site weekly. Currently, she personally handles the copyediting of all submissions, in addition to serving as a judge for the yearly story contests. Her professional affiliations include Gold membership at The Christian PEN, editing certifications from The PEN Institute, and copyediting and proofreading expertise at the Christian Editor Connection."

BROOKSTONE CREATIVE GROUP | SUZANNE KUHN

PO Box 211, Evington, VA 24550 | 302-514-7899

www.brookstonecreativegroup.com

Contact: website form

Services: substantive editing, copyediting, proofreading, coaching, one-sheets, book proposals, ghostwriting

Types of manuscripts: books

Charges: flat fee

Credentials/experience: Suzanne has more than thirty years of book-specific experience. Brookstone is an expansion of her business, SuzyQ, with a team of almost two dozen professionals who bring a wide range of knowledge and experience to help you get published.

BUTTERFIELD EDITORIAL SERVICES |
DEBRA L. BUTTERFIELD

4810 Gene Field Rd. #2, St. Joseph, MO 64506 | 816-752-2171

deb@debralbutterfield.com | TheMotivationalEditor.com

Contact: website form

Services: substantive editing/rewriting, copyediting

Types of manuscripts: articles, nonfiction books, devotions, short stories, novels, book proposals, adult

Charges: word rate

Credentials/experience: "Ten years experience as a freelance editor and six years combined experience as editor and editorial director for traditional publishers."

ByBRENDA | BRENDA WILBEE

4631 Quinn Ct. #202, Bellingham, WA 98226 | 360-389-6895

Brenda@BrendaWilbee.com | www.BrendaWilbee.com

Contact: email

Services: writing coach

Types of manuscripts: nonfiction books, academic, novels, adult

Charges: hourly rate

Credentials/experience: "Brenda Wilbee is an award-winning and best-selling author of 10 books, dozens of articles, short stories, and radio scripts with over 30 years of publishing experience as a writer, editor, and book designer, and she's taught in the public school system, specializing in homeschool connections—and has 7 years' experience teaching university and college composition. Her books have sold over 700,000 copies. MA: Professional Writing."

C. S. LAKIN

cslakin@gmail.com | *www.livewritethrive.com*

Contact: email, website form

Services: manuscript evaluation, substantive editing/rewriting, copyediting, proofreading, writing coach

Types of manuscripts: articles, nonfiction books, devotions, poetry, short stories, novels, query letters, book proposals, gift books, scripts, curriculum, Bible studies, adult, teen/YA, picture books, easy readers, middle grade, scene or chapter outlines

Charges: hourly rate, page rate

Credentials/experience: "With more than fifteen years' experience as a copyeditor, and having authored and published twenty novels and ten nonfiction books, I bring a wealth of experience and expertise to my critiques and editing. I critique more than two hundred manuscripts a year and have more than a million words of instruction for writers at my blog *Live Write Thrive*. More than a thousand writers have benefited from my online video courses at *cslakin.teachable.com*. Fast turnaround time, encouraging support, and dependability are the things I strive for with all my clients."

CALLED WRITERS CHRISTIAN PUBLISHING |
CHRIS MCKINNEY

1900 Rice Mine Rd. N. 401, Tuscaloosa, AL 35406 | 205-872-4509

chris@calledwriters.com | *calledwriters.com/christian-book-editor*

Contact: email

Services: manuscript evaluation, substantive editing, copyediting, proofreading, ghostwriting, coauthoring, back-cover copy

Types of manuscripts: articles, nonfiction books, devotions, short stories, novels, Bible studies, adult, teen/YA, easy readers, middle grade

Charges: word rate

Credentials/experience: "Chris McKinney is the founder and managing editor of Called Writers Christian Publishing. He was formerly the executive editor of *GODSPEED Magazine* and has written and edited for several ministry organizations. Chris has worked on many contract writing, editing, and proofreading projects for individuals as well as organizations. In addition to *GODSPEED Magazine*, Chris's writing has been featured by Crosswalk, *Engage*, and quite a few other publications and websites; he also has written several books. Chris is passionate about helping Christian authors succeed in their mission. In addition to Chris McKinney, Called Writers employs other editors who are highly skilled and experienced."

CARLA ROSSI EDITORIAL SERVICES | CARLA ROSSI

Texas

carla@carlarossi.com | www.carlarossi.com

Contact: email

Services: manuscript evaluation, substantive editing/rewriting, copyediting, writing coach, back-cover copy

Types of manuscripts: short stories, novels, adult, teen/YA

Charges: word rate

Credentials/experience: "Professional editor since 2014. Member of writing and editing organizations. Specialize in romance and fantasy fiction."

CHRISTI MCGUIRE

Christi@ChristiMcGuire.com | www.ChristiMcGuire.com

Contact: email, website form

Services: copyediting, proofreading

Types of manuscripts: nonfiction books, devotions, query letters, book proposals, curriculum, adult, articles, Bible studies

Charges: hourly rate, word rate

Credentials/experience: "Christi McGuire, freelance editor, writer, and publishing consultant, has been in the Christian publishing industry for more than nineteen years. Formerly an editor at LifeWay Christian Resources, Christi has published more than one hundred parenting magazine articles, dozens of children's devotionals, and ten years of VBS curriculum. She is a cofounder of the Christian Editor Network LLC, the former director of the Christian Editor Connection, and the former director of The PEN Institute. Currently, her primary focus is partnering with authors in the creative process to polish their manuscripts and book proposals and help them navigate the path to publishing."

CHRISTIAN COMMUNICATOR MANUSCRIPT CRITIQUE SERVICE | SUSAN TITUS OSBORN

3133 Puente St., Fullerton, CA 92835 | 714-313-8651

susanosb@aol.com | www.christiancommunicator.com

Contact: email, phone, website form

Services: manuscript evaluation, copyediting, proofreading, ghostwriting, book-contract evaluation, discussion questions for books, writing coach, coauthoring, back-cover copy

Types of manuscripts: articles, nonfiction books, devotions, poetry, short stories, novels, query letters, book proposals, curriculum, Bible studies, scripts, gift books, technical material, adult, teen/YA, picture books, easy readers, middle grade, academic

Charges: hourly rate, page rate

Credentials/experience: "Our critique service, comprised of 14 professional editors, has been in business for 37 years. We are recommended by ECPA, the Billy Graham Association, and a number of publishing houses and agents."

CHRISTIAN EDITOR CONNECTION | KATHY IDE
KathyIde@ChristianEditor.com | www.ChristianEditor.com

Contact: website form

Services: manuscript evaluation, substantive editing/rewriting, copyediting, proofreading, ghostwriting, coauthoring, writing coach, back-cover copy, indexing

Types of manuscripts: articles, nonfiction books, devotions, poetry, short stories, novels, query letters, book proposals, curriculum, Bible studies, gift books, technical material, adult, teen/YA, picture books, easy readers, middle grade, academic

Charges: custom

Description: "Christian Editor Connection has established, professional editors who have been extensively screened and tested. Fill out the website form to Request an Editor and you will be personally matched with members who best fit your needs. Those editors who are interested and available will contact you with detailed quotes so you can choose the right one for you."

CHRISTIANBOOKPROPOSALS.COM | CINDY CARTER
408-966-3998
ccarter@ecpa.org | www.ChristianBookProposals.com

Contact: website form

Service: online proposal-submission service

Types of manuscripts: book proposals for all kinds of books and all ages

Charges: $98 for six months

Description: Managed by the Evangelical Christian Publishers Association (ECPA).

COLLABORATIVE EDITORIAL SOLUTIONS |
ANDREW BUSS
info@collaborativeeditorial.com | collaborativeeditorial.com
>   **Contact:** email
>   **Services:** copyediting, proofreading
>   **Types of manuscripts:** articles, nonfiction books, devotions, Bible studies, technical material, adult, academic
>   **Charges:** hourly rate, page rate
>   **Credentials/experience:** "I'm a professional editor with more than five years of full-time experience working with authors and scholarly publishers such as InterVarsity Press, Reformation Heritage, P&R Publishing, Georgetown University Press, and Baylor University Press. Although I primarily work in the genre of scholarly nonfiction, I'm always keen to work with creative and thoughtful authors, whatever the topic or genre. I'm a member of the Editorial Freelancers Association and the Society of Biblical Literature."

COMMUNICATION ASSOCIATES | KEN WALKER
729 Ninth Ave. #331, Huntington, WV 25701 | 304-525-3343
kenwalker33@gmail.com | www.KenWalkerWriter.com
>   **Contact:** email
>   **Services:** copyediting, ghostwriting, coauthoring, discussion questions for books, back-cover copy
>   **Types of manuscripts:** articles, nonfiction books, devotions, Bible studies, adult
>   **Charges:** hourly rate, flat fee
>   **Credentials/experience:** "Started freelancing in 1983 and fulltime in 1990. Experienced in ghostwriting, substantive editing, and book editing."

CORNERSTONE-INK EDITING | VIE HERLOCKER
Goodlettsville, TN
vherlock@yahoo.com | www.cornerstone-ink.com
>   **Contact:** email
>   **Services:** manuscript evaluation, substantive editing/rewriting, copyediting
>   **Types of manuscripts:** articles, nonfiction books, devotions, short stories, novels, query letters, book proposals, adult, teen/YA, middle grade, gift books
>   **Charges:** word rate
>   **Credentials/experience:** "Vie Herlocker provides 'Tough-Love

Editing with a Tender Touch.' She is a member of Christian Editor Connection, Christian Proofreaders and Editors Network, ACFW, and Word Weavers, Int. Her experience includes: editing for a small Christian publisher (10 years), editing for a regional magazine, judging a national writing contest, and freelance editing. She uses *The Chicago Manual of Style, Christian Writers' Manual of Style*, and *Merriam-Webster* 11th."

CORPORATE PEN | CATHY STREINER
Orange Park, FL | 480-419-0356
info@thecorporatepen.com | www.thecorporatepen.com

Contact: email, website form

Services: substantive editing/rewriting, copyediting, proofreading, coauthoring, write discussion questions for books, writing coach, back-cover copy

Types of manuscripts: articles, nonfiction books, devotions, short stories, novels, scripts, gift books, technical material, poetry, curriculum, Bible studies, academic, picture books, easy readers, middle grade, adult, teen/YA

Charges: flat fee, page rate, word rate, hourly rate with a maximum amount, custom

Credentials/experience: "Extensive experience with the written word. Cathy began making her living as a writer prior to 1990, and in 2001 established her own company. She self-published a Christian novel in 2009 under a pseudonym and enjoys using her writing and editing skills to help other Christians."

CREATIVE EDITORIAL SOLUTIONS | CLAUDIA VOLKMAN
cvolkman@mac.com

Contact: email

Service: manuscript evaluation, copyediting, proofreading, writing coach, back-cover copy

Types of manuscripts: articles, nonfiction books, devotions, novels, Bible studies, gift books, adult, book proposals, picture books, easy readers, middle grade

Charges: flat fee, custom

Description: "With over 35 years of experience in the publishing industry, I offer high-level, creative editing solutions. I have worked for major publishers in the Christian and Catholic arena and now freelance full-time. I make sure my client's content flows well, is grammatically correct, and reads compellingly, all while making sure it retains each individual author's tone, style, and voice."

CREATIVE ENTERPRISES STUDIO |
MARY HOLLINGSWORTH
Bedford, TX | 817-312-7393
ACreativeShop@aol.com | CreativeEnterprisesStudio.com

> **Contact:** email
> **Services:** manuscript evaluation, substantive editing/rewriting, copyediting, proofreading, ghostwriting, coauthoring, write discussion questions for books
> **Types of manuscripts:** nonfiction books, devotions, short stories, novels, book proposals, curriculum, gift books, adult, teen/YA, picture books, easy readers, middle grade
> **Charges:** rates vary according to the work required, estimates provided
> **Description:** "CES is a publishing services company, hosting more than 150 top Christian publishing freelancers. We work with large, traditional Christian publishers on books by best-selling authors. We also produce custom, first-class books on a turnkey basis for independent authors, ministries, churches, and companies."

CREWS AND COULTER EDITORIAL SERVICES |
KAY COULTER
806 Hopi Trl., Temple, TX 76504 | 254-778-6490
bkcoulter@sbcglobal.net | www.crewscoultereditingservices.com

> **Contact:** email, phone, website form
> **Services:** manuscript evaluation, substantive editing/rewriting, copyediting, proofreading, ghostwriting, coauthoring, writing coach, working with non-native English speakers
> **Types of manuscripts:** nonfiction books, devotions, short stories, novels, book proposals, gift books, adult, teen/YA, Bible studies, academic
> **Charges:** hourly rate, custom
> **Credentials/experience:** "Kay is a published author and has been an editor since 2002, having worked with authors on over three hundred projects. Kay has been a Christian for more than fifty years and also served in a speaking/singing ministry for twenty-five years. She loves words and the Word and helping authors realize their dreams."

CROSS & DOT EDITORIAL SERVICES | KATIE VORREITER
San Jose, CA | 408-812-3562
Katie@CrossAndDot.net | www.CrossAndDot.net

> **Contact:** email, website form

Services: copyediting, proofreading

Types of manuscripts: articles, nonfiction books, devotions, short stories, novels, curriculum, gift books, technical material, adult, teen/YA, middle grade

Charges: flat rate

Credentials/experience: "Certificate in professional sequence in editing, U.C. Berkeley; MA in international management; BA in English and Spanish."

CYPRESS WIND | RACHEL HILLS

Mooresville, IN | 317-443-0019

rachel@cypresswind.com | www.CypressWind.com

Contact: website form, email

Services: substantive editing/rewriting, copyediting, proofreading, writing coach, web page and blog copyediting

Types of manuscripts: articles, nonfiction books, short stories, novels, adult, teen/YA

Charges: rates based on the project

Credentials/experience: "I have sixteen years of experience editing for academics and various certifications and training in editing and writing."

DILLER DESIGNS | LILA DILLER

128 Teak Dr., Statesville, NC 28625 | 980-829-5819

liladiller78@gmail.com | www.liladiller.com/editingservices

Contact: email

Services: copyediting, proofreading

Types of manuscripts: nonfiction books, devotionals, novels, Bible studies, adult, middle grade

Charges: word rate

Credentials/experience: "As a life-long reader and lover of grammar, I love to help new authors turn their book babies into professional and gripping prose."

"Lila did a wonderful job proofreading my middle grade fantasy adventure novel. She caught several things that would have been somewhat embarrassing mistakes. Even though Lila was primarily proofreading for me, she also mentioned a detail in one scene that was super helpful. I would use Lila again to proof one of my novels," R.V. Bowman.

DONE WRITE EDITORIAL SERVICES |
MARILYN A. ANDERSON
127 Sycamore Dr., Louisville, KY 40223 | 502-244-0751
shelle12@aol.com

> **Contact:** email, phone
> **Services:** copyediting, proofreading, substantive editing, writing coach
> **Types of manuscripts:** articles, nonfiction books, devotions, poetry, short stories, novels, curriculum, technical material, adult, children, book proposals, Bible studies, gift books, academic, query letters
> **Charges:** hourly rate
> **Credentials/experience:** "I am qualified by both bachelor's and master's degrees in English. I am also qualified because I have tutored more than thirty English/writing students since 2004. Most of them have been English-language learners. Also, I have taught English/writing as a classroom teacher. I have additionally conducted business-project editing for several corporations over the years. I currently copyedit for nonfiction and fiction independent writers, as well as for publishers and a few Christian ministries and am in the process of mentoring several other writers/editors. I copyedit both books (such as memoirs) and doctoral dissertations, theses, and other academic journal articles and papers.
>
> "I offer a free sample edit, and my rates are both reasonable and competitive. I am a Gold charter member of The Christian PEN proofreaders and editors' network, along with a tested member of the Christian Editor Connection. In addition, I have participated in over forty editing classes during five national Christian-editor conferences."

ECHO CREATIVE MEDIA | BRENDA NOEL
Smyrna, TN | 615-223-0754
bnoel@thewordeditor.com | echocreativemedia.weebly.com

> **Contact:** email
> **Services:** substantive editing/rewriting, copyediting, proofreading, ghostwriting, write discussion questions for books
> **Types of manuscripts:** articles, nonfiction books, devotions, short stories, book proposals, curriculum, gift books, adult, teen/YA, picture books, easy readers
> **Charges:** flat fee, hourly rate

Credentials/experience: "Sixteen years of experience in the Christian publishing industry."

EDIT RESOURCE, LLC | ERIC AND ELISA STANDFORD

19265 Lincoln Green Ln., Monument, CO 80132 | 719-290-0757
info@editresource.com | *www.editresource.com*

Contact: website form
Services: manuscript evaluation, substantive editing/rewriting, copyediting, proofreading, ghostwriting, coauthoring, write discussion questions for books, writing coach, back-cover copy
Types of manuscripts: nonfiction books, devotions, novels, query letters, book proposals, curriculum, Bible studies, adult, teen/YA
Charges: flat fee, hourly rate
Credentials/experience: "Eric and Elisa have a combined forty plus years of editorial experience, both as in-house employees and as independent service providers, and are well-recognized members of the Christian publishing community. They also represent other top indie editors; see the Team page on the website."

EDITING BY LUCY | LUCY CRABTREE

Lawrence, KS | 913-543-1782
editingbylucy@gmail.com | *editingbylucy.com*

Contact: email, website form
Services: copyediting, proofreading
Types of manuscripts: articles, nonfiction books, short stories, novels, query letters, book proposals, adult
Charges: word rate
Credentials/experience: "Polished writer and editor with nine years of professional experience in the publishing industry (seven years) and educational settings (two years). Well-versed in Microsoft Office and Adobe Creative Suite. Familiarity with Associated Press, American Psychological Association, and *Chicago Manual* style books. Experience with Drupal, WordPress, and Blogger."

EDITING GALLERY LLC | CAROL CRAIG

2622 Willona Dr., Eugene, OR 97408 | 541-735-1834
kf7orchid@gmail.com | *www.editinggallery.com*

Contact: email
Services: manuscript evaluation, substantive editing/rewriting, writing coach, copyediting, proofreading, back-cover copy

Types of manuscripts: novels, query letters, book proposals, adult, teen/YA, nonfiction books, short stories

Charges: hourly rate

Credentials/experience: "University of Oregon English Major. I have over twenty years of experience as an editor with a long list of published authors in both fiction and nonfiction."

eDITMORE EDITORIAL SERVICES | TAMMY DITMORE

501-I S. Reino Rd. #194, Newbury Park, CA 91320 | 805-630-6809
tammy@editmore.com | *www.editmore.com*

Contact: email

Services: manuscript evaluation, copyediting, proofreading

Types of manuscripts: articles, nonfiction books, devotions, curriculum, Bible studies, adult, academic

Charges: hourly rate

Credentials/experience: "A specialist in nonfiction, I offer manuscript consultations, critiques, developmental editing, copyediting, and proofreading services."

EDITOR FOR YOU | MELANIE RIGNEY

4201 Wilson Blvd. #110328, Arlington, VA 22203-4417 | 703-863-3940
editor@editorforyou.com | *www.editorforyou.com*

Contact: email

Service: manuscript evaluation

Types of manuscripts: nonfiction books, devotions, novels, book proposals, adult

Charges: flat fee

Credentials/experience: "Melanie has decades of professional editing experience, including time as editor of *Writer's Digest* magazine and a publishing manager for what was Hayden Books. Since 2003, her consultancy, Editor for You, has helped hundreds of publishers, agents, and authors. Melanie knows what it's like on the other side of the desk; she's authored several books for Catholic publishers."

EDITOR WORLD, LLC | PATTI FISHER

119 Blue Grass Trl., Newport, VA 24128 | 614-500-3348
info@editorworld.com | *www.editorworld.com*

Contact: email

Services: copyediting, proofreading

Types of manuscripts: articles, nonfiction books, devotions, poetry, short stories, novels, query letters, book proposals, curriculum,

Bible studies, scripts, gift books, technical material, adult, teen/YA, easy readers, middle grade

Charges: word rate

Credentials/experience: "Clients can choose a professional editor based on the editor's profile, such as qualifications, skills, number of pages edited, and previous client ratings. Our editing panel includes university faculty, professional editors, published authors, and retired professionals who love words more than anything else. Our editors are tested on their editing skills before being accepted to provide editing services through Editor World. Choose your own personal editor to improve your work based on his or her qualifications, expertise, skills, and ratings/reviews, benefiting from our strict deadlines and affordable fees."

EDITORIAL SERVICES | KIM PETERSON

1114 Buxton Dr., Knoxville, TN 37922

petersk.ktp@gmail.com | naturewalkwithgod.wordpress.com/about-kim

Contact: email

Services: manuscript evaluation, copyediting, proofreading, discussion questions for books, writing coach, back-cover copy

Types of manuscripts: articles, nonfiction books, devotions, poetry, short stories, novels, query letters, book proposals, curriculum, academic, Bible studies, gift books, technical material, adult, teen/YA, picture books, easy readers, middle grade, blogs

Charges: hourly rate

Credentials/experience: "Freelance writer; college writing instructor; conference speaker. MA in print communication from Wheaton College."

ELISABETH WARNER

Long Island, NY

editor@elisabethwarner.com | www.elisabethwarner.com

Contact: website form

Services: substantive editing/rewriting, copyediting, proofreading, discussion questions for books, indexing

Types of manuscripts: nonfiction books, devotions, novels, Bible studies, academic, adult, teens/YA, middle grade

Charges: page rate

Credentials/experience: "Years of editing experience in academic, faith-based fiction, and faith-based nonfiction writing. Gives personalized, encouraging feedback and fully edits your manuscript with meticulous attention to detail."

ELOQUENT EDITS, LLC | DENISE ROEPER

Port Orange, FL | 386-753-4488

denise.eloquentedits@gmail.com | www.eloquentedits.com

> **Contact:** email
> **Services:** copyediting, proofreading, substantive editing
> **Types of manuscripts:** nonfiction books, short stories, novels, teen/
> YA, middle grade
> **Charges:** word rate, also review a document and provide an estimate
> **Credentials/experience:** "I have edited and proofread print matter
> ranging from brochures, business print, website content to fiction
> manuscripts. Specialties are editing fiction, motivational, and spiritual
> print. Accepting projects that require a short turnaround time."

EMH INDEXING SERVICES | ELISE HESS

605-641-3014

emhess5@gmail.com

> **Contact:** email
> **Services:** indexing
> **Charges:** page rate
> **Credentials/experience:** "I have experience in subject, Scripture, and
> name indexes, as well as index updates. I have written indexes for
> Moody Publishers, Wiley Publishers, and many more. My husband
> and I are pastors, and I have a Biblical Studies degree so I am very
> familiar with Christian materials."

EXEGETICA PUBLISHING | CATHY CONE

312 Greenwich #112, Lee's Summit, MO 64082

editor@exegeticapublishing.com | exegeticapublishing.com/editing

> **Contact:** website form
> **Services:** manuscript evaluation, substantive editing, copyediting,
> proofreading
> **Types of manuscripts:** articles, nonfiction books, devotions,
> curriculum, Bible studies, academic
> **Charges:** page rate
> **Credentials/experience:** "Exegetica editorial staff have more than 30
> years editing experience with diverse media and publishers."

FACETS EDITORIAL SERVICES | DEBORAH CHRISTENSEN

PO Box 354, Addison, IL 60107 | 630-267-7874
dcfacets@earthlink.net | *www.Plowingthefields.wordpress.com*

Contact: email
Services: substantive editing/rewriting, copyediting, proofreading
Types of manuscripts: articles, nonfiction books, devotions, novels, adult, teen/YA
Charges: hourly rate
Credentials/experience: "I have over 30 years experience with editing and proofreading. I served as an editor for Christian Service Brigade and a mentor for the Christian Writer's Guild. I'm proficient with *The Associated Press Stylebook*, *The Chicago Manual of Style*, and *The Christian Writer's Manual of Style*."

FAITH EDITORIAL SERVICES | REBECCA FAITH

PO Box 184, Novelty, OH 44072 | 216-906-0205
rebecca@faitheditorial.com | *www.faitheditorial.com*

Contact: email, website form, mail
Services: substantive editing/rewriting, copyediting, proofreading
Types of manuscripts: articles, nonfiction books, technical material, adult, teen/YA, sermons, devotions, curriculum, Bible studies, academic
Charges: hourly rate
Credentials/experience: "My experience editing in the Christian market includes six years as managing editor for a Christian nonprofit; another six years editing and writing content for a global Christian ministry, including sermons and sermon transcripts; and copyediting nonfiction Christian books and devotionals. In addition, I edit technical, engineering, medical, and educational material for various independent and publishing clients. I hold membership in the EFA and Christian PEN."

FAITHFULLY WRITE EDITING | DAWN KINZER

dawnkinzer@comcast.net | *www.faithfullywriteediting.com*

Contact: email
Services: manuscript evaluation, substantive editing/rewriting, copyediting, proofreading
Types of manuscripts: short stories, novels
Charges: flat fee, page rate
Credentials/experience: "Dawn Kinzer launched Faithfully Write

Editing in 2010. She is currently focusing on editing fiction: full-length novels, novellas, and short stories. She is a member of the Northwest Christian Writers Association, American Christian Fiction Writers, The Christian PEN, and the Christian Editor Connection. Four of her own novels have been published, and her work has also been included in devotionals and magazines. Dawn co-hosts and writes for the Seriously Write blog, which is dedicated to encouraging and equipping Christian writers."

FAITHWORKS EDITORIAL & WRITING, INC. |
NANETTE THORSEN SNIPES

PO Box 1596, Buford, GA 30518 | 770-945-3093
nsnipes@bellsouth.net | www.faithworkseditorial.com

> **Contact:** email, website form
> **Services:** manuscript evaluation, copyediting, proofreading, work-for-hire projects
> **Types of manuscripts:** articles, nonfiction books, devotions, poetry, short stories, query letters, gift books, adult, picture books, easy readers, middle grade, memoirs, business
> **Charges:** hourly rate, page rate
> **Credentials/experience:** "Member: The Christian PEN (Proofreaders & Editors Network), Christian Editor Connection, Christian Editor Network. Proofreader for corporate newsletters, thirteen years. Published writer for more than twenty-five years. Published hundreds of articles in magazines and stories in more than sixty compilation books, including Guideposts, B&H, Regal, and Integrity. Twelve years of editorial experience in both adult and children's short fiction and books, memoirs, short stories, devotions, articles, business. Rates are generally by page but, under specific circumstances, by the hour. Editorial clients have published with such houses as Zondervan, Tyndale, and Revell."

FINAL TOUCH PROOFREADING & EDITING |
HEIDI MANN

Ely, MN | 701-866-4299
mann.heidi@gmail.com | www.FinalTouchProofreadingAndEditing.com

> **Contact:** email, website form
> **Services:** copyediting, proofreading
> **Types of manuscripts:** articles, nonfiction books, devotions, novels, curriculum, adult, teen/YA, picture books, easy readers, middle grade, Bible studies

Charges: flat rate, hourly rate

Credentials/experience: "Fourteen years of experience as a seminary-trained Lutheran pastor; excellent understanding of writing mechanics and style, honed through years of higher education and professional use; freelance editor since 2007 serving authors, publishers, and other entities; have completed multiple educational courses to enhance my knowledge and skills; passionate about writing that intersects with Christian faith. Member of The Christian PEN."

THE FOREWORD COLLECTIVE, LLC | MOLLY HODGIN
1726 Charity Dr., Brentwood, TN 37027 | 615-497-4322
info@theforewordcollective.com | *www.theforewordcollective.com*

Contact: email

Services: manuscript evaluation, substantive editing/rewriting, ghostwriting, coauthoring, writing coach, back-cover copy, book contract evaluation, discussion questions for books, acquisitions consulting

Types of manuscripts: nonfiction books, devotions, novels, query letters, book proposals, gift books, adult, teens/YA, picture books, easy readers, middle grade, poetry, short stories, Bible studies, curriculum, scripts

Charges: flat fee, hourly rate

Credentials/experience: "The Foreword Collective was founded by Molly Hodgin, a publishing professional with two decades of experience. Most recently, she served as the Associate Publisher for the Specialty Division of HarperCollins Christian Publishing working to acquire and create gift books, children's books, and new media products with authors and brands. Prior to that, she worked as an editor for Penguin Young Readers Group and a Senior Editor for Scholastic, Inc."

FREELANCE WRITING & EDITING SERVICES | ROBIN SCHMITT
Rockford, MI | 616-350-0576
schmitt.freelancer@sbcglobal.net | *robinschmitt.com*

Contact: email, phone

Services: manuscript evaluation, substantive editing/rewriting, copyediting, ghostwriting, coauthoring, write discussion questions for books, writing coach, back-cover copy

Types of manuscripts: articles, nonfiction books, devotionals, short stories, novels, curriculum, Bible studies, scripts, gift books, adult, teens/YA, picture books, easy readers, middle grade

Charges: flat fee, hourly rate, page rate, word rate

Credentials/experience: "More than 20 years of experience as a writer and editor in Christian publishing. I've edited many books, both fiction and nonfiction, for adults, teens, and children. In every project I take on, I always strive for the highest standard of excellence."

FRENCH AND ENGLISH COMMUNICATION SERVICES |
DIANE GOULLARD

3104 E. Camelback Rd. #124, Phoenix, AZ 85016-4502 | 602-870-1000
RequestFAECS2008@cox.net | www.FrenchAndEnglish.com

Contact: email, phone, website form, mail

Services: copyediting, proofreading, coauthoring, discussion questions for books; French to English and English to French proofreading, translating

Types of manuscripts: articles, nonfiction books, devotions, poetry, short stories, novels, query letters, book proposals, curriculum, Bible studies, scripts, gift books, technical material, adult, teens/ YA, picture books, easy readers, middle grade, scientific, lyrics

Charges: flat fee, hourly rate, page rate, word rate, custom

Credentials/experience: "Visit my website for bio, references, and experience."

GALADRIEL GRACE
galadriel@galadrielgrace.com | galadrielgrace.com

Contact: email, website form

Services: substantive editing/rewriting, copyediting, proofreading, ghostwriting, back-cover copy

Types of manuscripts: articles, nonfiction books, devotionals, poetry, short stories, novels, query letters, book proposals, curriculum, Bible studies, adult, teens/YA, picture books, easy readers, middle grade

Charges: flat rate, page rate, word rate

Credentials/experience: "PEN certified editor, several years working with authors to help them present their best work and market themselves better."

GINGER KOLBABA

ginger@gingerkolbaba.com | www.gingerkolbaba.com

Contact: email

Services: manuscript evaluation, substantive editing/rewriting, copyediting, proofreading, ghostwriting, coauthoring, discussion questions for books, writing coach

Types of manuscripts: articles, nonfiction books, devotions, novels, short stories, query letters, book proposals, adult, teen/YA, Bible studies, gift books

Charges: hourly rate for editing, flat rate for writing

Credentials/experience: "More than twenty-five years in the industry. Former editor of *Today's Christian Woman* and *Marriage Partnership* magazines and *Kyria.com*, all national, award-winning publications of Christianity Today International. Best-selling author; written or contributed to more than forty books and one thousand articles, both in print and online. Clients include many publishing houses and best-selling authors."

HANEMAN EDITORIAL | NATALIE HANEMAN

Franklin, TN | 615-712-4430

nathanemann@gmail.com | www.nataliehanemannediting.com

Contact: email, website form

Services: manuscript evaluation, substantive editing/rewriting, copyediting

Types of manuscripts: nonfiction books, novels, book proposals, adult, teen/YA, middle grade

Charges: flat fee

Credentials/experience: "Eleven years in-house at publishing houses, eight of those at Thomas Nelson in the fiction division under the tutelage of Allen Arnold. Since 2012, I've been freelance editing fiction and nonfiction (substantive and line), as well as helping authors get their synopses ready to submit to agents. I've edited more than three hundred manuscripts and particularly love working with newer authors or authors who are unsure if they should publish traditionally or indie. Certified by the Christian Editors Connection."

HAYHURST EDITORIAL LLC | SARAH HAYHURST

1441 Haynescrest Ct., Grayson, GA 30017 | 470-825-2905

sarah@sarahhayhurst.com | www.sarahhayhurst.com

Contact: email

Services: substantive editing/rewriting, copyediting, proofreading, website text

Types of manuscripts: articles, nonfiction books, devotions, Bible studies, adult

Charges: word rate

Credentials/experience: "Sarah graduated as the valedictorian of her class in high school, earned an associate degree in Secretarial Science in 1991, and pursued a bachelor's degree in Communication Arts in 2014, graduating cum laude. Sarah has enjoyed a variety of positions, such as editor/online teacher for a publishing company, managing editor for a university, computer/ESL teacher for a school, marketing manager for a law firm and an engineering firm, and communications director for a school. Sarah is a gold-level member of The Christian PEN and Christian Editor Network with whom she passed extensive testing and demonstrated expertise in the substantive editing, copyediting and proofreading of both fiction and nonfiction manuscripts as well as other nonfiction content. Sarah has over ten years of experience in editing and started her own editorial company in 2014."

HENRY MCLAUGHLIN

817-703-9875

henry@henrymclaughlin.org | www.henrymclaughlin.org

Contact: email, phone

Services: manuscript evaluation, substantive editing/rewriting, ghostwriting, writing coach

Types of manuscripts: nonfiction books, short stories, novels, adult

Charges: custom rate

Credentials/experience: "For the past several years I have served as a coach and editor to many writers in both fiction and nonfiction. I have also ghostwritten. My work is in both Christian and general markets. For me, building a relationship with the author is key to any editing. It's important for me to know the author's heart and desire for their work. As an editor, my goal is to help them achieve their dream by providing editing and coaching geared to helping them develop and grow as writers."

HESTERMAN CREATIVE | DR. VICKI HESTERMAN

PO Box 333, Napoleon, OH 43545

vhes@mac.com

Contact: email

Services: manuscript evaluation, substantive editing/rewriting, copyediting, proofreading, coauthoring, writing coach, back-cover copy

Types of manuscripts: articles, nonfiction books, devotions, novels, query letters, book proposals, Bible studies, gift books, adult

Charges: hourly rate, firm estimate with sample

Credentials/experience: "Writer, editor, photographer, college professor with 30 years experience in newspapers, magazines, books."

HONEST EDITING SERVICES | BILL LELAND

Bend, OR

bill@writersedgeservice.com | www.honestediting.com

Contact: email, website form

Services: "Honest Editing offers three specific editorial services for Christian manuscripts. (1) We can create professional proposals for enhancing your presentation to publishers; (2) We can do a full evaluation of a manuscript that identifies both strengths and weaknesses in a manuscript and points the author in the right direction to improve the manuscript/writing style; (3) We can perform a full edit, page by page, of an entire manuscript. All these are done by professional editors for a flat fee as outlined at our website."

Types of manuscripts: nonfiction books, devotionals, novels, book proposals, Bible studies, gift books, adult, teen/YA

Charges: flat fee

HONEYCOMB HOUSE PUBLISHING LLC |
DAVID E. FESSENDEN

dave@fessendens.net | www.davefessenden.com

Contact: email

Services: manuscript evaluation, substantive editing/rewriting, copyediting, book-contract evaluation, write discussion questions for books, writing coach, back-cover copy, coauthoring

Types of manuscripts: nonfiction books, devotionals, academic, novels, book proposals, Bible studies, gift books, adult, teen/YA , middle grade

Charges: flat fee

Credentials/experience: "David E. Fessenden, publisher for Honeycomb House Publishing LLC, has degrees in journalism and theology, and over 30 years of experience in writing, editing, and editorial management for Christian book publishers."

IEDIT.INK | BOBBIE TEMPLE

3328 Flagstaff Ln., Knoxville, TN 37931 | 954-559-9587

editingbox@outlook.com | iedit.ink

Contact: website form

Services: manuscript evaluation, substantive editing, writing coach

Types of manuscripts: adult, teen/YA, picture books, easy readers, middle grade, graphic novels

Charges: page rate, word rate

Credentials/experience: "I have several years of publishing, writing, editing, and graphic design experience as well as multiple certifications. Currently working as a middle-grade editor at Elk Lake."

INKSMITH EDITORIAL SERVICES | LIZ SMITH

336-514-2331

liz@inksmithediting.com | *www.inksmithediting.com*

Contact: email

Services: copyediting, proofreading, indexing, sermon transcription

Types of manuscripts: articles, nonfiction books, devotions, Bible studies, academic, adult

Charges: word rate, page rate

Credentials/experience: "Liz edits primarily Christian nonfiction. She works with self-publishing authors as well as writers preparing a manuscript for submission to traditional publishers. Her other services include general and Scripture indexes, sermon transcription, typesetting (interior design), and e-book formatting."

INKSNATCHER | SALLY HANAN

429 S. Avenue C, Elgin, TX 78621 | 512-351-5869

inkmeister@inksnatcher.com | *www.inksnatcher.com*

Contact: email

Services: substantive editing/rewriting, copyediting, proofreading, ghostwriting, coauthoring, discussion questions for books, back-cover copy, self-publishing help

Types of manuscripts: articles, nonfiction books, short stories, novels, curriculum, gift books, adult, teen/YA, middle grade, devotions, Bible studies

Charges: hourly rate, word rate

Credentials/experience: "Certified nonfiction copy editor by the Christian Editor Connection."

INSPIRATION FOR WRITERS, INC. | SANDY TRITT

Parkersburg, WV | 304-428-1218

IFWeditors@gmail.com | *www.InspirationForWriters.com/editorial-services*

Contact: email

Services: manuscript evaluation, substantive editing/rewriting, copyediting, proofreading, ghostwriting, writing coach, consulting

Types of manuscripts: nonfiction books, devotions, short stories, novels, query letters, book proposals, scripts, gift books, adult, teen/YA, middle grade, articles, academic, Bible studies, picture books, easy readers

Charges: flat fee, word rate

Credentials/experience: "Inspiration for Writers, Inc., is one of the oldest editing and writing services still operating today. All of our editors/writers are published authors, many with MFAs in Creative Writing. We have editors who specialize in specific genres and cover some technical and curriculum subjects. Just ask. We are active in the writing community, giving workshops at conferences and sharing our experience with those who are just now beginning their voyage into the writing world—and with those who are well-published and just need an extra eye. We provide many craft of writing tutorials on our website and on our blog, and we offer a free sample edit or a free consultation upon request."

JAMES WATKINS

759 S. Lenfesty Ave., Marion, IN 46953
jim@jameswatkins.com | jameswatkins.com/editing

Contact: email

Services: manuscript evaluation, substantive editing/rewriting, writing coach

Types of manuscripts: articles, nonfiction books, devotions, adult

Charges: page rate, hourly rate

Credentials/experience: "Thirty years of editorial experience with Wesleyan Publishing House and other publishers, five national editing awards, fifteen years teaching writing at Taylor University, plus over twenty traditionally published books earning two national awards and over 2,500 published articles with two national writing awards. Have worked with first-time authors as well as *New York Times* best-sellers."

JAMIE CHAVEZ, EDITOR

3035 Argyle Ave., Murfreesboro, TN 37127 | 615-948-4430
jamie.chavez@gmail.com | www.jamiechavez.com

Contact: email

Services: manuscript evaluation, substantive editing/rewriting, copyediting

Types of manuscripts: nonfiction books, novels, adult, teen/YA, picture books, easy readers, middle grade, devotions, gift books

Charges: flat fee

Credentials/experience: "Jamie Chavez worked for more than ten years in the Christian publishing industry and twenty as a professional copywriter before becoming a freelance editor in 2004. Books she's edited have become *New York Times* best sellers, won Christy and Carol Awards, and been finalists for many other awards and honors. She enjoys the collaborative nature of editing and finds long-term relationships especially rewarding—bring on the second, third, fourth book in the series! Jamie counts many national publishing houses as clients, many authors as friends, and spends her days making good books better."

JANIS WHIPPLE

9608 Regiment Ct., Land O Lakes, FL 34638 | 954-579-8545
janiswhipple@gmail.com

Contact: email

Services: manuscript evaluation, substantive editing/rewriting, copyediting, proofreading, coauthoring, discussion questions for books, writing coach

Types of manuscripts: articles, nonfiction books, devotions, query letters, book proposals, curriculum, gift books, adult, teen/YA

Charges: hourly rate, sometimes does fee projects

Credentials/experience: "Thirty years of editing, ten years as an in-house editor with B&H Publishers in acquisitions and managing editing, fifteen years as a freelance editor and writing coach."

JAY K. PAYLEITNER & ASSOCIATES | JAY PAYLEITNER

629 N. Tyler Rd., Saint Charles, IL 60174 | 630-377-7899
jaypayleitner@gmail.com | *www.jaypayleitner.com*

Contact: email, phone, website form

Services: ghostwriting, coauthoring, back-cover copy

Types of manuscripts: nonfiction books, devotionals, gift books

Charges: flat fee

Credentials/experience: "Author of 30 books with Harvest House, Broadstreet, DaySpring, Tyndale, Multnomah, Bethany House, and Worthy."

JEANETTE GARDNER LITTLETON, PUBLICATION SERVICES

3706 N.E. Shady Lane Dr., Gladstone, MO 64119-1958 | 816-459-8016 *jeanettedl@earthlink.net | www.linkedin.com/in/jeanette-littleton-b1b790101*

Contact: email

Services: manuscript evaluation, substantive editing/rewriting, copyediting, proofreading, book-contract evaluation, discussion questions for books, back-cover copy, indexing

Types of manuscripts: articles, nonfiction books, devotions, short stories, novels, query letters, book proposals, curriculum, Bible studies, gift books, technical material, adult, teen/YA

Charges: flat fee, hourly rate, page rate

Credentials/experience: "I've been a full-time editor and writer for thirty years for a variety of publishers. I've written five thousand articles and edited thousands of articles and dozens of books. Please see my profile at LinkedIn."

JEANETTE HANSCOME

jeanettehanscome@gmail.com | jeanettehanscome.com/services-for-writers

Contact: email, website form

Services: manuscript evaluation, copyediting, ghostwriting, coauthoring, writing coach

Types of manuscripts: articles, nonfiction books, devotions, short stories, novels, query letters, adult, teen/YA, middle grade

Charges: hourly rate, flat fee

Credentials/experience: "Jeanette Hanscome has written five books and hundreds of articles, devotions and stories, as well as contributing to over a dozen devotionals. As a freelance editor and coach, Jeanette has experience in a variety of genres including devotionals, women's contemporary fiction, historical romance, YA, memoirs, and general non-fiction."

JENNIFER EDWARDS COMMUNICATIONS |
JENNIFER EDWARDS

San Diego, CA

mail.jennifer.edwards@gmail.com | www.jedwardsediting.net

Contact: email, website form

Services: manuscript evaluation, copyediting, proofreading, discussion questions for books, back-cover copy, writing coach

Types of manuscripts: nonfiction books, curriculum, academic, book proposals, Bible studies, adult, query letters

Charges: hourly rate

Credentials/experience: "Jennifer Edwards is an established professional nonfiction editor, writer, and publishing coach serving Christian authors and publishers. She has worked with 40+ authors and numerous Christian publishers and ministries, including Penguin Random House, Faithlife (Lexham Press), Principles to Live By Publishing, BMH Books, Compel/She Speaks, FDM.World, Redemption Press, Gospel Advocate, The Sophos Group, and more. Her master's degree in Biblical and Theological Studies from Western Seminary has proven invaluable in helping Christian authors with their manuscripts by providing a critical eye for content, a thorough understanding of Scripture, and insightful theological thinking."

JENWESTWRITING EDITING & MARKETING SERVICES | JENNIFER WESTBROOK

14030 Connecticut Ave., #6813, Silver Spring, MD 20916 | 301-615-1123
jen@jenwestwriting.com | *www.jenwestwriting.com*

Contact: email, website form
Services: manuscript evaluation, substantive editing, copyediting, proofreading, ghostwriting, back-cover copy
Types of manuscripts: articles, nonfiction books, devotions, poetry, short stories, novels, technical material, academic, adult, teen/YA, picture books, easy readers, middle grade
Charges: flat fee, custom
Credentials/experience: "As a Christian Content Marketing Copywriter and Editor, I work with church leaders, business owners, and authors who need help growing their ministry, business, or online following. I also work with post-graduate students who need support as they complete their Master's or Doctoral programs. My author clients are in all genres, including fiction, religious and inspirational, children's books, business, and non-fiction.

"I've been serving clients as their trusted writer and editor for over 20 years. I earned a Bachelor's Degree in English from Hampton University in Hampton, Virginia, and a Juris Doctor Degree from Columbia Law School in New York City. Before becoming a full-time entrepreneur, I worked as a Washington, D.C. attorney for over a decade, where I became skilled at technical writing, project management, and client relations."

JHWRITING+ | NICOLE HAYES

Randleman, NC | 410-709-8549
jhwritingplus@yahoo.com | *www.jhwritingplus.com*
Contact: email, website form

Services: manuscript evaluation, substantive editing/rewriting, copyediting, proofreading, ghostwriting, coauthoring, discussion questions for books, writing coach

Types of manuscripts: articles, nonfiction books, devotions, poetry, short stories, novels, curriculum, gift books, technical material, adult, teen/YA

Charges: flat rate, word rate

Credentials/experience: "Bachelor's degree in English; PhD in education. Although I do most writing, editing, and proofreading projects, my niche is creative nonfiction (engaging, dramatic, factual prose). I have been writing and editing for more than twenty-five years."

JLC SERVICES | JODY L. COLLINS

1403 Newport Ct. S.E., Renton, WA 98058 | 425-260-0948
heyjode70@yahoo.com | *www.jodyleecollins.com*

Contact: email

Services: copyediting, proofreading, writing coach, back-cover copy, manuscript evaluation

Types of manuscripts: nonfiction books, devotions, book proposals, Bible studies, picture books, curriculum

Charges: custom

Credentials/experience: "BA in liberal studies, English major. Teaching credential, 1991. Twenty-five years of experience writing online and in print. Author of *Living the Season Well: Reclaiming Christmas*. Coach/consultant for multiple clients from editing to self-publishing."

JOHN SLOAN LLC | JOHN SLOAN

830 Grey Eagle Cir. N., Colorado Springs, CO 80919 | 719-888-0365
jsjohnsloan@gmail.com | *sloanhinds.com*

Contact: website form

Services: substantive editing/rewriting, ghostwriting, coauthoring, writing coach, consulting

Types of manuscripts: nonfiction books, devotions, Bible studies, gift books, academic, adult

Charges: flat fee; hourly rate; both, depending on job

Credentials/experience: "I have worked in publishing and editorial roles for 40 years, with Multnomah Press, HarperCollinsChristian Publishing, Zondervan. I am offering my services for freelance work in the areas of book development, collaboration, writer coaching, book doctoring, macro editing, content editing. I have worked with a broad spectrum of book and author types: I have edited the literary and general-market works of authors like Philip Yancey and Frederick Buechner; popular-issues volumes of writers like Chuck Colson; high-visibility authors like Lee Strobel and Ben Carson; broader-market authors and pastors like John Ortberg and Mark Batterson; and popular academic works of writers like Ravi Zacharias."

JOT OR TITTLE EDITORIAL SERVICES |
SAMUEL RYAN KELLY
sam@jotortittle.com | jotortittle.com

> **Contact:** email
>
> **Services:** manuscript evaluation, substantive editing/rewriting, copyediting, proofreading, writing coach, academic
>
> **Types of manuscripts:** articles, nonfiction books, devotions, short stories, novels, Bible studies, adult
>
> **Charges:** hourly rate
>
> **Credentials/experience:** "Sam has a double BA in English and biblical and religious studies and an MA in theology. He specializes in academic writing and has a background in biblical languages, but he likes to bring his expertise to a variety of projects. In addition to his freelance work, Sam does research for pastors and churches at Docent Research Group and serves as an associate editor with Wordsmith Writing Coaches."

JOY MEDIA | JULIE-ALLYSON IERON
PO Box 1099, Park Ridge, IL 60068
j-a@joymediaservices.com | www.joymediaservices.com

> **Contact:** email
>
> **Services:** manuscript evaluation, substantive editing/rewriting, proofreading, copyediting, ghostwriting, discussion questions for books, writing coach, back-cover copy
>
> **Types of manuscripts:** articles, nonfiction books, devotions, book proposals, gift books, adult, novels, Bible studies
>
> **Charges:** hourly rate, flat fee
>
> **Credentials/experience:** "Master's degree in journalism with more than thirty years in Christian publishing management, writing, and editing. Fourteen years as a mentor/master craftsman with the Jerry B. Jenkins Christian Writers Guild."

JR'S RED QUILL EDITING | JUDITH ROBL
PO Box 802, Lyons, KS 67554 | 620-257-3143
jrlight620@yahoo.com | *www.judithrobl.com/editing-2*
> **Contact:** email, website form
> **Services:** copyediting, proofreading, writing coach, back-cover copy, manuscript evaluation, discussion questions for books
> **Types of manuscripts:** devotions, short stories, novels, query letters, Bible studies, gift books, adult
> **Charges:** custom
> **Credentials/experience:** "Educated as a secondary English teacher decades ago, I've edited for people for many years. My first major accomplishment in editing was published in 2010. I use *The Chicago Manual of Style* unless another style guide is provided. No project is undertaken without a sample edit to see if we are a good fit. I believe the relationship between author and editor is second only to competence."

KACI LANE CREATIONS, LLC | KACI LANE HINDMAN
15900 Jackson Trace Rd., Coker, AL 35452
kacilane@gmail.com | *kacilane.com*
> **Contact:** email
> **Services:** proofreading, back-cover copy
> **Types of manuscripts:** articles, devotions, novels, short stories, Bible studies, gift books, adult
> **Charges:** hourly rate, flat fee
> **Credentials/experience:** "I have worked as a writer and editor since 2003 for various clients, both in-house at publishing companies and as an independent contractor."

KAREN APPOLD
Macungie, PA | 610-351-5400
kappold@msn.com
> **Contact:** email
> **Services:** copyediting, proofreading
> **Types of manuscripts:** articles, curriculum, academic
> **Charges:** flat fee, hourly rate, word rate
> **Credentials/experience:** "I am an award-winning journalist with a BA from Penn State University in English (Writing). I have more than 25 years of professional editorial experience. I mainly write on healthcare/medical and retail, but welcome Christian-themed work."

KATHY IDE DIVERSIFIED ENTERPRISES | KATHY IDE
Kathy@KathyIde.com | www.KathyIde.com

Contact: email

Services: manuscript evaluation, copyediting, proofreading, ghostwriting, writing coach, substantive editing/rewriting, back-cover copy

Types of manuscripts: articles, nonfiction books, devotions, short stories, novels, query letters, book proposals, Bible studies, scripts, gift books, adult, teen/YA

Charges: hourly rate

Credentials/experience: "Kathy Ide is the author of *Proofreading Secrets of Best-Selling Authors, Editing Secrets of Best-Selling Authors,* and *Capitalization Dictionary,* and she is the editor/compiler of the Fiction Lover's Devotional series. She's been a professional freelance editor since 1998 and owns Christian Editor Network, parent company to The Christian PEN: Proofreaders and Editors Network, Christian Editor Connection, The PEN Institute, and PENCON, which she founded."

KATIE PHILLIPS CREATIVE SERVICES | KATIE PHILLIPS
1500 E. Tall Tree Rd. #33202, Derby, KS 67037-6033 | 316-293-9202
morford.katie@gmail.com | www.katiephillipscreative.com

Contact: email, phone

Services: manuscript evaluation, writing coach, branding and business coaching and courses, social-media strategy, back-cover copy

Types of manuscripts: novels, short stories, query letters, book proposals, adult, teen/YA

Charges: word rate, hourly rate, custom

Credentials/experience: "Katie Phillips is a developmental editor, as well as a writing, branding, and business coach for women authors of YA sci-fi/fantasy looking to take their career to the next level. Her clients include multiple award winners and finalists, and have gone on to sign book deals, find agents, and profitably self-publish. She has a BA in Journalism and Mass Communications and worked over ten years as an editor for newspapers and in non-profit communications. She helped found indie publishing house Crosshair Press (now Uncommon Universes) and studied writing under agent Les Stobbe and author DiAnn Mills. She was an AWSA Editor of the Year finalist and studied business and branding strategies under coach Michelle Knight."

KEELY BOEVING EDITORIAL | KEELY BOEVING

Denver, CO | 303-916-7498
keely.boeving@gmail.com | *www.keelyboeving.com*

    Contact: website form
    Services: manuscript evaluation, substantive editing/rewriting, copyediting, ghostwriting, coauthoring
    Types of manuscripts: nonfiction books, novels, query letters, book proposals, adult, teen/YA, middle grade
    Charges: hourly rate
    Credentials/experience: "Experienced editor and copy editor, formerly worked in editorial for Oxford University Press. Have worked with independent clients, literary agencies, and publishers as a freelancer for the past several years."

KELLY KAGAMAS TOMKIES

Bexley, OH | 614-270-0185
kellytomkies@gmail.com

    Contact: email
    Services: substantive editing/rewriting, copyediting, proofreading, ghostwriting, writing coach
    Types of manuscripts: articles, nonfiction books, devotions, short stories, novels, query letters, book proposals, adult, teen/YA, picture books, easy readers, middle grade
    Charges: flat fee
    Credentials/experience: "I have nearly twenty years of editorial experience, including authoring seven books for different publishers, contributing chapters to two National Geographic books, serving as editor of three major business magazines, and years of experience writing and editing for publishers and individual authors. My client list includes HarperCollins, John Wiley & Sons, McGraw-Hill, Kirkus Editorial, Fountainhead Press, Barbour Books, Vantage Press, and Gadfly, LLC, as well as individual authors who wish to find publishers or self-publish."

KRISTEN STIEFFEL

kristen@kristenstieffel.com | *www.kristenstieffel.com*

    Contact: email
    Services: manuscript evaluation, substantive editing/rewriting, copyediting, proofreading, ghostwriting, coauthoring, writing coach
    Types of manuscripts: short stories, novels
    Charges: custom

Credentials/experience: "Fantasy and Science Fiction specialist. Trained in developmental editing and copyediting by the Editorial Freelancers Association and in substantive editing by the Christian Proofreader and Editor Network. Edited dozens of books, including more than 20 sci-fi and fantasy titles. Also an editor with Havok Publishing. Author of *Alara's Call* (fantasy) and *Tales of the Phoenix* (science fiction)."

LEE WARREN COMMUNICATIONS | LEE WARREN
leewarrenjr@outlook.com | *www.leewarren.info/editing*

Contact: email, website form

Services: copyediting, proofreading, manuscript evaluation

Types of manuscripts: nonfiction books, devotions, novels, articles, Bible studies, curriculum, gift books, adult

Charges: word rate, flat fee

Credentials/experience: "Lee Warren has more than twenty years of experience in the Christian publishing industry (both traditional and indie). He has been a contract editor for Barbour Publishing, Electric Moon Publishing, and Bold Vision Books, as well as editing manuscripts through his own service."

LESLIE H. STOBBE
201 E. Howard St., E46, Tryon, NC 28782 | 828-808-7127
lhstobbe123@gmail.com | *www.stobbeliterary.com*

Contact: email

Services: substantive editing/rewriting, ghostwriting, coauthoring, book-contract evaluation, writing coach, back-cover copy, manuscript evaluation

Types of manuscripts: nonfiction books, devotions, book proposals, curriculum, adult

Charges: hourly rate

Credentials/experience: "I've been writing articles, church materials, and curriculum; ghostwriting for prominent authors; editorial director at three publishers and president of one; literary agent for 25 years; mentor at hundreds of writers conferences; and book writer coach for many years. I can take a book idea development through rewrites and editing to book proposal for agents and editors."

LESLIE L. MCKEE EDITING | LESLIE L. MCKEE
lmckeeediting@gmail.com | *lmckeeediting.wixsite.com/lmckeeediting*

Contact: email

Services: copyediting, proofreading, discussion questions for books, back-cover copy

Types of manuscripts: nonfiction books, devotions, poetry, short stories, novels, adult, teen/YA, picture books, easy readers, middle grade, articles, gift books

Charges: page rate, word rate, per-project rate, flat rate

Credentials/experience: "Freelance editor and proofreader with various publishing houses (large and small) since 2012, working with traditionally published and self-published authors. Member of The Christian PEN and American Christian Fiction Writers. See website for details on services offered, as well as testimonials and a portfolio."

LESLIE SANTAMARIA

leslie@lesliesantamaria.com | www.lesliesantamaria.com

Contact: email

Services: manuscript evaluation, copyediting, proofreading, writing coach, back-cover copy

Types of manuscripts: nonfiction books, query letters, book proposals, picture books, easy readers, middle grade

Charges: page rate, flat fee

Credentials/experience: "Published author, freelance editor, and writing coach, with more than 200 pieces published in periodicals, specializing in children's literature."

LIBBY GONTARZ

Apache Junction, AZ | 480-278-4848

libbygontarz@gmail.com | www.libbygontarz.com

Contact: email, phone

Services: substantive editing/rewriting, copyediting, discussion questions for books

Types of manuscripts: articles, nonfiction books, curriculum, Bible studies, adult, middle grade, devotions

Charges: page rate, word rate, custom; free sample edit

Credentials/experience: "After a career of teaching and nation-wide educational training, I accepted a curriculum development position at an educational publishing company. Writing lessons and assessments gradually led into editing. After the layoff of my entire department during an economic downturn, I wrote for a weekly paper, focusing on business and local politics. God rewoke in me a desire I had first experienced as a child: to be an editor.

And since God always finishes what he starts, here I am, a freelance editor, available to make your project better."

LIFE LAUNCH ME | JANE RUBIETTA
418 W. Touhy Ave., Park Ridge, IL 60068 | 847-363-6364
jane@lifelaunchme.com | *www.LifeLaunchMe.com*
> **Contact:** email
> **Services:** manuscript evaluation, proofreading, ghostwriting, coauthoring, book-contract evaluation, writing coach, copyediting, discussion questions for books, back-cover copy
> **Types of manuscripts:** articles, nonfiction books, devotions, novels, query letters, book proposals, adult, Bible studies
> **Charges:** hourly rate
> **Credentials/experience:** "Jane Rubietta has written 21 books, 100s of articles, helped train writers and speakers for more than 20 years, and co-authored three books. Jane speaks internationally and also trains writers and speakers at conferences around the globe."

LIGHTHOUSE EDITING | DR. LON ACKELSON
13326 Community Rd. #11, Poway, CA 92064 | 858-748-9258
Isaiah68la@sbcglobal.net | *lighthouseedit.com*
> **Contact:** website form
> **Services:** manuscript evaluation, substantive editing/rewriting, copyediting, proofreading, ghostwriting, coauthoring, back-cover copy
> **Types of manuscripts:** articles, nonfiction books, devotions, query letters, book proposals, curriculum, Bible studies, adult
> **Charges:** flat fee, hourly rate, page rate
> **Credentials/experience:** "A professional editor for thirty-three years and a published writer for forty years."

LIGHTNING EDITING SERVICES | DENISE LOOCK
699 Golf Course Rd., Waynesville, NC 28786 | 908-868-5854
denise@lightningeditingservices.com | *www.lightningeditingservices.com*
> **Contact:** email
> **Services:** manuscript evaluation, copyediting, proofreading, ghostwriting, discussion questions for books, coauthoring, back-cover copy
> **Types of manuscripts:** articles, nonfiction books, devotions, book proposals, easy readers, picture books, Bible studies, adult, teen/YA, middle grade
> **Charges:** flat fee, hourly rate, custom

Credentials/experience: "After teaching English for almost thirty years on the high school and college level, Denise switched to an editing career. She has ten years' experience as a book editor for LPCBooks, and she also accepts freelance projects from both fiction and nonfiction authors."

LINDSAY A. FRANKLIN

Escondido, CA | 858-243-8134
Lindsay@LindsayAFranklin.com | lindsayafranklin.com

Contact: website form
Services: manuscript evaluation, substantive editing/rewriting, copyediting, proofreading, ghostwriting, coauthoring, writing coach
Types of manuscripts: nonfiction books, short stories, novels, adult, teen/YA, picture books, easy readers, middle grade
Charges: hourly rate, word rate
Credentials/experience: "Award-winning, published author; member of The Christian PEN."

LINORE BURKARD EDITORIAL SERVICES |
LINORE ROSE BURKARD

PO Box 674, Waynesville, OH 45068 | 513-331-0143
Admin@LinoreBurkard.com | www.LilliputPressllc.com

Contact: email
Services: manuscript evaluation, substantive editing/rewriting, discussion questions for books, writing coach, back-cover copy
Types of manuscripts: novels, teens/YA, easy readers, middle grade
Charges: flat rate, hourly rate
Credentials/experience: "Linore Burkard is a multi-published author with a love of literature. Since earning a magna cum laude degree from CUNY in English Literature, Linore has written novels, articles, a screenplay, poetry, blog posts, writing workshop curricula, and edited newsletters and books for numerous clients. After a low cost initial evaluation of a potential client's work, she will provide either a flat fee or hourly rate. Page and/or word rates can be negotiated if desired."

LISA BARTELT

Lancaster, PA | 717-673-7236
lmbartelt@gmail.com | lisabartelt.com

Contact: email
Services: copyediting, proofreading, coauthoring
Types of manuscripts: articles, nonfiction books, devotions, novels,

query letters

Charges: hourly rate

Credentials/experience: "Eight years of writing and editing for daily newspapers; member of American Christian Fiction Writers and The Christian PEN; published articles in *Thriving Family*, *Prayer Connect*, and *The Upper Room*; wrote curriculum for Group Publishing."

LISSA HALLS JOHNSON EDITORIAL |
LISSA HALLS JOHNSON

13926 Double Girth Ct., Matthews, NC 28105 | 479-220-8662
lissahallsjohnson@gmail.com | lissahallsjohnson.com

Contact: email, website form

Services: manuscript evaluation, substantive editing/rewriting, writing coach

Types of manuscripts: novels, memoir, teens/YA

Charges: hourly rate

Credentials/experience: "Editor for fiction, nonfiction narrative, memoir for 20+ years. Some writers have received Christy Award finalist awards or nominations, on bestselling lists, *Publishers Weekly* starred reviews."

LOGOS WORD DESIGNS, LLC | LINDA NATHAN
PO Box 735, Maple Falls, WA 98266-0735 | 360-599-3429
editor@logosword.com | www.logosword.com

Contact: email

Services: manuscript evaluation, substantive editing/rewriting, copyediting, ghostwriting, discussion questions for books, back-cover copy

Types of manuscripts: articles, nonfiction books, devotions, short stories, novels, query letters, book proposals, Bible studies, academic, gift books, technical material, adult, teen/YA

Charges: word rate, page rate, hourly rate, flat fee, custom

Credentials/experience: "Linda Nathan has over 30 years of experience as a professional independent freelance writer, editor, and publishing consultant, working with authors and institutions on a wide range of projects. She is a published author with 10 years of experience in the legal field and has spoken on the radio and at conferences and seminars. Since 1992 she has run her own company, Logos Word Designs, LLC. Linda has a B.A. in Psychology from the University of Oregon and master's level work. She is a freelance staff editor with Redemption Press, a Gold member of the Christian Editor Connection, and a member of four other professional writers' and editors' associations."

LOUISE M. GOUGE, COPYEDITOR

900 Jamison Loop #105, Kissimmee, FL 34744 | 407-694-5765
Louisemgouge@aol.com | louisemgougeauthor.blogspot.com

> **Contact:** email
> **Services:** copyediting, substantive editing/rewriting, manuscript evaluation, back-cover copy
> **Types of manuscripts:** short stories, novels, book proposals
> **Charges:** word rate
> **Credentials/experience:** "Louise M. Gouge is a retired college English professor and the author of twenty-five novels. For editing, she utilizes CMOS and MLA. Copyediting includes checking grammar, punctuation, spelling, and phrasing. Substantive editing includes making sure character arcs are balanced, the story is well-paced, and the conclusion is satisfying. Checking a client's research will raise the cost, the amount depending upon how much research is required. Novel editing $1,000-3,000."

LUCIE WINBORNE

116 Hickory Rd., Longwood, FL 32750-2708 | 321-439-7743
lwinborne704@gmail.com | www.bluetypewriter.com

> **Contact:** email
> **Services:** copyediting, proofreading
> **Types of manuscripts:** nonfiction books, devotions, poetry, short stories, novels, adult, teen/YA, middle grade
> **Charges:** hourly rate
> **Credentials/experience:** "Conversant with *Chicago Manual of Style, Merriam-Webster Collegiate Dictionary*, Google Docs and Microsoft Word, with experience in fiction, nonfiction, educational, and business documents. Demonstrated adherence to deadlines and excellent communication and organizational skills."

LYNNE TAGAWA

5606 Onyx Way, San Antonio, TX 78222 | 210-544-4397
lbtagawa@gmail.com | www.lynnetagawa.com/editing

> **Contact:** email
> **Services:** copyediting, proofreading
> **Types of manuscripts:** short stories, novels

Charges: word rate

Credentials/experience: "Educator, writer, and editor serving as proofreader for Chapel Library literature ministry for many years. Member, Christian PEN. Experience copyediting historical fiction."

MANYESHA BATIST INC. | MANYESHA BATIST

4071 Orleans Ct., Denver, CO 80249 | 303-253-0424
mybatistinc@gmail.com | *mybatistinc.journoportfolio.com*

Contact: email

Services: substantive editing/rewriting, copyediting, proofreading, ghostwriting, coauthoring, discussion questions for books, back-cover copy

Types of manuscripts: articles, nonfiction books, devotions

Charges: flat fee, hourly rate, page rate, word rate

Credentials/experience: "Manyesha Batist is a seasoned journalist with more than 17 years of experience as both an editor and writer."

MARCY WEYDEMULLER

San Francisco, CA | 925-876-4860
marcy@sowinglightseeds.com

Contact: email

Services: manuscript evaluation, substantive editing/rewriting, discussion questions for books, writing coach

Types of manuscripts: articles, nonfiction books, devotions, short stories, novels, curriculum, adult, teen/YA, picture books, easy readers, middle grade

Charges: hourly rate

Credentials/experience: "I have worked on more than forty published novels, and four of the authors I work with have published three or more series. My current edits have included historical fiction, historical Christmas novella, YA contemporary, middle-readers both historical and contemporary, suspense-mystery, woman's romance, and memoir. I have more than twenty-five years of experience writing, mentoring, and teaching, both in fiction and nonfiction, including Bible studies and college composition. I have completed a BA in history and sociology and an MFA in writing, with a special focus on fantasy, poetry, and children's literature."

MARK MY WORD EDITORIAL SERVICES, LLC |
VICKI ADANG
1176 Deliquia Dr. #14, Cincinnati, OH 45230 | 317-549-5176
vadang@outlook.com | www.mmwLLC.net

Contact: email

Services: manuscript evaluation, substantive editing/rewriting, copyediting, proofreading, writing coach, back-cover copy

Types of manuscripts: articles, nonfiction books, adult, teen/YA, devotions, short stories, novels, query letters, book proposals

Charges: hourly rate, flat rate

Credentials/experience: "As an editor and project manager, I provide development editing, copyediting, and proofreading services of fiction and nonfiction manuscripts. I enjoy coaching new authors and collaborating with seasoned authors. I focus on helping authors refine their writing, present clear and compelling messages, and achieve success through skilled editorial services."

MARTI PIEPER, COLLABORATIVE WRITER AND EDITOR
246 Maple Grove Rd., Seneca, SC 29678 | 352-409-3136
martipieper@gmail.com | www.martipieper.com

Contact: email, website form

Services: manuscript evaluation, copyediting, proofreading, ghostwriting, coauthoring, discussion questions for books, writing coach

Types of manuscripts: articles, nonfiction books, devotions, query letters, book proposals, curriculum, adult, teen/YA, Bible studies, gift books

Charges: custom

Credentials/experience: "Marti Pieper's eclectic publishing career includes ghostwriting a young adult memoir that made the ECPA bestseller list and traveling to six Latin American countries to share stories of teen mission trips and an award-winning missionary memoir. She has written seven traditionally published nonfiction books and edited several more, written and edited for both print and digital publications, and taught at multiple writers conferences."

MEGHAN BIELINSKI PROFESSIONAL WRITING AND EDITING SERVICES | MEGHAN BIELINSKI STOLL
mbielinski34@gmail.com
the-efa.org/membershipinfo/meghan-bielinski-21154

Contact: website form

Services: copyediting, proofreading

Types of manuscripts: nonfiction books, short stories, novels, adult, teen/YA

Charges: word rate

Credentials/experience: "Writing and editing are my passions. Since graduating with a bachelor's in English literature, I have gained four years of experience offering professional editing services. I work with both fiction and nonfiction, most notably self-help, lifestyle, personal finance, YA novels, Christian, and historical fiction."

MENTOR ME CAREER NETWORK | CHERYL ROGERS

Tampa, FL | 863-288-0802

cheryl@mentormecareernetwork.com | linkedin.com/in/cherylarogers

Contact: email, phone

Services: manuscript evaluation, substantive editing/rewriting, copyediting, proofreading, ghostwriting, coauthoring, writing coach

Types of manuscripts: articles, nonfiction books, adult, teen/YA, middle grade

Charges: flat rate, hourly rate, word rate

Credentials/experience: "BA in journalism and sociology; more than five years of book editing/freelancing; one year of newspaper copyediting; eleven years of newspaper reporting; four years of desktop design, including brochures, booklets, and flyers."

MISSION AND MEDIA | MICHELLE RAYBURN

715-382-6030

info@missionandmedia.com | www.missionandmedia.com

Contact: email

Services: substantive editing/rewriting, copyediting, proofreading, ghostwriting, discussion questions for books

Types of manuscripts: nonfiction books, Bible studies

Charges: flat fee, hourly and word rates

Credentials/experience: "Michelle Rayburn has been a freelance writer for 19 years and has edited for Christian publishers as well as for indie authors. Has also worked in the marketing and public relations industry. Michelle has an MA in ministry leadership and has published hundreds of articles and Bible studies as well as five books. She specializes in Christian living, Bible study, humor, and self-help."

MONICA SHARMAN EDITING | MONICA SHARMAN

2930 Coldwater Dr., Colorado Springs, CO 80919 | 719-357-6910
monicasharman@gmail.com | www.monicasharman.wordpress.com/monica-sharman-editing

Contact: email
Services: copyediting, proofreading
Types of manuscripts: articles, nonfiction books, devotions, poetry, short stories, curriculum, Bible studies, technical material, adult, teen/YA, picture books, easy readers, middle grade, novels, gift books, academic
Charges: hourly fee
Credentials/experience: "An engineer-turned-editor, Monica is known for her technical accuracy, her light touch preserving and enhancing the author's voice, and her encouragement. She has edited memoirs, essays, devotionals, fiction, children's fiction, poetry, and Bible studies for traditional publishers as well as self-publishing authors."

NATALIE NYQUIST

nyquist.n.m@gmail.com | natalienyquist.com

Contact: email
Services: copyediting, proofreading, bibliographies, citations
Types of manuscripts: nonfiction books, academic, adult, novels
Charges: flat fee, hourly rate
Credentials/experience: "Instructor and course developer, UC Berkeley Extension, teaching the Professional Sequence in Editing courses. Freelance editor since 2012. Clients have included HarperCollins Publishing, Baker Books, and Moody Publishing. Project portfolio: *pathbrite.com/natalienyquist/hhdM.*"

NEXT INDEX SERVICES | JESSICA MCCURDY CROOKS

876-354-4084 (Jamaica), 954-406-5426 (US)
Jessica@JessicaCrooks.com | www.next-index.com

Contact: email, website form
Services: copyediting, proofreading, indexing
Types of manuscripts: articles, nonfiction books, devotions, novels, adult, teen/YA, middle grade
Charges: flat fee, hourly rate, page rate, word rate
Credentials/experience: "My training as a librarian and records manager gives me an eye for detail and finding information. I also know how readers tend to search for information, a skill that helps

me arrive at keywords and phrases for the indexes I write. I have more than twenty years of indexing experience."

NOBLE CREATIVE, LLC | SCOTT NOBLE

PO Box 131402, St. Paul, MN 55113 | 651-494-4169
snoble@noblecreative.com | *www.noblecreative.com*

Contact: email

Services: manuscript evaluation, substantive editing/rewriting, copyediting, proofreading, ghostwriting, writing coach

Types of manuscripts: articles, nonfiction books, devotionals, query letters, book proposals, curriculum, adult

Charges: flat fee

Credentials/experience: "Nearly twenty years of experience as an award-winning journalist, writer, editor, and proofreader. More than 1,000 published articles, many of them prompting radio and television appearances. Won several awards from Evangelical Press Association. Worked with dozens of published authors and other public figures, as well as first-time authors and small businesses. Have a BA and MS from St. Cloud State University and an MA from Bethel Seminary."

NOVEL IMPROVEMENT EDITING SERVICES |
JEANNE MARIE LEACH

PO Box 552, Hudson, CO 80642
jeanne@novelimprovement.com | *novelimprovement.com*

Contact: email, website form

Services: manuscript evaluation, substantive editing/rewriting, copyediting, writing coach, ghostwriting, back-cover copy

Types of manuscripts: short stories, novels, query letters, book proposals, poetry, adult, teen/YA

Charges: flat fee, page rate

Credentials/experience: "Multi-published author, past coordinator and current gold member of The Christian PEN: Proofreaders and Editors Network; member of Christian Editor Network; and member of the American Christian Fiction writers, where I received the 2012 Member Service Award. I teach online courses through my website on editing fiction to editors and authors. I've been editing, mentoring, and critiquing for thirteen years and over a dozen of my clients have gone on to win numerous writing awards and have made various bestsellers' lists."

OASHEIM EDITING SERVICES, LLC | CATHY OASHEIM
800 Dillard Dr., Palm Bay, FL 32909 | 321-421-0933
admin@cathyoasheim.com | *www.cathyoasheim.wordpress.com*

> **Contact:** email, website form
> **Services:** substantive editing/rewriting, copyediting, proofreading, ghostwriting, writing coach, discussion questions for books, manuscript evaluation, back-cover copy
> **Types of manuscripts:** articles, nonfiction books, devotions, short stories, novels, gift books, technical material, adult, curriculum, Bible studies, academic
> **Charges:** custom
> **Credentials/experience:** "Has years of editing experience within the independent publishing industry. Specializes in Christian and wholesome nonfiction, memoirs, military, psychoeducational, self-help, and technical writing for critiques, books, blogs, and articles. Additional expertise with doctoral dissertations and Capstones in the areas of theology, apologetics, communications, psychology, and some engineering topics. Write and edit podcasts and speeches. Review up to 175 entries per year as an esteemed judge for the Next Generation Indy Book Awards (*https://www.indiebookawards.com*) in multiple categories. Rates on all editing services depend upon the scope of work required for the project (free estimates). Member of the Christian PEN, Editorial Freelancer Association, Nonfiction Authors Association, and Alliance for Independent Authors."

ODD SOCK PROOFREADING & COPYEDITING | STEVE MATHISEN
807 Maple St., Hoquiam, WA 98550 | 425-741-8392
scmathisen98037@hotmail.com | *oddsock.me*

> **Contact:** email, website form
> **Services:** substantive editing/rewriting, copyediting, proofreading, manuscript evaluation
> **Types of manuscripts:** nonfiction books, short stories, novels, adult, teen/YA, middle grade, devotions
> **Charges:** page rate
> **Credentials/experience:** "I am a writer, copyeditor, and proofreader with five years of experience on a wide variety of material. I trained with the PEN Institute and have a broad background in writing, spanning fiction, nonfiction, and technical documentation."

OFFSCRIPT EDITING | SHERRY CHAMBLEE
Sun Valley, CA | 818-767-8765
chambleeservices@gmail.com | *www.offscript.weebly.com*
- **Contact:** email, website form
- **Services:** copyediting, proofreading
- **Types of manuscripts:** articles, nonfiction books, devotions, poetry, short stories, novels, gift books, technical material, adult, teen/YA, picture books, easy readers, middle grade
- **Charges:** word rate
- **Credentials/experience:** "I am a freelance editor, working directly with authors for the past five years. I have edited both fiction and nonfiction, including works ranging from illustrated children's picture books and middle-grade chapter books to young-adult and adult Christian fiction."

OUR WRITTEN LIVES | RACHAEL HARTMAN
Universal City, TX | 318-319-6893
publisher@owlofhope.com | *www.OurWrittenLives.com*
- **Contact:** email, website form
- **Services:** manuscript evaluation, substantive editing/rewriting, copyediting, proofreading, ghostwriting, coauthoring, book-contract evaluation, discussion questions for books, writing coach
- **Types of manuscripts:** articles, nonfiction books, devotions, curriculum
- **Charges:** hourly rate
- **Credentials/experience:** "Member of Christian Indie Publishing Association. MS in human services, specialization in counseling; BA in liberal studies with a minor in writing; and certified life coach. Ten years in the writing and publishing industry; established Our Written Lives in 2013; author of three books."

PAMELA GOSSIAUX
Michigan | 734-846-0112
pam@pamelagossiaux.com | *BestsellingBookShepherd.com*
- **Contact:** email, phone, website form
- **Services:** manuscript evaluation, substantive editing/rewriting, copyediting, proofreading, discussion questions for books, ghostwriting, coauthoring, writing coach, back-cover copy, author consultation for publishing and social-media campaigns
- **Types of manuscripts:** articles, nonfiction books, devotions, short stories, novels, query letters, book proposals, gift books, adult,

teen/YA, picture books, easy readers, middle grade, Bible studies, poetry, blogs

Charges: custom fee, flat fee, hourly rate, packages

Credentials/experience: "Pamela Gossiaux is an international best-selling author, an Associated Press award-winning journalist, speaker, editor, ghostwriter and author consultant. Her clients are bestselling authors on the *USA TODAY, Wall Street Journal,* Barnes and Noble and Amazon bestsellers list, and she also loves working with new and unpublished authors and entrepreneurs. Fiction and non-fiction."

PEGGYSUE WELLS

3419 E. 1000 North, Roanoke, IN 46783 | 260-433-2817
peggysuewells@gmail.com | www.PeggySueWells.com

Contact: email, website form

Services: manuscript evaluation, substantive editing/rewriting, copyediting, ghostwriting, coauthoring, discussion questions for books, writing coach, back-cover copy

Types of manuscripts: articles, nonfiction books, devotions, short stories, novels, query letters, book proposals, curriculum, Bible studies, scripts, gift books, technical material, adult, teen/YA, picture books, easy readers, middle grade

Charges: hourly rate

Credentials/experience: "The bestselling author of 29 books, PeggySue Wells is the go-to person to create, write, or polish a project to be publish-ready. From idea to published manuscript, PeggySue provides coaching, writing, and finishing."

PERFECT WORD EDITING SERVICES | LINDA HARRIS

921 Green Star Dr. #407, Colorado Springs, CO 80905
lharris@perfectwordediting.com | www.perfectwordediting.com

Contact: email

Services: substantive editing/rewriting, copyediting, proofreading, back-cover copy, manuscript evaluation

Types of manuscripts: articles, nonfiction books, devotions, book proposals, curriculum, Bible studies, picture books, easy readers, middle grade

Charges: page rate

Credentials/experience: "Experienced editor for over 35 years, Gold Member of the Christian PEN, Instructor of Editing Children's Books at the PEN Institute."

PERPEDIT PUBLISHING INK | BECKY LYLES

PO Box 190246, Boise, ID 83719 | 208-407-9970
beckylyles@beckylyles.com | www.beckylyles.com

> **Contact:** email
> **Services:** manuscript evaluation, copyediting, proofreading, ghostwriting, writing coach
> **Types of manuscripts:** articles, nonfiction books, devotions, short stories, novels, query letters, book proposals, Bible studies, adult, teen/YA
> **Charges:** flat fee, hourly rate, word rate
> **Credentials/experience:** "15 years creating/proofing/editing articles, newsletters and magazines for government and corporate entities and 15 years freelance-editing fiction and nonfiction, including Bible studies, white papers, résumés, novels and short stories."

PICKY, PICKY INK | SUE MIHOLER

1075 Willow Lake Rd. N., Keizer, OR 97303 | 503-393-3356
suemihler@comcast.net

> **Contact:** email
> **Services:** copyediting
> **Types of manuscripts:** articles, nonfiction books, devotions, Bible studies
> **Charges:** hourly rate
> **Credentials/experience:** "Since 1998, I have edited for individuals, the majority of whom self-publish. I enjoy helping people write it right."

PLOT & PROSE | MARY KEANE

Park Ridge, IL | 773-691-7477
info@plotandprose.com | www.plotandprose.com

> **Contact:** website form
> **Services:** substantive editing/rewriting, copyediting, proofreading
> **Types of manuscripts:** short stories, novels, adult, teen/YA, easy readers, middle grade
> **Charges:** word rate
> **Credentials/experience:** "Completed Fiction Editing 1, 2, 3 from The Christian PEN. Writer and indie author. Specializing in independent authors, debut authors, e-book publishing."

PRATHERINK LITERARY SERVICES | VICKI PRATHER

107 Billy Byrd, Clinton, MS 39056 | 601-573-4295

pratherINK@gmail.com | pratherink.wordpress.com
Contact: email
Services: copyediting, proofreading, coauthoring, manuscript
evaluation, substantive editing, discussion questions for books
Types of manuscripts: nonfiction books, devotions, poetry, short
stories, novels, adult, teen/YA, articles, curriculum, Bible studies
Charges: hourly rate, word rate, flat fee, custom
Credentials/experience: "I've been freelance editing since 2014.
I've worked with around twenty authors on short, long, & repeat
projects. My clients praise me for taking their work & making
them shine!"

PROFESSIONAL PUBLISHING SERVICES |
CHRISTY CALLAHAN
PO Box 461, Waycross, GA 31502
professionalpublishingservices@gmail.com | professionalpublishingservices.us
Contact: email, website form
Services: manuscript evaluation, substantive editing/rewriting,
copyediting, proofreading, discussion questions for books, writing
coach, French-language editing, French to English translation
Types of manuscripts: nonfiction books, devotions, short stories,
novels, curriculum, Bible studies, gift books, technical material,
academic, adult, teen/YA, articles, poetry, picture books, easy
readers
Charges: flat fee, hourly rate, word rate
Credentials/experience: "Christy graduated Phi Beta Kappa
from Carnegie Mellon University and then earned her MA in
Intercultural Studies from Fuller Seminary. A gold member of
The Christian PEN: Proofreaders and Editors Network and
certified by the Christian Editor Connection and Reedsy, she
also completed the 40-hour Foundational Course (Christian
track) with the Institute for Life Coach Training."

PWC EDITING | PAUL W. CONANT
527 Bayshore Pl., Dallas, TX 75217-7755 | 214-289-3397
pwcediting@gmail.com | www.pwc-editing.com
Contact: website form
Services: copyediting, proofreading, brochures, newsletters, website
text
Types of manuscripts: articles, nonfiction books, devotions, short
stories, novels, query letters, book proposals, Bible studies,
technical material, adult, teens/YA, middle grade, academic

Charges: hourly rates; prefers a 2,000-word sample in order to make the most appropriate estimate for a manuscript

Credentials/experience: "Member of Christian Editors Connection, The Christian PEN, and *Thumbtack.com*. Fifteen years of experience with dissertations, twenty-two years with magazines, twenty years with books. Has worked with new or ESL writers, as well as publishers."

REBECCA LUELLA MILLER'S EDITORIAL SERVICES

rluellam@yahoo.com | rewriterewordrework.wordpress.com

Contact: email, website form

Services: manuscript evaluation, substantive editing/rewriting, copyediting, proofreading, writing coach, back-cover copy

Types of manuscripts: articles, nonfiction books, devotions, short stories, novels, query letters, adult, teen/YA, middle grade, academic

Charges: page rate, word rate

Credentials/experience: "Rebecca has worked as a freelance editor since 2004, editing books by such authors as Bryan Davis and Jill Williamson and working with AMG Publishers on other projects. Previously she taught English at the middle-school and high-school levels. She has a BA in English from Westmont College."

REFINE SERVICES | KATE MOTAUNG

kate@refineservices.com | www.refineservices.com

Contact: email, website form

Services: copyediting, proofreading, writing coach, discussion questions for books

Types of manuscripts: articles, nonfiction books, devotions, Bible studies, poetry, short stories, novels, query letters, adult, teens/YA, picture books, easy readers, middle grade

Charges: word rate

Credentials/experience: "Kate Motaung is an experienced copyeditor who enjoys helping authors refine their work to create an exceptional finished product. Kate is also a traditionally published and self-published author who can relate to the writing and publishing process and give insight into the right next steps."

REVISIONS BY RACHEL, LLC | RACHEL E. NEWMAN

Owasso, OK | 918-207-2833

Editor@RevisionsbyRachel.com | www.RevisionsbyRachel.com

Contact: email, phone

Services: manuscript evaluation, copyediting, proofreading, indexing, ghostwriting, coauthoring, discussion questions for books, writing coach, back-cover copy

Types of manuscripts: nonfiction books, novels, curriculum, adult, teen/YA, Bible studies, academic

Charges: word rate, custom

Credentials/experience: "Rachel is a gold member of The Christian PEN: Proofreaders and Editors Network, is an established freelance editor with Christian Editor Connection, is an instructor with The PEN Institute, and has served as a judge for the Excellence in Editing Award and as faculty for PENCON."

RICK STEELE EDITORIAL SERVICES | RICK STEELE

26 Dean Rd., Ringgold, GA 30736 | 706-937-8121

rsteelecam@gmail.com | steeleeditorialservices.myportfolio.com

Contact: email, website form

Services: manuscript evaluation, substantive editing/rewriting, copyediting, proofreading, coauthoring, book-contract evaluation, discussion questions for books, writing coach, back-cover copy

Types of manuscripts: nonfiction books, devotions, poetry, short stories, novels, query letters, book proposals, curriculum, Bible studies, gift books, adult, teen/YA, middle grade

Charges: flat fee, page rate, critiques are charged by the page

Credentials/experience: "With more than twenty years of experience working for a traditional, royalty publisher in the religious market, Rick Steele provides an array of freelance editorial services ranging from fiction and nonfiction manuscript editing, proofreading, and critiquing to help with query letters and proposal drafting."

ROBIN'S RED PEN | ROBIN PATCHEN

Austin, TX

robinpatchen9@gmail.com | robinpatchen.com/editing

Contact: email

Services: manuscript evaluation, substantive editing/rewriting, copyediting, writing coach

Types of manuscripts: nonfiction books, devotions, novels, adult, teen/YA, articles

Charges: page rate

Credentials/experience: "Nominated for ACFW's Editor of the Year three years in a row, Robin Patchen is a multi-published, award-winning author and freelance editor specializing in Christian fiction. She is one of the authors of *Five Editors Tackle the 12 Fatal Flaws of Fiction Writing*, an in-depth guide to self-editing. Patchen loves mentoring new authors and helping established authors polish their books. She enjoys reading and editing almost every clean YA and adult genre."

SALISBURY ALEXANDER COMMUNICATIONS |
KIRT G. SALISBURY

153 Monticello Ave., Rio Linda, CA 45673 | 760-212-2872
kirtwrites81@icloud.com

> **Contact:** email
> **Services:** ghostwriting, back-cover copy
> **Types of manuscripts:** technical material, articles, devotions, query letters, response letters, nonfiction books
> **Charges:** flat fee
> **Credentials/experience:** "Has written advertising and promotional materials for high-tech scientific equipment, Christian and biomedical magazines, and biomedical newsletters. Ghostwritten for more than twenty-four major Christian ministries for their partner communications, premium books, fundraising appeals, and response letters."

SARA LAWSON

423 N. Monterey St., Alhambra, CA 91801 | 530-933-9838
sarareneelawson@gmail.com | www.sarasbooks.com

> **Contact:** email, website form
> **Services:** substantive editing, copyediting, proofreading, discussion questions for books, back-cover copy
> **Types of manuscripts:** articles, nonfiction books, devotions, short stories, novels, Bible studies, scripts, academic, adult, teen/YA, middle grade
> **Charges:** custom
> **Credentials/experience:** "Sara Lawson has over 10 years of freelance editing experience working with fiction and nonfiction books, magazine articles, television scripts, and academic papers of all lengths. She has also served at both predominantly white and Asian American churches, so she understands a variety of ministry contexts. She loves to help writers because she believes that everyone has a story to tell and no one should have to let technical writing abilities get in the way of telling that story."

SARAH HAMAKER

Fairfax, VA

sarah@sarahhamaker.com | sarahhamakerfiction.com

Contact: email, website form

Services: copyediting, proofreading, ghostwriting, coauthoring, substantive editing

Types of manuscripts: nonfiction books, novels, adult

Charges: custom

Credentials/experience: "As an experienced writer and editor, Sarah has edited magazine publications, fiction and nonfiction books for both adult and children. In addition, she's ghostwritten articles and *Out of the Shadows: A Journey of Recovery from Depression.* As an experienced editor, she can take your book (both fiction and nonfiction) from start to finish, providing project management and guidance along the indie publishing route. On her website you can book a free, 15-minute consultation with her to discuss bringing your idea into a published book."

SCRIVEN COMMUNICATIONS | KATHIE NEE-SCRIVEN

22 Ridge Rd. #220, Greenbelt, MD 20770 | 240-542-4602

KathieScriven@yahoo.com

Contact: email, phone

Services: manuscript evaluation, copyediting, writing coach, back-cover copy

Types of manuscripts: articles, short stories, nonfiction books, book proposals, query letters, back-cover copy, devotions, poetry, Bible studies, adult, teen/YA, middle grade

Charges: flat fee

Credentials/experience: "I have edited more than eighty Christian nonfiction books and countless shorter pieces. Former editor of four Christian publications and freelance writer. Bachelor's degree in mass communication with a concentration in journalism from Towson University. My services include coaching and helping authors with their marketing and publicity strategies. I can email a document that goes over my background and experience in greater detail to anyone interested."

SHARMAN ENTERPRISES, LLC | SHARMAN J. MONROE

3431 S. Dakota Ave. N.E., Washington, DC 20018 | 240-353-8000

myjourneytome@gmail.com | www.sharmansedits.com

Contact: website form

Services: proofreading

Types of manuscripts: nonfiction books, devotions, novels, teen/YA, articles, Bible studies

Charges: custom

Credentials/experience: "I had over 25 years of experience writing, editing and proofreading before starting my own business in 2011. Today, I have edited and proofed more than 30 books, non-fiction and fiction, and of different genres ranging from Christian to devotionals, guides/handbooks to mystery to self-help to YA to urban, over the past few years. Moreover, I am an award-winning published author.."

SHARON HINCK

s.hinck@comcast.net | www.sharonhinck.com

Contact: email

Services: copyediting, manuscript evaluation

Types of manuscripts: novels, adult, teen/YA

Charges: word rate, hourly rate

Credentials/experience: "Sharon brings her experience as an award-winning novelist to her thorough-but-encouraging approach to giving feedback. For over a decade, she has edited for best-selling authors as well as beginning writers and also serves as an adjunct professor of a Creative Writing MFA program. She has special interest in Christian fiction and speculative fiction, but has helped writers in the general market and other genres as well."

SHERYL MADDEN

Seattle, WA | 206-919-2203

madden58sheryl@gmail.com | www.editorsherylmadden.com

Contact: website form

Services: copyediting, proofreading, discussion questions for books, back-cover copy

Types of manuscripts: articles, nonfiction books, devotions, short stories, novels, Bible studies, adult

Charges: page rate

Credentials/experience: "Certificate in professional editing, freelancing since 2015."

SHIRL'S EDITING SERVICES | SHIRL THOMAS

9379 Tanager Ave., Fountain Valley, CA 92708 | 714-968-5726
shirlth@verizon.net

Contact: email, phone
Services: manuscript evaluation, substantive editing/rewriting, copyediting, proofreading, writing coach
Types of manuscripts: articles, nonfiction books, devotions, poetry, short stories, novels, query letters, book proposals, gift books, adult
Charges: hourly rate, custom
Credentials/experience: "Shirl has been a successful freelance writer/editor since 1973 and has had 165 clients and students. Last published book: *My 36 Years in Space* (2018) has 5 stars on Amazon and has excellent reviews. Another: *Making My Way* is mandatory reading for the 9th grade."

SIGHTHOUND EDITORIAL SERVICES | MEGAN LEE

Herndon, VA | 703-229-2369
sighthoundeditorial@gmail.com

Contact: email
Services: manuscript evaluation, substantive editing/rewriting, copyediting, proofreading, discussion questions for books, writing coach
Types of manuscripts: novels, adult, teen/YA
Charges: flat fee, hourly rate, page rate, word rate
Credentials/experience: "I'm a published author with an MFA in creative writing from George Mason University. As an editor with Pelican Book Group, I evaluate manuscripts for acquisition and work closely with authors and other editors to ensure manuscripts meet their potential throughout the publication process. Additionally, I've taught English to high school and college students for the past fifteen years."

SO IT IS WRITTEN | TENITA JOHNSON

5172 Aintree Rd., Rochester, MI 48306 | 313-999-6942
info@soitiswritten.net | www.soitiswritten.net

Contact: website form
Services: copyediting, proofreading, ghostwriting, manuscript evaluation, writing coach, substantive editing, coauthoring, back-cover copy
Types of manuscripts: nonfiction books, devotions, poetry, short stories, novels, adult, teen/YA, easy readers, middle grade,

curriculum, Bible studies, scripts, gift books

Charges: page rate

Credentials/experience: "Authors worldwide write better thanks to editorial guru and authorpreneur, Tenita C. Johnson. Perfecting manuscripts for hundreds of best-selling authors, she's on a mission to end the prominent everyday abuse of the English language and rectify punctuation pet peeves. Tenita collaborates with industry professionals to take manuscripts to the marketplace, positioning authors for success in the literary world."

STARCHER DESIGNS | KARA STARCHER

Chloe, WV | 330-705-3399

info@starcherdesigns.com | *www.starcherdesigns.com*

Contact: website form

Services: manuscript evaluation, substantive editing, copyediting, ghostwriting, coauthoring, writing coach, back-cover copy

Types of manuscripts: nonfiction books, novels, curriculum, Bible studies, adult, teen/YA

Charges: word rate

Credentials/experience: "BA in publishing with a minor in English; twenty years experience as a freelance editor working for small publishing houses and independent authors; ten years experience as managing editor for various nonprofit organizations; other experience in high school English education and journalism. Member of American Christian Fiction Writers."

STEEPLE VIEW COACHING | ANDREA BOESHAAR

PO Box 33, Newberg, WI 53060 | 414-708-8930

Andrea@AndreaBoeshaar.com | *www.AndreaBoeshaar.com*

Contact: website form

Services: manuscript evaluation, substantive editing/rewriting, writing coach

Types of manuscripts: short stories, novels, teen/YA

Charges: page rate

Credentials/experience: "Author of more than thirty books, certified Christian life coach."

STICKS AND STONES | JAMIE CALLOWAY-HANAUER

Annapolis, MD | 510-972-3285

snsedits@gmail.com | *www.snsedits.com*

Contact: email

Services: manuscript evaluation, substantive editing/rewriting, copyediting, proofreading, ghostwriting, coauthoring, book-contract evaluation, discussion questions for books, writing coach

Types of manuscripts: articles, nonfiction books, devotions, poetry, short stories, novels, query letters, book proposals, curriculum, adult, teen/YA, easy readers, middle grade

Charges: flat fee

Credentials/experience: "Jamie has eighteen years of experience in the editing field. Previously a full-time public interest attorney who also edited part-time, she is now the owner-operator of Sticks and Stones, where she specializes in academic, legal, and faith-based fiction and nonfiction for adults and teens; ghostwriting; and proposal and query review and development."

SUE A. FAIRCHILD, EDITOR

512 Elm St., Watsontown, PA 17777 | 570-939-0318
sueafairchild74@gmail.com | suefairchild.wordpress.com

Contact: email, website form

Services: substantive editing/rewriting, copyediting, proofreading, discussion questions for books, writing coach, back-cover copy, indie publishing

Types of manuscripts: nonfiction books, devotions, short stories, novels, Bible studies, gift books, adult, teen/YA, middle grade

Charges: word rate

Credentials/experience: "I don't change voices. I make them louder. Editor for Elk Lake Publishing, writing coach and content editor for Redemption Press, proofreader for Iron Stream Media, Gold Member editor of The Christian PEN."

SUPERIOR EDITING SERVICE | JAN ACKERSON

611 S. Elm, Three Oaks, MI 49128 | 269-756-9912
jan_ackerson@yahoo.com | www.superioreditingservice.com

Contact: website form

Services: substantive editing/rewriting, copyediting, writing coach

Types of manuscripts: poetry, short stories, novels, gift books, adult, teen/YA, picture books, easy readers, middle grade

Charges: word rate

Credentials/experience: "Seven years editing (both freelance and for Breath of Fresh Air Press), author of *Stolen Postcards*, short stories in multiple anthologies."

SUSAN KING EDITORIAL SERVICES | SUSAN KING

Franklin, TN | 615-202-6019

susan@susankingedits.com | susankingedits.com

> **Contact:** email, website form
> **Services:** substantive editing/rewriting, copyediting, proofreading, ghostwriting, coauthoring, writing coach
> **Types of manuscripts:** articles, nonfiction books, devotions, poetry, short stories, novels, query letters, gift books, adult, book proposals, Bible studies, academic
> **Charges:** hourly rate
> **Credentials/experience:** "Of my more than 27 years in the industry, I served over 20 years as an editor for *The Upper Room*. For the past 20 years, I have trained writers at over one hundred Christian writers' conferences in the U.S. and Canada. My professional life has also included teaching composition, literature, and feature-writing classes at Lipscomb University, Biola University, and Abilene Christian University for a total of 27 years. Currently, I am the compiler and editor of the Short and Sweet book series."

SUSAN R. EDITORIAL | SUSAN RESCIGNO

PO Box 473, Crompond, NY 10517 | 914-844-5217

SusanR.Edit@gmail.com | srescigno7.wixsite.com/mysite

> **Contact:** website form
> **Services:** copyediting, proofreading, indexing, project management
> **Types of manuscripts:** nonfiction books, academic, adult
> **Charges:** hourly rate, page rate
> **Credentials/experience:** "30 years' experience in publishing industry. Copyedit using MS Word track changes. Create indexes using Sky Index Pro. Clients have included CLC Publications, Orbis Books, Twenty-third Publications."

TANDEM SERVICES | JENNIFER CROSSWHITE

PO Box 220, Yucaipa, CA 92399 | 414-465-2567

jennifer@tandemservicesink.com | www.tandemservicesink.com

> **Contact:** email, website form
> **Services:** manuscript evaluation, substantive editing/rewriting, copyediting, writing coach
> **Types of manuscripts:** nonfiction books, devotions, novels, adult
> **Charges:** custom, flat fee, hourly rate
> **Credentials/experience:** "We empower authors to improve their

craft, develop their writing careers, find community, and create effective commerce around their books. With twenty years' experience spanning both sides of the publishing desk, from author to former managing editor, we've worked with authors for Barbour, Zondervan, Thomas Nelson, Concordia, B&H, and others. Member of The Christian PEN professional editors association."

THREE FATES EDITING | SARAH GRACE LIU
28 Close Hollow Dr., Hamlin, NY 14464
sarah.grace@threefatesediting.com | www.threefatesediting.com
  Contact: email, website form
  Services: manuscript evaluation, substantive editing/rewriting, copyediting, proofreading, ghostwriting
  Types of manuscripts: nonfiction books, poetry, short stories, novels, Bible studies, academic, adult, teen/YA, middle grade
  Charges: word rate
  Credentials/experience: "I have an MA in Creative Writing and have run my own editing business since 2012. My true specialization is speculative fiction. For nonfiction, I am more comfortable with progressive texts."

TISHA MARTIN EDITORIAL | TISHA MARTIN
210 S. 66th Ave., Yakima, WA 98908
tisha@tishamartin.com | www.tishamartin.com/editing-services
  Contact: website form
  Services: manuscript evaluation, substantive editing/rewriting, copyediting, proofreading, discussion questions for books, writing coach, back-cover copy, ghostwriting
  Types of manuscripts: nonfiction books, devotions, short stories, novels, curriculum, adult, teen/YA, articles, book proposals, scripts
  Charges: flat fee, word rate, hourly rate
  Credentials/experience: "Although I have been immersed in the editing and writing world for over fifteen years, since 2017 I have worked on over 300 books and manuscripts in all levels of editing with new and published authors, publishers, and film producers. (Portfolio via website.) From contest judging and critiques to editing and proofreading to writing marketing copy and ghostwriting—it's my desire to work as a team and to deliver a professionally edited book you can be proud of. The top skills I

bring to the table in each project are the ability to hear the author's message and cultivate context to the story because editing is a pure gift to the writer and ultimately to the reader. Contact me for an introductory chat and let's go from there!"

TRAILBLAZE WRITING & EDITING | SARAH BARNUM
sarah@trail-blazes.com | trail-blazes.com
> **Contact:** email, website form
> **Services:** manuscript evaluation, substantive editing/rewriting, copyediting, proofreading, writing coach
> **Types of manuscripts:** articles, nonfiction books, devotions, short stories, novels, gift books, adult
> **Charges:** word rate, flat fee
> **Credentials/experience:** "Sarah Barnum is a member of Inspire Christian Writers and the Christian PEN (Proofreaders and Editors Network), and she serves on the board, leadership team, and faculty for the West Coast Christian Writers Conference. Sarah holds a bachelor's degree with highest honors and edits for both publishers and freelance authors."

TUPPANCE ENTERPRISES | JAMES PENCE
PO Box 99, Greenville, TX 75403 | 469-730-6478
james@pence.com | jamespence.com
> **Contact:** email, phone, website form
> **Services:** manuscript evaluation, substantive editing/rewriting, copyediting, proofreading, coauthoring, writing coach, ghostwriting
> **Types of manuscripts:** articles, nonfiction books, devotions, short stories, novels, query letters, book proposals, Bible studies, technical material, adult, teen/YA, middle grade
> **Charges:** word rate, hourly rate, flat fee
> **Credentials/experience:** "James has been writing and editing professionally since 2000, and is a traditionally published author of ten books. Publishers include Osborne/McGraw-Hill, Tyndale, Kregel, Baker (co-author), Thomas Nelson (ghostwriter), and Mountainview Books. Published works include textbooks, how-to, novels (adult and YA), Christian living, and memoir."

TURN THE PAGE CRITIQUES | CINDY THOMSON
PO Box 298, Pataskala, OH 43062 | 614-354-3904
cindyswriting@gmail.com | *cindyswriting.com/hire-me*

> **Contact:** email
> **Services:** manuscript evaluation, proofreading, critiques
> **Types of manuscripts:** articles, novels, query letters, book proposals
> **Charges:** flat fee
> **Credentials/experience:** "Published author both traditionally and independently of fiction and non-fiction, author of numerous magazine articles, and a former mentor with the Jerry B. Jenkins Christian Writers Guild, I can help you get a solid footing as you prepare to publish."

THE VERSATILE PEN | CHRISTY PHILLIPPE
8816 S. 73rd East Ave., Tulsa, OK 74133 | 918-284-7635
christy6871@aol.com

> **Contact:** email
> **Services:** manuscript evaluation, substantive editing/rewriting, copyediting, proofreading, discussion questions for books
> **Types of manuscripts:** articles, nonfiction books, devotions, short stories, novels, curriculum, gift books, adult, teen/YA
> **Charges:** hourly rate, word rate
> **Credentials/experience:** "More than twenty years of experience as managing editor, senior editor, and editorial director of various publishing companies and as the owner of The Versatile Pen."

WHALIN & ASSOCIATES | W. TERRY WHALIN
9457 S. University Blvd., Ste. 621, Highlands Ranch, CO 80126 | 720-708-4953
terry@terrywhalin.com | *terrywhalin.blogspot.com*

> **Contact:** email
> **Services:** substantive editing/rewriting, ghostwriting, coauthoring, discussion questions for books
> **Types of manuscripts:** nonfiction books, devotionals, book proposals, gift books, adult
> **Charges:** flat fee
> **Credentials/experience:** "Terry has written more than sixty books for traditional publishers, including one book that has sold more than 100,000 copies. He has written for more than fifty publications and worked in acquisitions at three publishing houses."

WHITE PENCIL PRODUCTIONS, INC. | KARLA DIAL

620 Dee Ct., Redding, CA 96002 | 719-930-3094

email through website | Karladial.com

> **Contact:** email
>
> **Services:** substantive editing/rewriting, copyediting, proofreading, ghostwriting, coauthoring
>
> **Types of manuscripts:** articles, nonfiction books, short stories, novels, adult, teen/YA
>
> **Charges:** $500 retainer, which sometimes covers the whole cost, then an hourly fee
>
> **Credentials/experience:** "I am an award-winning journalist with more than 20 years of experience as a reporter, writer, managing editor, and editor in chief at both daily and monthly, local and national publications. You have something to say; I can help you say it the best way possible."

WILDCAT WRITING SERVICES | JEFF ADAMS

3675 N. Verdugo Rd., Kingman, AZ 86409 | 928-716-9673

jeffadams@frontiernet.net | wildcatwritingservices.com

> **Contact:** email
>
> **Services:** manuscript evaluation, substantive editing/rewriting, discussion questions for books, writing coach, back-cover copy, book proposals
>
> **Types of manuscripts:** nonfiction books, devotions, query letters, book proposals, curriculum, Bible studies, gift books, adult
>
> **Charges:** custom
>
> **Credentials/experience:** "I'm a substantive editor certified by Christian Editor Connection. I've contributed to more than 25 books. I create, evaluate, and prepare book proposals, including chapter-by-chapter synopsis and sample chapters, for presentation to editors, publishers, and agents. I help writers write better."

A WORD IN SEASON | SAMANTHA HANNI

3400 Windsor Ter., Oklahoma City, OK 73122 | 405-642-7855

samantha.hanni@mrshanni.com | mrshanni.com

> **Contact:** email, website form
>
> **Services:** manuscript evaluation, substantive editing, copyediting
>
> **Types of manuscripts:** articles, nonfiction books, devotions, curriculum, Bible studies, adult, teen/YA
>
> **Charges:** flat fee, word rate

Credentials/experience: "I am passionate about wielding words for good, whether it be writing my own or refining the words of others. For the past decade, I've had the privilege of writing and editing, helping individuals and businesses share the content that's most important to them. As a freelance writer and editor, I have self-published four books for Christian teens and edited dozens of manuscripts for Christian authors, many of them debut authors. I have provided copy editing services for two Christian publishing houses and for The Odyssey Online. Specialty: non-fiction."

WORD MARKER EDITS | KATHRESE MCKEE

8765 Spring Cypress, Ste. L219, Spring, TX 77379 | 281-787-6938
kmckee@kathresemckee.com | *www.wordmarkeredits.com*

Contact: website form
Services: manuscript evaluation, substantive editing/rewriting, copyediting, proofreading, ghostwriting
Types of manuscripts: short stories, novels, adult, teen/YA, middle grade
Charges: hourly rate, page rate, word rate
Credentials/experience: "Kathrese is an editor, fiction author, former middle-school reading and ESL teacher, speaker, and blogger. She specializes in editing speculative fiction written from a Christian worldview but is also available to edit other genres and fiction for the general market. She is a silver member of The Christian PEN: Proofreaders and Editors Network."

WORDMELON, INC. | MARGOT STARBUCK

308-A Northwood Cir., Durham, NC 27701 | 919-321-5440
wordmelon@gmail.com | *www.wordmelon.com*

Contact: email
Services: manuscript evaluation, substantive editing/rewriting, ghostwriting, coauthoring, discussion questions for books, writing coach
Types of manuscripts: nonfiction books, book proposals, articles, query letters, Bible studies, theology
Charges: flat fee
Credentials/experience: "Margot Starbuck, a *New York Times* bestselling collaborator and an award-winning author of over 20 books, is a graduate of Westmont College and Princeton Seminary. Margot has had a hand in over 100 major publishing projects, serving publishers as a writer, collaborator, ghostwriter, editor,

and writing coach. Passionate about effective communication, she teaches at writing conferences across the country and delights in equipping writers to craft winning book proposals at *wordmelon. com.*"

WORDS FOR WRITERS | GINNY L. YTTRUP

PO Box 1650, Lincoln, CA 95648 | 916-276-7359
ginny@wordsforwriters.net | www.wordsforwriters.net
   Contact: email, website form
   Services: manuscript evaluation, substantive editing/rewriting, writing coach
   Types of manuscripts: nonfiction books, novels, query letters, book proposals, adult
   Charges: hourly rate, page rate
   Credentials/experience: "Ginny L. Yttrup is an award-winning author and writing coach. She has coached writers to publication and partners with writers to present their best work to agents and editors."

WRITE AWAY EDITING | JEFFREY PEPPLE

15317 Laurel Ridge, Leo, IN 46765 | 260-627-3003
jlepepple@gmail.com
   Contact: email
   Services: manuscript evaluation, substantive editing/rewriting, copyediting, proofreading
   Types of manuscripts: articles, nonfiction books, devotions, short stories, novels, curriculum, gift books, technical material, adult, teen/YA, easy readers, middle grade, academic, picture books, Bible studies
   Charges: flat fee, hourly rate, page rate
   Credentials/experience: "BA in professional writing, Taylor University. Have edited manuscripts and websites."

WRITE BY LISA | LISA THOMPSON

200 Laguna Dr. S., Litchfield Park, AZ 85340 | 623-258-5258
writebylisa@gmail.com | www.writebylisa.com
   Contact: email
   Services: manuscript evaluation, copyediting, proofreading, ghostwriting, discussion questions for books, writing coach, back-cover copy, creating citations
   Types of manuscripts: articles, nonfiction books, devotions, short stories, novels, query letters, book proposals, curriculum, Bible

study guides, adult, teen/YA, middle grade, picture books, easy readers

Charges: word rate, hourly rate, custom

Credentials/experience: "I have a degree in elementary education with a minor in English. I began writing and editing as a freelancer in 2009. Since then, I have written and sold more than 2,000,000 words and edited more than 200 books, mostly Christian nonfiction. I have experience editing other genres as well, including memoirs."

WRITE CONCEPTS, LLC | ALICE CRIDER

590 Highway 105 #107, Monument, CO 80132 | 719-651-0160
editoralicecrider@gmail.com | *www.alicecrider.com*

Contact: website form

Services: substantive editing/rewriting, ghostwriting, writing coach, back-cover copy

Types of manuscripts: nonfiction books, book proposals, adult

Charges: flat fee

Credentials/experience: "With more than twenty years of experience in traditional Christian publishing, Alice Crider has edited many bestselling books by top-level authors such as Kyle Idleman, Tricia Goyer, and Lisa Bevere. She specializes in nonfiction developmental, content, and line editing. She is skilled at analyzing a manuscript's strengths and weaknesses as well as suggesting improvements, clarifications, and revisions. As a certified life coach, Alice is brilliant at helping authors get in touch with the heart of their message in order to communicate powerfully. She is also a certified marketing copywriter and a competent collaborator on projects that need more than editing."

THE WRITE EDITOR | ERIN K. BROWN

510 Adirondac Ave., Hamilton, MT 59840 | 406-239-5590
thewriteeditor@gmail.com | *www.writeeditor.net*

Contact: email, website form

Services: manuscript evaluation, substantive editing/rewriting, copyediting, proofreading

Types of manuscripts: articles, nonfiction books, devotions, short stories, novels, query letters, book proposals, gift books, adult, Bible studies, academic

Charges: custom with free sample edit

Credentials/experience: "Erin Brown is a professional freelance editor, proofreader, and writer. Erin's formal training in editorial practices and procedures, ten years in Christian retailing, twenty-six years in education, and many years as a Christy Award judge afford her a wide knowledge and experience base. She combines her love of editing and teaching by mentoring new writers and teaching nonfiction editing skills to professional editors. She is the director of The PEN Institute, the premiere online educational institute for Christian editors."

WRITE HIS ANSWER MINISTRIES | MARLENE BAGNULL
951 Anders Rd., Lansdale, PA 19446 | 484-991-8581
mbagnull@aol.com | writehisanswer.com/editingmentoring

- **Contact:** email
- **Services:** manuscript evaluation, copyediting, proofreading, substantive editing
- **Types of manuscripts:** articles, nonfiction books, devotions, novels, adult
- **Charges:** flat fee, hourly rate
- **Credentials/experience:** "More than thirty-five years of experience in publishing, leading critique groups, and directing writers conferences; author of twelve books and more than a thousand sales to Christian periodicals; editor, typesetter, and publisher of eleven Ampelos Press books."

WRITE NOW EDITING | KARIN BEERY
PO Box 31, Elk Rapids, MI 49629
karin@karinbeery.com | www.writenowedits.com

- **Contact:** email, website form
- **Services:** copyediting, ghostwriting, writing coach, back-cover copy
- **Types of manuscripts:** novels, adult, teen/YA
- **Charges:** hourly rate, word rate
- **Credentials/experience:** "Karin Beery is a certified substantive fiction editor with the Christian Editor Connection, as well as an editing instructor with the PEN Institute. As a general editor with Smitten Historical Romance, all of her authors' books were nominated for awards. Her preferred genres are contemporary fiction, women's fiction, and contemporary and historical romance."

WRITE PATHWAY EDITORIAL SERVICES | ANN KNOWLES
Wilmington, NC | 910-231-9520
annknowles03@aol.com | write-pathway.blogspot.com

Contact: email

Services: copyediting, proofreading, ghostwriting, coauthoring, writing coach, transcription, Spanish translation

Types of manuscripts: articles, nonfiction books, devotions, poetry, short stories, novels, query letters, book proposals, curriculum, gift books, adult, teen/YA, picture books, easy readers, middle grade

Charges: project cost

Credentials/experience: "Retired educator, MA in education, certified ESL and Spanish; ESL training consultant for public schools and community colleges. I joined The Christian PEN: Proofreaders and Editors Network in 2005 and started Write Pathway in 2007. I have taken numerous courses from The Christian PEN, American Christian Fiction Writers, Write Integrity Press, and Christian Writers International."

WRITE WAY COPYEDITING LLC | DIANA SCHRAMER
diana@writewaycopyediting.com | www.writewaycopyediting.com

Contact: email

Services: manuscript evaluation, copyediting

Types of manuscripts: nonfiction books, devotions, Bible studies, novels, gift books, memoir

Charges: hourly rate

Credentials/experience: "I started my business in 2010 and have copyedited 100+ book-length manuscripts and have reviewed 200+ manuscripts. In addition, I have copyedited and reviewed front- and back-cover copy as well as business-related documents and blogs."

WRITER JUSTIFIED | JUDY HAGEY
Des Moines, Iowa
judy.hagey@gmail.com | judyhagey.com

Contact: email, website form

Services: copyediting, proofreading, substantive editing, back-cover copy

Types of manuscripts: articles, nonfiction books, novels, academic, adult, devotions

Charges: word rate

Credentials/experience: "I have filled various roles in Christian higher education and the nonprofit world, including ten years as the writing director of a ministry producing small-group discipleship materials. Editing credits include theological dissertations, fiction, and nonfiction manuscripts. I currently freelance for traditional publishers as well as individual clients. I have a BA degree in education from Dordt University and am a (certified) Gold Member of the Christian Professional Editors Network."

WRITER'S EDGE SERVICE | BILL LELAND

220 S. Pine St., Sisters, OR 97759 | 541-549-1139
bill@writersedgeservice.com | *www.writersedgeservice.com*

Contact: email

Services: manuscript evaluation, copyediting, proofreading, book-proposal creation

Types of manuscripts: nonfiction books, devotionals, novels, book proposals, Bible studies, academic, adult, teen/YA, easy readers, middle grade

Charges: $99

Description: "Professional editors with many years of experience in working with major Christian publishers evaluate, screen, and expose potential books to traditional Christian publishing companies."

THE WRITER'S TABLET AGENCY | TERRI WHITMIRE

4371 Roswell Rd #315, Marietta, GA 30062 | 770-648-4101
Writerstablet@gmail.com | *www.Writerstablet.org*

Contact: email, phone

Services: manuscript evaluation, substantive editing/rewriting, copyediting, proofreading, discussion questions for books, writing coach, back-cover copy

Types of manuscripts: articles, nonfiction books, devotions, short stories, novels, curriculum, Bible studies, technical material, adult, teen/YA, picture books, easy readers, middle grade

Charges: flat fee, hourly rate, word rate

Credentials/experience: "Owner, Terri Whitmire, and her team of skilled writers, editors, and marketers are diverse and prepared to fulfill your content needs. At The Writer's Tablet Agency, we believe that words are critical in communicating your unique message. Together, we will develop or edit your content to tailor fit your individual objectives. Whether you need to write a novel, perfect a presentation, or build an e-commerce website, Writer's Tablet will provide expertise and scrupulous attention to detail every step of the way.

"A seasoned author and successful writing consultant, Mrs. Whitmire earned a bachelor's degree in Information Technology from North Carolina's historic A&T State University. She pursued a writing certification from the Institute of Children's Literature. She is the author of five published books and passionately provides inspired written solutions to businesses and aspiring authors. Some of her clients have gone on to be best-selling authors, public speakers, and leaders in their industry."

WRITTEN BY A PRO | SHARLA TAYLOR
PO Box 223, Polk City, FL 33868 | 912-656-6857
info@writtenbyapro.com | *www.writtenbyapro.com*
   Contact: email, *calendly.com/writtenbyapro*
   Services: manuscript evaluation, copyediting, proofreading, ghostwriting, coauthoring, discussion questions for books, writing coach, résumé writing, back-cover copy
   Types of manuscripts: articles, nonfiction books, devotions, short stories, query letters, book proposals, Bible studies, gift books, adult, academic
   Charges: flat fee
   Credentials/experience: "Sharla Taylor is a published author whose short stories have been featured in *God Allows U-Turns, Hugs for the Heart, Chicken Soup for the Sister's Soul,* and *Chicken Soup Life Lessons for Women.* Taylor is a multi-certified résumé writer and career coach who has trained under three bestselling authors. She enjoys writing about job search strategies and offers career coaching programs for individuals and groups."

YO PRODUCTIONS, LLC | YOLONDA SANDERS
1543 Reynoldsburg, Columbus, OH 43068 | 614-452-4920
info_4u@yoproductions.net | *www.yoproductions.net*
   Contact: email, phone, website form
   Services: manuscript evaluation, substantive editing/rewriting, copyediting, proofreading, ghostwriting, coauthoring, discussion questions for books, writing coach, back-cover copy
   Types of manuscripts: articles, nonfiction books, devotions, poetry, short stories, novels, query letters, book proposals, curriculum, Bible studies, scripts, technical material, adult, teen/YA, academic

Charges: flat fee, hourly rate, word rate, custom
Credentials/experience: "More than thirteen years of professional editing and writing experience, editor and writer for a national publication."

INTERNATIONAL

AOTEAROA EDITORIAL SERVICES | VENNESSA NG
PO Box 228, Oamaru, New Zealand 9444 | +6 422 434 6995
aotearoa.editorial@gmail.com | www.aotearoaeditorial.com

Contact: email, mail
Services: manuscript evaluation, substantive editing/rewriting, copyediting, proofreading, writing coach
Types of manuscripts: short stories, novels, adult
Charges: page rate
Credentials/experience: "Fourteen years of experience working with Christian fiction authors. Member of The Christian PEN."

BOOK WHISPERS
Capalaba, QLD 4157, Australia | +61 07 3167 6513
info@bookwhispers.com.au | www.bookwhispers.com.au

Contact: email
Services: manuscript evaluation, structural editing, copyediting, proofing, back-cover copy, marketing copy, experienced, knowledgeable advice and recommendations on accessing the Australian educational and trade markets
Credentials/experience: The team has more than ten years of experience in traditional publishing.

CELTICFROG EDITING | ALEX MCGILVERY
Kamloops, BC, Canada | 250-819-4275
thecelticfrog@live.com | celticfrogediting.com

Contact: email, website form
Services: manuscript evaluation, writing coach
Types of manuscripts: articles, nonfiction books, devotions, short stories, novels, adult, teen/YA, middle grade
Charges: based loosely on word count
Credentials/experience: "I have been reviewing and critiquing books for more than three decades, and editing since 2014. One client

compared my work favourably with the editors at a traditional publisher."

CHRISTIAN EDITING SERVICES | IOLA GOULTON

Tauranga, New Zealand

igoulton@christianediting.co.nz | www.christianediting.co.nz

Contact: website form

Services: manuscript evaluation, copyediting, writing coach

Types of manuscripts: novels, adult, teen/YA

Charges: custom

Credentials/experience: "Iola is a member of The Christian PEN: Proofreaders and Editors Network, American Christian Fiction Writers, Romance Writers of New Zealand, and Omega Writers. She has completed fiction editing courses with The Christian PEN and Lawson Writers Academy, and won the 2016 ACFW Genesis Award (Novella), and edited the 2018 RITA Award winner (Romance with Religious or Spiritual Elements)."

EXTRA INK EDITS | MEGAN EASLEY-WALSH

Megan@ExtraInkEdits.com | extrainkedits.com

Contact: email

Services: manuscript evaluation, copyediting, proofreading, writing coach, back-cover copy, substantive editing, discussion questions for books, query and synopsis critique

Types of manuscripts: articles, nonfiction books, devotions, poetry, short stories, novels, query letters, book proposals, curriculum, Bible studies, gift books, academic, adult, teen/YA, picture books, easy readers, middle grade

Charges: flat fee, page rate, word rate

Credentials/experience: "Megan Easley-Walsh is an Amazon international multi-bestselling author of historical fiction, a researcher, and a writing consultant and editor at Extra Ink Edits with over ten years of experience. She is an award-winning writer and has taught college writing in the UNESCO literature city of Dublin, Ireland. Her degrees are in history-focused International Relations. She is American and lives in Ireland with her Irish husband."

IMMORTALISE | BEN MORTON

PO Box 656, Noarlunga Centre, SA 5168, Australia
info@immortalise.com.au | www.immortalise.com.au

> **Contact:** email
> **Services:** writing coaching, manuscript assessment, editing, proofreading
> **Charges:** page rate (where pages average 250 -300 words)
> **Credentials/experience:** "Published author, creative writing teacher, experienced editor and publisher, MA fiction writing supervisor."

NEXT LEVEL EDITING AND TRANSCRIPTION | DARLENE OAKLEY

248 Oakdale Ave., St. Catharines, ON, Canada L2P 2K6 | 289-696-2382
nextleveleditingandt@gmail.com | nextleveleditingandtranscription.com

> **Contact:** email
> **Services:** manuscript evaluation, substantive editing/rewriting, copyediting, proofreading, transcription
> **Types of manuscripts:** articles, nonfiction books, devotions, technical material, short stories, novels, Bible studies, teen/YA, adult
> **Charges:** word rate, page rate, custom
> **Credentials/experience:** "15+ years editing fiction/non-fiction, inspirational and mainstream; also urban fiction/non. 15+ transcription experience (interviews, videos, telecons). Past Acquisitions Editor, Project Manager, Social Media for 2 publishing companies. Go-to Editor for many clients."

NITPICKING WITH A PURPOSE | MARSHA MALCOLM

Savanna-la-mar, Westmoreland, Jamaica | 876-823-2092
purposefulnitpicker@gmail.com
www.linkedin.com/in/marsha-malcolm-4791549a

> **Contact:** email
> **Services:** copyediting, proofreading
> **Types of manuscripts:** short stories, novels, picture books, easy readers, middle grade
> **Charges:** word rate
> **Credentials/experience:** "Expert rating certification in Keys to Editing."

RED LOUNGE FOR WRITERS | CECILY PATERSON

19 Coora Ave., Belrose, NSW, Australia 2085 | +61410760271
cecilyapaterson@gmail.com | www.redloungeforwriters.com

Contact: website form
Services: writing coach
Types of manuscripts: specializes in memoir
Credentials/experience: "A published author of 12 books and a prize-winning memoirist, Cecily Paterson helps experienced writers as well as novice scribblers with memoirs."

SPLASHDOWN BOOKS | GRACE BRIDGES
New Zealand
gracebridges1@gmail.com | www.gracebridges.kiwi/hire-me
    Contact: website form
    Services: manuscript evaluation, copyediting, proofreading, substantive editing
    Types of manuscripts: short stories, novels, adult, teen/YA, middle grade
    Charges: word rate
    Credentials/experience: "Editor of dozens of published books; anthology editor of multiple short-story collections, including award-winning publications. Specialist in word flow, rhythm, clarity, and reader satisfaction. International perspective."

SUSAN J. BRUCE
Susan@susanjbruce.com | www.susanjbruce.com
    Contact: email
    Services: manuscript assessment, copyediting, proofreading
    Types of manuscripts: short stories, novels, nonfiction, devotions, teen/YA, adult
    Charges: flat fee, hourly rate
    Credentials/experience: "Master of Arts in Creative Writing. For more details see *www.susanjbruce.com/Editing.*"

VINEMARC COMMUNICATIONS | MARCIA LAYCOCK
PO Box 637, Blackfalds, AB, Canada T0M 0J0 | 403-885-9828
marcia@marciafeelaycock.com | www.marcialeelaycock.com
    Contact: email
    Services: copyediting, proofreading
    Types of manuscripts: short stories, novels, adult, teen/YA
    Charges: hourly rate
    Credentials/experience: "I have edited several books, both fiction and non-fiction, currently working with Siretona Creative."

WORDPOLISH EDITORIAL SERVICES | YVONNE KANU

1 Massey Sq., Toronto, ON M4C 2I2, Canada

yvonnei@wordpolish.net | www.wordpolish.net

> **Contact:** email, website form
>
> **Services:** manuscript evaluation, copyediting, proofreading, writing coach
>
> **Types of manuscripts:** articles, nonfiction books, devotions, short stories, novels, book proposals, academic, Bible studies, adult, teen/YA, easy reader
>
> **Charges:** word rate
>
> **Credentials/experience:** "A professional editor with nine years of experience in publishing, communications and technical writing."

THE WRITE FLOURISH | TIM AND NOLA PASSMORE

Toowoomba, Australia

nola@thewriteflourish.com.au | www.thewriteflourish.com.au

> **Contact:** email
>
> **Services:** manuscript assessments, structural editing, copyediting, proofreading, mentoring
>
> **Types of manuscripts:** adult and YA novels, poetry, memoirs, devotional books, creative nonfiction, academic, manuals, articles, short stories, book proposals
>
> **Charges:** hourly rate
>
> **Credentials/experience:** "Tim and Nola Passmore each have more than 20 years' experience as university academics. Nola also has a degree in creative writing. They founded The Write Flourish in 2014 and have edited a wide range of manuscripts across a variety of styles and genres. They have also had many of their own short pieces published including fiction, poetry, devotions, memoir, nonfiction and academic articles. They would love to help you add the right flourish to your manuscript."

Christian Writers Institute Courses
Editor Bundle

Courses in this bundle:
- When to Break the Rules of Writing
- What Editors Won't Tell You
- Working with Your Editor
- 10 Easy but Essential Self-Editing Tips
- 12 Ways to Please an Editor

Normal price: $45
Savings: 40%
Market guide price: $27

https://cwmg.link/editor2021

How to Scan QR Codes

Use the camera on your smartphone to focus on the above QR code to activate the discount. It will give you the option to visit the site, which you will want to accept. If you are using an older smartphone, you may need to download a QR-code scanning app. You can also visit the URL below the code to activate the discount on your computer.

20

PUBLICITY AND MARKETING SERVICES

THE ADAMS GROUP PUBLIC RELATIONS | GINA ADAMS
6688 Nolensville Rd., Ste. 108-149, Brentwood, TN 37027 |
888-253-3622
www.adamsprgroup.com
> **Contact:** phone, website form
> **Services:** social-media management, press kits, contributed content,
> media interviews, branding, media coaching, videos, press-release
> distribution
> **Books:** all faith-based genres
> **Charges:** flat fee
> **Credentials/experience:** "Gina Adams has served in the Christian
> marketplace for over 30 years representing singers, bands, films,
> authors, speakers, and major conference events. In 1994, Gina
> formed The Adams Group, an independent PR and marketing
> firm dedicated to working with Christian communicators who
> need assistance with promoting their products and increasing
> their national exposure. Her clients have appeared on a variety of
> Christian and mainstream media outlets, including Focus on the
> Family, TBN, *Fox News*, *60 Minutes*, American Family Radio,
> *The 700 Club*, *The New York Times*, CBN, Daystar, and *CBS This
> Morning*, among a myriad of other broadcast and print outlets.
> Gina holds a BS in business and marketing from Murray
> State University and a certificate of achievement in Christian
> apologetics from Biola University. She has also earned an Expert
> Rating Certification in Social Media Marketing."

ANNE RAUTH
3120 Karnes Blvd., Kansas City, MO 64111 | 913-710-8484
anne@annerauth.com | *www.annerauth.com*
> **Contact:** email

Services: marketing, public relations, strategic planning
Books: nonfiction
Charges: hourly rate
Credentials/experience: "Over 20 years of experience in marketing, public relations, and strategic planning for Fortune 500 companies, small businesses, nonprofit organizations, as well as individual authors."

AUDRA JENNINGS PR
2609 Sandy Ln., Corsicana, TX 75110 | 903-874-8363
ajenningspr@gmail.com | *www.audrajennings.com*
Contact: email
Services: publicity, blog tours, social-media management, graphics packages
Specialty: Christian books to Christian media
Books: nonfiction, fiction, children's
Charges: flat fees for publicity and blog tours, hourly rates for author assistance
Credentials/experience: "I have worked as a publicist in the Christian market since 2002. For 16 years, I worked for two different agencies before going freelance on my own and have worked with every major Christian publisher over the years. I currently work part-time on staff for New Growth Press but also take on projects on my own."

AUTHOR MEDIA | THOMAS UMSTATTD, JR.
PO Box 5690, Austin, TX 78763 | 512-582-7290
thomas@authormedia.com | *www.authormedia.com*
Contact: website form
Services: marketing consulting, web development, branding, web design
Books: fiction, nonfiction, children's
Charges: flat fee, hourly rate
Credentials/experience: More than ten years of experience, included in "101 Best Websites for Authors" by *Writer's Digest*.

AUTHOR SUPPORT SERVICES | RUSSELL SHERRARD
Carmichael, CA | 916-967-7251
russellsherrard@reagan.com | *www.sherrardsebookresellers.com/WordPress/ author-support-services-the-authors-place-to-get-help*
Contact: email

Services: Twitter and Facebook marketing, submitting URL to search engines, blog administration

Books: Christian ebooks, fiction, nonfiction

Charges: flat fee

Credentials/experience: Writing and editing since 2009; currently providing freelance services for multiple clients.

BANNER CONSULTING | MIKE LOOMIS

PO Box 1828, Winter Park, Co 80482

Mike@MikeLoomis.co | www.MikeLoomis.co

Contact: email, website form

Services: book-launch planning, branding, article curation and placement, web development, PR

Specialty: branding and marketing strategy

Books: nonfiction

Charges: custom fee

Credentials/experience: "I've worked with internationally known brands and *New York Times* bestsellers. I've helped clients get breakthrough PR, speaking engagements, and bestseller lists."

THE BLYTHE DANIEL AGENCY, INC . | BLYTHE DANIEL

email through website | www.theblythedanielagency.com

Blythe Daniel, publicist

Stephanie Alton, marketing manager

Contact: website form

Services: range of publicity campaigns utilizing broadcast and print media and the Internet, including blogs, podcasts, articles, TV and radio interviews, book reviews, and book launches

Books: primarily adult and young-adult nonfiction

Charges: customized by campaign

Credentials/experience: "We have personal relationships with hundreds of media outlets that we have developed over the last 20 years in the business. Through our relationships, understanding of the changing media landscape, and careful selection of content we promote, we are able to provide our clients more opportunities to bring recognition to their book(s)." Blythe worked five years as the publicity director and two years as the marketing director for Thomas Nelson.

BROOKSTONE CREATIVE GROUP | SUZANNE KUHN

PO Box 211, Evington, VA 24550 | 302-514-7899

www.brookstonecreativegroup.com

> **Contact:** website form
> **Services:** Amazon optimization, social-media assessment and consulting, video interviews, email and digital marketing, search-engine optimization, Facebook and Google ad management
> **Books:** all
> **Charges:** flat fee, custom rate
> **Credentials/experience:** Suzanne has more than thirty years of book-specific experience. Brookstone is an expansion of her promotion business, SuzyQ, with a team of almost two dozen professionals who bring a wide range of knowledge and experience to help you get published.

CHOICE MEDIA & COMMUNICATIONS | HEATHER ADAMS

231 Public Square, Ste. 300, PMB #45, Franklin, TN 37064-2552 | 404-423-8411

heather@choicepublicity.com | *www.ChoicePublicity.com*

Kerry Gardner, kerry@choicepublicity.com

Devin Lee Duke, devinlee@choicepublicity.com

Annie Cotter, annie@choicepublicity.com

Hannah Harter, hannah@choicepublicity.com

> **Contact:** email, phone
> **Services:** media relations, branding and strategy, social media, events
> **Books:** nonfiction
> **Charges:** retainer-based partnership or project fee
> **Credentials/experience:** "Choice Media & Communications is a boutique media and communications business dedicated to providing clients with quality public relations. Choice helps authors create a clear communications plan, gain media coverage, and receive guidance they won't get anywhere else. With more than two decades of high-level professional communications experience across varying industries and with many of today's tastemakers and thought leaders, Choice founder Heather Adams created a public relations business marked with warmth and enthusiasm, strategic development, clear communication, detailed execution, and thorough reporting."

CHRISTIAN INDIE PUBLISHING ASSOCIATION |
SARAH BOLME

PO Box 481022, Charlotte, NC 28269 | 704-277-7194

cipa@christianpublishers.net | *www.christianpublishers.net*

Contact: email

Services: resources and tools for publishing and marketing for independent authors

Specialty: marketing services

Books: all genres

Charges: membership dues

Credentials/experience: "Our mission is to support, strengthen, and promote independent authors and small publishers in the Christian marketplace. We have been doing this since 2004."

EABOOKS PUBLISHING | CHERI COWELL

3726 Christmas Palm Pl., Oviedo, FL 32765 | 407-712-3431

Cheri@eabookspublishing.com | *www.eabookspublishing.com*

Contact: website form

Services: marketing coaching is one-on-one for three to four months to lay a foundation

Specialty: websites, social media, e-newsletters, and marketing plan

Books: all genres

Charges: flat fee

Credentials/experience: "We don't believe marketing should be about you or your book; it should be about meeting readers' needs. Our websites, social media, and newsletter plan is reader focused and not author focused. Books sell when you meet readers' needs."

EPIC—A RESULTS AGENCY

Murfreesboro, TN | 615-829-6441

hello@epic.inc | *epic.inc*

Contact: phone, email, website form

Services: social-media management, email marketing, publicity campaigns, press materials, media training, platform development

Credentials/experience: Group of PR and marketing specialists with years of experience.

JONES LITERARY | JASON JONES

108 N. Public Sq. #204, Murfreesboro, TN 37130 | 512-720-2996

jason@jonesliterary.com | jonesliterary.com

Contact: email

Service: publicity, digital marketing strategy, podcast production

Specialty: areas of Christian faith, apologetics, persecution of the church, religious liberty, American history, conservative politics, culture, marriage/family

Books: nonfiction

Charges: custom

Credentials/experience: "Previously, Jason led one of the industry's premier Christian public relations firms, SERVE Literary & Media. Prior to that, he spent five years with Thomas Nelson Publishers. He has led campaigns for eleven *New York Times* bestselling titles and has managed some of the industry's most successful authors. He frequently works with producers and editors at *FOX News*, CNN, *Huckabee*, CBS, NBC, Moody Radio, Salem Radio, CBN, *Christianity Today* and numerous other national outlets."

KATIE BELL COMMUNICATIONS

Jackson, TN | 731-803-9056

hello@katiebellcommunications.com | katiebellcommunications.com

Contact: website form

Services: publicity campaigns, press materials, blog and social-media posts, media training

LOGOS PUBLICATIONS, LLC

PO Box 271, Lampeter, PA 17537 | 717-681-8452

customerservice@logospub.com | www.logospub.com

Contact: website form, email

Service: Catch Fire is a collaborative, subscription-based marketing service that is conducted via our website *FindChristianBooks.com*

Books: fiction, nonfiction, self-help; we reserve the right to reject any book we feel does not fit with our Christian worldview

Charges: six-month minimum subscription

Credentials/experience: "Logos Publications is a trusted ally to both indie and traditionally published authors. We are proud members of the Christian Indie Publisher's Association and the Southern Lancaster County Chamber of Commerce."

MCCLURE/MUNTSINGER PUBLIC RELATIONS |
PAMELA MCCLURE and JANA MUNTSINGER
PO Box 804, Franklin, TN 37065 | 615-595-8321
info@mmpublicrelations.com | *www.mmpublicrelations.com*

Contact: email
Services: customized publicity campaigns, including radio, TV, Internet, and social media
Books: any book they like
Charges: customized by campaign
Credentials/experience: "After more than 40 combined years of book publicity, we have long and strong relationships with dozens of editors, writers, and producers. We specialize in knowing how to place religious books in Christian and general-market media, traditional outlets, and online."

MEDIA CONNECT | SHARON FARNELL
301 E. 57th St., New York, NY 10022 | 212-593-6337
Sharon.Farnell@finnpartners.com | *www.media-connect.com*

Contact: email
Services: full-service book publicity firm with TV and radio campaigns, print, online, book tours, etc.
Books: primarily nonfiction but also children's and some fiction
Charges: custom rate
Credentials/experience: "Since joining the company in 1997, Sharon has been instrumental in helping faith-based authors and publishers reach both the Christian and mainstream audience. She has successfully placed her clients in a variety of top media outlets."

SIDE DOOR COMMUNICATIONS | DEBBIE LYKINS
224-234-6699
deb@sidedoorcom.net | *www.sidedoorcom.net*

Contact: email
Services: media relations, press-kit creation, consulting, publicity-plan development
Books: primarily nonfiction, also children's and fiction but highly selective
Charges: custom
Credentials/experience: "Side Door Communications is a national publicity agency that connects faith-based publishers and personalities with national and local media outlets as well as bloggers, with the goal of obtaining coverage in newspapers

and magazines, and on radio, television, and the Internet. Based in the Milwaukee area, founder Debbie Lykins has more than two decades of experience in marketing, publicity, and communications."

VERITAS COMMUNICATIONS | DON S. OTIS

PO Box 1505, Sandpoint, ID 83864 | 719-275-7775
don@veritasincorporated.com | *www.veritasincorporated.com*

Contact: email

Services: schedule radio and television interviews, write and distribute media releases, author training, website representation, travel tracking, select convention representation

Specialty: author training and media promotion

Books: prefers nonfiction and issues-related titles

Charges: flat fee

Credentials/experience: "Thirty years of publicity experience, scheduled more than 30,000 interviews and articles, author of five books, former host and producer for both radio and television."

WHO ARE YOU TRYING TO SERVE? | BRIAN ALLAIN

brian@writingforyourlife.com | *whoareyoutryingtoserve.com*

Contact: email

Services: marketing plans, platform development, courses, conferences

Specialty: marketing plans for authors

Books: all books for the Christian or general market

Charges: flat fee, hourly rate, custom

Credentials/experience: "Who Are You Trying To Serve? is led by Brian Allain, producer of Writing for Your Life, Publishing in Color, and Compassionate Christianity, and formerly Founding Director of the Frederick Buechner Center. At the Buechner Center he launched and managed Mr. Buechner's online presence, established strategic partnerships around the world, and launched new workshops and books.

"Through Who Are You Trying To Serve? (formerly known as Enliven Your Tribe!), Brian has supported several additional spiritual authors with their online marketing, including Kathleen Norris, the Madeleine L'Engle estate, Philip Yancey, Diana Butler Bass, Leslie Leyland Fields, Dominique Gilliard, and the Marcus Borg Foundation. He has also supported Drew Theological Seminary, Princeton Theological Seminary, Western Theological Seminary, and other companies on various marketing projects. His strengths are creating business transformation through innovation and high-trust relationships, with positive influence and great dedication."

WILDFIRE MARKETING | ROB EAGAR
3625 Chartwell Dr., Suwanee, GA 30024 | 770-887-1462
Rob@StartaWildfire.com | *www.StartaWildfire.com*

    Contact: email

    Services: Rob Eagar is one of the top experts on all facets of book marketing, including book launches, author websites, email marketing, social media, public speaking, and author-revenue growth.

    Specialty: book marketing

    Books: all genres

    Charges: flat fee

    Credentials/experience: "Rob Eagar is the founder of Wildfire Marketing, a consulting practice that has coached more than 450 authors and helped books hit *The New York Times* best-seller list in three different categories: new fiction, new nonfiction, and backlist nonfiction. His company has attracted numerous bestselling authors, including Dr. Gary Chapman, Lysa TerKeurst, DeVon Franklin, Wanda Brunstetter, and Dr. John Townsend."

Christian Writers Institute Courses Marketing Bundle

Courses in this bundle:
- How to Get Booked as a Podcast Guest
- How to Craft Amazing Blog Posts
- The Art of Persuasion
- 7 Secrets of Amazing Author Websites
- Sell Your Books Like Wildfire
- Book Marketing: How Everything Has Changed and Nothing Is New

Normal price: $355
Savings: 72%
Market guide price: $99.40

https://cwmg.link/mkt2021

How to Scan QR Codes

Use the camera on your smartphone to focus on the above QR code to activate the discount. It will give you the option to visit the site, which you will want to accept. If you are using an older smartphone, you may need to download a QR-code scanning app. You can also visit the URL below the code to activate the discount on your computer.

21

LEGAL AND ACCOUNTING SERVICES

CAROL TOPP CPA

10288 Amberwood Ct., West Chester, OH 45241 | 513-777-8342

Carol@TaxesforWriters.com | *TaxesforWriters.com*

Contact: email

Services: accounting, taxes

Charges: hourly rate

Credentials/experience: "Carol is a Certified Public Accountant (CPA) and author who offers consultations for writers. She is the author of 15 books, including *Business Tips and Taxes for Writers*. In addition, she was a contributing author to Writers Digest's *Writers Market* and *Guide to Self-Publishing*. She is available for private phone consultations."

CHRIS MORRIS CPA, LLC

11209 N. 161st Ln., Surprise, AZ 85379 | 623-451-8182

cmorris@chrismorriscpa.com | *chrismorriscpa.com*

Contact: email

Services: accounting, taxes, contract review

Charges: flat fee, custom

Credentials/experience: "Chris Morris CPA is a firm that has focused its resources on developing a deep understanding of the creative entrepreneur space. We have the privilege of counting photographers, authors, publishing presses, editors, virtual assistants, and bloggers among our clients. In other words, we live and breathe the world of the creative entrepreneur."

TOM UMSTATTD CPA

13276 Research Blvd., Ste. 101, Austin, TX 78750 | 512-250-1090

tom@taxmantom.com | *www.taxmantom.com*
> **Contact:** website form
> **Services:** accounting, taxes
> **Charges:** hourly rate
> **Credentials/experience:** More than 35 years of experience.

Christian Writers Institute Courses
Tax & Legal Bundle

Courses in this bundle:
- Tax & Business Guide for Authors
- Ghostwriting & Collaboration
- Understanding Copyright Law
- The Book Contract

Normal price: $117
Savings: 58%
Market guide price: $49.14

https://cwmg.link/taxlegal2021

How to Scan QR Codes
Use the camera on your smartphone to focus on the above QR code to activate the discount. It will give you the option to visit the site, which you will want to accept. If you are using an older smartphone, you may need to download a QR-code scanning app. You can also visit the URL below the code to activate the discount on your computer.

22

SPEAKING SERVICES

ADVANCED WRITERS AND SPEAKERS ASSOCIATION (AWSA)

PO Box 6421, Longmont, CO 80501

ReachOut2Linda@gmail.com | *awsa.com*

Contact: email, mail

Director: Linda Evans Shepherd

Services: website directory, online prayer group, coaching, online training and community, conference prior to the opening of Christian Product Expo, fall retreat at the Christian Booksellers Expo at Munce

Membership: women only, $40/year

Main membership qualifications: two major forms of communication from this list: national media (column, blog, podcast, radio or TV show), published book, speaking more than twice a year outside your community, making movies, acting; protégé membership for beginning to intermediate communicators

CHRISTIAN COMMUNICATORS ANOINTED & APPOINTED SPEAKER SUMMIT

contact@christiancommunicators.com | *www.ChristianCommunicators.com*

Contact: website form

Directors: Tammy Whitehurst, Lori Boruff

Services: annual conference to educate, validate, and launch speakers to the next level for beginning or seasoned speakers, July 28—August 1 in Texas; video listing on website

CHRISTIAN SPEAKER NETWORK

christianspeaker.net

Contact: website form

Service: web page that is listed in the online database

Fee: $39.95 per year

CHRISTIAN WOMEN SPEAKERS
womenspeakers.com
>**Director:** Marnie Swedberg
>**Contact:** website form
>**Service:** web page that is listed in the online database
>**Fees:** free; or $29.99 per month; $299 per year for higher ranking, extra features and benefits

DECLARE
info@wearedeclare.com | wearedeclare.com
>**Contact:** website
>**Directors:** Eryn Hall, Kristin Lemus, Michelle Acker, Megan Fish
>**Services:** annual conference in October to equip women to be effective communicators, blog, podcasts, community events

NEXT STEP COACHING SERVICES
info@nextstepcoachingservices.com | nextstepcoachingservices.com
>**Contact:** website form
>**Coaches:** Amy Carroll, Melanie Chitwood
>**Services:** coaching for women speakers to sharpen messages, develop marketing, and gain organizational tools; weekly speaking tips via email

NORTHWEST CHRISTIAN SPEAKERS
2818 Martin Rd., Bellingham, WA | 360-966-0203
Coordinator@NWSpeakers.com | nwspeakers.com
>**Director:** Christie Miller
>**Contact:** email, phone
>**Service:** speakers bureau, not limited to the Northwest
>**Qualifications/requirements:** attend training workshops/evaluation session

SHE SPEAKS CONFERENCE
Sponsored by Proverbs 31 Ministries. See the listing in "**Writers Conferences and Seminars.**"

SPEAK UP SPEAKER SERVICES
3141 Winged Foot Dr., Lakeland, FL 33803 | 586-481-7661
gene4speakup@aol.com | speakupspeakerservices.com
>**Contact:** email, mail

Director: Carol Kent

Service: speakers bureau, fee negotiation, contracts for services, speech and TV-interview coaching, SpeakUp Conference (see listing in "**Writers Conferences and Seminars**")

Qualifications/requirements: at least two books or CDs currently available in the Christian market and regularly speaking nationally; see list of application details to mail

Representation: exclusive, nonexclusive

ULTIMATE CHRISTIAN COMMUNICATORS CONFERENCE

ultimatechristiancommunicatorsconference.com

Contact: website

Director: Felice Gerwitz

Service: annual conference for women to train, coach, and provide networking for beginning and advanced speakers

Christian Writers Institute Courses
Public Speaking Bundle

Courses in this bundle:
- The Art of Persuasion
- How to Become a Successful Speaker
- Public Speaking for the Writer
- Speak So People Will Listen

Normal price: $67
Savings: 56%
Market guide price: $29.48

https://cwmg.link/speak2021

How to Scan QR Codes
Use the camera on your smartphone to focus on the above QR code to activate the discount. It will give you the option to visit the site, which you will want to accept. If you are using an older smartphone, you may need to download a QR-code scanning app. You can also visit the URL below the code to activate the discount on your computer.

23

WRITING EDUCATION RESOURCES

ANN KROEKER, WRITING COACH
annkroeker.com/podcasts
> **Type:** podcast
> **Host:** Ann Kroeker
> **Description:** "These writing podcast episodes offer practical tips and motivation for writers at all stages. . . . Tune in for solutions addressing anything from self-editing and goal-setting . . . to administrative and scheduling challenges."

CHRISTIAN EDITOR NETWORK LLC
www.ChristianEditorNetwork.com
> **Type:** organization
> **Owner:** Kathy Ide
> **Description:** "Our goal is to equip, empower, and encourage editors in the Christian market. Join our community of like-minded professionals in The Christian PEN. Advance your knowledge and skills through The PEN Institute. Attend the PENCON editors conference. Once you're established, apply to join Christian Editor Connection to get more job leads.
>
> The Christian PEN: Proofreaders and Editors Network, *www.TheChristianPEN.com*. Sharon Ford, director. "Whether you are a seasoned editor or thinking about becoming one, The Christian PEN will provide you with education, networking, and community. Become part of this community of like-minded professionals who share our knowledge and experience with one another."

CHRISTIAN PUBLISHING SHOW

www.christianpublishingshow.com

>**Type:** podcast
>**Host:** Thomas Umstattd, Jr.
>**Description:** "The Christian Publishing Show is a podcast to help Christian authors change the world. We talk about how to improve in the craft of writing, how to get published, and how to market effectively. Get expert advice from industry insiders."

THE CHRISTIAN SPECULATIVE FICTION PODCAST

www.buzzsprout.com/324404

>**Type:** podcast
>**Host:** Paul Regnier
>**Description:** "Author interviews and topic discussions about speculative fiction and how faith intersects with stories. Discussions cover writing craft, publishing, promotion, and everything related to the life of a speculative fiction author. Join us as we talk about storytelling in the genres of science fiction, fantasy, paranormal, superhero, and everything in between."

CHRISTIAN WRITERS INSTITUTE

christianwritersinstitute.com

>**Type:** courses
>**Director:** Steve Laube
>**Description:** "The Christian Writers Institute was created to help Christians become proficient in the skills, craft, and business of writing. To build the Kingdom of God word-by-word. It does so by providing audio, video, and pdf courses taught by some of the industry's best teachers. In addition, the Institute publishes a number of books on writing for writers, including *The Christian Writers Market Guide*. Originally founded in 1945, it is estimated that over 30,000 students have been trained by the Christian Writers Institute."

THE COMMUNICATOR ACADEMY PODCAST

www.communicatoracademy.com/podcast-2

>**Type:** podcast
>**Hosts:** Kathi Lipp, Michele Cushatt
>**Description:** "The Communicator Academy Podcast is for those who love God and want to share His story through writing, speaking,

social media—and yes—even marketing. Hosts Kathi Lipp and Michele Cushatt are both 'communication nerds' who love talking about God's message and how to share it better. Their refreshing and honest take on the 'industry' do's and don'ts as well as insight on what makes you stand out from the rest, will not only entertain, but will serve in helping you propel your career to the next level. If you are looking to clarify your calling, you will want to hang out with these two."

CREATE IF WRITING

createifwriting.com/podcast-and-show-notes

Type: podcast
Host: Kirsten Oliphant
Description: "Create If Writing is a weekly podcast for writers and bloggers dealing with authentic platform building online. You will hear from experts on list-building, connecting through Twitter, and how to utilize Facebook. But tools for building an audience would feel empty without a little inspiration, so these training episodes are balanced with inspirational interviews with writers who share their creative process, ups and downs, and how they have dealt with success or failure."

DECLARE PODCAST

declareconference.com/declare-podcast

Type: podcast
Host: Anne Watson
Description: "The mission of Declare is to equip women to walk in their callings as Christian communicators."

FIGHTWRITE PODCAST

fightwrite.net/podcast

Type: podcast
Host: Carla Koch
Description: "A writer's resource for writing action and fight scenes."

THE GATECRASHERS PODCAST

stitcher.com/podcast/amanda-luedeke/the-gatecrashers-podcast

Type: podcast
Hosts: Amanda Luedeke, Charis Crowe
Description: "Teaming up to talk about both sides of publishing

(self-publishing and traditional), Amanda and Charis share their combined twenty years of experience in the industry from both sides of the desk. They offer a glimpse behind the 'gates' as they share the realities, opportunities, and difficulties of the publishing world."

THE HABIT

thehabit.co/the-habit-podcast

Type: podcast

Host: Jonathan Rogers

Description: "Conversations about writing with writers."

HOME ROW: JUST KEEP WRITING

homerowpod.com

Type: podcast

Host: J. A. Medders

Description: "Get inspired to write from some of today's best writers. Listen. Learn. Just keep writing. You might learn how to get a book deal, write a best-seller, or quit your day job. Maybe you'll get that nudge you need to . . . write the blog, article, or book you've been thinking on for far too long. As Christians, our aim is to write in such a way that Jesus is made much of and the Church is encouraged to follow our risen Lord."

THE HOPE*WRITERS PODCAST

hopewriters.com/podcast

Type: podcast

Hosts: Emily P. Freeman, Brian J. Dixon, Gary Morland

Description: "Let's take the next step in your writing life! Maybe you're a beginner stumped about what to do first. Or you're experienced but aren't sure what to do next. The Hope*writers Podcast will help you skip the long learning curve we've struggled through and will put you ahead of the game. Each week you get answers to these questions, from us and from interviews with publishing pros, to help you have clarity for what's next for you."

THE JERRY JENKINS WRITERS GUILD

www.JerrysGuild.com

Type: courses

Director: Jerry Jenkins

Description: "The Writers Guild is like a writing conference you can access from anywhere 24/7. Instant access to video training on any writing topic. Additionally, several times each month Jerry answers your questions live, hosts new writing workshops, interviews industry experts, and so much more." Membership is open only periodically; join the waitlist for the next open period. Jerry also offers individual online courses at *jerryjenkins.com/online-creative-writing-courses.*

KICK-START YOUR AUTHOR PLATFORM MARKETING CHALLENGE

christianediting.co.nz/kick-start

Type: class
Director: Iola Goulton
Description: "Forty-day email challenge, with an email each day with a series of tasks to complete. Ongoing support is available via a private Facebook group. Topics: What is Marketing?; Understanding Your Brand; Know Your Genre; Know Your Target Reader; Design Your Visual Brand: fonts, colors, author photo, website logo; Create and Brand Social Media: Facebook, Instagram, Pinterest, Twitter; Create a Social Media Plan; To Blog or Not to Blog?; Create a Mailing List; Set Up, Design, and Configure Your Website."

KINGDOM WRITERS

authors.libsyn.com/podcast

Type: podcast
Hosts: CJ and Shelley Hitz
Description: "CJ and Shelley Hitz are passionate about equipping and empowering Christian writers of all genres to share their unique gifts with the world. This podcast is filled with spiritual encouragement as well as prayers to help you overcome the resistance you face as a writer. Your story matters!

"We believe that you have a specific role to play in the kingdom of heaven to impact lives for eternity. And because of this, we will pour out our lives encouraging writers like you to not only tell your stories but to take the courageous step of self-publishing your stories in books that will outlive you and leave behind a powerful legacy."

NOVEL MARKETING PODCAST

authormedia.com/novel-marketing

Type: podcast
Host: Thomas Umstattd Jr.
Description: "This is the show for writers who want to build their
platform, sell more books, and change the world with writing worth
talking about. Whether you self-publish or are with a traditional
house, this podcast will make book promotion fun and easy. Thomas
Umstattd Jr. interviews publishers, indie authors and bestselling
traditional authors about how to get published and sell more books."

PASTOR WRITER

pastorwriter.com/episodes

Type: podcast
Host: Chase Replogle
Description: "Join me as I interview pastors, authors, and writing
experts in my journey to better understand the calling and the craft
of writing, reading, and living the Christian life."

THE PEN INSTITUTE

PENInstitute.com

Type: courses
Director: Erin Brown
Description: "Lesson packs, group instruction, and individual
mentoring for aspiring and established freelance and in-house
editors. Instructors are all experienced industry professionals.
Established in 2004. "Whether you are just beginning your editing
career or are looking for an advanced class to update your skills,
The PEN Institute has courses for you. Group instruction, lesson
packs, one-on-one instruction, and mentoring are available."

THE PORTFOLIO LIFE

podcasts.apple.com/us/podcast/the-portfolio-life-with-jeff-goins/
id844091351

Type: podcast
Host: Jeff Goins
Description: "Jeff Goins shares thoughts & ideas that will help you
to pursue work that matters, make a difference with your art &
discover your true voice!"

THE PROLIFIC WRITER PODCAST

theprolificwriter.libsyn.com

Type: podcast

Host: Ryan Pelton

Description: "The Prolific Writer is about writing fast, often, and well. Follow writer and publisher Ryan Pelton as he discusses processes and strategies for writing, editing, publishing, and marketing your books. TPW podcast also interviews some of the most prolific writers in the world. Be inspired as they discuss their journey into writing, explore tips and tricks on the craft, and learn about the latest trends in publishing today."

SERIOUS WRITER, INC.

seriouswriter.com

Type: courses

Directors: Cyle Young, Bethany Jett

Description: "Serious Writer's mission is to set the industry standard for excellence for the clean and Christian writing markets through online courses, one-day book camps, and writers conferences." The Serious Writer Academy offers recorded classes and workshops. The Serious Writer Club offers weekly training, 80+ hours of recorded workshops, networking opportunities, and more.

THE STORY BLENDER PODCAST

www.thestoryblender.com

Type: podcast

Hosts: Steven James

Description: "We are passionate about well-told, impactful stories. We love to listen to them. Watch them. Create them. So, we decided to talk with premier storytellers from around the country. Hear their stories and get their insights. From novelists to comedians to film makers to artists. Stories are told through a variety of people in a variety of ways. And here they are. The secrets of great storytelling from great storytellers."

THE STORYTELLER'S MISSION

www.buzzsprout.com/872170

Type: podcast

Host: Zena Dell Lowe

Description: "A podcast for artists and storytellers about changing the world for the better through story."

WRITE FROM THE DEEP

writefromthedeep.com/write-from-the-deep-podcast

Type: podcast

Hosts: Karen Ball, Erin Taylor Young

Description: "Encouragement, refreshment, and truth from writers, for writers. Every writer, at some point, faces the deep places of crushing trials and struggles. But the deep is also a place where we can learn to abide in God as never before. This podcast reminds writers they're not alone, and equips and helps them to embrace the deep, to discover their truest voice and message, and to share it with refined craft and renewed passion."

THE WRITE HOUR

thewritecoach.biz/the-write-hour-podcast

Type: podcast

Host: Joyce Glass

Description: "How do I start writing a book? Why do I need to write a book? What is the process to write a book? What is next after I have written my book? Are you a personal development leader ready to expand your business with a book? Have your questions answered by Joyce Glass, The Write Coach For Personal Development Leaders. Learn from leaders in the publishing world and begin your writing journey or take your writing career to the next level. Dig deeper with step-by-step instructions and mini-workshops. Joyce's strong point is breaking down the overwhelm and guides you to the next step in your journey. In every episode, she gives practical advice you can implement immediately. Join The Write Hour each week for your dose of writing motivation!"

WRITING FOR YOUR LIFE

writingforyourlife.com

Type: webinars, downloadable resources

Host: Brian Allain

Description: "Writing for Your Life is committed to offering a wide variety of useful resources and services to support spiritual writers. We offer online videos featuring leading spiritual writers and publishing industry experts. Authors discuss and teach about various aspects of spiritual writing. Industry experts offer advice on how to get published and how to market. We also provide a host of services and resources to support your spiritual writing. We cannot guarantee that you will become a best-selling author, but we will help you take your best shot. Learn to tell your own story; write for your life!"

WRITING FOR YOUR LIFE PODCAST

writingforyourlife.com/writing-for-your-life-podcast

Type: podcast

Host: Brian Allain

Description: "If you write, or read, books that matter—books with substance and soul—then this is the place for you. We are here to help you gain inspiration and knowledge to empower your writing. Join us weekly for interviews and presentations from our author partners and industry professionals."

YOUR BEST WRITING LIFE

www.buzzsprout.com/1127762

Type: podcast

Host: Linda Goldfarb

Description: "Writing industry experts share weekly content for all levels of writers, from beginners to bestsellers. You receive practical information and how-to application you can use today to grow your writing career. Each month, Linda Goldfarb and her guests cover general issues about the craft of writing, fiction specific writing topics, nonfiction topics, self-care for writers, and topics specific to the business of writing. If you're an aspiring writer, we have content to help you excel in your craft. Seasoned writers, we have current content to make your next book proposal, manuscript editing, speaking event, and writer's conference worth your time and energy."

24

CONTESTS

A listing here does not guarantee endorsement of the contest. For guidelines on evaluating contests, go to *www.sfwa.org/other-resources/ for-authors/writer-beware/contests*.

 Note: Dates may not be accurate since many sponsors had not posted their 2021 dates before press time.

CHILDREN AND TEENS

CORETTA SCOTT KING BOOK AWARD
www.ala.org/awardsgrants/awards/24/apply

Description: Sponsored by Coretta Scott King Task Force, American Library Association. Annual award for children's books published the previous year by African-American authors and/or illustrators. Books must promote an understanding and appreciation of the "American Dream" and fit one of these categories: preschool to grade 4, grades 5–8, grades 9–12.
Deadline: December 1
Prize: $1,000 and plaque

SOCIETY OF CHILDREN'S BOOK WRITERS AND ILLUSTRATORS
www.scbwi.org/awards/grants/for-authors

Description: Sponsors a variety of contests, scholarships, and grants.
Deadline: varies by contest
Prizes: ten awards for published authors and five for unpublished authors, plus grants for emerging voices and student writers

FICTION

ALLIANCE AWARD

www.realmmakers.net/awards/the-alliance-award

> **Description:** Sponsored by The Faith and Fantasy Alliance to give readers their say in what speculative fiction novels they enjoyed most in the preceding year. Only readers may nominate books in this contest. Books may be traditionally published or self-published.
>
> **Deadline:** submit between April 5 and 22
>
> **Entry fee:** none
>
> **Prize:** certificate of recognition

AMERICAN CHRISTIAN FICTION WRITERS CONTESTS

www.ACFW.com/contests

> **Description:** Genesis Contest for unpublished Christian fiction writers in a number of categories/genres. First Impressions award for unpublished writers. Carol Awards for best Christian fiction published the previous year.
>
> **Deadline:** varies by contest
>
> **Entry fee:** varies by category and membership

BARD FICTION PRIZE

www.bard.edu/bfp

> **Description:** Sponsored by Bard College. Awarded to a promising, emerging young writer of fiction, 39 years or younger and an American citizen. Entries must be previously published.
>
> **Deadline:** June 15
>
> **Entry fee:** none
>
> **Prize:** $30,000 and appointment as writer-in-residence for one semester at Bard College, Annandale-on-Hudson, New York

BOSTON REVIEW SHORT STORY CONTEST

www.bostonreview.net/contests

> **Description:** Previously unpublished short stories no longer than 5,000 words.
>
> **Deadline:** October 1
>
> **Entry fee:** $20
>
> **Prize:** $500 plus publication

BULWER-LYTTON FICTION CONTEST

www.bulwer-lytton.com

> **Description:** Sponsored by San Jose State University English Department. For the worst opening line to a novel. Each submission must be a single sentence; multiple entries allowed. Entries will be judged by categories: general, detective, western, science fiction, romance, etc. Overall winners, as well as category winners.
>
> **Deadline:** June 30

THE EUPLE RINEY MEMORIAL AWARD

www.thestorytellermagazine.com/contests

> **Description:** Sponsored by *The Storyteller Anthology/Magazine*. Open genre contest but must be about family in some way and suitable for a family magazine. Length: 3,000 words maximum. Can enter multiple stories with separate entry fee for each one.
>
> **Deadline:** date varies
>
> **Entry fee:** $5
>
> **Prizes:** first place, $50; second place, $25; third place, $15; honorable mention, $10

FLANNERY O'CONNOR AWARD FOR SHORT FICTION

www.ugapress.org/index.php/series/FOC

> **Description:** Sponsored by University of Georgia Press. For collections of short fiction. Length: 40,000–75,000 words. Contestants must be residents of North America.
>
> **Deadline:** submit between April 1 and May 31
>
> **Entry fee:** $30
>
> **Prize:** $1,000 plus publication under royalty book contract

GET PUBBED CONTEST

scriveningspress.com/get-pubbed

> **Description:** Sponsored by Scrivenings Press. For unpublished novels in four genres: speculative, historical, contemporary, and mystery/suspense. Submit the first ten pages.
>
> **Deadline:** November 30
>
> **Entry fee:** $25
>
> **Prizes:** Grand prize, publishing contract, paid registration for annual author retreat, thorough critique of up to 25 pages of your manuscript, and $50 Amazon gift card. Entry with the highest score in each genre will receive a critique of up to 25 pages of your manuscript and $25 Amazon gift card.

GRACE PALEY PRIZE FOR SHORT FICTION
www.awpwriter.org/contests/awp_award_series_overview

> **Description:** Sponsored by Association of Writers and Writing Programs. Short-story collections. May contain stories previously published in periodicals. Length: 150-300 pages.
> **Deadline:** submit between January 1 and February 28
> **Entry fee:** $25
> **Prize:** $5,500 and publication

JACK DYER FICTION PRIZE
craborchardreview.siu.edu/submissions-annual-lit.html

> **Description:** Sponsored by Southern Illinois University Department of English. Annual competition for short stories twenty pages or fewer on a theme.
> **Deadline:** submit between December 1 and January 31
> **Entry fee:** $2
> **Prizes:** $500 each and publication in *Crab Orchard Review*

JAMES JONES FIRST NOVEL CONTEST
www.wilkes.edu/pages/1159.asp

> **Description:** Sponsored by Wilkes University. For a first novel or novel-in-progress by a US writer who has not published a novel. Submit a two-page outline and the first fifty pages of an unpublished novel.
> **Deadline:** March 15
> **Entry fee:** $30 plus $3 processing fee
> **Prizes:** first place, $10,000; two runners-up, $1,000 each; a selection from the winning work is published in *Provincetown Arts*

KATHERINE ANNE PORTER PRIZE IN SHORT FICTION
untpress.unt.edu/submitting-katherine-anne-porter-prize-short-fiction

> **Description:** Sponsored by University of North Texas Press. Quality unpublished fiction by emerging writers of contemporary literature. Can be a combination of flash fiction, short stories, and novellas from 100 to 200 pages (27,500-50,000 words). Material should be previously unpublished in book form.
> **Deadline:** submit between May 1 and June 30
> **Entry fee:** $25
> **Prize:** $1,000 and publication by UNT Press

NATIONAL WRITERS ASSOCIATION NOVEL-WRITING CONTEST

www.nationalwriters.shoppingcartsplus.com/f/Novel_Form4.pdf

Description: To encourage development of creative skills and recognize and reward outstanding ability in the area of novel writing. Any genre or category of novel manuscript may be entered. Only unpublished works in the English language. Maximum length: 100,000 words. Must be submitted via USPS.

Deadline: postmarked by April 1

Entry fee: $35

Prizes: first place, $500 and possible representation; second place, $250; third place, $150; fourth through tenth places, book of the winner's choice; honorable mentions, certificate

NATIONAL WRITERS ASSOCIATION SHORT-STORY CONTEST

www.nationalwriters.shoppingcartsplus.com/f/Short_Story_Contest1.pdf

Description: Any genre of story. Length: 5,000 words maximum. Submit only unpublished works in the English language via mail.

Deadline: postmarked by July 1

Entry fee: $15

Prizes: first place, $250; second place, $100; third place, $50; fourth through tenth places, recognition

NOVEL STARTS CONTEST

scriveningspress.com/novel-starts

Description: Sponsored by Scrivenings Press. For an unfinished novel in four genres: speculative, historical, contemporary, and mystery/suspense. Submit the first five pages.

Deadline: November 30

Entry fee: $25

Prizes: Grand prize, video-based novel writing course, invitation to submit novel for consideration by Scrivenings Press once it is finished, and thorough critique of up to 25 pages of your manuscript. Entry with the highest score in each genre will receive a critique of up to 25 pages of your manuscript and $25 Amazon gift card.

REALM MAKERS AWARDS

www.realmmakers.com

Description: Sponsored by The Faith and Fantasy Alliance. Realm Makers Genre Awards in these categories: debut, science fiction,

fantasy, young adult, supernatural/paranormal, and horror/other (for those who don't feel other categories accurately characterize their speculative work). Realm Award recognizes the most excellent speculative novel written by a Christian author in the previous calendar year. Length: 60,000 words minimum; 50,000 words minimum for young adult. Parable Award for Excellence in Cover Design is awarded to the best overall cover for a speculative novel written by a Christian author.
Deadline: submit between January 1 and 20
Entry fee: $35
Prizes: cash

SERENA MCDONALD KENNEDY AWARD
www.snakenation.press/contests

> **Description:** Sponsored by Snake Nation Press. Novellas up to 50,000 words or short-story collections up to 200 pages, published or unpublished.
> **Deadline:** August 31
> **Entry fee:** $25
> **Prize:** $1,000 and publication

TOBIAS WOLFF AWARD FOR FICTION
www.bhreview.org/contest-submissions-guidelines

> **Description:** Sponsored by Western Washington University's *Bellingham Review*. Length: 5,000 words maximum.
> **Deadline:** submit between December 1 and March 31
> **Entry fee:** $20
> **Prize:** $1,000 plus publication

ZOETROPE: ALL-STORY SHORT FICTION COMPETITION
www.zoetrope.com/contests

> **Description:** For all genres of literary fiction. Entries must be unpublished and strictly 5,000 words or fewer. More than one entry allowed.
> **Deadline:** October 13
> **Entry fee:** $30
> **Prizes:** first place, $1,000; second place, $500; third place, $250; plus publication of winning story and consideration for agency representation

NONFICTION

ANNIE DILLARD AWARD IN CREATIVE NONFICTION
bhreview.org/contest-submissions-guidelines

> **Description:** Sponsored by Western Washington University's *Bellingham Review*. Unpublished essays on any subject. Length: 5,000 words maximum.
> **Deadline:** submit between December 1 and March 31
> **Entry fee:** $20 for first submission, $10 each additional one
> **Prize:** $1,000

AWP PRIZE FOR CREATIVE NONFICTION
www.awpwriter.org/contests

> **Description:** Sponsored by Association of Writers and Writing Programs. Open to published and unpublished authors. Book collection of nonfiction manuscripts. Length: 150–300 pages.
> **Deadline:** submit between January 1 and February 28
> **Entry fee:** $15 for members, $30 for nonmembers
> **Prize:** $2,500 and publication with the University of Georgia Press

THE BECHTEL PRIZE
www.twc.org/publications/bechtel-prize

> **Description:** Sponsored by Teachers & Writers Collaborative. For unpublished essays that explore themes related to creative writing, arts education, and/or the imagination. Length: 2,500 words maximum.
> **Deadline:** January 6
> **Entry fee:** $20
> **Prize:** $1,000 and publication

EVENT NON-FICTION CONTEST
www.eventmagazine.ca/contest-nf

> **Description:** Unpublished creative nonfiction. Length: 5,000 words maximum.
> **Deadline:** October 15
> **Entry fee:** $34.95, includes a one-year subscription to *EVENT*
> **Prizes:** first place, $1,500; second place, $1,000; third place, $500 plus publication

GUIDEPOSTS WRITERS WORKSHOP CONTEST

www.guideposts.org/enter-the-guideposts-writers-workshop-contest

> **Description:** Contest is held in even years with a mid-June deadline. Submit an original, unpublished, true, first-person story (your own or ghostwritten for another person) in 1,500 words or fewer about an experience that changed your life. Show how faith made a difference. Twelve winners will attend an all-expenses-paid, weeklong writers workshop in Rye, New York, to learn about inspirational storytelling and writing for Guideposts publications.

INTREPID TIMES TRAVEL WRITING CONTEST

intrepidtimes.com

> **Description:** Sponsored by Exisle Publishing. For narrative travel writing that focuses on stories, places, and people.
> **Deadline:** May 19
> **Entry fee:** none
> **Prize:** $100, publication on website, possible publication in anthology

JOHN GUYON LITERARY NONFICTION

craborchardreview.siu.edu/submissions-annual-lit.html

> **Description:** Sponsored by Southern Illinois University Department of English. Annual competition. Literary nonfiction, 6,500 words.
> **Deadline:** submit between December 1 and January 31
> **Entry fee:** $2
> **Prize:** $500 and publication online

NEW LETTERS EDITOR'S CHOICE AWARD

www.newletters.org/editors-choice-award

> **Description:** For unpublished essays. Length: 8,000 words maximum.
> **Deadline:** May 18
> **Entry fee:** $24
> **Prize:** $1,500 and magazine subscription

RICHARD J . MARGOLIS AWARD

award.margolisaward.com

> **Description:** Sponsored by Blue Mountain Center. Given annually to a promising young journalist or essayist whose work combines warmth, humor, wisdom, and concern with social justice. Submit at least two examples of published or unpublished work and a short biographical note, including a description of current and

anticipated work. Length: 30 pages maximum.
Deadline: July 1
Prize: $5,000 plus a one-month residency at the Blue Mountain
Center in Blue Mountain Lake, New York

PLAYS, SCRIPTS, SCREENPLAYS

ACADEMY NICHOLL FELLOWSHIPS IN SCREENWRITING
www.oscars.org/nicholl/about

> **Description:** International contest open to any writer who has not
> optioned or sold a treatment, teleplay, or screenplay for more than
> $25,000. May submit up to three scripts, 70-160 pages.
> **Deadline:** submit between March 7 and May 1
> **Entry fee:** $45-85, depending on submission date
> **Prizes:** up to five $35,000 fellowships; recipients will be expected to
> complete at least one original feature-film screenplay during the
> fellowship year

AMERICAN ZOETROPE SCREENPLAY CONTEST
www.zoetrope.com/contests

> **Description:** To find and promote new and innovative voices in
> cinema. For screenplays and television pilots. No entrant may have
> earned more than $5,000 as a screenwriter for theatrical films or
> television or for the sale of, or sale of an option to, any original
> story, treatment, screenplay, or teleplay. Prizes, fellowships, awards,
> and other contest winnings are not considered earnings and are
> excluded from this rule. Length: film scripts, 70-130 pages; one-
> hour television pilot scripts, 45-65 pages; half-hour television
> scripts, 22-34 pages.
> **Deadline:** September 19
> **Entry fee:** $35-$50, depending on submission date
> **Prizes:** first place, $5,000, plus consideration for film option and
> development; ten finalists will also get this consideration

AUSTIN FILM FESTIVAL SCREENWRITERS COMPETITION
austinfilmfestival.com/submit

> **Description:** Offers a number of contest categories, including
> narrative feature, narrative short, documentary feature,

documentary short for screenplays, screenplay, teleplay, and scripted digital competition.
Deadline: varies by type
Entry fee: $35-70, varies by type and submission date
Prizes: $1,000-$5,000

KAIROS PRIZE FOR SPIRITUALLY UPLIFTING SCREENPLAYS

www.kairosprize.com

> **Description:** Sponsored by Movieguide. For feature-length screenplays. Judges consider not only a script's entertainment value and craftsmanship, but also whether it is uplifting, inspirational, and spiritual and if it teaches lessons in ethics and morality. Length: 87-130 pages; will accept scripts up to 150 pages (not counting the title page) for an additional $20.
> **Deadline:** October
> **Entry fee:** varies, depending on submission date
> **Prizes:** $15,000 each for first-time and professional screenwriters

MILDRED AND ALBERT PANOWSKI PLAYWRITING COMPETITION

www.nmu.edu/forestrobertstheatre/playwritingcompetition

> **Description:** Sponsored by Forest Roberts Theatre, Northern Michigan University. Unpublished, unproduced, full-length plays. Award to encourage and stimulate artistic growth among educational and professional playwrights. Provides students and faculty members the opportunity to mount and produce an original work on the university stage.
> **Deadline:** submit between June 1 and December 1
> **Prize:** $2,000, a summer workshop, a fully mounted production, and transportation to Marquette, Michigan

MOONDANCE INTERNATIONAL FILM FESTIVAL COMPETITION

www.moondancefilmfestival.com

> **Description:** Offers a variety of awards for films, screenplays, librettos, and features that raise awareness about social issues.
> **Deadline:** May 30
> **Entry fees:** $50-100
> **Prize:** promotion to film companies for possible option

SCRIPTAPALOOZA SCREENPLAY COMPETITION

www.scriptapalooza.com/competition/how-to-enter

> **Description:** Any screenplay from any genre considered; must be the original work of the author (multiple authorship acceptable). Shorts competition: screenplays fewer than 40 pages.
> **Deadline:** submit between December 16 and April 13
> **Entry fee:** $45-65
> **Prizes:** first place, $10,000; each genre winner, $500 (action, adventure, comedy, drama, family, science fiction, thriller/ horror, historical), plus access to more than fifty producers through Scriptapalooza's network

SCRIPTAPALOOZA TV COMPETITION

www.scriptapaloozatv.com/competition

> **Description:** Scripts for television pilots, one-hour dramas, reality shows, and half-hour sitcoms. Length: pilots, 30-60 pages; one-hour program, 50-60 pages; reality show, one- to five-page treatment; half-hour sitcom, 25-35 pages.
> **Deadline:** October and April
> **Entry fee:** $45-50, varies with deadline
> **Prizes in each genre:** first place, $500; second place, $200; third place, $100, plus access to more than fifty producers through Scriptapalooza's network

POETRY

ACADEMY OF AMERICAN POETS

poets.org/academy-american-poets/american-poets-prizes

> See the website for a list of multiple contests and prizes.

ANHINGA-ROBERT DANA PRIZE FOR POETRY

www.anhingapress.org/anhinga-robert-dana-prize

> **Description:** Sponsored by Anhinga Press. For poets submitting a manuscript of original poems in English. Length: 48-80 pages.
> **Deadline:** submit between February 15 and May 31
> **Entry fee:** $28 per manuscript
> **Prize:** $2,000, a reading tour, and publication by Anhinga Press

BALTIMORE REVIEW POETRY CONTEST

baltimorereview.submittable.com/submit

> **Description:** All styles and forms of poetry, directed toward an announced theme. Maximum of three entries.
> **Deadline:** November 30
> **Entry fee:** $10
> **Prizes:** $100-500 and publication

BARBARA MANDIGO KELLY PEACE POETRY AWARDS

www.peacecontests.org/#poetry

> **Description:** Sponsored by Nuclear Age Peace Foundation. Awards to encourage poets to explore and illuminate positive visions of peace and the human spirit. Poems must be original, unpublished, and in English. May submit up to three poems for one entry fee.
> **Deadline:** July 1
> **Entry fee:** adults, $15; youth ages 13-18, $5; none for ages 12 and under
> **Prizes:** adult winner, $1,000; youth winner, $200; ages 12 and under, $200

BLUE MOUNTAIN ARTS POETRY CARD CONTEST

www.sps.com/contest-5

> **Description:** Biannual contest. Original poems. May be rhymed or unrhymed, although unrhymed is preferred. Poems also considered for greeting cards or anthologies. Original creations in English only. No limit to number of entries.
> **Deadlines:** June 30 and December 31
> **Entry fee:** none
> **Prizes:** $350, $200, $100

BOSTON REVIEW ANNUAL POETRY CONTEST

www.bostonreview.net/contests

> **Description:** Submit up to five unpublished poems in English; no more than ten pages total. Submit manuscripts in duplicate with cover note.
> **Deadline:** May 31
> **Entry fee:** $20, includes a subscription to *Boston Review*
> **Prize:** $1,000 plus publication

CAVE CANEM POETRY PRIZE

cavecanempoets.org/prizes/cave-canem-poetry-prize

> **Description:** Sponsored by Cave Canem Foundation. Supports the work of black poets of African descent with excellent manuscripts and who have not found a publisher for their first book. Offered

every other year. Length: 48-75 pages.
Deadline: varies, with a spring season date
Entry fee: $15
Prize: $1,000 plus publication by a national press and copies of the book, with a feature reading in New York City

THE COMSTOCK REVIEW CHAPBOOK CONTEST
comstockreview.org/comstock-writers-group-chapbook

Description: Submissions must be unpublished as a collection, but individual poems may have been published previously in journals. Length: 25-34 pages. Poems may run longer than one page.
Deadline: submit between August 1 and October 31
Entry fee: $30
Prize: $1,000 plus publication and author copies

FLO GAULT STUDENT POETRY PRIZE
www.sarabandebooks.org/flo-gault

Description: Sponsored by Sarabande Books. For full-time Kentucky undergraduate students. Submit up to three poems.
Deadline: submit between October 1 and December 1
Prize: $500 and publication

49TH PARALLEL POETRY AWARD
bhreview.org/contest-submissions-guidelines

Description: Sponsored by Western Washington University's *Bellingham Review*. Up to three poems in any style or on any subject.
Deadline: submit between December 1 and March 31
Entry fee: $20; international entries, $30
Prize: $1,000 and publication

HOLLIS SUMMERS POETRY PRIZE
www.ohioswallow.com/poetry_prize

Description: Sponsored by Ohio University Press. For an unpublished collection of original poems written in English, 60-95 pages. Open to both those who have not published a book-length collection and to those who have.
Deadline: December 1
Entry fee: $30
Prize: $1,000 plus publication in book form by Ohio University Press

THE JAMES LAUGHLIN AWARD

www.poets.org/academy-american-poets/james-laughlin-award-guidelines

> **Description:** Sponsored by Academy of American Poets. To recognize a second full-length print book of original poetry by a US citizen, permanent resident, or person who has DACA/TPS status, forthcoming within the next calendar year. Author must have published one book of poetry in English in a standard edition (48 pages or more) in the United States or under contract and scheduled for publication during the current calendar year; publication of chapbooks (less than 48 pages) does not disqualify. Length: 48-100 pages.
> **Prize:** $5,000 plus publication

KATE TUFTS DISCOVERY AWARD

www.cgu.edu/tufts

> **Description:** Sponsored by Claremont Graduate University. Award presented annually for a first poetry volume published in the preceding year by a poet of genuine promise.
> **Deadline:** June 30
> **Prize:** $10,000

KINGSLEY TUFTS POETRY AWARD

www.cgu.edu/pages/6422.asp

> **Description:** Sponsored by Claremont Graduate University. Presented annually for a published book of poetry by a midcareer poet to both honor the poet and provide the resources that allow artists to continue working toward the pinnacle of their craft.
> **Deadline:** June 30
> **Prize:** $100,000

MURIEL CRAFT BAILEY MEMORIAL POETRY AWARD

comstockreview.org/annual-contest

> **Description:** Sponsored by *The Comstock Review*. Unpublished poems up to 40 lines. No limit on number of submissions.
> **Deadline:** submit between April 1 and July 15
> **Entry fee:** postal: $5 per poem for up to five poems; online: $27.50 for five poems
> **Prizes:** first place, $1,000; second place, $250; third place, $100

PATRICIA CLEARY MILLER AWARD

www.newletters.org/patricia-cleary-miller-award-for-poetry

> **Description:** Sponsored by *New Letters*. A single poetry entry may contain up to six poems, and the poems need not be related.
> **Deadline:** May 18
> **Entry fee:** $24 each entry; if entering online, add a $5 service charge to entry fee; includes a one-year subscription to *New Letters*
> **Prize:** $2,500 for best group of three to six poems

PHILIP LEVINE PRIZE FOR POETRY

www.fresnostate.edu/artshum/english/levineprize

> **Description:** Sponsored by California State University Department of English. An annual book contest for original English, previously unpublished, full-length poetry manuscripts. Length: 48-80 pages with no more than one poem per page.
> **Deadline:** submit between July 1 and September 30
> **Entry fee:** $28 online fee; $25 postal fee
> **Prize:** $2,000 and publication by Anhinga Press

POETRY SOCIETY OF VIRGINIA POETRY CONTESTS

poetrysocietyofvirginia.org

> **Description:** More than twenty-five categories for adults and students. Form and length vary according to the categories. All entries must be unpublished, original, and not scheduled for publication before the winners of the competition are announced.
> **Deadline:** submit between October 15 and January 15
> **Entry fee:** $5 per poem for nonmembers
> **Prizes:** $100, $50, $30, $20, varying according to specific competition

RICHARD PETERSON POETRY PRIZE

craborchardreview.siu.edu/submissions-annual-lit.html

> **Description:** Sponsored by *Crab Orchard Review*, Southern Illinois University, Carbondale Department of English, on an announced theme. Unpublished poems by a United States citizen, permanent resident, or person who has DACA/TPS status. Length: five pages maximum. Limit three entries.
> **Deadline:** January 31
> **Entry fee:** $2
> **Prize:** $500 and publication online

SLIPSTREAM ANNUAL POETRY CHAPBOOK COMPETITION

www.slipstreampress.org/contest.html

> **Description:** Sponsored by Slipstream Press. Entries may be any style, format, or theme. Length: 40 pages maximum.
> **Deadline:** December 1
> **Entry fee:** $20
> **Prize:** $1,000 plus fifty published copies of chapbook

SOUL-MAKING KEATS LITERARY COMPETITION: JANICE FARRELL POETRY PRIZE

soulmakingcontest.us/guidelines-rules

> **Description:** Sponsored by National League of American Pen Women. Three poems per entry. One poem per page, one-page poems only. Free verse, blank verse, and prose poems.
> **Deadline:** November 30
> **Entry fee:** $5 per entry
> **Prizes:** first place, $100; second place, $50; third place, $25

SUMMERTIME BLUES POETRY CONTEST

www.thestorytellermagazine.com/contests

> **Description:** Sponsored by *The Storyteller* magazine. Poems may be rhyming or nonrhyming and should be about summer, although this topic isn't mandatory. Length: 40 lines maximum. Multiple entries accepted.
> **Deadline:** postmarked by August 31
> **Entry fee:** $5 per three poems
> **Prizes:** first place, $25 plus publication; second place, $15; third place, $10

TOI DERRICOTTE & CORNELIUS EADY CHAPBOOK PRIZE

cavecanempoets.org/prizes/toi-derricotte-cornelius-eady-chapbook-prize

> **Description:** Sponsored by Cave Canem Foundation. Dedicated to the discovery of exceptional chapbook-length manuscripts by black poets. Presented in collaboration with the O, Miami Poetry Festival and The Center for the Humanities at the CUNY Graduate Center.
> **Deadline:** September 2
> **Entry Fee:** $12
> **Prize:** $500, publication, ten copies of the chapbook, a four-day writer residency, and a feature reading

TOM HOWARD/MARGARET REID POETRY CONTEST

winningwriters.com/our-contests/tom-howard-margaret-reid-poetry-contest

Description: Sponsored by Winning Writers. Poetry in any style or genre. Length: 250 lines maximum.

Deadline: submit between April 15 and September 30

Entry fee: $12 per poem

Prizes: Tom Howard Prize, $3,000 for poem in any style or genre; Margaret Reid Prize, $3,000 for poem that rhymes or has a traditional style; $100 each for ten honorable mentions in any style

UTMOST NOVICE CHRISTIAN POETRY CONTEST

www.utmostchristianwriters.com/poetry-contest/poetry-contest-rules.php

Description: Sponsored by Utmost Christian Writers Foundation. Unpublished poems may be rhymed or free verse, up to 60 lines. Need not be religious in content. Maximum of five entries.

Deadline: February 28

Entry fee: $20 per poem

Prizes: $1,000, $500, $300; ten honorable mentions, $100; best rhyming poem, $300; honorable mention rhyming poem, $200

VIOLET REED HAAS PRIZE FOR POETRY

www.snakenation.press/contests

Description: Sponsored by Snake Nation Press. Length: 50-75 pages. Previously published eligible.

Deadline: December 31

Entry fee: $25

Prize: $1,000 plus publication

WERGLE FLOMP HUMOR POETRY CONTEST

winningwriters.com/our-contests/wergle-flomp-humor-poetry-contest-free

Description: Sponsored by Winning Writers. Submit one published or unpublished humor poem up to 250 lines.

Deadline: April 1

Entry fee: none

Prizes: first place, $1,000; second place, $500; ten honorable mentions, $100; plus the top twelve entries will be published online

MULTIPLE GENRES

BLUE RIDGE CONFERENCE WRITING CONTEST

www.blueridgeconference.com/contest-info

> **Description:** Sponsors three book contests for fiction or nonfiction: Foundation Awards, Director's Choice, and The Selahs. Look for details about guidelines, deadlines, and entry fees on the website after January 1.

BRAUN BOOK AWARDS

wordalivepress.ca

> **Description:** Sponsored by Word Alive Press. For unpublished Christian books written by Canadian citizens and permanent residents in Canada. Categories: nonfiction and fiction.
> **Deadline:** March 15
> **Entry fee:** none
> **Prizes:** One fiction and one nonfiction manuscript will each receive a royalty-based book contract. A select number of secondary winners will also receive prizes, including credit toward publishing.

CHRISTIAN INDIE AWARDS

www.christianaward.com

> **Description:** Sponsored by Christian Indie Publishing Association. This award is designed to promote and bring recognition to quality Christian books by small publishers and independently published authors. Books must be printed in English, for sale in the United States, and promote the Christian faith. Awards are offered in eighteen categories. Publishers and authors may nominate titles, and Christian readers vote to determine the winners.
> **Deadline:** November 15
> **Entry fee:** $45

COLUMBIA JOURNAL CONTESTS

columbiajournal.org/submit/winter-contest

> **Description:** Fiction and nonfiction, 5,000 words maximum; poetry, five pages maximum.
> **Deadline:** December 1
> **Entry fee:** $15 per submission
> **Prizes:** $500 plus publication in each category

EDITOR'S REPRINT AWARDS

www.sequestrum.org/editors-reprint-award-fiction-and-nonfiction
www.sequestrum.org/editors-reprint-award-poetry

> **Description:** Sponsored by *Sequestrum* journal. Contest open to previously published manuscripts in prose (fiction and creative nonfiction up to 12,000 words) and poetry (up to 50 lines).
> **Deadline:** April 30
> **Entry fee:** $15
> **Prizes:** first prize awarded in both categories, $400 and publication; runners-up, $50 and publication

ERIC HOFFER BOOK AWARD

www.hofferaward.com

> **Description:** Eighteen categories for books from small, academic, and micro presses, including self-published, ebooks, and older books. The prose category is for creative fiction and nonfiction fewer than 10,000 words.
> **Deadline:** January 21
> **Entry fee:** varies by category
> **Prizes:** $2,500 grand prize, other prizes awarded in categories

THE EUPLE RINEY MEMORIAL AWARD

www.thestorytellermagazine.com/contests

> **Description:** Sponsored by *The Storyteller*. Open-genre contest but must be about family—good or bad. Can be fiction or nonfiction (indicate which). Length: 3,000 words maximum. No pornography, graphic anything, New Age, or children's stories will be accepted.
> **Deadline:** June 30
> **Entry fee:** $5
> **Prizes:** first place, $50; second place, $25; third place, $15; honorable mention, $10. Plus an editor's choice award.

EVANGELICAL PRESS ASSOCIATION CONTEST

www.evangelicalpress.com/contest

> **Description:** Higher Goals awards in a variety of categories for periodical manuscripts published in the previous year. Although most submissions are made by publication staff members, associate EPA members may also submit their articles.
> **Deadline:** January 17
> **Entry fee:** $50

EXCELLENCE IN EDITING AWARD
www.christianeditor.com/eie

Description: Sponsored by Christian Editor Connection. This award celebrates newly released books that are superbly written, well edited, and published by a CBA publisher or self-published by a Christian author. It is open to all books published in hardcover or paperback in 2020. Books must be written in English, have been released in North America, and contain a Christian worldview.
Deadline: December 31
Entry Fee: $35 before November 15, $40 after
Prizes: Winning authors and editors will each receive an award plaque, emblem stickers for marketing, and one selection from an array of Christian Editor Network benefits.

INSCRIBE CHRISTIAN WRITERS' FELLOWSHIP CONTEST
inscribe.org/contests

Description: Sponsors contests for InScribe members: Fall Contest, Winter Contest, Word Challenge, FellowScript Contests, Barnabas Award, Janette Oke Award, Post Conference Contest.
Deadline: varies
Entry fee: varies
Awards: vary by category

NARRATIVE MAGAZINE CONTESTS
www.narrativemagazine.com/submit-your-work

Description: Biannual contests in a variety of categories, including short stories, essays, memoirs, poetry, and literary nonfiction. Entries must be previously unpublished. Length: varies by category.
Deadline: varies
Entry fee: varies
Prizes: vary by category

NARRATIVE MAGAZINE 30 BELOW CONTEST
www.narrativemagazine.com/node/345528

Description: For writers ages 18-30. Fiction, nonfiction, poetry (up to five poems), essays, memoirs. Length: 15,000 words maximum. Restrictions on previously published works.
Deadline: November 19
Entry fee: $25 per entry
Prizes: $1,500, $750, $300, plus ten finalists will receive $100 each

NATIONAL WRITERS ASSOCIATION CONTESTS

www.nationalwriters.com/page/page/2734945.htm

> **Description:** Sponsors six contests: nonfiction, novel, young writers, poetry, short short, and David Raffelock Award for Publishing Excellence.
> **Deadline:** varies by contest
> **Entry fee:** varies by contest
> **Prizes:** vary by contest

NEW LETTERS AWARDS FOR WRITERS

www.newletters.org/writers-wanted/may-writing-contests

> **Description:** Sponsored by University of Missouri—Kansas City. Entries accepted in these categories: poetry, fiction, nonfiction.
> **Deadline:** May 18
> **Entry fee:** $24 for first entry; $15/additional entry
> **Prizes:** $2,500 for the best in poetry and fiction, $2,500 for nonfiction

NEW MILLENNIUM AWARDS

submit.newmillenniumwritings.org

> **Description:** Sponsored by New Millennium Writings. Fiction and nonfiction: 6,000 words maximum. Flash fiction (short-short story): 1,000 words maximum. Poetry: three poems to five pages total. No restrictions as to style or subject matter.
> **Deadline:** November 30
> **Entry fees:** $20, $45 for three entries, $72 for five entries
> **Prizes:** $1,000 plus publication for each category

OREGON CHRISTIAN WRITERS CASCADE AWARDS

oregonchristianwriters.org

> **Description:** Contests for novels; nonfiction books; memoir; young adult/middle grade fiction and nonfiction books; poetry; children's chapter and picture books; articles, columns, and blog posts; short stories/flash fiction; and devotionals. Separate divisions for published and unpublished authors. Awards are presented at the summer conference in Portland, Oregon.
> **Deadline:** submit between February 1 and March 15
> **Entry fees:** $30-35 for members, $40-45 for nonmembers

PROMISING BEGINNINGS CHRISTIAN WRITERS' CONTEST

www.KathyIde.com/promising-beginnings-contest

Description: This contest is open to both published and unpublished writers. Submit the first five pages of an unpublished or self-published book manuscript, fiction or nonfiction (any genre except poetry), for YA or adult readership (no children's). Must follow the formatting guidelines on the Promising Beginnings blog at *www. KathyIde.com*. Submissions will be judged on whether the quality of the writing shows promise.

Deadline: November 30

Entry fee: none

Prize: full scholarship to SoCalChristian Writers' Conference (including meals, dorm lodging, and travel expenses up to $300)

SOUL-MAKING KEATS LITERARY COMPETITION

www.soulmakingcontest.us

Description: Sponsored by National League of American Pen Women, Nob Hill, San Francisco Branch. Categories include flash fiction, short story, memoir vignette, humor, novel excerpt, intercultural essay, creative nonfiction, religious essay, young-adult poetry, and young-adult prose.

Deadline: November 30

Entry fee: $5

Prizes: in each category: first place, $100; second place, $50; third place, $25

TENNESSEE WILLIAMS/NEW ORLEANS LITERARY FESTIVAL

tennesseewilliams.net/contests

Description: Tennessee Williams gained some early recognition by entering a writing contest. The festival that bears his name now sponsors writing contests in poetry, fiction, very short fiction, and one-act playwriting.

Deadline: varies according to genre

Entry fee: varies

Prizes: vary by category

THE WORD GUILD CHRISTIAN WRITING AWARDS

thewordguild.com/contests

Description: The Word Awards recognize the best work published in the previous year in thirty-five categories of writing, including

446

novels, nonfiction books, articles, columns, poems, song lyrics, scripts, and screenplays. Fresh Ink Student Writers Contest for never-before-published student writers. In the Beginning for unpublished novice and emerging writers. The Grace Irwin Prize for Canadian writers who are Christians; recognizes the best book published in the previous year. The Leslie K. Tarr Award celebrates a major career contribution to Christian writing and publishing in Canada. The Partnership Award recognizes an individual or organization that has shown exceptional support and encouragement for Canadian writers and editors who are Christians.

Deadline, entry fees, prizes: vary according to the award and its guidelines

WORDS AND MUSIC WRITING COMPETITION

wordsandmusic.org/contest

Description: Sponsored by The Pirate's Alley Faulkner Society, Inc. Seven categories: novel, novella, book-length narrative fiction, novel-in-progress, short story, essay, poetry, and short story by a high-school student. For previously unpublished work only.

Deadline: May 15

Entry fee: varies by category

Prizes: $250-7,500, depending on category

WRITER'S DIGEST COMPETITIONS

www.writersdigest.com/writers-digest-competitions

Description: Every other month, *Writer's Digest* presents a creative challenge for fun and prizes, providing a short, open-ended prompt for short-story submissions based on that prompt. Winner receives publication in *Writer's Digest*. Also sponsors annual contests for feature articles, short stories (multiple genres), poetry, personal essays, and self-published books (categories vary).

Deadline: varies according to contest

Entry fee: varies

Prizes for annual contest: first place, $500; second place, $500; and more places for each contest; grand prize, $2,500

THE WRITERS' UNION OF CANADA AWARDS & COMPETITIONS

www.writersunion.ca/awards

Description: Short Prose Competition for Developing Writers for fiction or nonfiction by an author who has not yet published a book. Length: 2,500 words maximum. Danuta Gleed Literary Award for the best first collection of short fiction.

Deadlines: Short Prose, March 1; Danuta, January 31

Entry fee: $29

Prizes: Short Prose, $2,500; Danuta, $10,000, plus two finalist awards for $500 each

WRITERS-EDITORS NETWORK ANNUAL INTERNATIONAL WRITING COMPETITION

www.writers-editors.com/Writers/Contests/Contest_Guidelines/contest_guidelines.htm

Description: Nonfiction and fiction: 4,000 words maximum; children's literature (story, fiction-book chapter, poem, magazine article, or nonfiction-book chapter targeted to a specific age group): 4,000 words maximum. Poetry may be traditional or free verse. All entries must be unpublished or self-published and not accepted for publication by a traditional publisher at the time they are entered in the contest.

Deadline: March 15

Entry fees: poetry, $5 for members, $10 for nonmembers; prose: $10 for members, $20 for nonmembers

Prizes: $200, $150, $100, $75, plus one-year membership in Writers-Editors Network

RESOURCES FOR CONTESTS

These websites are sources for announcements about other contests.

DAILY WRITING TIPS
www.dailywritingtips.com/25-writing-competitions

FREELANCE WRITING
www.freelancewriting.com/writingcontests.php

FUNDS FOR WRITERS
fundsforwriters.com/contests

NEW PAGES
www.newpages.com/classifieds/big-list-of-writing-contests

POETS & WRITERS
www.pw.org/grants

TETHERED BY LETTERS
tetheredbyletters.com/resources/contest-list

THE WRITE LIFE
thewritelife.com/writing-contests

THE WRITER
www.writermag.com/writing-resources/contests

DENOMINATIONAL PUBLISHERS

ANGLICAN
The Anglican Journal

ASSEMBLIES OF GOD
God's Word for Today
Influence
Light Magazine
LIVE
My Healthy Church
Take 5 Plus

BAPTIST
B&H Publishing
The Brink
CommonCall
Facts & Trends
Faith on Every Corner
HomeLife
Judson Press
Mature Living
On Mission
Parenting Teens
ParentLife
Point
Randall House Publications
The Secret Place
Word&Way

BRETHREN
BMH Books

GraceConnect

CATHOLIC
America
American Catholic Press
The Arlington Catholic Herald
Ave Maria Press
Catholic Book Publishing House
Catholic New York
Catholic Sentinel
Celebrate Life
Christ Is Our Hope
Columbia
Commonweal
Franciscan Media
Image Books
LEAVES
Liguorian
Liturgical Press
Living Faith
Living Faith for Kids
Loyola Press
Our Sunday Visitor, Inc.
Our Sunday Visitor Newsweekly
Paraclete Press
Parish Liturgy
Pauline Books & Media
Paulist Press
Resurrection Press

Scepter Publishers
St. Anthony Messenger
U.S. Catholic

CHARISMATIC
See Pentecostal.

CHRISTIAN CHURCH/ CHURCH OF CHRIST
Christian Standard
College Press Publishing
Leafwood Publishers

CHURCH OF GOD
Bible Advocate
The Church Herald &
Holiness Banner
The Gem
Gems of Truth
Now What?
Pathways—Moments with God
Warner Christian Resources

EPISCOPAL
Forward Day by Day
Forward Movement
The Living Church

EVANGELICAL COVENANT
The Covenant Companion

LUTHERAN
Beaming Books
Broadleaf Books
Canada Lutheran
The Canadian Lutheran
Christ in Our Home
Fortress Press
Lutheran Forum
The Lutheran Journal

The Lutheran Witness
Northwestern Publishing House
The Word in Season

MENNONITE
Canadian Mennonite
The Messenger

MESSIANIC
The Messianic Times

METHODIST
Abingdon Press
Christian Living in the
Mature Years
Light + Life Magazine
Methodist History Journal
The Upper Room

NAZARENE
The Foundry Publishing
Holiness Today
Reflecting God
Standard

ORTHODOX
Ancient Faith Publishing

PENTECOSTAL/CHARISMATIC
Charisma
Charisma House
Charisma Leader
Empowered Publications, Inc.
Testimony/Enrich
Whitaker House

PRESBYTERIAN
byFaith
Presbyterians Today
These Days: Daily Devotions for

Living by Faith
Westminster/John Knox Press

QUAKER/FRIENDS
Friends Journal
Friends United Press
Fruit of the Vine

REFORMED
Christian Courier
Faith Alive Christian Resources
P&R Publishing

SALVATION ARMY
Faith & Friends
New Frontier Chronicle

Peer
SAConnects
War Cry

SEVENTH-DAY ADVENTIST
Guide
Journal of Adventist Education
Ministry
Our Little Friend
Pacific Press
Primary Treasure
Vibrant Life

WESLEYAN
Light from the Word

PUBLISHING LINGO

My first week working in a bookstore I learned a valuable lesson. I had a stack of books in my arms that I had taken from a shipment in the back room. My boss walked by, said, "Steve, please put those in the dump," and kept walking.

I paused and thought, *Why should I throw these away? They are brand new books!* To my chagrin, I discovered that, in bookstore lingo, a dump was a cardboard display in the front of the store.

The lesson I learned is that knowing the lingo can keep you from being confused or potentially misunderstanding some instructions. Like bookstores, writing and publishing have their own lingo. The following definitions will acquaint you with some of the more important terms.

ABA: American Booksellers Association. This acronym has come to mean the general market, as opposed to CBA, the Christian market.

Advance: Money a publisher pays to an author up front, against future royalties. The amount varies greatly from publisher to publisher and is often paid in two or three installments (on signing the contract, on delivery of the manuscript, and on publication).

AE: An abbreviation for Acquisitions Editor. Not all publishing houses use this abbreviation, but they all have people who acquire in their editorial departments.

All rights: An outright sale of a manuscript. The author has no further control over any subsidiary rights or reusing the piece.

Anecdote: A short, poignant, real-life story, usually used to illustrate a single thought. It need not be humorous.

ARC: Advance Reader Copy. An early paperback (or ebook) version of a book sent out for reviews around four to six months prior to publication.

Assignment: When an editor asks a writer to create a specific manuscript for an agreed-on price.

As-told-to story: A true story you write as a first-person account about someone else.

Audience: The people who are expected to be reading your manuscript, in terms of age, life experience, knowledge of and interest level in the story or subject. Editors want to be sure writers understand their assumed audiences well.

Audiobooks: Spoken-word books available by streaming via the Internet, on compact disc, or MP3 file.

Backlist: A publisher's previously published books that are still in print a year or more after publication.

Bible versions:
AMP—*Amplified Bible*
ASV—*American Standard Version*
CB—*Confraternity Bible* (Catholic)
CEB—*Common English Bible*
CEV—*Contemporary English Version*
CJB—*Complete Jewish Bible*
CSB—*Christian Standard Bible*
ESV—*English Standard Version*
GNB—*Good News Bible*
GW—*GOD'S WORD Translation*
HCSB—*Holman Christian Standard Bible* (replaced by CSB)
ICB—*International Children's Bible*
KJV—*King James Version*
KJV21—*21ˢᵗ Century King James Version*
MEV—*Modern English Version*
MSG—*The Message*
NAB—*New American Bible*
NABRE—*New American Bible Revised Edition*
NASB—*New American Standard Bible*
NCV—*New Century Version*
NEB—*New English Bible*
NET—*New English Translation*
NIrV—*New International Reader's Version*
NIV—*New International Version*
NJB—*New Jerusalem Bible*
NKJV—*New King James Version*

NLT—*New Living Translation*
NRSV—*New Revised Standard Version*
PHILLIPS—*J.B. Phillips New Testament*
RSV—*Revised Standard Version* (replaced by NRSV)
TEV—*Today's English Translation* (aka *Good News Bible*)
TLB—*The Living Bible*
TNIV—*Today's New International Version*
VOICE—*The Voice Bible Translation*

Bio: Brief information about the author.

Bluelines: The last printer's proofs used to catch errors before a book or periodical is printed. May be physical pages or digital proofs in PDF.

BOB: Back-of-Book ad for the author's previous book(s) or a similar book released by the publisher. It uses the blank pages in the back of a book or extra pages at the end of an ebook.

Book proposal: Submission of a book idea to an agent or editor. It usually includes a hook, summary and purpose of the book, target market, uniqueness of the book compared to similar ones in the marketplace, chapter-by-chapter summaries or plot synopsis, marketing and promotion information, your credentials, and delivery date, plus one to three sample chapters, including the first one.

Byline: Author's name printed below the title of a story, article, etc.

Camera-ready copy: The text and artwork for a book that are ready for the press.

Category romance: Novels of around 50,000-60,000 words that are published in categories and according to strict guidelines. For example, Love Inspired novels, the Christian division of Harlequin.

CBA: Christian Booksellers Association. The acronym has come to describe the Christian market as opposed to ABA, the general market. As an entity, the CBA folded in 2019, but the acronym still applies when referring to the Christian publishing industry.

Chapbook: A small book or pamphlet containing poetry, religious readings, etc.

Circulation: The number of copies sold or distributed of a periodical.

Clips: Copies of articles you have had published in newspapers or magazines.

Colophon: The publisher's emblem or imprint used on the title page or spine of a book or a statement at the end of a book with information about its production, such as the type of font used.

Column: A regularly appearing feature, section, or department in a periodical with the same heading. It's written by the same person or a different freelancer each time.

Comp copies: Complimentary copies given to the author by the publisher on publication.

Comps: Shorthand for "comparable." The publisher may have comps on cover designs or titles to help position the book in the marketplace.

Concept statement: A 50- to 150-word summary of your proposed book.

Contributing editor: A freelance writer who has a regular column or writes regularly for the periodical.

Contributor's copy: Copy of an issue of a periodical sent to an author whose work appears in it.

Copyedit: The editor checks grammar, punctuation, and citations to make sure the work is accurate. More detailed than a developmental edit. Some publishers refer to this as the line edit.

Copyright: Legal protection of an author's work. A manuscript is automatically copyrighted in your name when you produce it. You don't need to register it with the Copyright Office unless you are self-publishing a book or other publication since a traditional publisher registers it for you.

Cover copy: Or "copy." The text on the back cover of a book, in the online description, or in marketing materials. For a hardcover, it can also include flap copy, the text on the inside dust-jacket flaps.

Cover letter: A letter that accompanies some manuscript submissions. Usually it's needed only if you have to tell the editor something specific, to give your credentials for writing a manuscript of a technical nature, or to remind the editor that the manuscript was requested or expected. Often used as the introduction to a book proposal. Rarely used for an article submission; query letters are used instead.

Credits, list of: A listing of your previously published works.

Critique: An evaluation of a manuscript.

Defamation: A written (libel) or spoken (slander) injury to the reputation of a living person or organization. If what is said is true, it cannot be defamatory, but that does not prevent the injured party from bringing a lawsuit.

Derivative work: A work derived from another work, such as a condensation or abridgment. Contact the copyright owner for permission before doing the abridgment, and be prepared to pay that owner a fee or royalty.

Developmental edit: Usually the first round of editing done on a manuscript. The editor helps "develop" the book by shaping its content and structure. Also called a substantive edit or line edit.

Devotion: A short manuscript based on a Scripture verse or passage that shares a personal spiritual discovery, inspires to worship, challenges to commitment or action, or encourages. A book or periodical of devotions is called a devotional.

Ed board: Editorial board meeting. The editors meet to discuss the new proposals they received to determine which ones should go to the pub board.

Editorial guidelines: See "Writers guidelines."

Em dash (—): Used to create a break or set off material in a sentence instead of using a comma. *The Chicago Manual of Style* calls this punctuation mark "the most versatile of the dashes."

En dash (-): An en dash is longer than a hyphen but shorter than an em dash. Often used in-between numbers and dates to show a range. It was called the "en" dash because in the early days of typesetting it was same width as the capital letter N.

Endorsements: Flattering comments about a book, usually printed on the back cover or in promotional material.

Epub: Term for a specific file format used by ebooks. Mobi is used for Kindle (Amazon). Epub is used by everyone else (Nook, Kobo, Apple, Google Play, etc.).

Essay: A short composition expressing the author's opinion on a specific subject.

Evangelical: A person who believes that one receives God's forgiveness for sins through Jesus Christ and believes the Bible is the authoritative Word of God. This is a broad definition for a label with broad application. Often mistakenly used as a synonym for "Christian."

Exegesis: Interpretation of a Scripture passage.

Feature article: In-depth coverage of a subject, usually focusing on a person, an event, a process, an organization, a movement, a trend, or an issue. It's written to explain, encourage, help, analyze, challenge, motivate, warn, or entertain, as well as to inform.

Filler: A short item used to "fill" a page of a periodical. It could be a joke, anecdote, light verse, short humor, puzzle, game, etc.

First rights: A periodical editor buys the right to publish a manuscript that has never been published and to do so only once.

Foreign rights: Selling or giving permission to translate or reprint published material in another country.

Foreword: Opening remarks in a book to introduce the book and its author. Often misspelled as *forward*.

Freelance: Supplied by freelance writers.

Freelancer or freelance writer: A writer who is not on salary but sells his or her material to a number of different periodicals and publishers.

Galley proof: A typeset copy of a book or magazine used to detect and correct errors before printing.

General editor: Usually, the person who oversees a large work that has multiple authors writing individual chapters for a book or a series of books. This person is not an employee within a publishing house.

General market: Non-Christian market, sometimes called secular market.

Genre: Refers to a type or classification, as in fiction or poetry. For instance, westerns, romances, and mysteries are fiction genres.

Glossy: A photo with a shiny, rather than matte, finish. Also, a publication printed on such paper.

Go-ahead: When an editor tells you to write or submit your article.

Hard copy: A printed manuscript, as opposed to one sent via email.

460

Independent book publisher: A book publisher who charges authors to publish their books or buy a certain number of copies, as opposed to a royalty house that pays authors. Some independent publishers also pay a royalty. Sometimes called a subsidy, vanity, or custom publisher.

ISBN: International Standard Book Number, an identification code needed for every version of a book.

Journal: A periodical presenting information in a particular area, often for an academic or educated audience.

Kill fee: A fee paid for a completed article done on assignment that is subsequently not published. The amount is usually 25-50% of the original payment.

Libel: A published false statement that is damaging to another person's reputation; a written defamation.

Line edit: See "Developmental edit" and "Copyedit." Check to see how your editor defines each process.

Little/Literary: Small-circulation periodicals whose focus is providing a forum for the literary writer, rather than on making money. Often they do not pay or pay in copies.

Mainstream fiction: Other than genre fiction (such as romance, mystery, or fantasy). Stories of people and their conflicts handled on a deeper level.

Mass market: Books intended for a wide, general market, produced in a smaller format, usually with smaller type and sold at a lower price. The expectation is that their sales will be higher.

Matte finish: A nonglossy, nonreflective finish on a book cover. Has a textured feel.

Mobi: Term for a specific file format used by ebooks. Mobi is used for Kindle (Amazon). Epub is used by everyone else.

Ms: Abbreviation for manuscript.

Mss: Abbreviation for more than one manuscript.

NASR: Abbreviation for North American serial rights. Permission for a periodical targeting readers in the US and Canada to publish a manuscript.

New-adult fiction: A developing fiction genre with protagonists ages 18-25. In the general market, these novels often explore sexual themes considered too "adult" for the YA or teen market. They tend to be marketed to older teen readers.

Novella: A short novel, usually 20,000–35,000 words. The length varies from publisher to publisher.

On acceptance: Editor pays a writer at the time the manuscript is accepted for publication.

On assignment: Writing a manuscript at the specific request of an editor.

On publication: Publisher pays a writer when his or her manuscript is published.

On speculation/spec: Writing something for a periodical editor with the agreement that the editor will buy it only if he or she likes it.

Onetime rights: Selling the right to publish a manuscript one time to more than one periodical, primarily to nonoverlapping audiences, such as different denominations.

Over the transom: Unsolicited manuscripts sent to a book editor. Comes from the old transom, which was a window above the door in office buildings. Manuscripts could be pushed "over the transom" into the locked office.

Overrun: The extra copies of a book printed during the initial print run.

Pen name/pseudonym: A name other than your legal name used on a manuscript to protect your identity or the identities of people included or when you wish to remain anonymous. Put the pen name in the byline under the title and your real name with your contact information.

Perfect binding: When pages of a paperback are glued together (bound) on the spine and the cover is then attached.

Periodical: A magazine, newsletter, or newspaper.

Permissions: Asking permission to use text or art from a copyrighted source.

Personal experience: An account based on a real-life experience.

Personality profile: A feature article that highlights a specific person's life or accomplishments.

Plagiarism: Stealing and using the ideas or writing of someone else as your own, either as is or rewriting slightly to make them sound like your own.

POD/Print-on-demand: A printing process where books are printed one at a time or in small numbers instead of in quantity. The production cost per book is higher, but no warehousing is necessary.

POV: Point-of-view. A fiction term that describes the perspective of the one telling the story, such as first person or third person.

Press kit: A compilation of promotional materials for a book or author, used to publicize a book.

Pub board: A formal meeting where people from editorial, marketing, sales, finance, and management meet to discuss whether or not to publish a book.

Public domain: Work for which copyright protection has expired. Copyright laws vary from country to country; but in the US, works published more than 95 years ago have entered the public domain. Because the U.S. copyright law has changed several times, check with the Copyright Office (*copyright.gov*) to determine if a work is in public domain or not. Generally, since 1978, copyright endures for the author's life plus seventy years.

Query letter: A letter sent to an editor about an article or book you propose to write and asking if he or she is interested in seeing it.

Recto: The right-hand page in printing.

Reprint rights: Selling the right to reprint an article that has already been published. You must have sold only first or onetime rights originally and wait until it has been published the first time.

Response time: The number of weeks or months it takes an editor to get back to you about a query, proposal, or manuscript you sent.

Review copies: Books given to reviewers or buyers for bookstore chains and online sellers.

Royalty: The percentage an author is paid by a publisher on the sale of each copy of a book.

Running head: The text at the top of each page that can show the author's name, book title, chapter, or page number.

SASE: Self-addressed, stamped envelope. Always send it with a hard-copy manuscript or query letter.

SASP: Self-addressed, stamped postcard. May be sent with a hard-copy manuscript to be returned by the editor to indicate it arrived safely. Rarely used.

Satire: Ridicule that aims at reform.

Second serial rights: See "Reprint rights."

Secular market: An outdated term for the non-Christian publishing market.

Serial: Refers to publication in a periodical, such as first serial rights.

Sidebar: A short feature that accompanies an article and gives additional information about the topic, such as a recommended reading list. It is often set apart by appearing within a box or border.

Signature: All books are printed in 16-page increments or signatures (occasionally in 32-page increments for large books like Bibles). A large sheet of paper is printed, then folded multiple times. Three sides are cut (top, side, and bottom). The fourth side holds eight double-sided pages. The signatures are compiled and bound into the finished book.

Simultaneous submissions: Sending the same manuscript to more than one editor at the same time. Usually this action is done with nonoverlapping periodical markets, such as denominational publications or newspapers in different cities, or when you are writing on a timely subject. Most periodical editors don't accept simultaneous submissions, but they are the norm in the book market. Be sure to state in a cover letter that it is a simultaneous submission.

Slander: The verbal act of defamation.

Slanting: Writing an article to meet the needs of a particular market.

Slush pile: The stack of unsolicited manuscripts that arrive at an editor's desk or email inbox.

Subsidiary rights: All the rights, other than book rights, included in a book contract, such as translations, audiobooks, book clubs, and movies.

Subsidy publisher: See "Independent book publisher."

Substantive edit: See "Developmental edit."

Synopsis: A brief summary of a work, ranging from one paragraph to several pages.

Tabloid: A newspaper-format publication about half the size of a regular newspaper.

Take-home paper: A small periodical given to Sunday-school students, children through adults. These minimagazines are published with the curriculum.

Think piece: A magazine article that has an intellectual, philosophical, or provocative approach to a subject.

Trade book: Describes a 5½" x 8½" paperback book (sometimes 6" x 9"). This is a typical trim size for a paperback. Mass-market books are smaller, around 4" x 6".

Trade magazine: A magazine whose audience is in a particular business.

Trim size: The size of a book after being trimmed in the printing process. (See "Signature" for more information.)

Unsolicited manuscript: A manuscript an editor did not specifically ask to see.

Vanity publisher: See "Independent book publisher."

Verso: The left-hand page in printing.

Vignette: A short, descriptive literary sketch of a brief scene or incident.

Vita: An outline of one's personal history and experience.

Work-for-hire: A manuscript you create for an agreed payment, and you give the publisher full ownership and control of it. You must sign a contract for this agreement to be legal.

Writers guidelines: Information provided by an editor that gives specific guidance for writing for the publication or publishing house. If the information is not offered online, email or send an SASE with your request for printed guidelines.

INDEX

D

N

O

NOTES

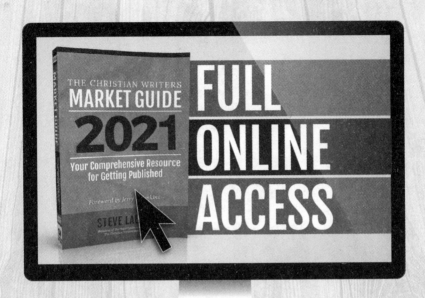

CHRISTIAN WRITERS INSTITUTE

We Teach Writers

AUDIO COURSES • VIDEO COURSES • BOOKS

Taught by some of the industry's best teachers

ChristianWritersInstitute.com